Changing Ideals in Modern Architecture
1750-1950

by the same author

*

CONCRETE: THE VISION OF A NEW ARCHITECTURE

CHANGING IDEALS
IN
MODERN ARCHITECTURE
1750-1950

PETER COLLINS

Professor of Architecture
McGill University, Montreal

Montreal
McGILL UNIVERSITY PRESS
1965

Printed in Great Britain

Acknowledgments

First of all, I should like to acknowledge my indebtedness to Professor John Bland, Professor Jonas Lehrman and Professor C. C. Bayley for the many improvements they suggested to the manuscript, and to my wife who, with indefatigable zeal, corrected the proofs.

Secondly, I should like to express my thanks for the financial assistance which enabled me to carry out the preliminary research, and which was given me by McGill University, the Canada Council, and the Royal Institute of British Architects' Henry Florence Architectural Book Scholarship.

Finally, I should like to acknowledge the kindness of the editors of *The Architectural Review*, *Progressive Architecture*, *The Journal of the Royal Architectural Institute of Canada* and *The Canadian Architect* in allowing me to republish fragments which have already appeared in their periodicals.

Contents

CONTENTS

RATIONALISM

THE INFLUENCE OF THE ALLIED ARTS

List of Illustrations

LIST OF ILLUSTRATIONS

Preface

THE changing ideals in architecture during the last two hundred years were many, varied, and at times flimsy. The old established basis of architecture was practically dissolved, and architects were more than usually victims to any ideas that appeared worthy to be guides for them. Architects, being partly artists, can be expected to be more than ordinarily sensitive to such changes, and may indeed need their stimulus more than others. For example, whether or not there have been changing ideals in, say, railway or ship design, they have certainly not been as influential as with buildings, because scientific and technical considerations have been clearly dominant and the lines of possible development limited.

Because architecture is partly an art, involved with feelings, it seems inevitable that both the architect and his client are moved by ideals external to architecture and that such ideals of one sort or another continually appear and change. Yet although it is inevitable that foreign notions should act upon architectural theory from time to time, the phenomenon of the last two centuries was clearly unique, in that it not only embraced so many such notions, but that they were taken so seriously. These changing ideals, by virtue of their diversity and intensity, charted for architecture a crooked path even when they merged and grew out of one another.

The important thing to note is that when such objectives are measured against established architectural customs, they become subordinate considerations which do not deflect the course of architecture so much as flavour it. Thus it now seems that, as we enter the second half of the twentieth century, the zigzags become less, and one senses a new stable body of opinion which betokens the commencement of the classic age of modern architecture. It is this new development which gives a sudden pertinence and meaning to the architectural ideas of the last two hundred years, and makes this book particularly welcome and opportune.

JOHN BLAND

Introduction

THE limits of the history of modern architecture are as difficult to define satisfactorily as the limits of any other kind of modern history, since each age has a different idea of what it means historically by 'modern'. Thus, in the seventeenth century, the architects of the early Renaissance were called 'modern' to distinguish them from the architects of Antiquity. Nowadays, modern architecture is usually considered to be the kind of architecture peculiar to the twentieth century, but all recent writers on the subject have recognized that its origins go back much further, even though they may not agree as to where exactly they begin. Some authorities (such as Nikolaus Pevsner) are content to trace the roots back to the work of William Morris in the 1860s. Others (such as Henry-Russell Hitchcock, Sigfried Giedion, Vincent Scully, Hans Sedlmayr and Leonardo Benevolo) trace it back a century earlier. It would of course be simple to prove that no architectural forms or materials are ever confined to the age in which they are most popular, in the sense of having no precedent whatsoever in earlier periods. It is possible to contend that modern concrete was invented by the Romans if one is content to overlook the fact that the material was itself overlooked for fifteen hundred years before the researches of Cointereau. At the same time, it can hardly be disputed that radical changes took place in the middle of the eighteenth century which so profoundly altered subsequent theories of architecture as to make the ideals of architects differ henceforth quite markedly from what they were before.

From 1750 onwards, architects were motivated by a number of notions which had previously played little or no part in the formation of their ideals, and these new notions did not simply succeed one another as an evolutionary sequence; they were to recur continually, in various combinations and with various expressions, during the whole of the following two centuries. The fondness of late eighteenth century architects for historical allusions, for analogical justifications, for asymmetrical landscaping, for brutal detailing, for oriental prototypes, and for pictorial techniques does not simply cut them off from the tradition of earlier centuries; it relates them intimately to the architects of today, and it is this which gives unity to the period 1750–1950, and allows us to treat it as a single architectural age.

INTRODUCTION

The changes which occur in the appearance of buildings during these two centuries have been fully analysed by Henry-Russell Hitchcock, just as the sources of contemporary architecture have been fully analysed by Sigfried Giedion, and since the books of both these authors are standard texts (which may eventually be elaborated by additional evidence, but which will always remain classic expositions of their subjects), it might seem pretentious to suggest that a third approach can contribute to a full understanding of the period. Yet works of the type just mentioned inevitably possess one inherent limitation in that they are concerned essentially with the evolution of forms, rather than with the changes in those ideals which produced them, and this tends to minimize one of the most important factors in architectural design, namely the motives which dictate the character of an architect's work.

'Forms', wrote Philip Johnson in his review of Reyner Banham's *Theory and Design in the First Machine Age*, 'beget more forms, whereas ideas barely have influence on them'. But forms do not beget more forms by a mechanical evolutionary process. It is precisely the *idea* of what forms may most appropriately be selected which creates the architecture of a particular age. Architectural historians are quite right in emphasizing the importance of architecture as an end product; in concerning themselves mainly with what a building looks like, how it is constructed and how efficiently it fulfils its purpose. But the architects who created such buildings were obliged to be equally concerned with more philosophical problems, such as why anyone should choose one form, material or system rather than another. An architect does not arrive at his finished product solely by a sequence of rationalizations, like a scientist, or through the workings of the *Zeitgeist*. Nor does he reach them by uninhibited intuition, like a musician or a painter. He thinks of forms intuitively, and then tries to justify them rationally; a dialectical process governed by what we may call his theory of architecture, which can only be studied in philosophical and ethical terms.

The type of history he needs is thus what César Daly, a century ago, called 'a philosophical history of architecture'; a history which will attempt 'not to pass in review a list of the executed works and technical improvements effected since the end of the eighteenth century, but to set in relief the evolution and revolution in architectural thoughts and architectural sentiments which have succeeded one another in this period, and have left in their train so many hesitations and doctrinal uncertainties in architects' minds, that the efficacious criticism of buildings becomes virtually impossible, through lack of definite principles mutually acceptable to artists, critics and the general public'.

'It is not knowing what people did but understanding what they thought that is the proper definition of the historian's task', wrote R. G. Collingwood in his *Idea of History*, and this book is similarly intended to be a history of thoughts about architecture, rather than a history of architecture itself. It is concerned more with ideas than with buildings, and its intention is to convey an idea of what architects

16

have been trying to achieve since the modern age started, rather than to analyse stylistically all the buildings they built, and which in any case have now become so numerous as to be archaeologically unclassifiable. Unlike the more orthodox kind of history specifically devoted to modern architecture, it does not exclude from consideration those nineteenth century ideals which are now unfashionable. On the contrary, it asks the reader to decide for himself what modern ideas are valid, and what aspects of nineteenth century theory have been unjustifiably neglected or condemned. In this way, an attempt has been made to lead the way towards an architectural philosophy evolved in the spirit of true eclecticism. 'An eclectic', wrote Diderot in 1755, 'is a philosopher who tramples underfoot prejudice, tradition, seniority, universal consent, authority, and everything which subjugates mass opinion; who dares to think for himself, go back to the clearest general principles, examine them, discuss them, and accept nothing except on the evidence of his own experience and reason; and who, from all the philosophies which he has analysed without respect to persons, and without partiality, makes a philosophy of his own, peculiar to himself.'

Part One

ROMANTICISM

I

Revolutionary Architecture

In the mid-nineteenth century, the general opinion regarding the nature of architectural development could probably best be summarized by a quotation from *The Course and Current of Architecture*, written by Samuel Huggins, a Liverpool architect, and published in 1863. In a chapter entitled 'The Style of the Future', he wrote: 'To me, the whole history of the rise and mutations of styles conspires to show the folly of hankering after a new style. Every style of whose origin we have any knowledge has arisen not from an act of the will, or someone setting about the invention of a new style, but spontaneously, out of circumstances, brought on by some great political, intellectual or religious revolutions'.

There were however other architects, of more radical temper, who made precisely the opposite deductions from these same lessons of the past. They agreed that great intellectual and political revolutions had in fact occurred; and they agreed that as a result of such intellectually revolutionary works as the *Encyclopédie*, or the political revolutions in America and France, there was every reason why great changes should occur in architecture. But these changes, like those which had occurred in thought, politics and the mechanical arts would not, according to them, be the automatic result of natural forces, but would be brought about by the will of individual men.

The architecture of the end of the eighteenth century is distinguished by the work of four such architects: John Soane, E. L. Boullée, C. N. Ledoux and J. N. L. Durand, whose attitudes were unmistakably revolutionary rather than evolutionary, and whose aim was not to maintain tradition by applying and re-interpreting old principles in the light of changing conditions, but to re-evaluate the very principles themselves. They did not have a large following, nor were their principles systematically pursued for a long period; indeed, the architectural shapes by which their ideals found expression were soon abandoned, and were not to attain popularity again for another hundred years. But these architects can with justice be regarded as pioneers of modern architecture, for whilst the vast gulf of Revivalism separates their architecture from the architecture of Le Corbusier and the Bauhaus, it can fairly be claimed that it had no precedent, and was literally the architecture of a new age.

Before studying the new ideals these men propagated, it may be as well to reach some conclusions as to what is meant by 'traditional principles', such as those against which they reacted. If we take, for example, the most traditional definition of good architecture, namely Vitruvius's *utilitas*, *firmitas*, *venustas*, it is clear that none of these three essential constituents of good architecture can ever be rejected entirely, since obviously commodious planning, sound construction and pleasing appearance can never be replaced by anything else. It follows therefore that revolutionary architecture can only be based on notions added to these three, on unusual emphases given to one or two of these three at the expense of the third, or on changes in the meaning attached to the idea of architectural beauty. As will be shown eventually, the only notion added to the Vitruvian trinity was the idea that 'space' is a positive architectural quality, and that it possessed as much, if not more architectural interest than the structure by which it was confined. Other revolutionary theories, especially in the mid-nineteenth and early twentieth centuries, were based either on unusual emphases on the notion of *firmitas* (whereby great value was attached to the exhibition of structural honesty, which led at times to a striving for exaggerated structural virtuosity for its own sake) or on unusual emphases on the notion of *utilitas* (whereby the plans of buildings were regarded as of prime importance and the 'functional' expression of a programme was taken as the principal criterion of good architectural design). But a great deal of revolutionary theorizing was based on new interpretations given to the notion of architectural beauty, and since these theories were particularly prevalent at the beginning of the period under discussion, it is with them that the first few chapters will be mainly concerned.

Soane's ideas will be discussed first, because although he was not born until 1753 (and was thus younger than Ledoux and Boullée by seventeen and twenty-five years respectively), he made use of several aesthetic devices which had already appeared in England at the very beginning of the eighteenth century in the work of John Vanbrugh and Nicholas Hawksmoor. Neither of these two architects (who worked in partnership) could be described as modern, for both were popularly employed by typical members of the late Stuart and early Georgian aristocracy, and both designed in an architectural idiom that was close enough to contemporary work in Europe to be called Baroque. Yet perhaps because neither of them was properly trained, perhaps because both of them were English, perhaps because Vanbrugh was more a writer than an architect, their designs had a somewhat eccentric flavour which was to characterize many buildings of the new age.

First we find in their work a character which some may call eclecticism, but which it would be far better to describe as 'indifferentism'; that is to say, they were quite happy to design in any style, whether Classical or Gothic, without considering that any matter of principle was involved. Secondly, we find (in Hawksmoor's work in particular) what John Summerson has described as a 'morbid passion for archaeology'. Thirdly, we find a deliberate search for sculptural and picturesque effects; a technique particularly admired by Soane, who asserted that Vanbrugh's inventiveness had no equal in England, and that 'the young architect, by studying the picturesque effects of his works, will learn to avoid the dull monotony of minor artists and be led to think for himself and acquire a taste of his own'. Lastly, we find in both Hawksmoor's and Vanbrugh's work a delight in achieving novel compositions by mixing Classical elements into eccentric combinations, or by reversing the normal tectonic relationship of Classical motifs; devices which correspond to some extent to what, with reference to sixteenth century architecture, is sometimes called Mannerism, but which were here far more radical in that they produced virtually a new architectural vocabulary of sculptural forms.

Soane took over many of Vanbrugh's and Hawksmoor's notions, just as he took over many of their compositional techniques. He designed churches indifferently in the Gothic or Classical 'styles'; his taste for archaeology led him to design part of the Bank of England like the temple of Vesta at Tivoli and to build his own house as a large museum; and he considered that a building could only be beautiful if it formed 'an entire whole from whatever point it is viewed, like a group of sculpture'. In addition, his designs also displayed two qualities found in the contemporary work of Boullée, Ledoux and their followers: namely, a lugubrious fondness for blank walls and blocked windows, and an equally lugubrious Piranesian fondness for sarcophagi, the latter forming the inspiration for some of his pediments, as for example on the Bank of England roof.

Yet it will be perceived that although Soane's ideals were certainly not Classical, in that they were very different from those we generally associate with the Classicism of, say, Inigo Jones or François Mansart, they were revolutionary only in a negative sense, since although he rejected the disciplined use of antique tectonic elements, he did not substitute any positive body of principles in their place. Nevertheless, there is a modernity in his very perversity, as we may see by comparing George Godwin's assessment of Soane, written in 1855, with John Summerson's assessment of Le Corbusier, written a century later. 'Soane supported the doctrine of predominant novelty', wrote Godwin, 'and his details were produced by very simple means; they usually consisted in the reverse of the ordinary'. Of Le Corbusier, Summerson wrote: 'For to him, the obvious solution of a problem, however charming, cannot possibly be the right solution; a building by Le Corbusier is a ruthless dismemberment of the building programme and a reconstruction on a plane where the unexpected always, unfailingly, happens'. We thus see that although the forms are different, the technique used is very much the same.

Similar parallels can be made between the works of Le Corbusier and those of Boullée or Ledoux, and have been so made at considerable length by Emil Kaufman. Here the evidence is far more telling, since not only do the forms resemble one another very closely, but the correspondence of doctrines is attested

23

by documentary sources. For example, in *Towards a New Architecture* (1927), Le Corbusier deliberately defined architecture not in Vitruvian terms (i.e. as good planning, sound construction and pleasing appearance) but in terms of the sculptural effects of light and shade. 'Architecture', he wrote, 'is the masterly, correct and magnificent play of masses brought together in light. Our eyes are made to see forms in light. Thus cubes, cones, spheres, cylinders or pyramids are the great primary forms which light reveals to advantage; they are not only beautiful forms, but the most beautiful forms'. Now this is almost an exact, though unconscious, paraphrase of Boullée's definition of architecture, contained in a manuscript that was written in the last quarter of the eighteenth century, though not fully published until 1953. 'Shall I,' Boullée asks, 'like Vitruvius, define architecture as the art of building? No, for this would be to confuse causes and effects. The effects of architecture are caused by light', and he goes on to claim that the first principles of architecture are to be discerned in symmetrical solids, such as cubes, pyramids, and, most of all, spheres, which are, in his view, the only perfect architectural shapes which can be devised.

It is possible that some of Boullée's aesthetic ideas may have been derived from contemporary philosophers such as Lord Kames, for in the latter's *Elements of Criticism* (1762) a globe is described as the most pleasing of figures, since it exhibits the maximum variety conjoined to the greatest uniformity, whilst simplicity is praised because 'it permits a single and more telling stroke upon the mind, and because the mind in elevated mood descends only with reluctance to minute ornaments'. But Boullée nevertheless expounded an architectural aesthetic which was revolutionary in its most real sense, for he boasted his scorn of the ancient masters, and sought instead, by the study of nature, to enlarge his thoughts on an art which he considered 'still at its dawn'. He disdained to limit his imagination to what was constructable or commodious, and some of his projects for great spherical buildings, such as his cenotaph to Newton, or his completely impracticable opera house, not only had little relevance to *utilitas*, but could not have been constructed with the materials or techniques available at the time.

Ledoux was a disciple of Boullée, and like him, exploited the dramatic effects of cubic and spherical masses. Like him also, he displayed a fondness for blank walls and a dislike of traditional fenestration patterns which has characterized modern architecture in more recent years, and which caused even Frank Lloyd Wright to remark: 'Often I used to gloat over the beautiful buildings I could build if only it were unnecessary to cut windows in them'. He also showed a predilection for what J. F. Blondel called 'male simplicity', an idea which Ledoux may well have learnt directly from Blondel when he attended his school of architecture in the rue de la Harpe.

Ledoux's most revolutionary designs are to be found in his book entitled: *Architecture considered with respect to Art, Customs and Legislation* (1804), a series of projects intended to constitute an ideal city, and comprising all sorts of utopian

J. Soane: The Art Gallery Mausoleum, Dulwich (1811)

REVOLUTIONARY ARCHITECTURE

Illustrating the simplification of the Classical Orders in terms of abstract sculpture

I

E. L. Boullée: Project for a cenotaph to Newton (1784)

REVOLUTIONARY ARCHITECTURE

Illustrating the new emphasis on arbitrary, simple and grandiose compositional forms

II

E. L. Boullée: Design for a theatre (1781)

V. Louis: Theatre at Bordeaux (1777)

REVOLUTIONARY ARCHITECTURE

Illustrating the formalism of Boullée's compositions, by comparing the different ways 'revolutionary' and 'evolutionary' architects approached the same problem. (see also Plate XXV)

III

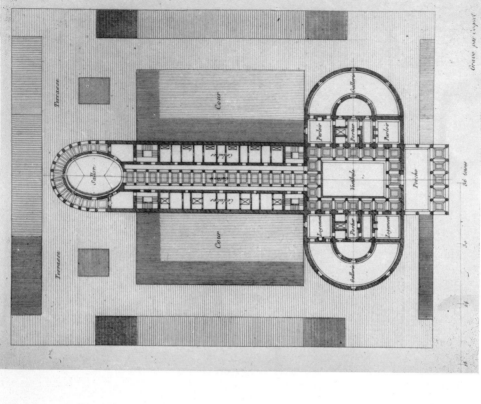

J. N. L. Durand: Method of planning by the use of squared paper
(1802)

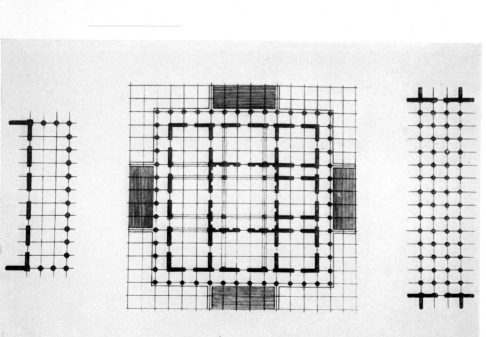

C. N. Ledoux: Plan for a 'house of pleasure' (1804)

REVOLUTIONARY ARCHITECTURE

*Illustrating the new tendency to plan buildings geometrically or
symbolically without close reference to functional requirements*

IV

buildings, including various temples to abstract virtues (such as a *Maison d'Union* consecrated to the worship of moral values, and a Temple of Conciliation) as well as more practical buildings such as brothels, schools, workshops, apartment houses and public baths. From an inspection of these 'ideal' compositions it is evident that his main contribution to modern architecture was his concept of a building as something *symbolic*. For him, the plan of an edifice was not something *resulting* from its function but was deliberately designed to *express* its function by the association of ideas. His plan for a House of Pleasure, for example, is not so much functional as phallic. At that time, the technique was known as *architecture parlante*, but in recent years it has been given the name of Expressionism, when it has again become influential, as may be seen from many of Eric Mendelsohn's projects, from Viljo Rewell's executed design for the Toronto City Hall, and from Eero Saarinen's T.W.A. Terminal at the John F. Kennedy Internationl Airport, New York.

The last of the four revolutionary architects, J. N. L. Durand, was also influenced by Boullée, since he worked in his office; but his doctrine differed considerably as a result of his having been a pupil of Perronet (the director of the French school of civil engineering) and it was the latter who doubtless helped him secure the post of professor of architecture at the newly formed École Polytechnique. Like Boullée, he considered a circle the ideal plan form, but for totally different reasons; indeed, a comparison of the work of these two men cannot better demonstrate the advantage of studying the history of modern architecture in terms of ideals, rather than of shapes. Both Boullée and Durand preferred circular plans; but whereas Boullée preferred them because they produced a perfect sculptural shape externally, Durand preferred them because they were more economical, in that they contained the greatest volume for a given area of enclosing wall. There were, he said, only two problems in architecture; firstly, the problem of private building, which was how to provide the optimum accommodation for the smallest sum of money; secondly, the problem of public building, which was how to provide the maximum accommodation for a given sum. He thus avoided the opulent megalomania characteristic of Boullée's more imaginative schemes, and based his criteria of architecture solely on the notions of utility and minimum cost.

Durand's theories were doubtless influenced very much by the fact that he was engaged in teaching engineering students, and that he was living in a period when utilitarian buildings were all that the French treasury could then afford. But it is immensely significant that instead of chafing under these restrictions, he eagerly accepted them, and made them the essence of his architectural doctrine. Ornament, he claimed, had nothing to do with architectural beauty, since a building was only beautiful when it satisfied a need. 'Whether we consult our reason, or examine ancient monuments', he wrote in his published lecture course, 'it is evident that the primary purpose of architecture has never been to please, nor has architectonic decoration been its object. Public and private usefulness, and the happiness and preservation of mankind, are the aims of architecture'. Similarly, he considered that originality should derive entirely from the unique functional quality which every building possessed. 'Does not one building automatically differ from another building if it is planned in a manner suited to its destined usage?' he rhetorically asked, 'and do not the different parts of that building, by being destined for different usages, necessarily differ from one another? Thus one should not strive to make a building pleasing, since if one concerns oneself solely with the fulfilment of practical requirements, it is impossible that it should not be pleasing. Architects should concern themselves with planning and with nothing else'. The doctrine of functionalism could hardly have been expressed more forcibly, and it has certainly never been expressed so unequivocally, even in recent years.

There is no need to describe the individual works of these four architects, nor those of their numerous disciples, since they have been amply documented by Henry-Russell Hitchcock in *Architecture, Nineteenth and Twentieth Centuries*. It is however necessary to mention an even more radical concept which emerged in the mid-eighteenth century (mainly in the works of other architects, such as J. F. Blondel), since though little noticed, it was to influence modern architecture in later years more than anything else. I refer to the new awareness of the qualities of architectural space.

A great deal of cant is talked nowadays about space in architecture, but behind the extravagant phrases and recondite terms one indisputable fact emerges; namely, that architects today consider that modern buildings possess spatial relationships of quite a different order from those possessed by the buildings of the past. There are even some theorists who contend that this new attitude towards space constitutes the basic principle which distinguishes the style of the modern age.

The most recent theories of architectural space will be discussed in the final chapter; but it is important to note here that a new theory had in fact already emerged as part of the Rococo. Before the mid-eighteenth century, the interior of a building was essentially a kind of box-like enclosure, or a series of box-like enclosures, either divided by visibly solid walls, or else interspersed by colonnades. But after about 1730, this attitude changed, although it is evident that the enclosures were still solidly bounded, and could only be fully experienced by walking through them, this being indeed a characteristic of all masonry structures of all times.

It would be wrong to assume, as some writers have assumed, that Classical volumes were spatially dull. Even the most symmetrically arranged box-like room could, when richly adorned, give different visual and emotional sensations as one moved around in it, and perceived its walls from different angles. Moreover, large rooms subdivided by columns produced even more exciting impressions as a result of parallax. But whatever the extent of this variety, its nature was still essentially the same as that produced since remote antiquity by the walls, porticoes and hypostyle halls of the monumental buildings of the past, and the new attitude towards space inevitably depended on changes of a more radical kind.

REVOLUTIONARY ARCHITECTURE

The change which occurred in the mid-eighteenth century concerned new devices for achieving parallax. Parallax is defined by the dictionary as 'the apparent displacement of objects caused by an actual change in the point of observation'. In ordinary experience this means, for example, that as one rides in a fast car, distant objects seem to be travelling at the same speed as the car relative to, say, nearby trees or poles which line the road. In architecture, it means that as one moves through or past a colonnade, the columns not only appear to change position relative to one another, but also appear to change position relative to whatever is perceived through them or behind them.

The multiplication of real (as opposed to illusionistic) effects of parallax was to prove impossible until developments in steel and reinforced concrete construction made every large building essentially a sequence of free-standing columns, and until the manufacture of large sheets of plate glass and the invention of modern heating equipment made buildings of every sort capable of becoming vast glazed hypostyle halls. But already in the middle of the eighteenth century we find an increase in the number of artificial effects of parallax, and also a new and sudden interest awakened in the aesthetic implications of the phenomenon itself, though only in general terms.

These artificial effects were produced by the use of large mirrors, which it became fashionable for Rococo decorators to place opposite one another on the walls of rooms. Now at first sight it might appear that the effect thus produced would differ little from the effect of the *trompe l'oeil* perspectives which it had long been traditional to use as wall decoration; but on further reflection—and this phrase may be taken quite literally—it will be perceived that whereas a painted perspective in no way adapts itself to the movements of an observer, the perspective image in a mirror does. Thus wherever the visitor walked in a mid-eighteenth century Rococo salon, he apparently saw, not enclosing walls, but a series of open arcades through which architectural spaces extended in an infinite parallactic sequence beyond the confines of the room.

Architectural effects of parallax intrigued the more acute observers of the period whenever they were to be found out of doors. Such effects did not occur very often, and were of course impossible to achieve deliberately with habitable buildings because of the constructional limitations of the era; but they were invariably to be seen in ruins, and this may be one of the reasons why ruins became so popular in that age. Robert Wood, when visiting the ruins of Palmyra in 1751, was as much impressed by their aesthetic as by their archaeological qualities, and remarked that 'so great a number of Corinthian columns, mixed with so little wall or solid building, afforded a most romantic variety of prospect'. In England, such effects were later to be widely appreciated by visitors to the numerous monastic ruins which dotted the countryside, and where, to quote from Sigfried Giedion's *Space, Time and Architecture* (though these words are used in a very different context), 'the interior and exterior of the building are presented simultaneously'.

The fondness at this time for multiplying free-standing Classical colonnades inside buildings, as well as outside buildings, may also be explained by the new delight in parallax. Boullée's more grandiose projects were to show many variations on this theme, but it had been exploited as early as 1757 by Soufflot in his great church of Ste. Geneviève (a building which, when it became the Panthéon, became even more Boulléesque in appearance through having all its forty-nine windows blocked up to produce completely blank walls). Soufflot had noticed that in the cathedral of Notre-Dame, 'the spectator, as he advances and as he moves away, distinguishes in the distance a thousand objects, at one moment found, at another lost again, offering him delightful spectacles'. He therefore attempted to produce the same effect inside Ste. Geneviève; for as Wolfgang Hermann has remarked, 'while the visitor moves forward, the cluster of columns seems to move too, opening up constantly changing views'—an effect actually described by Soufflot's successor Brébion in a letter dated 1780.

We thus find that by the end of the eighteenth century, the character of European architecture had been leavened by a completely new body of ideals. The fact that these were temporarily abandoned at the beginning of the nineteenth century in favour of other ideals, no less new and no less radical, is immaterial, for it is characteristic of stylistic changes in art that they result from the alternation of antithetical ideas rather than from any evolutionary process developing along a constant path. The important thing to note is that all these ideas were quite different from the ideas which constituted the architectural principles of earlier ages; for as Vincent Scully has perspicaciously remarked: 'it is an image we can recognize as ourselves that we must seek as we attempt to define the beginning of an art that is our own. First we might travel backward in time until we reach a chronological point where we can no longer identify the architecture as an image of the modern world. This point occurs, not at nineteen, or even eighteen hundred, but about the middle of the eighteenth century.'

2

The Influence of Historiography

Every student of eighteenth century architecture must have been struck by the number of epoch-making though apparently disconnected events which occurred round about the year 1750. In 1747, Perronnet founded the *École des Ponts et Chaussées* which formed the educational basis of modern civil engineering. In 1750, Walpole began to gothicize Strawberry Hill, the first substantial building of the Gothic Revival. In the same year, Baumgarten introduced the word 'aesthetics'. In 1751, Stuart and Revett and Soufflot made the first serious attempts to record Greek ruins. In 1752, Blondel published the first modern history of architecture. In 1754, Laugier published the first book equating architecture with rational construction. Examples could be multiplied, and will in fact be multiplied during the course of this book. It is sufficient here to say that it was these events rather than technological innovations which first produced the theory of modern architecture, and which prepared the way for the architecture which was to come when the Industrial Revolution eventually caused the old ways of living to be modified, and caused the old structural systems to be replaced.

The various positive changes which began to occur at this time are too complex to be summarized in a few phrases, but the negative qualities which they engendered, and which were to characterize architecture for the next two centuries, are very obvious. The first was the sudden uncertainty as to which of a wide variety of architectural elements were most appropriate or 'correct'. The second, resulting from it, was the abandonment of standardized components in architectural composition. There had of course been controversies about architectural 'correctness' in earlier centuries, such as those which discussed whether the proportions of the Orders given by one author were preferable to those given by another. But whereas before 1750, such arguments seem to have been concerned mainly with the proper use of standard elements, and the interpretation of accepted and clearly formulated values, by the end of the eighteenth century it is the values and elements themselves that are in dispute. As a result, a new importance was attached to variety, which the architects of the old school, such as Sir William

Chambers, dismissed as a mere search after novelty, but which the younger architects exploited with considerable success, especially when building houses for the bankers and other beneficiaries of the new capitalist system then being established. And as wealth became more abundant and more widespread, and the number of patrons and their architects increased, the difficulty of achieving originality in domestic architecture became more acute. It was inevitable that the resultant variety should eventually come to be justified by new doctrines, and that standardization, so essential a feature of classical doctrine, should ultimately go by the board.

Yet influential as these economic factors eventually proved to be, the immediate source of the changes in architectural ideas was more philosophical, and stemmed primarily from a new kind of awareness which we may call the awareness of history. For it would be quite wrong to assume that the study of history is a natural, inherent, inevitable kind of human activity, or that it has been regarded in all ages as a distinctive form of thought. The Greeks were not interested in history because it is concerned with what is transient and changing, with facts located in both space and time, whereas the scholars of Antiquity were concerned with what was permanent and immutable, such as is expressible by mathematics. Aristotle, for example, considered that poetry was more scientific than history, for history was to him a mere collection of empirical facts, whereas poetry extracted from such facts a universal judgement. Herodotus wrote only of what could be ascertained from eye-witnesses, and his aim was simply to chronicle glorious deeds which might be in danger of being forgotten with the passage of time.

The Roman historians such as Livy did indeed begin their histories at a more remote period of the past, but without any greater sense of historical development. On the contrary, their aim was to show the Eternal City as having existed ready-made from all time, so that they could hold up the mythical morality of its first citizens as an example to their contemporaries. They had an elemental awareness of historical cycles, but since they accepted the Greek view that there can be no science of transitory things, they considered history worth studying only because it constituted a good form of training for political life.

Mediaeval scholars had no more awareness of history, in its modern sense, than the scholars who preceded them, since they merely substituted the authority of theology for that of mathematics, and thought it incumbent on them to interpret the past entirely in terms of the Divine Plan. They did, however, introduce two concepts into historiography which were to affect historical thought in the period with which we are concerned: one was the notion of historical periods, the other was the idea that the past and the future both form some intelligible sequential pattern of events. These historical periods were based on religious foundations, such as the Redemption and the Day of Judgement. But once history was divided into periods, these led the way to a division of architecture into styles. Once history was thought of as apocalyptic, it tempted architectural historians to become theorists, and to try to determine the future as well as the past.

With the advent of the Renaissance, historical thought developed in different ways. Those interested in politics based their studies on classical writers. Those interested in science based their studies on classical methods. In the latter respect, the philosophical speculations of Descartes exerted a wide, even though somewhat negative influence on historiography. He himself was antagonistic to historical studies; but his purely rational methods encouraged a more scientific approach to the assessment of historical evidence, such as is to be found in the works of Bayle. It was in this age that manuscripts were first accurately dated and scientifically evaluated by means of the new sciences of palaeography and diplomatics, and that non-literary documents such as inscriptions and coins were first used to check and illustrate the narratives of early writers, thus leading the way to the archaeological researches of the modern age.

It is a curious fact that although the study of ancient buildings had formed an inevitable counterpart to the revival of Antiquity, it had little decisive influence on seventeenth and early eighteenth century thought, because people then, like those of Antiquity, were more interested in the present than in the past. History was rarely taught in schools before about 1760, when it was introduced into the Dissenting Academies by such teachers as Joseph Priestley. Chairs of modern history had been founded at Oxford and Cambridge in 1724 for political reasons, but no lectures were delivered at Cambridge until 1773, whilst at Oxford, the chair was usually occupied by poets, such as Thomas Gray and Joseph Spense. In Germany, there was a similar Aristotelian conviction that poetry and history were interchangeable, as seems clear from the career of J. F. Christ at the University of Leipzig. No chair of history was established at the Collège de France until 1769. The first French professorship in the history of architecture was that created at the École des Beaux-Arts in Paris in 1822.

The first modern historian, according to Eduard Fueter, was Voltaire, whose *Age of Louis XIV* appeared in 1751, and whose *Essay on the General History of Manners* was published in 1754. Now although neither of these books was directly concerned with architecture, they both provide us with useful clues as to how the new awareness of history created new trends in architectural thought. For example, if we examine the *Essay on Manners*, we find that, unlike previous history books, the text treats change as more characteristic of nature than permanence, and implies that this change is effected either gradually (i.e. by evolution) or suddenly (i.e. by revolution) as a direct result of human agency and will. Now this is the essence of the modern architectural concept of history. We now accept the word 'evolution' as meaning natural, gradual, and progressive changes in the structure of organized entities; but the original meaning of the word *evolutio* was simply the unrolling of a scroll (i.e. in order to read it), so that the English word 'evolution' at first meant the unrolling of the pre-ordained records of time. 'The whole Evolution of Ages', wrote the founder of the Cambridge Neo-Platonists, in 1667, 'is represented to God at once'. Similarly, the word 'revolution' has also had its original meaning reversed. A revolution was originally a mathematical or astronomical term meaning a rotation round an axis, and hence was also used figuratively to mean any cycle, such as the biological or historical cycles of growth, maturity and decay. But from the time of the English civil war it had begun to mean a radical political change, and today it means any radical change, as when we use the term 'industrial revolution'. It was not until the middle of the eighteenth century that architects began to think of architecture as a sequence of forms which evolve, and it was at this same time that some of them deliberately sought to accelerate the process of historical change by devising revolutionary shapes.

Secondly, Voltaire's text is concerned more with the general cultural progress of humanity than with political and military events, and it is for this reason that Voltaire is regarded as the first social historian, and hence the first to regard the arts as important aspects of national development. He had little interest in the visual arts, and in his three short chapters on the Fine Arts in his *Age of Louis XIV* scarcely mentions architecture at all. But in his article on 'History' in the *Encyclopédie*, he claimed that the history of the arts was perhaps the most useful of all, and he was probably the first historian to assert that the history of a civilization comprises the history of its art, and is mirrored in the works of art it produces. The first book to explore systematically this aspect of history was A. Y. de Goguet's *Origin of the Laws, Arts and Sciences, and their Progress among the most Ancient Nations*, published in 1758, but the author did not take his lengthy dissertation beyond 536 B.C., so that its influence on architecture was exerted indirectly, as for example through James Elmes' *Lectures in Architecture*, published in 1821.

Thirdly, Voltaire's text is critical to the point of scepticism. Myths are ruthlessly exposed, and all those fables which according to him fanaticism, romanticism and credulity have created throughout the ages are singled out for contempt. This attitude (which had already become manifest in 1723 when Levesque de Pouilly declared before the Academy of Inscriptions that nothing in Roman history was certain before Pyrrhus (316 B.C.)—for which he was denounced by one cleric as an atheist) eventually led to a completely critical approach towards the theory of architecture. Until this time students of architecture would no more have thought of questioning Vitruvius's mythical account of the origin of the Roman Orders than of questioning Livy's account of the origins of Rome itself, but once scorn was poured on Roman mythology, it was not long before architects sought more rational justification for using Roman architectural shapes.

Fourthly, Voltaire's text is concerned with determining the authenticity of origins, and it thus encouraged that respect for primitive cultures which is such a well-known characteristic of the present age. The historians of Antiquity had already established the tradition of idealizing primitive civilizations, but with Voltaire, Rousseau, Montesquieu, and in fact all the *Encyclopédistes*, new rational arguments were substituted for the old mythology, whereby instead of being merely pious superstitions, the forms of antiquity could now be cited as factual prototypes.

It is significant that it was not until 1750 that any architect thought of examining the ancient Greek temples at Paestum, which were only a few miles from Naples, or of studying the origins of architecture independently of Vitruvian texts.

Fifthly, Voltaire's text is concerned with progress, which he, like the other *Encyclopédistes*, conceived as essentially the advancement of the human race in and towards complete rationality, and hence towards perfection. Today, when the word 'progress' is almost invariably used in the sense of improvement, and when the word 'progressive' has come to be synonymous with 'beneficial', this attitude will not seem particularly worthy of note. But this figurative sense of the word (which in itself simply means physical movement forward), did not really become absolute until Voltaire's day. Fontenelle, in his *Digression on the Ancients and the Moderns*, published in 1688, held that although there is progress in science and industry, where development is cumulative, there is none in the Fine Arts which are chiefly a spontaneous expression of the human spirit. But it was precisely the progress in science and industry which most impressed philosophers in the mid-eighteenth century, and which they thought most likely to effect a general improvement in everything. The *Encyclopédie*, of which the first volume was published in 1751, has as its sub-title: *Reasoned Dictionary of the Sciences, Arts and Crafts*, and it defined 'Progress' in both its literal sense and in its figurative sense with specific reference to the Arts and Sciences. It is true that Rousseau, in his famous prize essay of 1750, claimed that 'the progress of sciences and arts has corrupted manners', but there is good evidence to show that he took this deliberately perverse attitude on Diderot's advice, because the latter perceived that the easiest way to win the prize was to be different from everyone else, and that in any case such contrariness was congenial to Rousseau's temperament.

Sixthly, Voltaire's text regards history as universal. Writers of the previous century, such as Bossuet, had already written what they called 'Universal Histories', but these were concerned essentially with the history of Christianity, and hence devoted most of their space to the sources from which it had grown. In the same way, writers on architecture, when they referred to the past, had tended only to concern themselves with those early architectural forms from which the architectural elements in current use were derived. But by criticizing Bossuet for not mentioning Mahometans or Hindus, and proceeding to rectify his omission, Voltaire led the way to the historical study of all civilizations, irrespective of their relationship to Graeco-Roman culture, and hence to the universal study of architectures as well.

Finally, Voltaire's text devotes about a third of its space to the Middle Ages, the rejection of which had been the primary requirement for all the architectural theories of the Renaissance. Voltaire thus strove not only to include the manners of all countries, but of all eras, and although he had, like most Frenchmen of the time, little sympathy with mediaeval literature, he recognized the historical importance of the period, and its formative influence on the national character of the

French. He specifically tells us that he wrote his *General History of Manners* to help Madame du Châtelet overcome the disgust which the earliest periods of the monarchy, before and after Charlemagne, inspired in her. Within a few years, histories and novels about the Middle Ages became widely fashionable, and these in turn led to the first scholarly studies of the mediaeval buildings which formed the settings for so many mediaeval events.

It was in England that the interest in mediaeval studies most quickly and most fully developed, and where the popularity of historical romances first prompted the new industrialists to adopt the Gothic style for their suburban homes. It was thus in England that modern architectural Romanticism really began. But before analysing the various reasons for this, it will be appropriate to mention here another important mid-eighteenth century trend exemplified in Voltaire's writings (which was also of great influence on architectural thought) namely, the new attitude towards the Orient.

Despite the apparent disparity of the two ideas, Historicism and Exoticism were very closely related. The essence of the modern awareness of history was the introduction of the notion of evolution, so that once philosophers such as Voltaire had shown that the nature of European institutions could be traced back as a continuous sequence of developments to primitive societies, the public became familiar with the evolutionary idea of chronology. But these same philosophers also drew attention to the fact that this chronology was purely relative, for they showed that primitive societies were still to be found in America, whereas there were civilizations in the Orient which, they claimed, were superior in many respects to that existing in Europe at that time. Thus the idea of evolution appeared contemporaneously with the idea of relativity, and these two concepts effectively combined together to destroy the faith in absolute and permanent values on which all the notions of Classical architecture were based.

In the polemical writings of Voltaire and Montesquieu, oriental personages were used simply as literary devices for making objective criticisms of the institutions then existing in France, and the vogue did not last long. But in the middle of the eighteenth century, several architects were also accepting the idea that Chinese architects could design ornament which was as good as Roman ornament for interior decorations; that Chinese gardens contained architectural features which might well be incorporated into English gardens; and that Chinese lack of symmetry (or *sharawaggi*, as it was erroneously called, under the delusion that this was the Chinese name for it) was as appropriate in buildings as it was in gardens. This latter view was put forward by Horace Walpole, and it was borne out by the writings of a French Jesuit, Frère Attiret, whose letters from China were published in 1749 and translated into English in 1761. Large Chinese structures, he said, such as public buildings, were symmetrical, but in Chinese pleasure-houses (i.e. villas) 'there reigns almost everywhere a beautiful disorder and asymmetry'. Little wonder that William Chambers's book on Chinese architecture, published in 1757, should have been so popular, or that he should have built a pagoda in the garden at Kew for his royal patron.

Naturally interest did not stop at China, so that by the middle of the nineteenth century, many European villas showed evidence of the variety of decorative motifs to be found in Indian and other Far Eastern monuments, especially as Fergusson's *History of Architecture* dealt very thoroughly with these countries, and several well-illustrated publications about their antiquities appeared at that time. The trend was particularly marked in America, where there were obvious chauvinistic reasons for deliberately disregarding the authority of traditional European prototypes. The tendency did not however become really marked until the beginning of the present century, when Frank Lloyd Wright, under the influence of the current concern with Japanese art, designed houses strongly influenced by the traditional architecture of Japan (though he himself claimed to have been influenced only by Japanese paintings). Today, exoticism has become so strong that a Japanese architectural magazine is now published in the English language, and even such radical theorists as Walter Gropius, who during the whole of their careers have fought strenuously against allowing the study of traditional architecture to influence the theory of modern design, now welcome books on the history of Japanese architecture as exemplifying the principles to be adopted in architecture today. It must be emphasized, however, that during the past two centuries, the ideals of Western architects have seldom been actually *derived* from the Orient. Exotic influences have usually been confined either to the borrowing of such ornamental motifs as could satisfy the current desire for novelty, or to the imitation of forms and dispositions which Western architects were already prone to adopt for reasons ignored by their oriental originators.

*   *   *

In the middle of the eighteenth century, the terms 'Chinese' and 'Gothic' were virtually interchangeable, since both were then merely synonyms for strange, outlandish, or bizarre, and, with respect to the then current classification of ornamentation, were merely branches of that general style of decoration then known derisively as Baroque. If we look for example at some of William Halfpenny's designs for temples in the Chinese taste, published in 1750, we can see that, apart from a slight waviness of the eaves, and bells suspended at the ends of them (both features derived more from the *chinoiseries* and *arabesques* of Rococo interior decorators than from any genuine oriental prototypes) all the details are Gothic. As late as 1780, Le Camus de Mézières was denouncing 'Gothic extravagances' by attributing them to the 'spirit of novelty' and the 'ease of doing Baroque', and he dismissed so-called 'Chinese' ornamental motifs as simply abstract shapes suggested by the grain of wood. The reason for this lack of stylistic discrimination was partly ignorance, but mainly indifference. What mattered to the nobility of that time was that the designs of their decorations should seem romantically remote, and whether this remoteness was expressed chronologically or geographically was immaterial to them. Nevertheless, since the effect eventually aimed at was (for reasons which will be discussed later) intended less to satisfy the intellect than to satisfy the imagination, they ultimately found it more congenial to associate their ideas with chronological remoteness related to their own national and historical traditions, and this was especially so when architectural patronage came into the hands of the newly rich, and when the historians and archaeologists began, for the first time, to explain to the public what those traditions really were.

Until 1750, nothing could have been more remote to a cultivated Englishman than the Middle Ages, for as its name implied, the mediaeval period was regarded simply as the thousand culturally-deserted years which occurred between the fall of Roman civilization and its revival during the Renaissance. But three events served to make him begin wondering whether it was not, in fact, a subject for serious research. The first was the attention given it by French political reformers, who recognized the mediaeval origins of all that was best in English law; the second was the attention given it by literary critics, who suddenly became interested in mediaeval poetry; and the third was the fact that most of the sources of classical history were by now exhausted, whereby the Middle Ages offered an exciting new field of documentary and archaeological research.

Popular attention was first drawn to the mediaeval origins of the British con-stitution by Montesquieu, who saw the latter as a model of that political liberty so signally lacking in France. Montesquieu himself had no more sympathy with the cultural aspects of mediaeval life than Voltaire, but he managed to show that the manners and institutions currently thought to be barbaric and irrational must be viewed in relation to their period, and to the historical needs and circumstances out of which they had grown. By presenting the idea that in at least one respect the Middle Ages were not barbaric, and that they possessed institutions which formed a valuable part of the English heritage, he suggested to British scholars that they should begin wondering whether the culture of the era was really as insignificant as they had hitherto supposed, or whether it might not, like Chinese civilization, be simply a worthy culture of a different kind.

This view was especially tempting to English literary critics, whose greatest national poet had written his plays before the Renaissance rules had been fully established. Voltaire, with his typically French Classical prejudices, not unnaturally considered Shakespeare's plays to be without the slightest spark of good taste, since they showed a complete lack of any knowledge of the rules. Similarly Pope, with his typically English Classical prejudices, shared this view, and could only defend Shakespeare's disregard of the Classical unities by saying that it was as unfair to judge Shakespeare by Aristotle's rules as it would be to try a man by the laws of one country if he had acted under the laws of another (a plea later echoed by Warton when, in 1754, he published his observations on Spenser's *Faerie Queene*). The distinction between Shakespeare's plays and more regular dramas, he said, was like that between an ancient majestic piece of Gothic architecture and a neat modern building. But in 1765 Dr. Johnson, goaded by Voltaire's sarcasm, not only defended Shakespeare's style wholeheartedly on its own merits, but suggested that it was perhaps time the whole question of the validity of Classical rules was re-examined. If Classical rules could be applied by a playright without harming his play, so much the better, he said, and the playright deserved as much applause as an architect who managed to display all the Orders of architecture in a citadel without diminishing its strength. But the principal beauty of a citadel, he added, was to exclude the enemy, just as the greatest graces of a play were to copy nature and instruct life. This vigorous analogy between architecture and military engineering was perhaps the first to suggest so plainly that function was more important than the observance of Classical forms.

The renewed interest and pride in Shakespeare's plays naturally awakened curiosity in the sources from which Shakespeare's mediaeval histories had been taken, especially after Bishop Percy published, in the same year as Dr. Johnson's preface, his *Reliques of Ancient Poetry* (containing many of the mediaeval ballads from which, according to Dr. Johnson, Shakespeare obtained much of his raw material). The result was that by the time Warton published his *History of English Poetry* in 1774, the Middle Ages were no longer regarded as a period of illiteracy and barbarism, with nothing in them worth noticing, but as a respectable and important period of English literature.

The inevitable effect of such views on the architectural thought of the period is evident from the analogies then used by the literary critics. In 1715 John Hughes had defended Spenser by saying that to compare the *Faerie Queene* with the models of Antiquity would be like comparing Gothic with Roman architecture; the latter undoubtedly contained more natural grandeur and simplicity, and gave a totality of greater majesty, whilst the former only derived its beauty from the surprising ornaments which constituted its lesser parts. But by 1765 it was accepted amongst the *literati* that neither the poetry nor the architecture of the two ages was comparable, and hence that such terms as 'barbarism' were out of place. For example, in Bishop Hurd's *Idea of Universal Poetry*, published in that year, he asked rhetorically why Spenser and Milton were charmed by mediaeval romances. Was it caprice or absurdity, he asked, or was there something in them suited to the ideas of a genius and the purposes of poetry? The answer he gave is similar to that made by Pope with regard to Shakespeare, but he expresses it with a more sympathetic metaphor than Pope's, and in a more phlegmatic way than Hughes: 'If you judge Gothic architecture by Grecian rules', he says, 'you find nothing but deformity, but when you examine it by its own the result is quite different'. In the same way, Hazlitt compared Sophocles to Shakespeare by comparing a Doric temple with a Gothic cathedral. The principle of the one, he says, is simplicity and harmony; that of the other is richness and power. The one owes its charm to a certain unity and regularity, the other attains its effect by complexity and the combination of the greatest extremes. 'Both', he concludes, 'are founded in essential and in-distructible principles of human nature'. In other words, all buildings can be judged aesthetically only with reference to their origins, and to the rules in force when they were built; a theory of relativity which has been of the utmost influence in the history of modern architectural thought.

The mid-eighteenth century interest in mediaeval literature naturally encouraged a more sympathetic regard for mediaeval history and antiquities. As early as 1741 Lord Lyttelton had complained to Pope that Bolingbroke and his friends had written everything worth writing about Classical history, leaving him nothing but 'the rubbish of monkish annals' and 'rude Gothic ruins'. By the 1760s historians were coming to the conclusion that these annals were not really such rubbish after all, and whereas their precursors, such as Voltaire and Hume, had written about the Middle Ages rather patronizingly, later historians such as Robertson now described them with considerable respect. By the beginning of the nineteenth century the Middle Ages were being approached with an enthusiasm bordering on adulation, and from being regarded as an era of barbarism, they came gradually to be vested with all the prestige and authority attributed formerly only to Greece and Rome. The publication of Hallam's *View of the State of Europe during the Middle Ages* in 1818 marked the stage in the transformation when the revision of scholarly opinion may be said to have been complete.

This change of view would not, however, have been appreciated by the general public had it not been for the sudden popularity of historical novels, written mainly by, and essentially for, women. The first Gothic novel was Horace Walpole's *Castle of Otranto*, published in 1764, but the great age of the 'Gothic romance' was from 1785 to the first decades of the nineteenth century, when a spate of titles appeared such as *Emmeline, the Orphan of the Castle*, over such names as Sophia Lee, Charlotte Smith, Ann Radcliffe, Eliza Parsons, Catherine Selden, Maria Edgeworth, Harriet Lee, and so on. The main purpose of these romances was to impart impressions of strangeness, mystery and glamour in the context of an unfamiliar environment; but their effect was often paradoxically the very opposite, for whether they dealt imaginatively with historical situations (like those of Ann Radcliffe) or with contemporary situations (like those of Charlotte Smith) they frequently implanted a desire in their more impressionable readers to continue experiencing these impressions in their daily lives.

The medium by which this transition from fantasy to reality was most easily effected was by architecture; especially by Gothic villas. All the romances contained frequent references to buildings, which performed much the same function in the dramatic action as stage-sets in a Shakespearian play, and it was the fascinating gloom and thrilling awfulness of the mediaeval architectural settings which gave these romances their most exciting character. Moreover, these buildings were more than just literary back-cloths; they actually contributed elements which formed the essential parts of the plots. Emmeline lived in a remote tower—the favourite habitation of the heroines of such novels—as did Monimia, the heroine of Charlotte Smith's *The Old Manor House*, and the latter's turret had the added convenience of a secret staircase which allowed her to visit her hero Orlando. Similarly, in Ann Radcliffe's *The Castles of Athlin and Dunbayne*, a loose stone in the pavement of Alleyn's cell, and a movable panel in the wainscot of Osbert's prison, afforded the crucial means of escape for these two captives by way of a subterranean passage leading under the moat. Tunnels, dungeons, garrets, and all the other features popularly but indistinctly associated with mediaeval architecture constituted the essential framework of the stories, and became glamorized through transmutations effected by impressionable and gentle minds. 'How widely different are my sensations in this charming retirement!', exclaims the heroine of Eliza Parsons's *Caroline Merton*. 'The venerable antiquity of the fabric, the pleasing gloom that reigns around, and the several pieces of rusty armour which adorn the lofty hall, fill my mind with new and delightful ideas.' It was inevitable that the readers themselves should eventually feel a desire to experience these same widely different sensations, and to enjoy that same emotion of 'romantic-ness' which Clarissa Harlowe, the heroine of Richardson's *Clarissa* (1748), had experienced in her Uncle Antony's moated house. All that was needed was a precedent, and this was already provided by Horace Walpole, the son of George II's prime minister and a leader of aristocratic fashion, who had indulged in a similar whimsicality by gradually converting his country house at Strawberry Hill into a Gothic villa, beginning in 1750 and continuing for the next twenty years.

It was the desire to live the experiences of a novel which constituted the original essence of architectural romanticism, even though romanticism itself eventually became complicated by many other factors whereby the word acquired all sorts of meanings, some of them contradictory. We know what the word meant in the early eighteenth century, for 'romance' had long been used for mediaeval stories written in the vernacular, and Chaucer used the term 'romaunce' when describing a tale embodying the adventures of some hero of chivalry. Hence by the seventeenth century the word 'romantic' had also acquired the meaning of 'fictitious' as when Pepys, in 1667, remarked that certain events were 'almost romantique, and yet true'. Soon after 1750, however, a radical change of meaning began to occur, as is shown in the writings of the Vicomte d'Ermenonville, who commented in his book on the composition of landscapes, published in 1777, that he preferred the English word 'romantique' to the French word '*romanesque*', since the latter designated the fable of a novel, whereas the former corresponded to qualities he had earlier classified as '*pittoresque*'.

The close relationship which developed between romanticism and the picturesque will be examined in the next chapter. But meanwhile it is appropriate to remark on the importance of the term romanticism in nineteenth century artistic (and hence architectural) ideas, especially after it had been adopted by German literary critics. In Friedrich Schlegel's studies of poetry, written in the early 1790s, the word was used freely to denote mediaeval literature, as distinct from the poetry of Antiquity, at a time when Schlegel still accepted the validity of Classical standards, and was only concerned to distinguish between the relative values of 'the ancient' and 'the modern' (i.e. mediaeval) so that the latter could be more effectively condemned. But like Johnson before him, he was faced with the problem of classifying Shakespeare, and he eventually concluded that although the distinctive quality of Classical poetry would always be its objective beauty, the poetry of Shakespeare (which he classified as both 'modern' and 'romantic') nevertheless had the subjective virtue of possessing greater interest. By the end of the decade he had decided that he actually preferred Romanticism to Classicism, 'the modern' to 'the ancient', the subjective to the objective, the freedom of expression to the rules of taste. As a result, the words 'modern' and 'romantic' shared entirely new meanings, for the former, instead of being a chronological distinction between Antiquity and the period which immediately followed its decline, now acquired aesthetic and moral implications whereby it was distinguished not only from what was ancient, but from what was displeasing, reactionary, academic, unfashionable, or possessed any other qualities which its devotees equated with what was ethically or aesthetically bad.

The heyday of Romanticism was the 1830s, when in the writings of Goethe, Wordsworth, Pushkin, Balzac, Victor Hugo, Stendhal and Dickens, in the music of Berlioz and Schumann, and in the paintings of Constable and Delacroix, Romanticism seems to find its most luxuriant expression, and even appears to some as the expression of a collective will. Yet even then, Romanticism was by no means universally accepted, and the words Romantic and Classical were still used to express the basic antithesis between two fundamentally antagonistic ideals. This was because they corresponded to two aspects of human nature from which all problems of morality ultimately spring, and thus they meant not only the difference between Greek and Gothic, but the difference between emotional and rational, between sensual and intellectual, between sentiment and judgement, and between freedom and the rule of law. Most moderate architects of the time, like most moderate men, managed to achieve some harmony and balance, or at least a compromise, between these conflicting forces. But in architecture, as in life, it is the extremists who attract the most attention; and by flouting their excesses in each other's faces, they managed to maintain a series of controversies which continued in different forms during the ensuing hundred years.

We thus find that one of the most characteristic features of the theory of modern architecture has been its concern with morality, whereby the ethical bases of architectural design have obsessed modern propagandists in a way formerly unknown. Why this change should have occurred in the middle of the eighteenth century is not entirely clear, but it is evident that as soon as architects became aware of architectural history, and of the architectures of exotic civilizations (and hence of architectural 'styles'); as soon as they became uncertain as to which of a wide

Pl. 54. The Elevation of a Temple partly in the Chinese Taste.

W. Halfpenny: A garden temple partly in the Chinese taste (1750)

HISTORICISM AND EXOTICISM

Illustrating the confusion which existed in the mid-eighteenth century regarding the characteristics of mediaeval and exotic 'styles'

V

Lord Herbert and R. Morris: Mrs. Howard's villa at Marble Hill (1721)

C. N. Ledoux: Madame du Barry's villa at Louveciennes (1771)

THE NEW FASHION FOR VILLAS

*Illustrating the type of aristocratic pleasure-houses which became the model for
domestic architecture during the following century*

F. J. Belanger: Comte d'Artois' Bagatelle, Paris (1777)

P. Rousseau: Hôtel de Salm, Paris (1786)

THE NEW FASHION FOR VILLAS

*Illustrating how some villas were influenced by more monumental
compositional forms, such as Roman thermae*

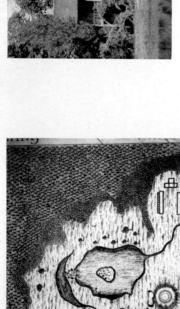

Hubert Robert: Hameau de la Reine, Versailles (1783)

J. Wyatt: Fonthill Abbey (1795)

R. Castell: Part of Pliny's villa garden
at Tuscum (published in 1728)

SUBLIMITY AND THE PICTURESQUE

Illustrating the two most powerful ingredients of eighteenth-century Romanticism

VIII

variety of tectonic elements they might appropriately use; they were obliged to make basic decisions involving moral judgements, and to discuss fundamental problems which their more fortunate forbears had disregarded because in their ignorance of history, and the security of their traditions, they did not know that these fundamental problems existed, and hence were blissfully unaware that there were any ethical decisions to make.

3

The Influence of the Picturesque

In each architectural era there is usually one building-type which dominates all others, and which, because of the attention lavished on it by influential patrons, tends to affect the design of buildings contemporary with it. In ancient Greece the dominant building-type was the temple; in mediaeval Europe it was the church; in Renaissance Europe it was the palace. After 1750 the dominant building-type is not so obvious, since the variety of different building-types became suddenly more numerous—a development which in itself was yet another characteristic distinguishing the modern age. But in so far as any one building-type could, more than another, be said to influence the general theory of architecture after 1750, it was the villa, defined by J. C. Loudon, in his *Encyclopedia of Cottage, Farm and Villa Architecture*, as 'a country residence with pleasure garden attached'. A villa was however more than this, for once it was adopted as the favourite type of dwelling for the newly enriched merchants and industrialists, it became a medium for expressing architecturally many of the most powerful aspirations of the age, and it was doubtless for this reason that Loudon added that a villa was also a means of adding to comfort 'the gratifications resulting from the display of wealth and taste'.

Villas, because of their multiplicity, their relatively modest dimensions and their unrestricted sites, allowed the current propensity for romanticism to be most fully exploited and expressed, and the importance of their subsequent influence cannot be exaggerated. Not only at the beginning of the modern era, but throughout the whole period from 1750 to 1950, architectural theory was dominated by factors more strictly appropriate only to domestic architecture; and it is by no means coincidental that the most influential architectural pioneers of the present century, such as Wright, Gropius, Mies van der Rohe and Le Corbusier, originally gave expression to their theories by building either villas for wealthy connoisseurs or, after the 1918 war, modest dwellings for artisans or impecunious artists. The romantic suburban villa was not so much a minor building-type characteristic of the early nineteenth century, as a paradigm for the architecture of the whole age. Many features of contemporary design, such as asymmetry, and the consequent irregularities of plan, fenestration and silhouette, were originally characteristic only of these villas, even though it was many years before they spread from this limited use to become integral parts of the general concept of architecture as we understand it today.

The general idea of a villa, in the sense of a country dwelling, could be traced, if one so wished, back to ancient Rome, but it was not until about 1720 that it was used in its modern and more restricted sense, so it would be more accurate to find its modern origins in the country houses constructed by the mid-eighteenth century aristocracy to entertain their friends. Forty years later, even sumptuous palaces were being designed like villas, and the plan of Keddleston, for example, was, as John Summerson has observed, a most important indication of the extent to which the villa idea had obtained a hold by 1759.

The fashion for building small houses probably started in England, and spread to the Continent as part of the general anglomania which also introduced the English informal garden, horse-racing, five o'clock tea, and other recreations for which the English names still survive in France. Its earliest royal prototypes were probably Marble Hill in England (built by George II for Mrs. Charles Howard) and the Petit Trianon in France (built by Louis XV for Madame de Pompadour); but the great period for 'follies' was about 1775, when the rise of capitalism and the fashion for theatregoing added bankers to the ranks of such ladies' protectors, and actresses to the ranks of the illustrious kept.

Amongst the most characteristic late eighteenth century 'follies' may be instanced those by Ledoux and Bélanger, such as Madame du Barry's charming little house at Louveciennes, the villa which the Prince de Soubise built in Paris for the ballet-dancer Marie-Madeleine Guimard, and the elegant 'Bagatelle' which Louis XVI's brother had constructed in six weeks on the outskirts of Paris as a result of a bet with Marie Antoinette. All three buildings were extremely Classical in composition and detail, with simple geometric elements and Classical mouldings, but such aristocratic formality was not necessarily congenial to the English manufacturers of the following century, who had neither noble ancestors nor educated tastes, and were moreover building villas for their wives. These sturdy matrons probably had little sympathy with the culture of Classical antiquity, but were very susceptible to the architectural qualities extolled in the novels they read, and it was this susceptibility, combined with the emergence of a new science called aesthetics, which created the roots of a new architectural theory which English suburban villas were to be the first to express.

The new aesthetic theory ostensibly embraced all the arts, but in fact its premises were based primarily on two of them, namely literature and landscape painting. The English had for some time been particularly fond of both, but until the middle of the eighteenth century neither had much direct influence on architecture. Thus to understand the new theory, and why it spread so rapidly throughout Europe and America, we must first examine briefly the English attitudes towards art and nature, and then consider why they should have influenced so strongly the general theory of architectural design when they did.

Whatever the origin of the new mid-eighteenth century theory of aesthetics (and clearly, since no idea is ever entirely original, anyone so inclined might trace its philosophical germs back to the most remote times) there can be little doubt that it received its first popular expression in Joseph Addison's periodical *The Spectator*, when, under the inspiration of Locke's *Essay on Human Understanding*, he published a series of daily articles entitled 'The Pleasures of the Imagination' in 1712. He began by explaining that the most perfect of all our senses is that of sight, since the mind not only receives most of its ideas by this means, but retains, alters and compounds these images into all the varieties of picture and vision which are most agreeable to the imagination. Thus the pleasures of the imagination (which are, he tells us, neither as gross as sensual pleasures nor as refined or as subtle as intellectual pleasures) arise in two ways: firstly, from such objects as are before our eyes, and secondly, from the thought of visible objects when these are not actually present. But as the article proceeds, this distinction is not in fact maintained, and the originality and importance of Addison's contribution to modern aesthetics lies in his fusion—or perhaps one might say confusion—between vision and imagination, between art and nature, between the objective and the subjective, and between the emotions peculiar to the various different media of art.

That he does not intend to make any distinction between art and nature, between visible form, the depiction of visible form and the description of visible form, or even between the different branches of art, is clear at the very beginning of the series, for in the sixth paragraph of his first article Addison refers casually to 'delightful scenes, whether in nature, painting or poetry', as if these were all generically the same thing. By his third article, he also makes clear that he does not intend to maintain the distinction originally made between what is seen and what is purely imaginary. Things, he tells us, would give a poor optical impression if we saw them only in their proper figures and motions, and man can only assume that they appear beautiful because God has given almost everything about him the power of raising an agreeable idea in the imagination. Thus our souls are constantly being delightfully lost and bewildered in a pleasing delusion, and we walk about, he says, like the enchanted hero in a romance, who sees beautiful and fantastic castles which, upon the breaking of some secret spell, will vanish. All beauty is thus, he implies, romantic beauty, whether it be found in landscapes, landscape paintings or pastoral poetry; for scenes and objects are only beautiful in so far as they imaginatively stimulate our minds.

But beauty is not, for him, the only pleasure of the imagination, and here he introduced another idea which was further to confuse and undermine the current objective Classical notions about taste. The pleasures of the imagination, he says, proceed not only from the sight of what is beautiful, but also from the sight of what is great or uncommon. Now the statement that visual pleasure arises from beauty was a commonplace at this time, since it had been the accepted basis of all artistic theory since the Renaissance, and was indeed implicit in the term *beaux-arts* (mistranslated into English as Fine—instead of Beautiful—Arts) and in the current notions of *la belle nature*. But the suggestion that size and novelty were also in themselves sources of aesthetic emotion, and of comparable importance to beauty, was revolutionary, since it not merely reduced the role of beauty as a criterion of artistic excellence, but asserted that the standards of taste were related less to what was objective and tangible than to the subjective manner by which objects were perceived. Indeed, Addison went so far as to insist on the aesthetic merits of ugliness, for, as he observed, 'novelty bestows charms on a monster, and makes even the imperfections of nature please'.

All the notions so far mentioned have referred to the pleasures of the imagination arising from the contemplation of actual objects or scenes. But in the sixth instalment of his essay, Addison begins discussing what he calls the 'secondary pleasures' which arise from the contemplation of what is imaginary, and are often expressed in works of art. These latter pleasures, he says, proceed from an action of the mind which compares the ideas prompted by original objects with the ideas prompted by the statue, picture, description, or sound that represents them, or, in other words, by 'the affinity of ideas'; and this, he claims, explains why different readers react in different ways to descriptive poems, for only those born with a good imagination can truly relish their emotional power. Thus whether we consider buildings as actual visible objects or as works of the imagination, their aesthetic value, according to Addison, is the same; their merits derive not from the possession of beautiful proportions or from their conformity to any standards of ideal perfection, but from their power to inspire romantic images by conjuring up thoughts in the observer's mind. Architecture, like the other arts, becomes a kind of poetry, and from now onwards its eloquence can only be evaluated in terms of the association of ideas.

Such theories (though their influence extended, according to Elie Halévy, even into the realm of economics) were mainly applicable to literature (and by extension, in an age which accepted Horace's dictum that a poem is comparable to a painting —*ut pictura poesis*—to genre paintings and landscapes) and it is not therefore surprising that the earliest contributions to the new science of aesthetics, such as G. B. Vico's *Scienza Nuova* published in 1725, and A. G. Baumgarten's *Aesthetica* published in 1750 (the first work in which the word aesthetics appears) were essentially, like the second half of Addison's articles in *The Spectator*, concerned mainly with verse. But by the end of the century, Addison's basic thesis had been established as an extensive philosophical system embracing all the arts (on the traditional though by no means well-founded assumption that all the arts must be explicable by one unique law) and the most lucid expression of its application to architecture occurred with the publication, in 1790, of Archibald Alison's *Essays on the Nature and Principles of Taste*.

Alison began by re-asserting Addison's claim that the association of ideas is the essential source of what he calls 'the emotion of Taste', and the primary cause by which all aesthetic emotions are to be ultimately explained. Matter itself, he insists, is unfitted to produce any kind of emotion, yet material objects may produce this effect from their association with other qualities, of which they become signs or expressions. Thus the admiration paid to the architecture of antiquity originates, he claims, in the associations which the majority of mankind connects with these forms, as being evocative of the glories of ancient Greece and Rome; or, as para- phrased by his disciple Joseph Gwilt: 'ancient architecture of whatsoever class, country or period cannot be separated, in a just estimation of its merits, from the history of the nation in which it flourished'.

Alison was clearly convinced, like most of his contemporaries, of the superiority of Classical forms, but he nevertheless considered that his preference was purely subjective and relative, and that other men might just as validly prefer some entirely different architecture which had associations more congenial to their cultural upbringing and temperament. Indeed, such a conclusion was to some extent forced upon him by the many radical changes which had occurred in the seventy-eight years since Addison's essays first appeared (although one may suspect that in order to further his argument, Alison here minimized the distinction —which he elsewhere insists upon—between fashion and taste). There are cases, he says, where the taste of a nation undergoes an absolute change, from associations of a different kind becoming fashionable. To illustrate this point, he shifts the argument from architecture to furniture and dress. Some years before, he says, every article of furniture was made in what was then called the Chinese taste, but this was subsequently succeeded by the Gothic taste. Gothic furniture was not made in imitation of genuine mediaeval furniture, but of the forms and ornaments of Gothic halls and cathedrals; nevertheless this slight association was sufficient to give beauty to such forms, because it led to ideas of Gothic manners and adventure made fashionable by reading beautiful compositions in prose and verse.

Now apart from his illogicality of defining fashion as 'the custom of the great' (the associated idea of which is simply snobbery) and then using the word as interchangeable with taste, it is clear that even such a cultivated and thoughtful man as Alison, in his anxiety to reinforce his philosophical arguments, was already, by praising such furniture, losing his sense of values, and showing an extraordinary lack of discrimination in judging of what was beautiful, or of the kind of artistic qualities which were likely to last. There is thus little wonder that less cultivated men, long before the Victorian era, also admired anything, however incongruous, which could stimulate their imaginations, and such doctrines, working in con- junction with the current popular enthusiasm for Gothic romances, were in them- selves quite sufficient to explain the sudden desire for romantic villas which appeared at this time.

It will now be appropriate to consider the implications of one other important aspect of the new theory of aesthetics, namely the decision to classify aesthetic stimuli into such categories as beauty, sublimity and the picturesque. Not all the philosophers of the time acknowledge these classifications, or agreed with one another as to how they applied. But the terms were soon widely accepted by the general public, and are intimately associated with the new architectural ideals which were then being introduced.

The first to be considered, without getting involved in all those wearisome shades of meaning given it by competing philosophers since remote antiquity, is the notion of beauty. It is fair to say that before 1750, architectural beauty was generally regarded, on the authority of Vitruvius, as a matter essentially of proportion, related absolutely to a harmonious system of abstract mathematical intervals, and related analogically to the proportions of man. This interpretation was accepted by Addison, who, like Vitruvius, attributed beauty to the symmetry and proportion of parts. But it was rejected by many later philosophers, notably Edmund Burke, who, in his *Philosophical Enquiry into the Origin of our Ideas of the Sublime and Beautiful* published in 1756, claimed that neither proportion nor utility had anything whatsoever to do with beauty, and justified his remark by referring to the various species of animals and plants.

According to Burke, beauty resulted from such qualities as smallness, smoothness and delicacy. He therefore rejected the Vitruvian notion that architectural beauty was related to the proportions of the human body (i.e. that the Doric Order was deliberately based on a man, the Corinthian Order on a maiden, and the Ionic Order on a stout lady whose girth was the average between the two); and although the reasons he gave for rejecting such an obviously irrational tradition were surprisingly obtuse, this did not lessen the revolutionary character of his attack. Today, we regard this analogy as not merely naïve and inept but pointless, and find it difficult to understand why Classical architects should have persisted in according it such uncritical belief. But in the Classical era it was regarded as the justification for a standardization of proportions which would otherwise have been impossible. For as J. D. Leroy observed in his book on the ruins of Greece, published in 1758, if the Greeks had thought to take any other natural object as the model for the form of their columns, as for example the trunk of a particular species of tree, they would have been obliged, because of its slender proportions, to use very hard materials such as granite or marble when building durably, and thus, in countries where such materials were not to be found, classical monuments could not have been built.

Burke's widely publicized views thus not only undermined the authority of the Classical Orders, but paved the way for those who held that the proportions of tectonic elements should be related to the strength of the materials of which they were made. Even by 1759 these ideas began to be tentatively introduced by architectural theorists. In Chambers's *Treatise on the Decorative Parts of Civil Architecture*, published in that year, the author accepted, as the origin of many

47

proportions, their aptitude for the purpose they serve, and also insisted on the importance of the association of ideas.

Alison, writing thirty years later, did not take such a radical approach to these problems as Burke, since he accepted the traditional view that beauty was derived from proportion. But in pursuing his theory of the association of ideas, he advanced the notion (which can also in its general terms be traced back to the ancient Greeks) that good proportions are simply an expression of the idea of fitness. Thus his conclusions were not merely, in fact, in harmony with Burke's, but were much more explicit, since he specifically asserted that architectural proportions were based on the association existing between the dimensions of a structural element and the material's resistance to the load. 'What we mean by proportion', he wrote, 'is merely fitness for the ends of stability and support'. This fitness could not at the time be very accurately measured, and since, of its nature, it was capable of wide limits, there were accordingly no accurate proportions of this kind. Moreover, as Alison observed, our sentiments regarding the proportions of buildings depend upon the nature of each building, as well as the materials of which they are composed.

Yet although the associational value attributed to the relationship between proportion and fitness varied, none of these theorists disputed the notion that the most powerful associations, and hence the most poignant aesthetic emotions, were derived not from beauty but from sublimity and the picturesque. Sublimity had long been identified as one of the main emotional qualities of certain kinds of poetry. But it was not easy to create it in architecture, even though Alexander Gerard, in his *Essay on Taste* of 1759, considered that since the principal source of grandeur in architecture is association, columns must inevitably introduce sublime ideas by suggesting strength and durability. Similarly Madame de Staël admired the dome of St. Peter's, Rome, because when seen from inside it inspired in her a sentiment of terror. Sublimity was a quality usually ascribed to cavernous mountains and other awe-inspiring scenic events, and the only characteristic of sublimity which, in an age devoted to melancholy poetry, could be related to architecture, was gloom. Therefore Burke considered that all edifices calculated to produce an idea of the sublime should be gloomy, and 'pleasing gloom' was, as has already been pointed out, one of the principal literary devices by which the novelists of the period created their most striking architectural effects.

The type of gloom envisaged was of the sort exemplified in Charlotte Smith's novel *The Banished Man* (1794), where the immense hall of Castle Vaudrecour was so obscure because of its great height, its time-blackened oak beams and its high narrow windows that it was with difficulty that the hero could make out the objects with which he was surrounded. In Ann Radcliffe's *Sicilian Romance* (1790), it was the high Gothic windows of one of the halls which gave the 'air of proud sublimity' which characterized the place. Similarly, in this same author's *The Mysteries of Udolpho* published in 1794, the heroine was able to gaze with melancholy awe at Montoni's castle because its mouldering walls of dark grey stone rendered it 'a gloomy and sublime object', and its extensive Gothic hall was obscured by 'the gloom of evening'. Not everyone could afford an extensive Gothic hall, but the gloom of evening was easily obtainable even if it could not be permanently simulated, whilst instructions for creating mouldering walls were available to everyone in J. C. Loudon's *Encyclopedia of Cottage, Farm and Villa Architecture*.

Probably the most striking attempt to exploit architecturally the poetic emotion of sublimity was to be seen in Fonthill Abbey. Built originally as a gigantic summer-house from 1796 onwards for William Beckford, an eccentric and romantic millionaire, it was designed from the first as essentially a grandiose piece of scenery, and consisted eventually of vast and extravagant wings which radiated from an octagonal tower 276 ft. high. This tower, which in its lower part constituted the salon, was approached by a stair hall 120 ft. high, and it is easy to believe that its carved timber painted in imitation of old oak, and its stained glass windows, produced what a contemporary visitor described as 'an effect little removed from the sublime'. This sublimity was considerably heightened at night on gala occasions, as for example when Lord Nelson, with Sir William and Lady Hamilton, visited it in 1800. Then, the staircase was lighted by mysterious living figures dressed in hooded gowns, and as the company entered the gallery, mysterious music struck the ear from some invisible quarter. It is not surprising, therefore, that when leaving this strange nocturnal scene of vast buildings and extensive woods, rendered dimly and only partially visible by the diminishing light of lamps and torches, the company seemed as if 'waking from a dream', or 'just released from the influence of some magic spell'.

Fonthill undoubtedly exerted a tremendous influence, even before the numerous books about it were published, and before it was visited by over seven thousand people when it was sold by auction in 1822. But the difficulty of achieving a comparable sublimity on a less extravagant scale caused it to have few imitators, so that the aesthetic value which had the most influence on early nineteenth century domestic architecture was not sublimity but the picturesque.

The notion of 'the picturesque' was probably the most important aesthetic idea ever exerted by England over European architecture, and since, for that reason, it has been exhaustively dealt with by several distinguished authors, it can be discussed here quite summarily. It derived essentially from the English fondness for natural scenery, and, by extension, from their fondness for paintings of natural scenery as exemplified in the highly prized Elysian or Vergilian landscapes by Nicholas Poussin and Claude Lorrain—hence the term 'picturesque'. This led to a widespread desire for less rigid layouts of gardens and private parks, which before 1740 had usually been based either on the Jacobean tradition of angular geometric parterres and topiary work, or on remote travesties of Le Nôtre's gardens, with straggling avenues of trees radiated across ploughed land and pastures, instead of cutting through densely timbered woods. As early as 1685 popular attention had been drawn to the merits of informality, and to the delights of novelty and surprise, with reference to Chinese gardens or 'sharawaggi', whilst in his fourth article on the *Pleasures of the Imagination*, Addison himself had lamented the fact that British gardens did not introduce those agreeable mixtures of garden and forest, and other kinds of 'artificial rudeness', such as were to be seen in French and Italian gardens. It was not surprising, therefore, that under the added impulsion of the revived popularity of pastoral and mediaeval poetry, and in view of the new concepts of political freedom then being romanticized by Whig aristocrats who had recently come to power, the landed gentry should encourage a kind of gardening which seemed more in harmony with so many aspects of national taste.

Yet since this was a time when the rules of Palladian architecture were unquestioned, the change could only be effected by two very special contributory circumstances which few authorities seem to have remarked upon. Firstly, there was the fact that the new English country mansions, unlike the French, were usually situated far from a main road in the middle of large parks, and thus their horticultural environment could not be visually restricted to the same manageable areas. Secondly, and most important, there was the fact that Pliny the younger had described the surroundings of his villa at Tuscum by stating that 'you would think it not a real but a painted landscape, drawn with exquisite beauty'. Hence Robert Castell in his illustrated *Villas of the Ancients* (a book which was published in 1728 and dedicated to Lord Burlington, and which even William Kent himself referred to as 'Pliny's Gardens') took the liberty of assuming that Pliny must have been aware of the type of garden described by Sir William Temple in 1685 as Chinese, so that when Pliny wrote that 'a sudden imitation of the country seems accidentally introduced into the middle of the garden', he was, according to Castell, implying a type of garden in which hills, rocks, cascades, rivulets, woods and buildings were thrown into such an 'agreeable disorder' as to please the eye from several points of view 'like so many landscape paintings'. Thus in his carefully delineated reconstruction of Pliny's villa, Castell depicted a garden in which winding paths threaded their way through natural features and in which decorative buildings crowned the more prominent hills.

The effect of introducing buildings amongst artificially established rocks and cascades as part of the landscape, was thus, as far as architecture was concerned, merely a first step towards establishing the general idea that rural architecture ought essentially to be thought of as making natural scenery more 'picturesque', i.e. more like a landscape painting; for according to Joseph Addison, the works of nature appear still more pleasing the more they resemble those of art, and according to Archibald Alison, a scene is picturesque only if it is such as to awaken a train of associations (comparable to the ostensibly mythological subjects of Poussin's or Claude's pictures) additional to those which the scene itself is calculated to excite. Thus, since buildings are clearly more likely than vegetation to awaken historical or romantic associations, architecture was the most important associational device of picturesque landscape design.

THE INFLUENCE OF THE PICTURESQUE

The kinds of building introduced by the seventeenth century painters into Italian landscapes were of three types: reconstructions of antique temples, ruins of antique temples, and rustic dwellings characteristic of the Italian countryside—or in other words, buildings associated with antiquity in its glory, buildings associated with antiquity in its decline, and buildings associated with an idealized pastoral life. The importance of these three on the developments of archaeological Revivalism (or more specifically on the development of the Roman Revival, the Greek and Gothic Revivals, and the Renaissance Revival) will be dealt with in due course. Their effect on the design of villas was of a totally different order, since it concerned general ideas rather than specific forms, and the result was nothing less than the establishment of a new set of aesthetic principles, whereby a small country house, instead of being considered as a geometrically complete object in a landscape disciplined to harmonize with it, was now thought of as being complementary to an existing or artificial rural scene. Thus the technique of designing houses could no longer invariably be based on the adornment of simple volumes derived from equally simple geometric interior spaces, but was henceforth, on the contrary, to be as often a matter of assembling projections and shadows into balanced compositions, and then fitting behind them an appropriate structure and plan.

This is clearly a very simplified, and perhaps even tendentious way of explaining it, and since neither side in the ensuing controversy considered that the technique of designing an arbitrary façade and putting a building behind it was ethically wrong, it would be unfair to make too radical a differentiation between these two schools of thought. Apart from the fact that good architectural design has never at any time been a simple mechanical progression from plan and section to elevation, there were many Classical compositions, such as the Place Vendôme in Paris, where the façades were not only established in advance, but were actually built before the plans of the rooms behind them were designed. The point at issue, therefore, is not that there was anything new in designing façades independently, but that these particular façades were composed in accordance with radically new ideals.

These new ideals effected a change in the whole attitude of the architectural profession towards minor domestic architecture. The new techniques for designing romantic rural constructions were at first applied only to summer-houses, or to the dwellings of a nobleman's more humble tenants, when they would usually be built by local craftsmen using copy books. They might occasionally be designed by painters, as when Hubert Robert designed the Hamlet for Marie Antoinette at Versailles. But before 1750, no fashionable architect would have dreamt of designing such buildings; not necessarily because they were beneath his dignity, but simply because he would not have considered them architecture. It is therefore immensely significant of the changing ideals of the period that Robert Morris should have included designs for farmhouses in his *Select Architecture* (1755), that Isaac Ware should have discussed the potential aesthetic value of barns, stables and cowhouses in his *Complete Body of Architecture* (1756) and that so ambitious a young architect as John Soane should have thought fit to launch his career with a book of designs for cottages and villas, which he published under the title of *Sketches in Architecture* in 1793.

Until the end of the eighteenth century, the popular conception of how to design cottages and villas was well exemplified in a book on the composition of landscapes published in 1777 by R. L. Gerardin, Vicomte d'Ermenonville, the protector of Jean-Jacques Rousseau. Instead, he says, of racking one's brains trying to make geometric plans, and then getting a carpenter to go to all the trouble of tracing out the disposition of the structural frame, it is much more expedient to have the main elevation built straight away and supported provisionally by timber props. What has so far retarded the progress of architectural taste, he continues, is the bad practice of trying to get the effect of a picture from geometric projections instead of deriving the plan from the pictorial effect; for composition, he concludes, is a matter for painters, whereas the purpose of geometry is simply to construct.

This attitude soon spread from rustic 'fabricks' to permanent dwellings, and it was not long before Payne Knight would assert, in his *Analytical Enquiry into the Principles of Taste*, that when choosing the site of a house, it was more important that the building should be in a picturesque setting than that the occupants should be assured of a good view.

Now the result of applying the criteria of pictorial composition to architectural composition, and assuming that the two must necessarily be the same, led to a complete reversal of traditional values. Once it was decided that a number of things which had formerly been condemned by architectural theorists were in fact permissible, it was inevitable that certain theorists would demand a complete revision of the rules. Indeed, the more radical theorists, such as Payne Knight, even went so far as to suggest that there were no valid rules, and that in all matters of taste and criticism, general rules appeared to be as futile as general theories in government and politics: 'never safe but when they are useless'.

This attitude was particularly prevalent amongst those philosophers who demanded a return to the simple life, as for example when Rousseau, in his famous *Discourse* of 1750, derided the current French notions about taste (which he considered over-subtle and finical) because they had reduced the art of pleasing to principles, and made 'vile and deceitful uniformity' permanent. But whereas even those members of the aristocracy who were sympathetic towards such views continued to build their mansions in the Classical manner, in accordance with their upbringing, the newly enriched merchants, whose notions of literature were necessarily limited to what was written in their own language, and whose artistic standards were unexacting, welcomed these ideas as an unhoped-for opportunity of overcoming the disadvantages of humble birth. For as Horace Walpole observed, one must have taste to be sensible to the beauties of Grecian architecture, whereas one only wanted passions to feel Gothic. Similarly, d'Alembert, in 1757, distinguished between the charms of sublimity, which affect all men in all ages, and that species of beauty which can only be perceived by men of taste.

Another notion introduced into architectural theory by the cult of the picturesque concerned the importance of novelty, which until this time had had a strictly pejorative sense, not only amongst the leaders of the profession, but amongst the intelligentsia; for it implied in their minds a deliberate flouting of the Classical rules to attain either cheap notoriety, or a superficial reputation for originality and inventiveness. Thus Voltaire, in his *Essay on Taste*, considered it a sign of degeneration when artists, through fear of being regarded as mere imitators, struck out into new and uncommon paths, and turned aside from 'the beautiful simplicity of nature which their predecessors invariably kept in view'. But by this time Addison was already proclaiming that novelty was one of the three primary sources of pleasure for the imagination, and that it operated by gratifying curiosity and filling the soul with an agreeable surprise. Subsequent philosophers were to disagree as to whether novelty was or was not classifiable as an aesthetic emotion; but by the end of the century most people would have agreed with Burke that some degree of novelty must necessarily subsist in anything in art or nature which operates upon the mind. Already by 1773, Robert Adam thought it a virtue to have 'transfused the beautiful spirit of antiquity with novelty and variety' in all the numerous works he had constructed within the previous ten years.

It would be untrue to say, as some critics still do say, that there was no element of novelty in the Classical garden of the seventeenth century, but it is nevertheless indisputable that the Classical notion of design, whether in gardens or buildings, regarded the totality of such schemes as forming a single unified and immediately intelligible composition, of which the elements were subdivisions constituting smaller but still harmoniously related parts. Whatever the variety of the occasional enclosures and fountains dispersed among the bosquets at Versailles, there is no doubt that the general arrangement of the principal features was intended to be appreciable at the first breath-taking inspection, and thus further exploration could only provide deeper awareness of a composition already generally known. But the so-called 'Chinese garden' was on the contrary designed in accordance with a diametrically opposite intention, for here the overall concept was carefully hidden, and the whole aim was to establish a sequence of different scenes in which disparity was deliberately introduced to constitute the element of 'surprise'.

The wits of the time were not slow in pointing out that this term ceased to be so appropriate the second time round the garden, and one might similarly argue that novelty of this sort would be even more ephemeral if applied to buildings, since the journey of discovery must necessarily be so short. But the virtues of disparity were nevertheless widely exploited in the larger Gothic villas of the nineteenth century, even though the arrangement was more often justified on archaeological grounds by reference to the stylistic disparity of elements joined together at different periods. Thus the most picturesque habitable buildings, according to Uvedale Price, were old castles, and it was not improbable, he said, that many owed the extreme picturesqueness of their appearance to their having been built at different times.

Another interpretation of novelty was in terms not of widely spaced impressions, but of the irregularity, intricacy and variety of specific picturesque scenes. Uvedale Price defined intricacy as 'that disposition of objects which, by a partial and uncertain concealment, excites and nourishes curiosity', and his friend Payne Knight, who held similar views, went to some trouble to distinguish this quality (which he termed 'permanent novelty') from the novelty of mere fashion, caprice or innovation. But like most of these authors, Knight was confused by the inevitable difficulty of distinguishing between space and time; of novelties which succeed one another at relatively distinct intervals, and novelties which are juxtaposed; of what is apprehended in measured sequence and what is apprehended at a glance. Difficulties of this order inevitably arose, because buildings are half-way in size between sculpture and landscape, and although they must be walked round and through to be spatially comprehended they are, at the same time, usually small enough and compact enough to be seen as a whole. But this particular difficulty was enhanced by the theorists of the picturesque because they insisted on treating such aesthetic extremes of space and time as landscape gardening and landscape painting as if they were the same thing. Naturally the landscapes on which the new techniques of gardening were modelled inevitably provided a sequence of ever-changing novelties which might last several hours; but landscape paintings were composed from a single fixed point of view, demanding other kinds of novelty (if in fact they really were such) to be effective, and it was the inability, arising from the nature of their basic premises, to decide what kind of novelty they were really seeking that prevented the establishment of any new principles of architectural composition comparable in authority to the old.

Nowhere is this more noticeable than in the new attitude towards symmetry, the essential meaning of which is generally misunderstood today precisely because of the confusion of thought which arose at this time. Before the middle of the eighteenth century, the word was generally accepted by architects as meaning what it had meant to Vitruvius, namely the proper agreement and relation between the different parts of a building and the whole scheme, in accordance with a selected module. But in popular language, it meant something much less precise, so that Canon de Cordemoy, an amateur theorist whose *New Comprehensive Treatise on Architecture, useful for Contractors and Workmen* was published in 1736, insisted that in common parlance it meant simply 'the relationship which the right side, for example, has with the left, the upper parts with the lower parts and those at the back with those at the front'. Twenty years later, another amateur, Father Laugier, could claim that symmetry meant simply the relationship between the right side and the left, as when he asserted that although a public square should be symmetrical, it should also display a 'certain disorder', contributed by differences in the size and shape of the buildings, which would vary and augment the view. By

1777, repetition with respect to a central axis had become its sole meaning for those who disliked it, and who, in accordance with the new aesthetic theories, considered that 'a certain disorder' was the principal aesthetic merit to be sought. Thus the Vicomte d'Ermenonville, writing in that year, defined symmetry scornfully as 'the manner of cutting the left and right of a building according to the same pattern'.

It is evident that all architects from the Renaissance onwards did in fact insist on a visible correspondence between laterally equidistant elements (except in rare instances, as for example the Grand Trianon at Versailles), even though they had no special word to describe it, for they considered it something essentially implicit in the whole notion of design. To them it was no more conceivable that anyone should deliberately design a building in which the left side and right side were disparate than that nature should design an animal which was lopsided. Their justification for assuming the validity of this biological analogy was, to say the least, inconclusive (as later theorists were to demonstrate by reference to organisms which do not move, such as plants) but their reasons for adopting such arrangements in buildings and gardens were not as naïve or superficial as the protagonists of the picturesque made them appear.

For example, according to the Vicomte d'Ermenonville, 'this blessed symmetry', as he sarcastically called it, contributed nothing to the commodity or solidity of buildings, and far from contributing to their appearance, there was not, he said, a single painter who could render a symmetrical building endurable in a picture. This was because the fundamental viewpoint of symmetry was the centre, which, he claimed, necessarily flattened all objects, just as a human face, viewed from the central point, and painted from straight in front, would also be perfectly flat. But in making this assertion about symmetry (which was later quoted approvingly by Repton) d'Ermenonville clearly missed its whole significance, even though this was fully grasped by most of his contemporaries such as Montesquieu (whom Repton also quotes approvingly) and whose *Essay on Taste* had been published posthumously eighteen years before. Symmetry, said Montesquieu, is necessary where a multitude of objects are presented to us in one point of view, because it thus aids us in forming quickly an idea of the whole. In other words, symmetry is not a relationship seen by the eye but perceived by the mind, whereby whatever the angle from which a group of symmetrically disposed objects is seen, the geometric disposition or plan is immediately grasped. Thus perspective compositions on a flat plane, such as we find in pictures, are not merely irrelevant to an understanding of symmetry in gardens, buildings, and other three-dimensional constructions, but demonstrate completely opposite principles. For as Montesquieu goes on to observe, if any two of the corresponding parts of the human body are depicted in exactly the same direction, such studied symmetry is uninteresting because it produces a perpetual and insipid sameness of attitude. And for this reason no painter ever makes the configurations on the left of a canvas duplicate those depicted on the right, because such an arrangement would convey no significant information to the mind, and would merely amount to painting the same composition twice.

There is thus no advantage in standing and examining a symmetrical garden or building from a point on its central axis, but since a fixed viewpoint was the basis of the picturesque landscape, in the sense that it was designed to look like a picture when seen from the mansion it surrounded, this was something which those hostile to the traditional Classical garden refused to accept. Deliberately ignoring the fact that a walk round a formal garden also furnished a sequence of asymmetrical images (even though these were all related by the mind to the unity of an axial grid) they insisted that the only conceivable kind of garden was a series of picturesque views composed like a painting by Salvator Rosa or Nicholas Poussin.

The confusion created by these conflicting doctrines is well exemplified in Payne Knight's *Analytical Enquiry into the Principles of Taste*. On page 197 of the 1805 edition, he puts forward the traditional notion that the regular conformation of animals is perceived rather by the mind than the eye, for as he correctly observes there is no object composed of parts, either in nature or art, that can appear regular to the eye unless seen at right angles, and this, he says, is the point of sight which a painter of any taste always studiously avoids. But fifteen pages further on, he deplores symmetrical country houses on the grounds that the beauties of symmetry are only perceived when the building is shown 'from a point of sight at right angles with one of the fronts'; hence for this reason he now recommends asymmetry as being the only way in which buildings will correspond with the natural environment of mountains, lawns and woods.

When applied to rural architecture, a preference for asymmetry was frequently well justified, especially when the landscape was in fact designed to be seen as a series of carefully controlled vistas from a large mansion, or from some other single point of view. But when applied dogmatically to architecture in general the results were not always so successful, for an architect can rarely limit the positions from which his building will be seen. However it was not until the middle of the nineteenth century that asymmetry was generally applied to any but domestic buildings, by which time its original purpose had been forgotten, and its philosophical significance lost; for whereas in the eighteenth century asymmetry was considered as having nothing to do with beauty, but as having relevance only to the picturesque, it was eventually regarded by many as an established principle of composition, and hence accepted unquestioningly as one of the basic rules of art.

In practice, the only result of all this philosophizing was to establish Gothic between 1800 and 1860 as the most suitable style for surburban villas, even though some authors, such as Loudon, thought Greek equally susceptible to picturesque treatment on the somewhat inconsequential grounds that the details of the Gothic style were as much taken from cathedrals as details of the Grecian style were taken from temples, so that it would be no more logical to be guided by the symmetry of the latter than of the former. But Gothic was generally accepted as the quintessence of the picturesque because it had always been considered the quintessence of variety when variety was despised. Montesquieu, in his *Essay on Taste*, had criticized the complexity, confusion and minuteness of Gothic ornament, because he considered that its variety had the same effect on the eye as a riddle on the understanding, and it was therefore natural that writers like Uvedale Price should consider this confusion (or, as he called it, splendid confusion) to be a great merit, and that he should praise the roughness, variety and irregularity of Gothic cathedrals as being on an aesthetic par with paintings by Salvator Rosa of shaggy goats. He also considered Gothic more beautiful than Greek on the grounds that a ruin is more picturesque than a new building, doubtless because Gothic was essentially thought of as ruined in his day.

It has already been pointed out that most authorities regard Strawberry Hill as the first Gothic villa of any importance, but this building was, like its immediate successors, essentially a piece of rococo whimsy, and was architecturally of no more consequence in its own day than any of the other examples of rococo fantasy and asymmetry, except that these had hitherto been kept indoors. The first serious development of the Gothic villa, though inspired by it, did not occur until thirty or fifty years later, when suburbs began to develop concurrently with mercantile expansion and with the construction of new roads, and when romantic novels first began to have their wide popular effect. It increased rapidly as the wealth of the new patrons increased, and as the character of the novels changed from romantic extravaganzas to the more scholarly and convincing novels of Sir Walter Scott. For whereas the earlier romances treated the Middle Ages as something remote, and hence unreal, Scott's novels gave them a vividness as of the present; and the buildings which Charlotte Smith described as in a state of gloomy dilapidation were, in Scott's novels, sturdy structures actually used for worship or defence.

Whether an architect should design a suburban villa like one of Sir Walter Scott's castles or of his churches (the only choice available at a time when the character of mediaeval houses was unknown) depended, according to Repton and Loudon, on the external qualities of the site, since in either event the Gothic style seldom penetrated further than the entrance hall. If it was to be built on a rude rocky eminence of irregular surface it was, in theory at least, to be in 'castle Gothic', and if in a fertile valley, in 'abbey Gothic'; for as Loudon pointed out, in so far as architecture was entitled to be considered a fine art, the style adopted must necessarily exercise some influence on the imagination, and a mansion with towers and battlements would, he thought, more powerfully affect the imagination when placed in a position favourable to defence. Needless to say most local architects and speculative builders, when faced with the dilemma of deciding whether a two and a half acre lot on the outskirts of Birmingham or Liverpool was a rude rocky eminence or a fertile valley, designed each villa in any way they fancied. The main thing was that it should not be insipid, for if there was one thing the vigorous merchants and manufacturers of the nineteenth century abhorred it was insipidity, and as Loudon pointed out, it was far better that there should be a 'strong relish', though even of a 'questionable quality', than those 'insipid decencies' which he found hazardous to censure, yet utterly impossible to commend.

When we look now at these once proud homes, standing in dilapidated abandon amongst more recent factories, or converted into shoddy warehouses and tenements, it is difficult to believe that such grotesque parodies of mediaevalism, with their incongruous crockets and crenellations, could still have any relevance to the ideals of modern architecture as we understand them today. Yet in these structures originated the notion of free planning, and although the numerous projections, recessions, oriels and turrets were often designed purely for effect, and frequently produced extremely awkward if not useless spaces inside, the more perspicacious theorists were not slow to realize the potential advantages stemming from such freely designed shapes. Uvedale Price had early remarked on the fact that by simply insisting that windows should face the best view, one could force an architect into inventing a number of picturesque forms and combinations which might never have occurred to him. Repton went even further, and pointed out that irregularity is not only eminently pictorial, but often the handiest manner of accommodating a variety of sizes and shapes for rooms, and permitting additions with greater grace. Utility and picturesqueness thus in great measure coincided, to such an extent that for the next century it proved almost impossible to distinguish between the two.

Part Two

===

REVIVALISM

4

The Awareness of Styles

One of the most popular notions twenty years ago concerning the meaning of the term 'modern architecture' was that it meant the twentieth century victory over Revivalism, or, in other words, over the earlier practice of 'imitating past styles'. Before 1750, architecture was a straightforward matter of building in accordance with established principles, whereby an architect's imagination and artistic sense could be fully exercised whilst keeping within the limits of certain acknowledged rules. But after 1750 (so the story goes) and particularly throughout the whole of the nineteenth century, architects were no longer content to build in this straightforward way, and preferred to waste their energies designing historical trappings which reduced architecture to little more than the elaboration of ornamental silhouettes and façades. Between 1920 and 1940, as a result of a revolution instigated by a number of well-known pioneers, a return was gradually made to the traditional philosophy of building as understood before 1750, even though there were radical differences in appearance because of changes in structural techniques. Hence the decades from 1750 to 1920 must be regarded, according to this theory, simply as an unhappy interlude interrupting an otherwise continuous architectural tradition; an interlude of little relevance to contemporary architecture except in so far as it nourished the seeds of rebellion which eventually directed architecture back to its proper path.

There is a good deal of truth in this interpretation (even though it is clearly too negative to be accepted as an adequate explanation of what modern architecture is really all about), but it is misleading in two respects. Firstly, it implies that there is something disreputable and decadent in the whole idea of Revivalism, whereas this is a phenomenon which has occurred in several culturally active and artistically sensitive periods of history, as in the ninth century, when an attempt was made to revive Roman architecture by Charlemagne, and in the fifteenth century, during what was actually called the Renaissance or re-birth. Secondly, it implies that there was some obvious alternative to Greek, Roman, Gothic or Renaissance architecture between 1750 and the time when steel and concrete frames were introduced, whereas in fact the building conditions which had originally created and favoured these masonry forms continued unchanged.

In fact, the singularity of nineteenth century Revivalism, as compared with earlier revivals, was that it revived several kinds of architecture at the same time, and none of them was ever authoritative or fashionable enough to vanquish its competitors, or even to supersede the kind of architecture which had previously been built. In the ninth and fifteenth centuries the forms revived were regarded at the time as the sole resuscitable expressions of an unchallengeable set of architectural principles; and had the Western world in the nineteenth century followed the leadership of, let us say, the Gothic Revivalists (who, for various reasons to be discussed later, demanded the reinstatement of the architectural traditions interrupted by the Renaissance), the Revivalism of the nineteenth century would never, in retrospect, have constituted anything peculiar as an intellectual phenomenon. As it was, the theorists of the nineteenth century could never even collectively agree as to what were its basic principles, let alone agree as to the forms which the expression of any one particular principle should ideally take. This was partly due to the democratization of artistic criticism (whereby patronage was no longer in the hands of a cultural élite) and to the current fondness for public controversy (facilitated by the rapid expansion of the popular press); but it was due essentially to the new attitude towards history which expressed itself architecturally as a self-conscious awareness of what was then, and is still, known as 'style'.

Style has been defined in recent years by J. M. Richards as the fashion which each generation can promptly recognize as its own, and by Nikolaus Pevsner as 'what ties together the aesthetic achievements of the creative individuals of one age'. According to another recent definition, it is the expression of a prevailing, dominant or authentically contemporary view of the world by those artists who have most successfully intuited the quality of human experience peculiar to their day, and who are able to phrase this experience in forms deeply congenial to the thought, science and technology which are part of that experience. Originally, however, the word 'style' meant those features of literary composition which belong to the form and expression rather than to the substance of the thought or matter expressed. In other words style, according to Classical theorists, was simply the literary aspect of those rules of decorum which required that the manner of doing something should be in harmony with what was done; hence Furetière, in his dictionary of 1690, defined it by explaining that the lofty or sublime style should be used for public utterances, the medium or familiar style should be employed in conversation, whilst the low or popular style was to be reserved for comedies and burlesque. By the middle of the eighteenth century, the number of recognized styles had been multiplied to provide more delicate distinctions, whereby in addition to the three styles just mentioned (the sublime, familiar and popular), were those indicative of certain moods, emotions and even defects, such as elegant, gay, pompous, turgid and dry. Certain theorists were also extending the term to cover the styles appropriate to the various recognized types of poetry, such as the epic, sacred or pastoral styles; but it should be noted that this interpretation was not given by any of the French, English or Italian dictionaries of this date.

There were other notions connected with the word style, such as the quality which might give literature its excellence, as when Swift defined style as 'proper words in proper places', or when Racine remarked that style was 'thought expressed with the minimum of words'. Moreover as early as 1589, George Puttenham, in *The Art of English Poetry*, had considered that whilst style was essentially related to matter and subject, there remained a pervasive individuality of language independent of the internal requirement of a work, which expressed the author's character —a view shared by Dr. Johnson. But even as late as the early nineteenth century, such a romantic critic as Coleridge could still claim that style was nothing else than the art of conveying a meaning appropriately and with perspicuity, and that Swift's style was perfect because not only were the terms appropriate, but because the manner was a complete expression of the matter, and the artifice was concealed.

It will be clear, then, why a Classical theorist such as J. F. Blondel, when lecturing in his school of architecture from 1750 onwards, should tell his students that style, in architecture, meant the authentic character which should be chosen relative to the purpose of a building, and was thus the poetry of architecture. Just as there was sacred, epic and pastoral poetry, so there was sacred, heroic and pastoral architecture, and just as some poetry was elegant, some gay and some pompous, so architecture likewise could express moods which might either be appropriate to a building's purpose or inept. For him, it was not only important to distinguish between buildings of widely different functions, such as churches and mansions, but between different types of churches and different types of mansions, so that a parish church should, he thought, be manifestly different from a monastic church, a banker's mansion different from a soldier's mansion, and the palace of a king different from one built by a prince or even by a queen. Many of his notions concerning the manner in which these distinctions were to be effected were impractical and arbitrary, and the French Academy of Architecture, which at that time was quite a realistically-minded body, did not hesitate to tell him so when he lectured to them on the subject in 1766. But his ideal was clearly, in itself, very sound, for it arose from the belief that, as a matter or principle, every edifice should bear the imprint of its particular purpose, and have a character, irrespective of any sculptural symbols, which determined its general form and announced the building for what it was.

Yet even as Blondel wrote this definition, new ones were coming into effect. They even appear in the revised text of his own lecture course. Such new definitions can be traced certainly as far back as the second volume of Colen Campbell's *Vitruvius Britannicus*, which appeared in 1717, and where the word style occurs on several occasions in a new sense, as for example with reference to a design for a house in 'the theatrical style' (which Campbell says 'admits of more Gayety than is proper either for the Temple or Palatial style') and to a design for a house 'in the style of Inigo Jones'. Now this first use of the word is clearly already perverse, since it suggests that a house can best be made gay by using the style only appropriate for a theatre; for by definition the term 'theatrical style', according to a Classical theorist, would have meant that since this style was appropriate for a theatre, it was by that very fact inappropriate for anything else. By labelling his other design as being 'in the style of Inigo Jones', Campbell was actually reversing the main Classical meaning, for he was asserting that style did not necessarily refer to the purpose of the building, but could apply equally well to the personality of the architect who prepared the design.

Such a change of attitude was clearly very much in harmony with the new aesthetic ideas being introduced into English thought at this time by the literary critics and philosophers who followed Addison. Thus by 1783, Hugh Blair, one of the later leaders of this new school of philosophers, could define style simply as 'a characteristic expression of a writer's manner of thinking and peculiarity of temperament'. Moreover even the classical notion of style, which related it to the matter dealt with (as in the 'epic' style or 'pastoral' style) was soon distorted to imply that one style might be preferable to all the others, irrespective of the nature of the ideas expressed. Thus in 1756 Thomas Gray, the poet, archaeologist and friend of Horace Walpole, claimed that the true lyric style, with all its flights of fancy, ornaments, heightening of expression and harmony of sound, was in its nature superior to every other style.

The mental climate was thus set for the philosophers of the mid-eighteenth century to wonder whether it was not rather pretentious to refer to Classical architecture simply as 'architecture', as had been done for the last two hundred years, since this implied that every other form of building—whether mediaeval or oriental—was non-architecture. Might it not be, they suggested, that Classical architecture was in fact simply that style of architecture which was superior to every other style? Thus whereas Classical architects, like Sir William Chambers, merely described Chinese architecture as 'a singular stile of *building*', later authors generally referred to it quite simply as 'the Chinese style'. Similarly, Gothic was also categorized as a style, and once novelists such as Henry Fielding began describing houses as being in 'the Gothic stile', architects were not long in following suit.

As yet, no one referred to the normal current architecture as 'the Classical style', or considered that there was any purpose in qualifying a kind of building by a stylistic epithet (e.g. according to country or period) except to indicate that it was alien, romantic or grotesque. But by 1762, the notion occurred to some architects that the term 'style' could also be applied to indicate the fluctuations which had taken place in the development of Classical architecture itself. Stuart and Revett's *Antiquities of Athens*, published in that year, referred to the differences between 'the Grecian and Roman style of building', whilst in Robert Adam's introduction to his *Ruins of the Palace of the Emperor Diocletian at Spalatro*, published in 1764, he claimed not merely that Diocletian had trained architects capable of successfully imitating 'the stile and manner of a purer age', but that he had also 'revived a taste in architecture superior to that of his own times'. Why, suggested Adam in his dedicatory preface to George III, should not royalty do the same again?

Inevitably these two ideas, acting in conjunction with all the other explosive theories then circulating among philosophers, poets and historians, effectively set a bomb under the whole theoretical fabric of Classical architecture. The Renaissance had admittedly also gone back to what might have been called the style and manner of a purer age, and revived a taste in architecture considered superior to that of its own times; but it had done so in reaction to what it had suddenly conceived to be an age of absolute cultural barbarism. It had never occurred to any Classical writer, from Alberti to J. F. Blondel, to doubt that true architecture had always, apart from this interlude, progressed. Even Sir William Chambers, who admitted that the Roman arts, like those of other nations, had had their rise, their era of perfection, and their decline, thought it a sufficient refutation of the Greek Revivalists' pretensions to claim that if Greek architecture was defective in the time of Alexander, it must have been more so some two centuries earlier. It was in fact a basic tenet of the early eighteenth century that Greek architecture had been inferior to Roman, and that Roman architecture had been inferior to what they were building themselves.

The radical new meanings of 'style' were accepted only gradually, so that during the second half of the eighteenth century the old and the new meanings often occur in the same written work. Even in J. F. Blondel's lecture course we find the statement that 'one must not only compare the grandeur of the massing of the Egyptians, the precious details of the Greeks, the beautiful planning of the Roman works and the ingenious structures of the Arabs (i.e. Gothic), but also the particular *style* which characterises them'. Similarly in a guide to the gardens at Ermenonville published anonymously in 1788, we are told both that one of the Classical temples is in 'the noble and elegant style', and that a garden structure called Gabrielle's Tower is 'of a style which suggests that it in fact existed at the time of Gabrielle d'Estrées'. But by the end of the century the victory of the new meaning was virtually complete, as is clear from Millin's *Dictionary of the Fine Arts*, published in 1806. This defines civil architecture in terms of 'the styles as they have differed according to peoples and epochs', and lists these as Egyptian, Persian, Indian, Phoenician, Hebrew, Greek, Roman, Arabic, Gothic, Saxon and Chinese. By 1821, James Elmes, in his *Lectures in Architecture*, not only accepts these stylistic divisions according to peoples, but also divides Graeco-Roman architecture chronologically into five 'styles' corresponding to the Homeric age, the age from 700 B.C. to Pericles, the age from Pericles to Alexander the Great, the age from Alexander to Augustus, and the age from Augustus to A.D. 324. For him modern architecture was no longer a further stage in an evolutionary progression, because he himself believed in the superiority of Periclean Greece, and favoured the revival of that style.

E

REVIVALISM

All this emphasis on the chronology of architectural styles was fostered by the cult of ruins. This cult had also been a phenomenon characteristic of the fifteenth century revival of Roman forms, but whereas the fifteenth century romanticization of ruins was short-lived, and quickly superseded by a more practical concern with the intact elements of which they were constituted, the romanticism of the eighteenth century, nourished by the new awareness of history, and by the many drawings and paintings of ruins produced by such artists as Pannini, Piranesi, Hubert Robert and Zucchi, lasted quite a long time, and expressed itself in a manner peculiar to the age. Firstly, it aroused a concern for classification, whereby a new science of archaeology was developed, comparable to diplomatics and palaeography, which treated buildings like documents of historical research; secondly, it encouraged a pedantic observance of many Vitruvian rules which, until then, had been disregarded because they were of no practical value; and thirdly, it introduced a fashion for imitating Roman compositions, however alien these might be to the purpose the new building was intended to serve.

5

Primitivism and Progress

The issues raised by the new interest in Classical archaeology drew attention to two fundamental dilemmas which all modern theorists have had to cope with, namely whether architecture evolves progressively or by cycles, and whether it evolves automatically by environmental influences or in accordance with stylistic determinants chosen by the designers themselves. These issues had never been of importance in any previous revivals, since although Vasari, for example, had observed that the arts of design resembled nature as shown in our bodies, and had, like them, their birth, growth and decay, he, like the other theorists of the period, was convinced that he lived during a time when the arts were not only progressing, but had attained all the perfection which could be expected in the circumstances. The problem as to how decadence was to be avoided in the future had no more meaning for them than how maturity had been achieved in the remote past. They regarded the rules of good architecture as immutable, and accepted the mythological explanation of the origins of architecture with the same lack of historical curiosity as they accepted the idea that decadence could only result from the decree of Heaven, the malignity of the age or the negligence of men.

The reaction to this view occurred as soon as architects became conscious of being instruments of an evolutionary process. It was initiated partly by that romanticization of everything primitive resulting from the English interest in mediaeval poetry, and partly by the sociological and political speculations of Rousseau and Montesquieu. It was encouraged by the popularity of what was then called Conjectural History, whereby the intellectual achievements, opinions, manners and institutions of current society were compared with those prevailing amongst savage tribes.

To the more traditional philosophers, such as Dugald Stewart, the value of this type of historical study was that it showed by what gradual steps the transition had been made from the first simple efforts of uncultivated nature to a state of things which was 'so wonderfully artificial and complicated'. It showed how civilization had developed from the first rudiments of the arts to 'their last and most refined improvements'. But Rousseau and Montesquieu questioned whether the artifice and complication of contemporary life really was so wonderful, and whether the arts really had been refined and improved. According to them, current political, social and cultural conditions were not the result of gradual improvement, but were due, on the contrary, to an inevitable decadence which overcame every society once it abandoned the simple life. The ideal political situation was that which still existed in the smaller Swiss cantons, where citizens assembled to vote publicly on every important issue. The ideal legal situation was that which still existed among American Indians, where justice was administered according to simple natural laws by the elders of the tribe sitting under a tree. The ideal poetry was that which was extemporized by the ancient bards and transmitted to posterity by word of mouth. Before art fashioned manners, wrote Rousseau in 1750, and taught passions to speak a borrowed language, customs were rustic but natural; and it was the renaissance of Roman culture which had deprived his contemporaries of the privilege of living the simple life.

The effect of this glorification of 'the noble savage' was clearly more influential in reviving Greek and Gothic architecture than in giving philosophical support to a revival of early Roman; but even so its effects on the current traditions of Classical architecture, which took Roman prototypes as their model, were too important to be ignored. Whether they liked it or not, the Classicists were obliged to choose between deliberate progress and deliberate retrogression; between the search for a new architecture or the return to a recognized 'golden age'. Even if they still believed in evolution, the awareness of history had made them too conscious of the mechanism of the evolutionary process to let them allow architecture to evolve at its own rate and of its own accord. But there were some who now began to question whether art did in fact obey the same evolutionary laws as science. As we have seen, Fontenelle had suggested in his *Digression on the Ancients and the Moderns* that since the Fine Arts are chiefly a spontaneous expression of the human spirit, their development cannot be cumulative, and therefore there can be no law of progress such as we find in the practical arts. Perhaps, therefore, architecture was no longer to be judged according to principles applicable to the progress of science, but was to be judged by reference to buildings constructed in an ideal age?

In practice the architects of the new age thus had a choice between four attitudes, the first of which was evolutionary, the last revolutionary, and the remainder a cross between the two. In other words, they could continue to believe that forms evolved naturally, they could make a deliberate break with the past, or they could insist that evolution should be directed in one way or another by the human will. Firstly they could maintain the traditional Classical philosophy that architecture inevitably evolved automatically by virtue of the fact that it fulfilled the needs of an evolving society, but in so doing they ran the risk of being dismissed by critics as simple-minded reactionaries, out of step with the most progressive trends. Secondly, they could revive early Roman, early Greek or early Renaissance architecture, and join those reformers who wished to return to an idealized period of Classical history, either in order to stay there for ever or to return to it so as to start another and purer evolutionary branch. Thirdly, they could join those reformers who wished to revive a mediaeval national architecture, and reject Classical architecture because it was alien to their climate, their geology and their ethnic traditions. Lastly, they could join those reformers who contended that unless the nineteenth century could produce a distinctive architecture of its own, the archaeological records of the future would be falsified, and that since the normal evolutionary processes were obviously failing to produce a distinctive contemporary style (or at any rate failing to produce one quickly enough) a new architecture must be deliberately sought.

The various attempts to achieve these aims will be dealt with in the following chapters. Meanwhile, it should be pointed out that whilst the problems they raised affected all architects, there were many, especially at the beginning, who regarded the whole matter with indifference, and who were too occupied with their practices to give any time to such speculation themselves. Some architects, indeed, were frankly cynical, and regarded style much as a tailor regarded fashion in clothes. For them, as for their clients, Lord Chesterfield's definition of style as 'the dress of thought' would have seemed entirely appropriate; and since it is not a far step from dress to fancy-dress, it can readily be comprehended why the Society of Dilettanti, who by 1741 had decided to dress their president in a scarlet toga and their secretary in the costume of Machiavelli, should decide to build a replica of the temple at Pola for their headquarters. This was the period when impresarios were already being expected to provide period costumes for their dramas, and similarly the more compliant architects accepted style as simply the kind of costume which a client wanted for his building. So long as draftsmen could be found to do the necessary details, or books could be found from which they could copy them themselves, they were indifferent as to the ethical implications which the choice of style necessarily raised for their more scrupulous colleagues. Whether or not such arbitrariness was justified is clearly a matter of opinion; but it was in opposition to this attitude that most of the theories of the last two centuries were formulated, thereby producing the kind of buildings we see around us today.

6

The Roman Revival

Between 1550 and 1750, architects who visited Rome found the sight of the ruins no more attractive than the sight of the debris of a city mutilated by war, and far from trying to draw reconstructions and date them, they simply regarded them as conglomerations of standardized elements, which could provide useful information concerning the details and refinements of the Classical Orders. Even the Italian architects of this period viewed the antiquities of their native country as little more than fragments to be studied methodically in conjunction with the Vitruvian text (of which the original illustrations had been lost), or as store yards of second-hand tectonic components to be incorporated into their clients' buildings. Lanciani has calculated that nearly eight thousand antique columns are to be found in various Renaissance buildings in the city. Most of the chapel of Gregory XIII in St. Peter's was built, for example, with marble taken from the mausoleum of Hadrian. If the marble was not used in this way it was burnt into lime, or cut into slabs, like the blocks from the Thermae of Titus used to adorn the Gesù.

Sentimentality towards Roman ruins did not really appear until the second decade of the eighteenth century, when the sudden interest in melancholy literature was making English poets aware of the evocative possibilities which architectural fragments possessed. In such circumstances, ruins were not admired because they were beautiful but because they were sublime; this is why it was thought at the time that the best ruins were Gothic, since these contained no elements of beauty at all. Roman ruins were admired in the paintings of Claude and Poussin; but until the second half of the eighteenth century they suggested to the mind the triumph of barbarity over taste—a gloomy and discouraging thought—whereas Gothic ruins suggested the idea of the triumph of time over strength (considered by Lord Kames, in his *Elements of Criticism*, to be equally melancholy but less unpleasant) or even of the triumph of nature; for as John Gilpin observed: having been rooted in the soil for ages, and assimilated to it, a ruin could be regarded more as a work of nature than a work of art.

The English poets and philosophers had little choice but to concentrate on the Gothic ruins scattered around them, but the wealthier and more influential members of society at that time, that is to say the nobility and landed gentry, also studied ruins on the Grand Tour, and such diversions became increasingly popular after 1750, when it became politically respectable to visit the city of Rome itself. Before 1714 the city had been avoided by Englishmen because it was officially regarded as the principal centre of Catholic intrigue against the Protestant succession. But with the accession of the House of Hanover, and especially after the failure of the Young Pretender's uprising in 1745 (when the unpopularity of the Jacobite cause was clearly demonstrated, and official recognition of the Young Pretender was withdrawn by the King of France) Whig aristocrats rightly considered that they could go there without incurring suspicion. They had little interest in examining the Catholic churches. So they spent their time looking at what was left of Antiquity instead.

By 1755 antiquarian British noblemen had already become an accepted joke, as is clear from the character of Lord Nicknackerton in John Shebbeare's novel *Lydia*, where his lordship spends all his time measuring up antique remains. Indeed, so distinctive were they that a number of those who had visited Italy formed themselves into a society called The Dilettanti, which, though originally little more than a drinking club, was eventually to play an influential role in subsidizing archaeological publications and research. Continental novelists also regarded the antiquarian British nobleman as a characteristic and distinctive type. Thus Corinne, in Madame de Staël's novel of that name, conducts her Scottish friend Lord Nelvil round the ruins of Rome in much the same spirit as when, in the fifteenth century, Poliphilus, in Colonna's *Hypnerotomachia*, had conducted Polia through the ruins in his dream. However, the reflections they prompted were markedly different. According to Corinne, the purpose of such tours was to learn history, for ruins, she says, teach it far better than books, in that they affect the mind through the imagination and by sentiment. The reflections excited by stones in disorder, and by ruins mixed together with new structures, act more powerfully, she claims, on the human soul than mere reading, and the marvellous charm of Rome is not only due to the real beauty of its monuments, but to the fact that they excite us to think. She has little patience with erudite scholars who occupy their time simply assembling a collection of names which they call history, since they overlook the fact that the value of ruins is to excite the imagination into guessing and discovering those secrets which reflections and study can reveal. She would thus certainly have approved Lessing's distinction between an antiquary and an archaeologist, according to which the former inherited the fragments of antiquity whereas the latter inherited its spirit; 'for the former scarcely thinks with his eyes, whereas the latter can see even with his thoughts'.

On the continent of Europe, the most notorious antiquarian pedant of the time was the Comte de Caylus, who spent four-fifths of his large income on the patronage of antiquarian research and filled his house three times over with Greek, Roman, Etruscan and Egyptian fragments and utensils, which on each occasion he eventually presented to the State. His findings were lavishly published in 1750 under the title of *Collection of Antiquities*, but despite the curiosity they aroused, his work did not always meet with the approval of his contemporaries. D'Alembert, the apostle of rationalism and progress, made unflattering comparisons between philosophers (whom he called the students of the future) and antiquaries, who, he said, spent their time scavenging among the rubbish-heaps of Antiquity, and accumulating useless facts about the past. Marmontel, secretary to Louis XV's Director of Buildings, dismissed de Caylus as a charlatan, especially with regard to the antiquarianizing influence he claimed to exercise over contemporary art. Diderot particularly detested him, partly because he was jealous of his rivalry as an art critic, but also because he sensed that antiquaries of de Caylus' type did not in fact set much value on beauty, and were only interested in what was old.

Even so, these new antiquarian researches seem to have attracted wide public attention. One of the first and almost certainly the dullest publication on this subject was Montfaucon's ten-volume *Antiquity Explained*; yet it was sold out within two months of publication, so that another edition of 2,000 copies, making a total of 40,000 volumes in all, had to be printed in the same year. Other works of a similar type followed, or were contemporary with it, one of the most influential being the studies of Italian antiquities and inscriptions published at intervals by Lodovico Antonio Muratori in seventy-nine volumes up to 1750, the year he died.

The most important result of all this research was to provide material for that new concept of history which regarded the past in terms of what would now be called social history, and which therefore prized artefacts more highly than official documents, because they enabled the imagination to picture more vividly how people lived. In 1750, Lessing, who was then at the beginning of his career as a literary critic, had initiated the direct scholarly study of social life in ancient times by means of their literature, whilst at this same time his former teacher, Johann Friedrich Christ, the professor of history at Leipzig University, began a memorable course of lectures in which he urged his audience to become familiar not only with the literature, the inscriptions, and the coins of the ancients, but also with their architecture, sculpture, gems, vases, and other works of art. In 1767, the first formal lectures on Classical archaeology were given by Christian Gottlob Heyne, despite the fact that his shortness of sight disqualified him from being a good judge of any but the smallest varieties of ancient sculpture. The techniques of art-historical study were at this time still in their infancy, and even Lessing had no compunction about writing his *Laocoon* before he had seen the original sculpture about which he wrote. Winckelmann also, at first, based his studies of this statue on plaster casts, and it was not until the publication of his *History of the Art of Antiquity* in 1764 that the scientific study of works of art, and hence the modern

F. Sandys: Ickworth House (1796)

Payne Knight: The dining room at
Downton Castle (1775)

J. Gondoin: The auditorium of the Medical
School, Paris (1771) (see Pl. XXVI)

THE ROMAN REVIVAL

Illustrating the influence of Roman monumental compositional forms

C. Campbell: 'Church in the Vitruvian Style' (1717)

T. Jefferson: Virginia State Capitol (1785)

THE ROMAN REVIVAL

Illustrating the new tendency to fit public buildings into Antique temples

X

L. von Klenze: Museum of sculpture (Glyptothek), Munich (1816)

THE GREEK REVIVAL

*Illustrating the new tendency to incorporate the compositional forms of
Antique temples into public buildings*

XI

The Temple by the Ilyssus as reconstructed by Stuart and Revett

The Temple by the Ilyssus as it existed in 1750

THE GREEK REVIVAL

Illustrating the influence of graphic 'restorations' in encouraging the adoption of ancient Greek forms

XII

techniques of dating according to stylistic characters, could be said to have really begun.

In view of these developments, it was only to be expected that architects would also awake to the apparent advantages which Classical archaeology seemed to offer, and whilst few of those with busy practices had time to indulge in original researches or explorations, a great deal of work was carried out by wealthy amateurs, or by students at the French Academy in Rome. As a result, several important books on Roman architecture were published at this time, the first of which was a splendidly engraved series of picturesque views and measured drawings of the extensive Roman ruins at Palmyra and Baalbek, published by Robert Wood in 1753 and 1757. The second, to which reference has already been made, was Robert Adam's book on the ruins at Spalatro, published in 1764. The third was Charles-Louis Clérisseau's *Antiquities of Nîmes*, first published in 1778 and republished in 1804. The fourth was the series of books published from 1751 onwards concerning the discoveries at Herculaneum and Pompeii. And the fifth was the series of engravings, numbering several hundreds, which G. B. Piranesi published on the antiquities of Rome.

The *Ruins of Palmyra* and the *Ruins of Baalbek* might not at first appear to have contributed anything very novel, for measured drawings of Roman antiquities had been published since the Renaissance. But they were important because they made architects particularly conscious of the variations which had existed between Roman architecture in different parts of the Empire and in different stages of its development; of the fact that in the East, under Hellenistic influences, the ornamentation was freer, the use of columns was more lavish, and the compositions were on a much grander scale. This was not the first time anyone had published an account of these two abandoned cities, for they had been described in travel books published in the previous century, and illustrated, though somewhat crudely and at second-hand, by Marot. But now, for the first time, European architects could study these buildings by means of carefully measured drawings and reconstructions, and speculate, by means of the literary evidence provided, concerning the periods in which they had originally been built.

The importance of the *Ruins of the Palace of the Emperor Diocletian at Spalatro* (measured under Adam's supervision, but actually drawn by Clérisseau) was that it was the first archaeological study to deal with a type of composition still currently being built. Robert Adam does not seem to have chosen this subject with any deep awareness of its practical implications; indeed, his avowed purpose in publishing a book at all was simply to impress potential clients and establish himself in public esteem. After toying with the idea of revising one of the existing books on Roman temples or Roman baths, he eventually decided to go to Egypt, but was prevented, through lack of funds, from traversing the Mediterranean, and so limited himself to crossing the Adriatic instead. Nevertheless, the fact remains that whereas earlier books of measured drawings, such as Desgodetz's *Antiquities of Rome*, had been devoted to such buildings as temples, basilicas and other types of structure foreign to eighteenth century social usages, the *Ruins of the Palace of the Emperor Diocletian*, by dealing with domestic architecture, did suggest that at least some Roman compositions might be as relevant to contemporary dwellings as were the details of the Roman Orders, on which architectural theorists had mainly concentrated in the past.

The importance of Clérisseau's *Antiquities of Nîmes* was that it roused Europeans to take an interest in the antiquities on their own soil. Two centuries earlier, J. P. d'Albenas had published an illustrated *Historical Discourse on the Ancient and Illustrious City of Nîmes*, but the illustrations (later copied by Palladio) were inaccurate, and although Desgodetz had measured the buildings again in 1674 when on his way to Rome, his drawings were lost when he was captured at sea by pirates, and detained for sixteen months in Algiers. In 1682 a local academy was founded to study the antiquities, and even tried to get the Maison Carrée as a headquarters and museum, but without success. Such buildings were by no means universally admired. Marmontel, for example, considered it unattractively massive and heavy, and in 1778 this famous building was still being used as a monastic church. By the time Clérisseau measured it, it was so mutilated inside and encumbered outside that it was in fact impossible to appreciate its composition. His published reconstructions thus not only familiarized architects with probably the most complete Roman temple in Europe apart from the Pantheon, but were instrumental in starting the campaign whereby such historical monuments would be properly preserved.

The most influential publications (apart from Piranesi's popular engravings) were those dealing with Herculaneum. The site of this buried town had been accidentally discovered in 1719, but serious excavations did not start until 1750 (two years after those at Pompeii) when privileged visitors were made suddenly and dramatically aware, as they clambered through the torch-lit tunnels, of the character of Roman interior design. Curiously enough, interiors of this type had been well known during the early Renaissance, and had even been imitated by artists like Raphael, who, because the antique prototypes were buried underground in what were called 'grottoes', referred to these kinds of design as 'grotesques'. But subsequent architects showed little interest in such remains, and it is characteristic of their attitude that when Fontana tunnelled an aqueduct through Pompeii in 1592, he had not sufficient curiosity to examine further what lay buried. Similarly, interior decorators between 1550 and 1750 relied on their own inventiveness and resources, and were completely indifferent to antique fashions, which they would have considered without authority over their own work. Even Palladio, the most fervent of all sixteenth century students of Roman architecture, neglected to follow Roman examples in domestic interiors, and when his English imitators designed interiors, they either adorned the walls with standard Orders, or adopted whatever Baroque or Rococo motifs were popular at the time.

This attitude towards antique interiors was reflected in the first reactions of the early visitors to Herculaneum and Pompeii. In Cochin and Bellicard's *Observations upon the Antiquities of the Town of Herculaneum*, published in both English and French editions in 1754, Cochin described the frescoes with obvious distaste. A number of these pictures, he said, depicted architecture in ruins, but they scarcely deserved notice because they were altogether out of proportion. Generally speaking, the pillars were double or triple the natural dimensions, whilst the profiles were, he said, 'of a wretched Gothic taste, as ridiculous as any of the Chinese designs'. Similarly, when the official *Antiquities of Herculaneum*, published privately by the King of the Two Sicilies, was presented to the French Academy in 1768, that body declared it of more use to the history of architecture than to its progress, since the buildings depicted there were more related to Chinese and Arab (i.e. Gothic) architecture than to the beautiful architecture of the Greeks and Romans—a remark repeated almost word for word by J. F. Blondel in the lectures he gave his students, published in 1771.

But by the middle of the 1760s, Robert Adam had not merely made these motifs fashionable for the decoration of English palatial interiors, but was taking similar liberties with proportions on external façades. 'Nothing is more sterile and disgustful', he wrote, 'than to see for ever the dull repetition of Dorick, Ionick and Corinthian entablatures in their usual proportions'. Adam's initiative was of particular importance because, as compared with the abstract views expressed earlier by Burke, and later by Alison, his preference for slenderness and lightness constituted a practical attack on the Vitruvian theory of proportion. No longer simply speculative, it offered a challenging example of how these proportions could be modified and perhaps improved. Yet the new fashion was not in fact to bear any real fruit until the use of cast iron columns made the problem of column proportions a practical issue in the following century. Meanwhile, the most common result of all this antiquarian research was, paradoxically enough, to establish the Vitruvian rules more strongly, since however slenderly the Romans might have proportioned the columns in the painted interiors of their buildings, there was no doubt that, externally, the structural columns at Palmyra and Baalbek not only conformed to Vitruvian standards, but were much more closely spaced than was customary at a later date. The architects of the seventeenth and early eighteenth centuries, recognizing the practical advantages of wide intercolumniations, and always ready to increase them whenever, by so doing, they could demonstrate their technical skill at constructing entablatures of wide span, never bothered with the Vitruvian rules in this respect, since for one thing they seem to have been based on no authority except the word of Hermogenes (a Hellenistic architect from whom Vitruvius copied them), and in any event they referred only to the peristyles of temples. Now, however, the younger architects insisted on keeping rigidly to these antique formulae, as when Gondoin used a eustyle intercolumniation on the temple-like portico of his new medical school, constructed in Paris in 1771.

Another paradoxical effect of all this research was to create an equally irrational and formalistic attitude towards Roman compositions. Between 1720 and 1770 the leading European architects, particularly the French, had prided themselves on the ingenuity and functional efficiency of their domestic planning, and the first book to be entitled *Architecture Moderne* was given its name, so the author tells us, because it dealt with mansions designed with such functional ends in view. Yet despite the examples of Roman domestic planning recently discovered, the fashionable French 'anticomaniacs' of the next generation designed mansions not even on the model of imperial palaces, but with features recalling the Roman thermae, as for example Pierre Rousseau's Hôtel de Salm, which has a caldarium-like rotunda in the middle of its garden façade. Even Robert Adam himself copied antique compositions without any regard for their original purpose, as at Kedleston, where although the design for the salon was based internally on the vestibule of Diocletian's palace, it was made externally to look like a Roman triumphal arch.

This fashion for indiscriminately using antique compositional forms in situations for which they were never intended seems to have originated in England, and was probably due initially to Nicholas Hawksmoor, who was simply perverting and misapplying a technique he had picked up from his master, Sir Christopher Wren. Wren, being originally untrained as an architect, had been obliged when designing his first buildings to base his compositions on drawings found in books, and there is no doubt, for example, that the plan of the Sheldonian Theatre at Oxford was derived from Serlio's reconstructed plan of the theatre of Marcellus, just as the façade was based on Cesariano's reconstruction of the basilica at Fano, illustrated in the Vitruvius edition of 1521. As Wren became more experienced, he naturally depended far less on such models, but he still retained his interest in trying to reconstruct the composition of antique buildings from literary descriptions, as when he reconstructed the mausoleum at Halicarnassus, or the tomb of Porsenna in 1677.

Perhaps because he had had little formal education before becoming Wren's draftsman at the age of eighteen, Hawksmoor seems to have mistaken Wren's scholarly amusements for serious architectural research. In any event, he certainly set great store by Classical erudition, for he took a childish pleasure in titling his drawings with long far-fetched Latin equivalents for English words, despite the fact that they would be unintelligible to most of those for whom they were intended. But whatever the cause, he evidently regarded the imitation of classical compositions as a special virtue in itself, for whereas Wren, in his actual buildings, had based his designs on Roman structures used for similar purposes, Hawksmoor seems to have been quite indifferent to such niceties, and used the mausoleum at Halicarnassus for a church steeple, the Roman clock tower at Athens for the details of another church, and in general delighted in the incongruous and heterogeneous sources from which his compositions were concocted.

Yet although Hawksmoor was a particularly flagrant practitioner of this technique, he was by no means the only one. In 1717, Colen Campbell published what he called a 'church in the Vitruvian Style' which was simply the Maison Carrée at Nîmes with an Ionic substituted for a Corinthian Order, and a Venetian window cut into the east end. In 1727 John Wood, under the romantic impulsion of his own archaeological studies, designed terrace houses on the model of the Roman Colosseum at Bath. In 1752 the Society of Dilettanti, having decided to abandon its patronage of the Star and Garter Tavern in Pall Mall and build proper premises of its own, resolved 'to fix upon some Antique Building as a model for that intended by the Society according to the most exact proportions and measurements that can be procured', and gave as their reason the fact that having been approved for many ages, the design would naturally be beyond criticism. This practice of using an irreproachable antique building (in this instance the temple at Pola) as a standard shell in which to cram every type of accommodation became in fact so influential and widespread at the beginning of the nineteenth century that it soon constituted almost an architectural tradition in itself, and it was particularly prevalent in America, where Thomas Jefferson, a fervent admirer of the Maison Carrée at Nîmes (which he knew only from drawings), had used a replica of that building as a receptacle for the Virginia State Capitol in 1785. Jefferson was quite explicit about his motives. 'In the execution of those orders', he wrote on January 26th, 1786, in reply to a demand from Virginia that he procure designs for the public buildings there, 'two methods of proceeding presented themselves to my mind. The one was to leave to some architect to draw an external according to his fancy, in which way experience shows that about once in a thousand times a pleasing form is hit upon; the other was to take some model already devised and approved by the general suffrage of the world. I had no hesitation in deciding that the latter was best.'

Nevertheless these various competing fashions regarding the choice of ideal prototypes were as nothing compared with the more fundamental philosophical conflicts which this general concern with archaeology soon raised. For one thing, there were still many theorists who specifically condemned direct imitations, and who continued to subscribe to the Classical doctrine enunciated by J. F. Blondel to the effect that 'the ancients can teach us to think, but we must not think as they did'. Clérisseau himself, the author of the very book which inspired so much facile copying, protested against the practice of making buildings destined for public utility or amusement resemble monuments consecrated to divinities, and claimed that the former should 'announce themselves by a style which distinguishes them absolutely from all others'. Those who copied exactly the forms of ancient buildings, he continued, showed simply that they had failed to study adequately the spirit in which these monuments were composed.

Even laymen and philosophers such as Payne Knight, a prominent member of The Dilettanti, pointed out that the fundamental error of all such imitators was that they servilely copied the effects which they saw produced, instead of studying and adopting the principles which guided the original artist in producing them. For the principles of art, he contended, were no other than the trains of ideas which arose in the mind of an artist out of a just and adequate consideration of all the circumstances, so that if the circumstances or purposes changed, his ideas must change with them, or his principles would be false and his work incongruous. Sir Joshua Reynolds put forward a similar view, and in fact it was frequently repeated by many writers who, prompted by the new attitude towards history, felt compelled to emphasize the difference which had always been implicit between thoughtful imitation and mere mimicry. Lord Aberdeen, the most vigorous propagandist of the Greek Revival, insisted that he was not recommending the servile imitation of any particular species of the remains of antiquity—'such as would evince the frigid pedantry of the mechanic'—but an adherence to those general principles of excellence in which the Greeks worked. Loudon, also writing at the beginning of the nineteenth century, insisted that when imitating a style one was not required to copy particular forms, but to enter into the spirit of the subject or style to which they belonged, and thus to form new compositions in that spirit. 'Any builder may copy a style', he concluded, 'but it takes an artist to compose it.' Hence despite such apparently authoritative precedents as those set by Ludwig II of Bavaria, who insisted on adorning his capital with reproductions of every foreign historical monument which took his fancy, servile copying was usually subject to ridicule by the more thoughtful observers, even at the time the fashion was introduced.

In conclusion, then, the Roman Revival may be summarized as the effect of the new antiquarianism on the more traditional architects' attitudes towards proportions and composition. As regards their attitude towards the proportions of the Orders, they either adopted a completely rigid and pedantic system, based on the teaching of Vitruvius, or, in complete contrast to this, adopted the proportions authorized by Pompeiian wall paintings, which were so slender and widely spaced that they led the way to the proportions later associated with metal construction. As regards the new attitude towards composition, a far greater interest was now shown in the reconstructions of buildings used by the Romans, to such an extent that the compositional forms of thermae and temples were adapted, however incongruously, for uses for which they had never been intended. All these tendencies may be regarded as retrogressive compared with the Classical doctrines of earlier generations, but they are peculiarly modern, in that they show the powerful influence exerted on architects by the new awareness of history, and display the first indications of a modern tendency towards 'formalism'—the preference for certain shapes, not because they are functional, but because they enjoy a current vogue.

7

The Greek Revival

 mong the many conflicting ideals which have influenced Western architecture
during the last two centuries, perhaps none has produced such a variety of
expressions as those emanating from the ruins of ancient Greece. This
diversity was particularly apparent in the United States, where Greek inspiration
was most prevalent, and where later historians have therefore classified the whole
period between 1820 and 1860 as 'Greek Revival', despite the fact that the number
of factors common to all the buildings constructed there at that time were necessarily few, even if we exclude those which were deliberately non-Classical. A similar
if not a greater diversity is to be found in European countries. Thus the Greek
Revival illustrates better than any other the narrowness of judging Revivalism as
if it were a simple affectation of forms, instead of the result of a complex mixture
of conflicting motives related to varying local circumstances, to widespread cultural
changes and to traditional architectural beliefs.

In so far as the Greek Revival originated in a newly acquired knowledge of Greek
architecture, it may properly be attributed to the appearance of J. D. Leroy's
Ruins of the Most Beautiful Monuments in Greece, published in 1758, to Stuart and
Revett's *Antiquities of Athens*, published in 1762, and to G. M. Dumont's *Sequence
of Plans, Sections &c. of Paestum*, published in 1764. Yet all three books can be
ascribed to the sudden interest in Paestum which occurred between 1748 and 1750,
in that the motives and circumstances of the visits there typified those which
prompted eighteenth century architects to engage in this kind of research.

Admittedly, one factor which encouraged such enterprises, as far as the visit to
Greece itself was concerned, was the increasing tolerance shown by the Turks in
allowing foreigners to visit their territories. But it would be wrong to consider this
a decisive influence, or to assume that only Turkish hostility had prevented Greek
ruins from being examined sooner. As early as 1625, the Earl of Arundel had sent
an agent to Greece to collect antique marbles, whilst in 1674, the French ambassador
to Turkey, the Marquis de Nointel, had been so impressed by the sculptures of the
Parthenon when passing through Athens that he had commissioned a pupil of

Lebrun to make careful drawings of all those which had survived. At this latter period also, the two most famous antiquarians of the time, Jacob Spon and George Wheler, were touring these territories to obtain material for their *Voyage in Italy, Dalmatia, Greece and the Levant*, published in 1678.

The Greek ruins at Paestum, about seventy miles by land from Naples, were clearly visible from boats sailing through the Gulf of Salerno, yet it was not until 1750 that any architect of importance thought of visiting them. The numerous Greek temples in Sicily were similarly accessible, yet no one thought of exploring them before d'Orville went there in 1724, and no drawings of them were published until G. M. Pancrazi's *Antiquities of Sicily* appeared in 1751.

The new notion of visiting Paestum seems to have been partly due to its proximity to Herculaneum, but was mainly due to the fact that it was considered picturesque. When Payne Knight visited the ruins, he found them romantically overgrown with moss and weeds, and since they were neither blackened by smoke nor disfigured by modern accretions like those he had seen in Rome, he commented on how much more colourful, harmonious and picturesque they appeared. When the ruins were visited by Goethe (who had been attracted to them by Payne Knight's description, and who subsequently translated Knight's book on the Sicilian antiquities into German) there was a similar appreciation of their unquestionable picturesqueness, but there was also a marked concern with their very unorthodox proportions, since, as Goethe remarked, his whole being was prepossessed in favour of a 'lighter style' of architecture. Nevertheless, within an hour he was reconciled to them, and had decided that although, at first sight, these crowded masses of stumpy pillars appeared 'heavy, not to say frightful', it was simply due to the fact that man's tastes evolved throughout the centuries from the severe to the pleasing, in harmony with the architecture produced.

The real beginning of the Greek Revival thus only occurred in architecture when Goethe's generation reconciled its tastes with those of primitive antiquity; a reconciliation which was tantamount to reversing the evolutionary process to which he referred.

The first architect to visit Paestum (apart from one living in the vicinity) was Jacques-Germain Soufflot, who went there in 1750 as a result of accompanying Madame de Pompadour's brother, the Marquis de Marigny, on a tour of Italy. On this occasion they naturally went to visit the newly discovered subterranean Roman remains near Naples, and whilst they were there, an Italian acquaintance of Marigny recommended a visit to Paestum, the ruins of which had been first described by D. G. Antonini in 1745 and of which drawings had been made in 1748. Marigny himself evidently did not consider that they offered much interest, and so Soufflot reluctantly accepted the invitation alone. Once there, however, he was so impressed by the remains that he made the complete set of measured drawings later engraved and published by Dumont, but he did this, he said, not because he thought the ruins particularly beautiful but in order that they might be admired 'in spite of the material and their proportions', and to show by their dimensions 'the progress subsequently made' by the Doric Order amongst the Greeks (i.e. as described by Vitruvius) and the Romans.

His avowed interest was thus purely historical, but the strange proportions of these columns and entablatures must nevertheless have suggested to him an affinity with certain problems in design then occupying his mind. For some time, the leading French architects had been showing a growing distrust of the sinuous compositions and effeminate ornamentations which had been popularized by Rococo interior decorators, and a growing fear that these would eventually cause the degeneration of architecture itself. In fact, the application of Rococo fashions to the exteriors of buildings had proved more congenial east of the Rhine than in France; but Meissonier's design for St. Sulpice, and the 'caprices' engraved by Cuvillies and Lajoue, seemed to be a warning of what might happen in France if French tastes were not disciplined. Hence teachers such as J. F. Blondel began to preach with increasing insistence the virtues of 'male simplicity'—a doctrine which the leading architects such as Ange-Jacques Gabriel and Soufflot himself were beginning to put into effect.

Now clearly, whatever the defects of the proportions and adornments of the Doric Order at Paestum compared with Vitruvian standards, they were certainly masculine to the point of brutality, and in an age which had never before seen Classical columns less than seven diameters high, they seemed to bear out the contention of the reformers that Classical architecture was essentially severe. The proportions found at Paestum were never in fact incorporated into new buildings until after 1785, when romantic architects like Ledoux occasionally considered them appropriate for such structures as customs houses and factories. Even the more slender Athenian Doric, as illustrated by Leroy, was viewed with disfavour by practising architects in the eighteenth century, and was only normally acceptable in gardens, where the heavy proportions were thought to be more in keeping with the romantic natural surroundings when seen from far away.

But though Neapolitan Doric could be dismissed without embarrassment as archaic and provincial, it was less easy to reject the Doric of Attica as irrelevant to contemporary architectural design. Theorists such as Blondel might well conclude, after examining Leroy's book, that its only value was historical, and that its principal merit was to demonstrate the progress which architecture had made since the time of the Greeks. This was something of which he was convinced already. Similarly, Sir William Chambers might well attribute the many 'deformities' he detected in Athenian buildings, such as 'gouty columns, narrow intercolumniations and disproportionate architraves' to the Greek lack of proficiency in construction. But Leroy himself, who was much younger and was excited by his own discoveries, was by no means sure that these buildings were only of historical value, since his purpose in visiting Greece had not been primarily archaeological, but had been intended to complete his architectural studies at the French Academy in Rome, where he had gone at the age of twenty-three after winning the *Prix de Rome*.

Being an architect by training, Leroy was faced with a dilemma, new to the age, of deciding whether the ruins of antiquity were to be studied as architectural history or architectural theory; for he had the perspicacity to see that the two were not the same thing. He therefore divided his book into two parts, and in the second, dealing with theory, he suggested that the whole question of the proportions of the Orders might require renewed study in the light of his own research. He cautiously and wisely refrained from suggesting that Periclean Doric was better than contemporary Doric; but at the same time he claimed that there was no evidence to show that Vitruvius's judgement was impeccable or that the few surviving examples of Roman Doric were the most typical or the most correct, since apart from the fact that the proportions of the columns on the theatre of Marcellus did not comply with Vitruvius's prescriptions, there were not enough examples left to prove that the Romans in Italy had ever abandoned completely the proportions of the fifth century B.C. On the contrary, the evidence of the Forum of Augustus in Athens proved that the Romans still used such columns when building in Greece.

Leroy's views did not begin to make any marked impression until he was appointed professor of architecture at the Academy school in Paris in 1774, and even then, the effects of his influence did not really appear until the students of that generation reached maturity at the end of the century. Meanwhile, French awareness of Greek architecture was derived mainly from popular literature, such as P. A. Guys' *Literary Journey through Greece*, Choiseul-Gouffier's *Picturesque Voyage in Greece*, and Barthélemy's *Journeys of Young Anacharsis in Greece*.

The *Literary Journey through Greece* sought to establish that the genius of ancient times still existed among the modern inhabitants—an idea which was to have particularly important implications after the Greek War of Liberation. The same idea is to be found in Madame de Staël's *Corinne*, for as Corinne remarks to Oswald, when gazing rapturously eastwards from the top of the campanile in Venice: 'it is very moving to contemplate that beyond the horizon there are men with a lively imagination and enthusiastic character who, despite the degradation imposed on them by destiny, may one day join us in bringing back life to their ancestors' dust'.

The *Picturesque Voyage in Greece* was a description of the country in its actual state as seen by Choiseul-Gouffier when he accompanied a naval cartographical expedition to the Peloponnese, and it shows a romantic and essentially oriental aspect of Greece which was very attractive to the tourists of that time, with its turbanned peasants and its Turkish minarets. Looking at the illustrations, it is easy to understand why the members of the Society of Dilettanti so liked having their portraits painted in oriental costumes, for Greece became their special interest after 1764, when they financed an expedition to Ionia. Some of them, such as Lord Bessborough and Lord Sandwich, had been there as early as 1739, and the latter wrote a book about it, though this was not published for another sixty years.

82

Barthélemy's *Journeys of Young Anacharsis* was the only book of the three to show any real concern with ancient Greek buildings, but the descriptions were all derived from Classical texts since the author had never been to Greece. Most important of all, it characteristically disregarded the notion—which today is usually taken for granted—that the fifth century B.C. was Greece's golden age. The hero of this historical novel began his journey in 363 B.C., finishing it in 337 B.C., and this, according to the translator of the English edition, was considered to be the period when the arts and literature of Greece were at their height.

The emphasis on the post-Periclean age is especially apparent in the most famous of all books on Classical archaeology published during this period, namely J. J. Winckelmann's *History of the Arts of Antiquity*, which appeared in 1764. Winckelmann, who had been a pupil of A. G. Baumgarten (the originator of the term 'aesthetics'), visited Paestum shortly after 1755, and published an essay about Greek architecture (including a description of the temples at Girgenti, which he had never seen but which were described to him by Robert Mylne) with the help of Clérisseau in 1760. But his real interests lay in the critical analysis of sculpture, which formed both the substance of his famous book and of an earlier pamphlet on the *Imitation of Greek Painting and Sculpture*, published in 1755. Hence his influence on architecture was due to the fact that the Greeks themselves had regarded architecture as a kind of sculpture, and to a growing belief that a single theory could explain all the arts.

In his general attitude towards the history of art, Winckelmann did not differ radically from his precursors, since he considered, like Vasari, that the object of such a study was to go back to art's first origins, to follow its progress and variations to the era of its perfection, and to mark its decadence and fall to the point where it became extinct. Where he differed from Vasari was in his notion of what constituted perfection, and in his scientific method of identifying it, whereby instead of regarding the history of art as simply an anecdotal and biographical miscellany, he concentrated on the evolving stylistic character of the works of art themselves, which led him to assert not only that much of what then passed for Greek works of sculpture were nothing but Roman forgeries or imitations, but that an era when such imitations could be considered permissible constituted the ultimate decadence of art.

The fact that his *exposé* caused a mania for the slavish imitation of Greek art which proved more devastating than anything before known in history need not for the moment detain us. The crucial importance of his thesis was that, by attacking the traditional evolutionary theory of development, he challenged the assumption that in architecture, as in all the arts, the Romans had improved on the Greeks. Yet it should be noted that Winckelmann did nothing towards substituting Periclean standards for those of Augustan Rome, since according to him, antique sculpture was to be classified in four periods of which the greatest was not the fifth but the fourth century B.C. The first of these four periods he called the 'direct and severe style', up to the time of Phidias; the second he called the 'grand and angular style', up to the time of Praxiteles; the third he called the 'beautiful and flowing style', up to the decline of the school of Praxiteles; and the last was the 'style of imitations', up to the time of Imperial Rome. Thus for him, as for Barthélemy, and also for artists such as Mengs, the century of Alexander the Great represented the summit of Greek art.

Winckelmann's influence on the whole of European thought was widely recognized. Madame de Staël, for instance, contended that by revolutionizing the manner of considering art, he had revolutionized the manner of considering literature, for a better understanding of sculpture had produced a better understanding of poetry. But this remark was made in her book entitled *About Germany*; for it was not unnatural that the main impact of his theory occurred in the country where his book had first appeared, and where a spontaneous trend towards philhellenism was becoming widely evident by the beginning of the nineteenth century. Why this interest in Greece should have arisen there is not entirely clear, although it may well have been, as E. M. Butler has suggested, because the Germans have long cherished a passion for the absolute, and thus have often been tempted to seek artistic inspiration in metaphysics rather than in nature itself. For there can be little doubt that it was the scientific precision with which Winckelmann identified perfect beauty, rather than any deep conviction that this type of beauty was necessarily adaptable or appropriate to the changing circumstances of their national culture, that attracted his compatriots, and made Goethe, for example, abandon Gothic for Greek as the appropriate symbol of a Teutonic golden age.

Greek Revival architecture did not become really popular in Germany until after the end of the Napoleonic wars, when peace and the elation of victory combined with the so-called 'New Humanism' to cause a large number of public buildings to be fashioned after Greek models. But a prototype had been constructed in 1789, when K. G. Langhans began the Brandenburg Gate in Berlin. This was the first important public building in Germany to revive self-consciously the ideals of ancient Greece, yet although it undoubtedly bears a resemblance to the propylaea on the Athenian Acropolis, it has many other features, such as its gigantic size and the details of its superstructure, which relate it equally directly to quite different ideals being popularized at that time by the followers of E. L. Boullée. Indeed, the main problem in identifying any Greek Revival building is to distinguish the Greek elements from all the others with which they are so often mixed, so that before studying how the new idealization of Greece manifested itself architecturally in the nineteenth century, and why this idealization occurred when it did, it will be appropriate to examine both the influence of Stuart and Revett's *Antiquities of Athens*, and the events which determined that only the Periclean age should have the right to be considered typically Greek.

Initially, the *Antiquities of Athens* not only contributed little towards identifying the Golden Age of Greece, but tended to support the traditional view that Greek architecture had been surpassed by the Romans. In his preface to the first volume, Stuart asserted that the purpose of the book was to give an idea of the state of architecture in the best ages of Antiquity, since despite the progress made since the Renaissance, architecture had not yet recovered all its former perfection. But far from illustrating the notion that this perfection was characterized by the buildings on the Acropolis, or even by buildings constructed before the Roman conquest, his first volume contained a heterogeneous collection of Hellenistic monuments, few of which were of great artistic or archaeological value, and some of which had been built after 86 B.C. The only fifth century building was the Temple by the Ilyssus (which he was unable to identify and hence unable to date); the only other building we should now classify as Greek was the choragic monument of Lysicrates; the rest comprised two Roman gateways, Julius Caesar's 'Tower of the Winds' and a Hadrianic colonnade.

In the preface to the second volume (1789), Stuart changed his ground slightly, and claimed that the selection given in the first volume had been deliberately designed to exhibit specimens of all the various kinds of columns used in Greece at different times. But the main reason for his strange miscellany was undoubtedly the fact that Leroy had forestalled Stuart and Revett with his own publication, even though his visit to Athens had followed their own widely publicized tour by two years. We thus find that the part played by the first volume of the *Antiquities of Athens* in awakening an interest in Periclean Greece was very small. When fifth century Ionic details were used by interior decorators before 1789, their source could only be Leroy, and although James Wyatt (following Hawksmoor's example of romantically incorporating archaic compositional elements into new buildings) used Stuart and Revett's book as the source for his new observatory at Oxford, the prototype he chose was the Roman 'Tower of the Winds'. Thus except for garden temples and interiors, the use of Periclean prototypes was almost completely neglected during the eighteenth century, and its adoption at the beginning of the nineteenth century was due less to the influence of copy-books than to the propaganda of wealthy connoisseurs and amateur architectural historians, such as Thomas Hope and the Earl of Aberdeen.

Thomas Hope was typical of the men who most powerfully influenced English architectural taste at this period. From the time he was a small boy, he had been passionately interested in art and architecture, so that when he came of age and inherited his fortune, he decided to go on various tours to study the arts of Antiquity, and embarked on a series of journeys through Italy, Greece and Egypt which lasted eight years. On his return, he was not content simply to catalogue all the treasures he had collected, or with designing neo-Egyptian decorations for his house. He wished also to figure as an arbiter of architectural taste, and his big opportunity came when he was invited by the first master of a new Cambridge college to pronounce on the plans for the college buildings which had been prepared in 1804.

Hope's opinion was published in a lengthy report entitled *Observations on the Plans and Elevations designed by James Wyatt for Downing College, Cambridge*. In it he insisted on the necessity of adopting certain definitive and unalterable Classical principles which were to be considered indispensable to the elegance and beauty of college buildings—a plea which might have been strikingly apt if made with reference to Oxford (where both Gothic and Classical had been used indifferently for centuries, and where neo-Gothic had been given a great impetus by Hawksmoor) but which seemed somewhat inept in the present circumstances where neo-Gothic had been specifically forbidden by George III (who had been well trained by his tutor, Sir William Chambers), and where the design was consequently in the standard manner which had been traditional in Europe for the last three hundred years.

Yet it was precisely with the current Classical forms that Hope took issue. Instead of 'the degraded architecture of the Romans', he asserted, Wyatt should have preferred 'the purest style of the Greeks'. Most architects who designed public buildings had never, he said, travelled beyond Italy, and as a result they copied Roman models as being the only style known to them which had been 'in vogue amongst the ancients'. But had they had his own advantage of visiting Greece, they would have perceived that the Order used in the Parthenon was superior to Roman Doric, and in support of both the orthodoxy and progressiveness of his opinion, he cited the new town gate he had recently seen in Berlin. It would, he said, be especially appropriate in the present instance, since a university college might well be thought of as a temple dedicated, like the Parthenon, to the goddess of Wisdom. If it was considered essential to give the columns a base rather than a stylobate, he could refer them to a Greek temple with this feature recently measured by William Wilkins (a graduate of the University, a fellow of Caius College, and a mathematician, who was eventually given Wyatt's job). Even if Doric were to be finally considered inacceptable (as in fact it was) Greek Ionic would be preferable to any Roman Order, for apart from its aesthetic advantages, especially as regards the association of ideas, an English building in the true Grecian style would, he said, have the tremendous advantage in this instance of being absolutely *unique*.

Lord Aberdeen's views on architecture were less bigoted, and as a result they lacked the influence of Hope's irrational preference for what he himself regarded simply as a superior 'vogue'. But as president of the Athenian Society, which he had founded on his return from a three-year stay in Greece in 1803, he naturally preferred Greek to Roman architecture, and regarded the Athenian temples as 'the full perfection of the art'. He was however by no means fanatical about them, and in his introduction to Gwilt's 1823 edition of Vitruvius, disclaimed any wish to prescribe the exclusive or servile imitation of any particular species of the remains of antiquity, and simply sought to recommend the general principles of excellence on which the Greeks worked. These remains, he said, should not be imitated with the servility of a copyist, but should have their beauties transferred to English soil whilst preserving a due regard for the changes of customs and manners, for the differences of climate, and for the traditions of modern society. He did not consider that architects should concentrate so much on the details of these buildings as on the spirit with which they were originally planned and erected. Nor did he insist that Greek architecture was only perfect in the age of Pericles, but, like Winckelmann and James Stuart before him, dated its decline after the death of Alexander, assuming, in view of the difficulties of dating Greek ruins, that the period of greatness had lasted for at least two hundred years.

The event which brought about the exclusive insistence on the artistic supremacy of mid-fifth century Athens, and which has caused even recent archaeologists to claim that Greek architecture 'began to decline towards the end of the fifth century because nothing new or better could be achieved in the same line', was the controversy aroused by the proposed purchase of the Elgin Marbles in 1805. In 1799, the year the Earl of Elgin was appointed ambassador to Turkey, his architect suggested that the mansion then being built for him in Fifeshire might appropriately be adorned with copies of the sculptures gracing the Parthenon, which were already well-known through the publication ten years earlier of the second volume of Stuart and Revett's *Antiquities of Athens*, and known before that through the publication of de Nointel's drawings in Montfaucon's *Antiquities*, and by the engravings of Leroy. But Lord Elgin was not content simply with plaster casts, and purchased the whole lot from the Turkish government, subsequently offering them to the British Museum at half-price.

Immediately, a controversy arose as to whether they were in fact worth the £35,000 requested. Payne Knight, who liked to consider himself the leading expert in such matters, followed the opinion of Jacob Spon by insisting that they were Roman restorations, and hence comparatively worthless; but artists such as Haydon, Fuseli and West asserted not only that they must be the original statues praised by Pausanias, Cicero and Pliny, but that they were the most beautiful examples of sculpture they had ever seen. The Society of Dilettanti loyally supported Knight (who was a member), but Haydon, Fuseli and West were supported by a large number of foreign artists and connoisseurs such as Canova and Visconti, and the result was that by 1820, the triumph of the Periclean faction was complete. From then onwards, Classical opinion (as expressed by Plutarch) to the effect that sculpture and architecture attained their highest degree of excellence at Athens under Pericles' leadership was considered irrefutable, and mid-fifth century Athens became not merely the standard of artistic excellence, but almost an epitome for everything Greek.

All these various events forcing awareness of Greek achievements on the public imagination culminated in the Greek rebellion against the Turks, which began in 1820 and came to its victorious climax seven years later, as soon as France, Russia and England officially intervened. The liberation of Greece had been a romantic theme in Western Europe for half a century, especially after the rising of 1769, when

Russia, then at war with Turkey, had sent an unsuccessful expedition to the Peloponnese. But at that time only Voltaire was moved to celebrate the event in verse. By 1820, however, European Romanticism was at its height, and although there were few poets who followed Byron to join the insurgents at Missolonghi, there were many who harnessed their muse to the popular enthusiasm, and who gave the insurgents unstinting verbal support. Patriotic poems were written by republican poets such as Victor Hugo and Lamartine, Rossini composed *The Siege of Corinth*, and even the French Academy was moved to propose 'Greek Independence' as the subject for one of its annual poetry prizes. Subscriptions were raised by the various Philhellenic Committees in England, Switzerland and France, and although in France philhellenism was viewed officially with suspicion (since the restored Bourbons associated it with liberal sympathies and pagan beliefs) it was promoted with great enthusiasm in the United States, where for nearly fifty years a romantic sense of solidarity had been felt for any nation fighting to be free.

More thoughtful American citizens might well have considered that an attempt by an indigenous population to free itself from foreign rule was more analogous to the Red Indians' struggle against armed efforts to attain their subjugation (then being vigorously resisted near what is now Chicago) than to the earlier rebellion by British colonists against troops of their own religion, allegiance and race; but the fact is that in America, the Greek War of Independence symbolized the inevitable triumph of republicanism and democracy. It did not matter to them that the Greek leaders lost no time in asking for a foreign king to rule them once victory was achieved; nor did they care whether or not the new government was democratically elected. All they knew was that a victory had been won which was comparable in significance to the earlier famous victory over Xerxes, and their determination to see it in this light was reinforced by the fact that an English historian, William Mitford, had equated the principles of the American revolutionaries (which he detested) with those of Greek democracy in the fifth century B.C.

This is why the revival of Greek architecture of this period became so prevalent in America, and also why it should have enjoyed a certain official popularity in Bavaria (whose royal family had provided Greece's first king) and in Denmark (whose royal family had provided its second). It was also, for even more compelling reasons, well represented in Athens itself, though the most ambitious Greek Revival building to be projected there, namely Friedrich Schinkel's design for a royal palace on the Acropolis, was never built. Schinkel was not perhaps one of those architects most distinguished for their integrity. Obliged by the paucity of building activities during the Napoleonic War to concentrate on designing stage scenery, he had become adept at representing all the different historical 'styles', and this may explain why he indulged in so many of them. But his major works were all inspired by Greek principles as he understood them, and like all the other more vigorous exponents of Greek Revivalism, he showed no sign of being intimidated by the achievements of the ancients, but clearly believed that his own

88

A. Roos: Lodge at Shrubland Park (1841)

G. G. Scott and D. Wyatt: The Foreign Office, London (1861)

THE RENAISSANCE REVIVAL

Illustrating the influence of Italian rustic villas on monumental compositions

XIII

C. Barry: The Palace of Westminster (1840)

GOTHIC NATIONALISM

Illustrating how, despite archaeological detailing, Revivalist buildings often incorporated rational features such as standardized fenestration patterns and ventilation ducts

XIV

A. W. N. Pugin: Scarisbrick Hall (1837)

GOTHIC ECCLESIOLOGY

Illustrating the influence of ecclesiastic architecture on Gothic Revival mansions

XV

W. Butterfield: Keble College, Oxford (1868)

G. G. Scott: St. Pancras Hotel, London (1865)

GOTHIC POLYCHROMY

*Illustrating the variegated patterns which it became fashionable to introduce
by means of differently coloured building materials*

XVI

work was just as good. Whereas more recent Hellenists would be seized with apoplexy at the thought of desecrating the Acropolis with anything contemporary, and have even been known to destroy quite respectable Byzantine or mediaeval structures if there was hope of unearthing Bronze Age foundations beneath, Schinkel blithely proposed to mingle his own buildings with the ancient ruins, and visualized the latter as constituting simply an appropriate patriotic *décor*. For he was not nearly as romantic as some of his designs might suggest, and it is symptomatic of the attitude of such men that the many crisply drawn reconstructions of Greek temples which were produced in the nineteenth century, and which give such pain to those who admire the original ruins for their picturesque effect, were often indistinguishable in character from the drawings for new buildings then being designed.

The same attitude is shown in the works of Schinkel's equally distinguished contemporary, Leo von Klenze. He also displayed a certain lack of artistic integrity in the indifference with which he indiscriminately adopted various 'styles' in accordance with his clients' wishes. But when not subjected to the demands of eccentric patrons like Ludwig II, he showed an ingenuity and resourcefulness not usually associated with Revivalism of this type. The Walhalla at Ratisbon, though so similar in appearance to the Parthenon that it excited the uttermost contempt of outspoken contemporary critics such as James Fergusson, was nevertheless one of the first monumental buildings to make an extensive use of structural cast iron beams in the ceiling. Conversely, his Greek Revival Technological Museum was an extremely original composition of Greek tectonic elements, even though designed to be built of traditional materials, and was planned asymmetrically with full appreciation of the unusual needs the building was expected to fulfil.

For it is one of the paradoxes as well as one of the strengths of the Greek Revival that just as Greek literature could at this time be considered both Classical, and Romantic, so Greek architecture could be considered both Classical and Picturesque. By some, Greek proportions and details were regarded, like Greek temples, Greek statues and Greek poems, as the epitome of Classical perfection, and were imitated for the same reason that the Society of Dilettanti had proposed imitating the temple at Pola, and that Thomas Jefferson had imitated the Maison Carrée at Nîmes—namely, because having been approved for many ages, they were beyond criticism. Yet by others, the asymmetrical siting of the buildings on the Athenian Acropolis, and the asymmetrical composition of the Erechtheion, were regarded as proof that Greek art was essentially naturalistic, and that these buildings proved how appropriately Classical forms could be arranged in a picturesque way. Fergusson pointed out in his *Historical Inquiry* that the Greeks were obviously too intelligent to make their domestic or civic buildings pedantically symmetrical, even though at this time no remains of early Greek dwellings had been excavated. But this was simply the rationalization of an opinion held since the late eighteenth century, for fifty years before this Payne Knight had decided on purely aesthetic grounds that there could be no impropriety in employing the elegances of Grecian taste in asymmetrical compositions. By the middle of the nineteenth century a whole series of asymmetrical Greek villas had already been built.

It would be tedious to enumerate all the various ways in which Greek Revivalism expressed itself, but there is something to be gained in studying the main groups into which they can be classified, since these show how complex the whole Greek Revival was, and why its influence was so lasting and so great. First, there was the general concern with simplicity. This could be justified in terms of 'male simplicity' or of 'republican simplicity', or the two ideas could be combined, as when Choiseul-Gouffier wrote of the 'male character which the Greeks imprinted on the Doric Order during the splendid centuries of their liberty'. As early as 1758, de Goguet had observed in his *Origin of the Laws, Arts and Sciences* that 'exterior modesty is the appendage and favourite virtue of republicans', so that it was particularly prized in the United States, especially in those newly developed townships with Greek names, where lavish expenditure on ornamentation would in any event have been out of the question. Simplicity thus excluded not only Imperial Roman but Hellenistic prototypes, for as Lord Aberdeen pointed out, the buildings constructed after the Macedonian conquest seemed to have been inconsistent with 'the chaste severity of republican taste'.

The idealization of severity expressed itself in a preference for the Doric Order, and in fact it was by the use of Greek Doric that Greek sympathies were most usually and most clearly shown. But the other two Greek Orders were also used, in which case the preference for Greek rather than Roman was probably motivated by the new belief in the virtues of variety. Whereas the more traditional architects were still content, especially after the abortive seventeenth century attempts to design a 'sixth Order', with the standard Roman designs for capitals, and only varied the Corinthian Order as regards the choice of leaves, there were several who saw in the Ionic and Corinthian details of early Athenian buildings an opportunity of appearing highly original without at the same time risking condemnation for showing corrupt Classical tastes. This tendency increased with the spread of archaeological research and discovery, so that by 1841 we find archaic and even eccentric prototypes being conscribed for service with the Greek Revival, such as the Ionic capitals of the remote temple of Apollo at Bassae (discovered as early as 1765, but unknown in Europe until 1811 because its original discoverer was murdered while attempting to make a more detailed examination), or the Corinthian capitals of the Tholos at Epidaurus.

When elements other than Greek ornaments or Greek Orders were used, the motive was probably simply a reflection of an uninhibited fascination for archaeological exactitude, and here the difference in ideals between the Greek Revivalists and the more traditional Classical architects was particularly marked. Before 1750 it was well known, for example, that the Greeks had made their windows narrower at the top than at the bottom, since not only was this arrangement described by

Vitruvius, but it could be seen in such Roman ruins as the round temple at Tivoli. But such authorities and prototypes had been generally disregarded because the arrangement was so ill-suited to hinged or sliding windows (although it is characteristic of the spirit of English Palladianism that it was used by Lord Burlington in the courtyard of his own house). When the French Academy, for example, discussed the matter on March 30th, 1676, March 8th, 1683, May 7th, 1691, and December 15th, 1698, it formally disapproved of doors 'which are made larger at the bottom than at the top, even though a few examples of these proportions are to be found in the buildings of Antiquity'. Its reintroduction by William Wilkins was due simply to the fact that he copied it, like the rest of his details for Downing College, from the illustrations of the Erechtheion in Stuart and Revett.

This type of window was not however copied very often. The more moderate Greek Revivalists recognized its practical disadvantages, whilst the more fanatical and punctilious did not use windows at all, considering that hypaethral temples, or those lit only by the doorway, were more characteristic and hence more correct. Nor did they adopt the Erechtheion's pilasters and engaged columns, but preferred façades consisting predominantly of porticoes and blank walls. Certain architects, such as Schinkel, had the ingenious idea of arranging fenestration as if it were simply a sequence of free-standing pilasters with the intercolumniation filled with glass, but all these treatments of walls and fenestration patterns were equally characteristic of several other contemporary ideals, and will be dealt with in a more appropriate place. It is sufficient to say here that the destruction of traditional fenestration patterns has been one of the most persistent architectural characteristics of the whole modern age.

Another way in which Greek influence was expressed was in the imitation of Greek compositional forms such as tholoi. Smaller cylindrical structures, as for example the monument of Lysicrates, might also be taken as models; but since all such shapes were difficult to adapt to contemporary needs, it was more usual to find half a tholos used. Such a half-cylinder might be employed to terminate one end of a building, for example, and it could be crowned perhaps with the monument of Lysicrates, as in William Strickland's Philadelphia Exchange. The most popular model for compositions was of course the Parthenon, which was used for all sorts of different buildings, but especially for banks, throughout the length and breadth of the United States.

The idea of the Parthenon as the most perfect building ever constructed is now so ingrained in architectural thought that it is seldom questioned, and there have been few general theories of architecture enunciated in the last hundred years which have omitted to put forward this building as the supreme example of its application. Indeed, when one considers the constant popular attitude towards this building since 1850, few things are more remarkable than the veneration it has aroused, or the persistence and ingenuity with which its qualities have been interpreted to justify every change in architectural fashion, from the servile duplication of its composition and details to the most individualistic creations in reinforced concrete and steel. Yet before Leroy's reconstructions were published it was virtually unknown, and even then, its merits took considerable time to achieve recognition. Before Leroy's book appeared, J. F. Blondel considered that the four most important Greek temples were those of Diana at Ephesus, Apollo at Miletus (i.e. Didyma), Demeter at Eleusis and Olympian Zeus at Athens, on the strength of the descriptions given by Pliny, Strabo, Pausanias and Spon. By 1771 he still had not included any illustrations of the Parthenon in his lecture course, even though Leroy was his assistant. On the contrary, he used Leroy's book to demonstrate how much superior Vignola's Doric was to the Doric of the gate to the Roman Forum in Athens. It was not until the beginning of the nineteenth century that any authors suggested that the Parthenon was the most perfect Classical temple ever constructed, and not until the middle of the century was it widely considered to be the most perfect of all time. In 1823, even such an enthusiast as Lord Aberdeen claimed only that the Parthenon was probably the most beautiful building of antiquity. Yet in 1855, Fergusson's *History of Architecture* stated that in its own class it was undoubtedly the most beautiful building in the world, and by this time even Ruskin and Viollet-le-Duc, the most uncompromising advocates of the Gothic Revival at that period, felt compelled to speak of it with respect.

Curiously enough, the qualities of the Parthenon which aroused most enthusiasm amongst the *cognoscenti*, and which were largely responsible for the veneration in which it was universally held, were completely disregarded by practising architects. These were the so-called 'refinements', by which the surfaces were imperceptibly curved and the component elements imperceptibly displaced. Such refinements had been described by Vitruvius (although the only one used by the Romans seems to have been that known as entasis), but they had been generally dismissed by Classical architects as either impractical or unnecessary, so that before 1800 no one thought of looking for them on any antique temples because no one cared whether they were there or not. But the nineteenth century saw the flowering of archaeology as an exact science, and in 1829, T. L. Donaldson established by careful measurement the fact that the columns of the Parthenon were inclined in accordance with Vitruvius's rules. In 1837 James Pennethorne noticed the curvature of the stylobate; by 1852, with the publication of F. C. Penrose's *Investigation of the Principles of Athenian Architecture* (measured at controlled temperatures to a thousandth of a foot), the full complexity of Ictinus's systematic deviations had been disclosed. Yet the nineteenth century stonemasons seem to have continued in their traditional use of plumb-lines, squares and levels, and seem to have laid their architraves no less horizontally and their columns no less vertically than they had done for the previous three hundred years.

Thus as far as actual building was concerned, the result of all the lip-service paid to the Parthenon amounted to little more than the transformation of the standard temple-like composition (or 'stuffed specimen', as Fergusson called it) from

Roman to Greek. But as far as the example of the Parthenon's site on the Acropolis was concerned, its influence was to prove quite revolutionary. Earlier architects, working in the Classical tradition, had preferred level sites for public buildings, because being concerned mainly with the enclosure of space, and with making such buildings form part of those spaces, the ideal position for a public building was at one side of a public square. But once picturesqueness had become fashionable, the dramatic quality of the Parthenon's site on the Acropolis made them regard all public buildings more as potentially objects *in* space rather than as objects *enclosing* space. For as Joseph Gwilt explained in his preface to the 1825 edition of Chambers's *Civil Architecture*, one of the most important qualities of Greek temples, apart from their size and strength, was the fact that their sites were 'almost invariably well chosen, and calculated to display their beauties to the greatest advantage'. Hence there can be little doubt that such buildings as St. George's Hall, Liverpool, and the High School at Edinburgh, as well as more obvious examples such as the Walhalla at Ratisbon or the parliament building in Vienna, derive much of their Greek Revival flavour from the fact that they were deliberately conceived with this sculptural isolation in mind. Where a hilly site was not forthcoming, a Greek Revival architect could compromise, as at London University or Leeds Town Hall, by placing his entrance at the top of a precipitous flight of steps.

Yet another characteristic of Greek Revivalism (which seems to have been first exploited by von Klenze in 1816 in his Glyptothek at Munich) was the insistence on making pediments correspond to the structural reality of a pitched roof, whereby this was placed only on the long axis of the principal block, the pediments of which spanned the full width of the façade. When a building was simply a replica of an antique temple, such an arrangement could hardly be avoided, but the vast majority of architects objected to always cramming the accommodation for public buildings into a single porticoed or peristyled prism, and so such buildings were usually designed as a sequence of concatenated blocks. Sometimes an entirely new type of composition resulted, as for example at Downing College, where an arrangement was devised similar to that later fully executed for Thomas Jefferson at the University of Virginia. More frequently, it was simply an adaptation of the typical Anglo-Palladian palace, whereby instead of having hipped roofs, the constituent pavilions were designed as a series of pedimented 'temples'. Frequently, for added piquancy, the axes of these 'temples' were placed at right angles, so that whereas the pediment of the central block would face the oncoming observer, those of the lateral blocks would only be seen by turning to the left or right. But any arrangement was acceptable provided that the pediments protruded above the adjoining links, and really constituted gables rather than decorative centrepieces. As James Elmes, one of the earliest writers of what he called the 'Greek persuasion' expressed it: 'the portico, according to the best examples of the Greeks, and to the natural fitness of things, is not a mere *appliqué* stuck on as an afterthought, but a natural continuation of the roof.'

But whatever the expressions resulting from this new and complex awareness of the implications of Greek archaeology, they all sprang essentially from a belief in the virtues of Primitivism; for in contrast to the progressive intentions proclaimed, however fruitlessly, by most of the other Revivalists, advocates of the Greek persuasion never disguised the fact that their eyes were fixed steadfastly towards the past. James Stuart had expressed uncertainty as to whether architecture was progressing or retrogressing; but in the minds of his more dedicated disciples there was no doubt at all. Unmoved by those who for various reasons demanded a new architecture, and unconvinced by those who claimed that technological developments would inevitably cause architectural components to reflect the changes of the times, they accepted no shapes or proportions which had not been approved by their most remote progenitors, and instead of being prompted by the new enthusiasm for history to trace the progression of Greek culture forward, they seem to have taken a delight in tracing its ancestry further and further back.

This was perhaps due to the peculiar relationship which had then developed between classical literature and classical archaeology; for it is a curious fact that in no other branch of linguistics has archaeology—and hence architecture—been so closely related to literature as in the study of Greek. On the one hand, late eighteenth century scholars such as Wolf were beginning to pay renewed attention to primitive Greek society as described by Homer, either by popularizing his poetry in new translations or by analysing it to discover the nature of primitive art. On the other hand the liberation of Greece now allowed the sites described in this poetry to be scientifically excavated, so that nineteenth century Greek scholars, having exhausted the possibilities of textual criticism, abandoned their books for pick-axes, and now spent their energy gathering shards. So infectious was their enthusiasm that when L. H. Le Bas was appointed professor of the history of architecture at the École des Beaux-Arts in Paris in 1840, he devoted the largest part of his lecture course to speculating on the type of buildings which might be excavated at Troy.

Today, architects no longer concern themselves with Greek archaeology, but it would be wrong to assume from this that the preoccupation with Primitivism is only characteristic of the beginnings of modern architecture and is foreign to the ideals we possess today. For it still influences us in three ways. Firstly, it has established a belief that there is a heuristic value in primitivism, whereby the best way to initiate young people to the practice of architecture is to ask them to design aboriginal dwellings, or study the social conditions of primitive tribes. Secondly, it has established a belief that the word 'natural' means simple and unsophisticated, spontaneous and unreflecting, and that naturalness can best be achieved by leaving rough, leaving plain or leaving out. Thirdly, it has established a belief that there is some peculiar virtue of innocence in primitive art which is lost once it has become mature.

There was nothing new, at the beginning of the nineteenth century, in considering that the Greeks, by their simplicity, were closest to nature, for this opinion had been expressed, for example, in the first course of lectures ever given at the French Academy school. But whereas in the seventeenth century this was regarded as a reason for not following them too closely, in the nineteenth century it was regarded in precisely the opposite light. The change of view was clearly related in large measure to the new attitude towards aesthetics, whereby primitive poetry was considered to be the most natural kind of poetry, as well as the key to an understanding of the nature of every kind of art, and it is no coincidence that Greek Revival architecture should have been contemporary with Wordsworth, as well as with Shelley and Keats. It was also very much influenced by French Primitivism, especially as expressed architecturally by Laugier, according to whom the only permissible elements were the four (namely columns, beams, pediments and blank walls) to be found in primitive huts. But whatever the various causes (many of which also influenced other Revivals) the result was to equate primitiveness with perfection, and to suggest that material progress had no relevance to man's spiritual progress, which demanded only a constant reference to those natural virtues best exemplified in the remote past. Such a view might have been quite valid when related to poetry, painting, music and sculpture, but its inapplicability to architecture became increasingly obvious as the industrial revolution aggravated the dichotomy which had always existed between architecture as a science and architecture as an art. As a result, the influence of the Greek Revival became progressively smaller as building technology became more complex (even though the ruins which inspired it continued to symbolize the authority which History exerted over every effort to find a viable theory of design), and Robert Kerr was probably right in claiming, in 1872, that Alexander Thomson was the last of the Greeks.

8

The Renaissance Revival

The term 'Renaissance Revival' may seem at first a nonsensical tautology, since the word 'Renaissance' itself clearly means a revival or, more literally, a rebirth. Yet not only does this title fittingly express the nature of one of the most important aspects of nineteenth century Revivalism; it expresses the very essence of Revivalism as understood by the more progressive, practical, least romantic and least sentimental architects of the age.

The ideal which created all aspects of Classical Revivalism (if we disregard the work of those many architects and patrons who merely imitated antique forms for the sake of variety) sprang essentially from the urge experienced after 1750 to avoid what was considered defective in the standardized architectural forms of the mid-eighteenth century by reverting to forms produced earlier in the evolutionary process. The aim was, as it were, to sprout a new and more vigorous off-shoot by pruning back to the very trunk of the architectural tree. Those who were most attracted towards archaeology, or who were especially interested in abstract aesthetic problems of form, tended to favour a return to the architecture of Imperial Rome or to that of the fifth century B.C., for reasons just explained. But the leading architectural practitioners, being necessarily most deeply involved with the rapidly changing needs of their clientele, generally took a different view, and those who still accepted the validity of Classical traditions preferred to return not to a remote period of sculpturesque perfection, whether Periclean or Augustan, but to a more recent period which was itself conditioned by uncertainties of social, economic and political change, of development and growth.

They argued that the flexibility necessitated by new building-types, by new decorative materials and by new mechanical inventions could best be paralleled historically in the works of the fifteenth and early sixteenth century architects of Tuscany, Lombardy, the Romagna, Venetia and France who, whether from an inability to rid their minds of mediaeval precedents, or from an unfamiliarity with Antique prototypes, had used antique forms with the greatest possible freedom. They argued that the way to design buildings suited to a transitional age was to

96

admit as wide a variety of window shapes, as unrestricted a system of ornamentation, as free a system of planning and as liberal a mixture of compositional forms as were to be found in the works of Brunelleschi, Raphael, the Lombardi, or the Métézeaux. It will be noticed incidentally that, in the spirit of the age, they sought a historical precedent for what they did.

Before about 1820, the term 'Renaissance Revival' would have been meaningless, since the word 'Renassiance' was not originally used to indicate a stylistic period, but was used only as part of such phrases as 'the renaissance of the arts of antiquity'. In other words, the term referred only to the initial impetus by which the architecture of the sixteenth, seventeenth and early eighteenth centuries had come into being. The first use of the word 'Renaissance', in its modern sense, seems to have been in Coussin's *Génie de l'Architecture* (1822), whilst its first occurrence in English seems to have been in Ford's *Handbook of Spain*, published in 1845. Its first use as a term of scorn, so far as I can discover, was Raoul Rochette's criticism of his fellow architects who wanted to 'faire de la Renaissance dans un temps tel que le nôtre'; a phrase which occurs in an article published in the *Revue Générale de l'Architecture* in 1841. Yet even so, an interest in the Renaissance period, a new tendency to isolate it stylistically from seventeenth century architecture, can already be discerned round about 1750 in the writings of Marc-Antoine Laugier, and it is even more evident in the researches of Jacques-Germain Soufflot, and the designs and teaching of Jacques-François Blondel.

Eighteenth century ignorance of the importance of Brunelleschi and his school is exemplified by the fact that J. D. Leroy, who was professor of architecture at the French Academy during the last quarter of the century, knew of no Renaissance use of pendentives earlier than 1483. Even so, Laugier had gone out of his way to draw attention to Brunelleschi's importance in his *Essay* (1753), where he calls him 'the first of the moderns', and in his *Observations* (1765), where he refers to him as the architect 'to whom we are foremost obliged for the renaissance of the Five Orders'. Laugier's references are all the more important in that he specifically excluded arcades from the structural system he himself advocated; thus he certainly did not admire Brunelleschi's churches wholeheartedly. But he was an admirer of 'Gothic lightness' when allied to Classical forms, and it was this aspect of Brunelleschi's work which mainly attracted the attention of leading French architects at this time.

Soufflot and Blondel are both good examples of architectural theorists interested in the buildings of the early Renaissance because, whilst being completely in accordance with Classical principles, they nevertheless had all the lightness and structural virtuosity of Gothic (as compared with the system of massive supports used, for example, in the Colosseum and copied in most French churches between 1650 and 1750). In March 1761, the French Academy of Architecture discussed the church of St. Augustine, Piacenza, and 'remarked especially on the extreme lightness of its construction'. In November 1762, Soufflot obtained from Italy the plans and sections of this church, together with a memorandum on its construction, 'so that the Academy could see to what degree of delicacy the construction of this building had been pushed by using the Greek Orders'. 'It proves', he said, 'that by using these Orders it is possible to approach that degree of lightness which the Academy has admired in several Gothic monuments, so as to attain a great saving of materials'. In February 1767, J. F. Blondel showed the Academy a church which he himself had designed on this system and which presented, he said, 'in some way the elegance one finds in Gothic edifices of the best type'. There is every reason to believe that he and his friends were working on this system independently of Soufflot, for Nicholas Nicole, who had been one of J. F. Blondel's fellow pupils in the office of the latter's uncle, had actually built a church in this manner in Besançon in 1748.

It was not however until the nineteenth century that the 'Renaissance' really became a popular source of inspiration, partly because of the newly awakened historical interest in the period, and partly because so few Antique buildings remained to be studied. Even the students of the French Academy in Rome were turning their attention to buildings of the fifteenth and early sixteenth centuries, and it was their published drawings which first made this kind of architecture widely known. In 1809, Percier and Fontaine published a book on the country houses of Rome and its neighbourhood. In 1815, their pupils Montigny and Famin published a book on early Tuscan architecture. In 1818, M. P. Gauthier, another pupil of Percier, published a book on the most beautiful buildings in Genoa. By the 1840s, 'Renaissance' architecture was so well known that its details could be, and were, copied all over Europe and in the United States.

Examples of the Renaissance Revival (or *Rundbogenstil*, as it was called in Germany) are so numerous that it would require a series of volumes to document those of which records survive. Henry-Russell Hitchcock has given an extensive selection in *Architecture, Nineteenth and Twentieth Centuries*, but even here he has only had space to list the more famous monuments. Let it suffice to say that the Renaissance Revival was probably the most popular of all the Revivals, especially for urban domestic architecture, and for public buildings such as hotels and government offices, and that it eventually developed into what was termed the 'Queen Anne Revival' (which will be discussed under the heading of Eclecticism), so as to last in popularity for nearly a hundred years.

This popularity of the Renaissance Revival was due to its immense adaptability. For whereas the Greek Revival, and to some extent the Roman Revival, demanded that the required accommodation be fitted into restricted and rigidly preconceived compositional shapes, lit by a limited choice of standardized windows, and adorned in accordance with a strict canon of decoration, the Renaissance Revival allowed an architect to select—and even to invent for himself—such compositional and decorative forms as might be considered suitable for the occasion. Assuming, therefore, as we must assume, that in the nineteenth century there was seldom any pressing need to forgo using traditional building materials, and that, for nearly every architectural programme, the most convenient and sensible structural material was load-bearing masonry, the logic of the Renaissance Revivalists can hardly be disputed, and it was not until the development of steel and reinforced concrete frames that their theoretical position could be seriously challenged.

The skill of the best Renaissance Revival architects is thus not to be found in the archaeological accuracy of their façades, but in the freedom with which they used their Classical tectonic vocabulary, in the ingenuity with which they planned orderly sequences of accommodation on awkward sites, in their skilful combination of different and often new building materials, and in their incorporation of such primitive mechanical equipment as existed at the time. There were of course writers such as Victor Hugo and Théophile Gauthier who admired early Renaissance architecture, and hence Renaissance Revival architecture, for purely romantic reasons, because it was picturesque, and lacked the order and symmetry of Classical architecture. But architects and architectural journalists admired it for more materialistic reasons. According to César Daly, for example, Charles Barry's Reform Club was not an inert mass of stone, brick and cast iron, but 'almost a living body, with its complex circulation systems; for in its walls, which appear so immobile, there circulate gases, vapours, and fluids through the hidden ducts and wires'. 'These latter constitute the arteries, veins and nerves of a new organized being', he lyrically exclaimed; 'heat is conveyed by them in winter, fresh air in summer, and in every season they supply light, hot and cold water, food, and all those numerous accessories which an advanced civilization requires'.

'Superabundant strength and simple planning characterize all primitive architectures', Daly concluded, 'whereas calculated strength, related to the resistance of materials, and relatively complex plans correspond to the complexity of advanced civilizations. This type of architecture thus characterizes already the architecture of our time, and can only be developed more and more in the future'. As he well observed, the Renaissance Revival was quite different from the Greek and Roman Revivals in that, though it used what might superficially appear to be the same tectonic elements, it really did produce an architecture which sought to be in harmony with the age. As James Ferguson put it: 'it introduced common sense into architectural design'.

9

Gothic Nationalism

Probably the most rational theory of Revivalism formulated during the nineteenth century was that used to justify the Gothic Revival, but it is important to appreciate that rationalism was not the Gothic Revival's only support. On the contrary, no other stylistic revival drew its strength from so many varied, and at times conflicting, sources.

It is common for art historians to classify all buildings ornamented with pseudo-mediaeval details as simply 'Gothic Revival', and to catalogue them within a single stylistic group. By so doing, they exemplify to perfection the drawback of studying modern architecture simply as a sequence of forms rather than as a series of ideals. Not only were the ideals which were used to justify the Gothic Revival immensely varied; they were often diametrically opposed. A. W. N. Pugin urged the adoption of Gothic architecture on the grounds that it was the architecture of Catholicism. John Ruskin, who hated Catholicism, urged its adoption because it expressed for him the essence of Protestantism, and the ideal of a happy working-class society. Eugène Viollet-le-Duc, who was a liberal and a free-thinker, urged its adoption because for him it was the only rational system of masonry construction (whereas Ruskin, on the contrary, considered that Gothic construction interfered with 'the purity and simplicity of the reflective element', and regarded ornament as the essence of architecture). There were in fact five principal ideals pursued: romanticism, nationalism, rationalism, ecclesiology and social reform. Romantic ideals of Gothic Revivalism have already been dealt with. Rational ideals of Gothic Revivalism will be dealt with in a section dealing with Rationalism in both its Classical and Gothic manifestations. It is proposed here to deal only with nationalism, ecclesiology and social reform, in that order.

The nationalist argument in favour of a Gothic Revival was based ostensibly on the historically irrefutable fact that Gothic architecture was far more indigenous to northern Europe than Greek or Roman architecture. As such, it could be supported by the kind of argument put forward by Montesquieu and de Goguet in the mid-eighteenth century, namely that since all good architecture is related to climate, steep Gothic gables and water-shedding string-courses are more appropriate to England, France and Germany than flat roofs and classical cornices. 'The admired façade of the Louvre may be excellent in its kind', wrote Friedrich von Schlegel in 1804, 'but what can be more out of place than twenty or thirty Grecian or Italian columns in a strange land and climate? Gothic architecture is the style of building best adapted to a northern climate and a colder zone'.

Nevertheless, this argument was in fact seldom taken to its logical conclusion by English theorists. Ruskin's fondness for Italian architecture made him urge on his countrymen the adoption of a type of Gothic which was as alien to England as the Classical architecture he abhorred. It became popular because Italy had more Gothic civic and domestic buildings than any other country. It was favoured because (to quote Eastlake) 'there can be little doubt that Italian Gothic lends itself more readily than most styles to the treatment of a façade in which the relation of wall space to aperture is restricted by modern requirements'. It was favoured, as will be seen later, because of the current interest in polychromy. As a result, English Gothic Revival buildings were predominantly Italian in character, and Italian Gothic was even chosen for Canada when the Ottawa Parliament Building was designed in 1859.

After the publication of Viollet-le-Duc's dictionary of French mediaeval architecture, and after the international competition for the new church of Notre-Dame, Lille, held in 1856, French Gothic became fashionable in England in some circles, and was exploited assiduously by Shaw and Nesfield at the beginning of their careers. But whatever the motives for defining Gothic so widely, the great weakness of the English architects' claim to be resurrecting an indigenous style was their disinclination to base their designs on national prototypes. This was especially so as Gothic became more popular, and as the urge to introduce greater variety increased.

Such was not however the case at the beginning. The first and most important Gothic Revival building to be constructed under nationalistic impulses was the Palace of Westminster, built after fire destroyed the original buildings in 1834. The original buildings were not entirely Gothic, for the old Palace of Westminster had consisted of a heterogeneous congerie of buildings constructed over a period of several hundred years. But the main buildings (namely Westminster Hall, which survived the fire, and St. Stephen's chapel, which had been transformed into a House of Commons) were Gothic, and the site was next to Westminster Abbey, with the main entrance facing Henry VII's chapel. It is not surprising therefore that despite a spate of propaganda in favour of Antique prototypes, the authorities decided, when drawing up rules for the competition, that the new building should be 'Gothic or Elizabethan', allowing considerable latitude to the interpretation of the latter term.

The competition was won by Charles Barry who, as has already been pointed out, was in fact the chief exponent of the Renaissance Revival. Indeed, as many writers have remarked, the Palace of Westminster, with its symmetrical façade facing the river, and its basically symmetrical plan, is essentially a classical building dressed in Gothic details. That the brilliance of this detailing both inside and out was mainly due to the skill of A. W. N. Pugin may be a criticism of Barry; but it would be a grave mistake to despise the detailing as superficial decoration without putting forward an alternative, just as it would be foolish to dismiss the whole building as a mediaeval *pastiche* without considering the technological advances which it incorporated, and the complex planning requirements which it fulfilled.

What, after all, was the alternative to a Revivalist building in 1834? Barry created a structure which at least harmonized with the surrounding mediaeval monuments, and expressed, by its adornment at least, the mediaeval origins of the great constitutional principles which it was built to administer and maintain. Though the floors and roofs were of an advanced type of metal construction, there was no question of building the walls of this vast edifice, covering nine acres, of any material other than masonry. The only alternative to the accepted design would thus have been a building modelled on antiquity, or a building left absolutely plain. Every architect of the time shrank from the latter alternative, and recognized the truth of the editorial on the Palace of Westminster published in *The Builder* in 1844, which pointed out that 'zealously were it to be wished that in architecture some standard of taste could periodically in modern times be so promulgated among the public, that whatever should be done in innocence of heart by various designers should be accepted, and become the one method or style of the day, what an end would then be put to the incessant babbling which is at present held upon architectural taste! But devoutly as all this were to be wished, it is at present hopeless'.

A later chapter will deal with the insuperable problems confronting those who, in the mid-nineteenth century, demanded a new architecture. Similarly, a chapter will discuss the contributions made by the Palace of Westminster to the new sciences of heating, ventilation and acoustics. But it is opportune here to challenge Fergusson's assertion that Barry and Pugin, by using detailing comparable to that of Henry VII's chapel, were asking the public to believe 'that Henry VII foresaw all that the Lords and Commons and committees would require in the nineteenth century, and provided this building for their accommodation accordingly'. Nothing is plainer to twentieth century eyes than that this is a nineteenth century building. Indeed, few nineteenth century buildings look so modern as this, with its rectilinear grid of windows and infilling panels stretching nine hundred feet; and although, even when first built, it doubtless lacked certain contemporary comforts, it had then, as it has now, a dignity, richness and freshness which few public buildings are ever likely to achieve again.

Nevertheless, it is probably true to say that, in general, the Gothic Revivalists, as opposed to the Renaissance Revivalists, paid too little attention to contemporary planning requirements. Hence Fergusson was doubtless right in saying, with respect to the Ruskin-inspired Oxford Museum: 'the lecture rooms are cold, draughty and difficult to speak in; the library is a long ill-proportioned gallery; the windows are glazed in the least convenient manner; and the bookcases are arranged, not to accommodate books, but to look monkish'. Despite their protestations to the contrary, the Gothic Revivalists' aim was usually the attainment of archaeological exactitude rather than the fulfilment of contemporary needs.

This obsession with archaeology was an obvious symptom of that new awareness of history which, as has already been explained at length, was the primary intellectual force of the age. It affected all the Revivals, Classical as well as Gothic, but it had a particularly noxious influence on Gothic architecture, since whereas the passage of time had left relatively few substantial antique monuments standing (all of which had long been catalogued and explored), Gothic architecture was a relatively new field of research. It was not until 1819 that Rickman published his *Attempt to Discriminate the Styles of English Architecture*, though as early as 1816, Repton had remarked that 'by the recent works of professed antiquaries, a spirit of inquiry has been excited respecting the dates of every specimen that remains of ancient beauty or grandeur'. It was not until the 1820s that Arcisse de Caumont, under the influence of English archaeological studies and of Linnaeus's *Species Plantarum*, decided to classify the mediaeval buildings of Normandy as if they were botanical specimens. But once these scholars had paved the way, a horde of enthusiasts, both amateur and professional, rapidly followed their example, and libraries became filled with books of measured drawings from which imaginative architects could draw inspiration, and from which less imaginative architects could extract their cribs. St. John's church at Salford, for example, was composed of the tower and spire of Newark, the nave of Howden and the choir of Selby. The porch of Montreal Cathedral (1856) was based on that of St. Mary's church, Snettisham, Norfolk, the nave of St. Mary's being the prototype for the Anglican Cathedral at Fredericton (1845). Few architects learnt to assimilate the Gothic spirit and design original buildings of their own.

The copy books were harmless to antiquaries who regarded architecture as an aspect of the social life of the past. But to the architectural profession, these publications had the unfortunate effects of giving excessive importance to skill in draftsmanship, and of placing undue emphasis on the value of chronology. Before 1750, the chronology of antique monuments was of no interest to architects, whilst detailing had been largely left to craftsmen who, recognizing that their first obligation was to become familiar with the traditional mouldings and ornaments of the Five Orders, could be relied upon to execute details without having large scale drawings supplied. But with the advent of the Gothic Revival, all this changed. Now, unfamiliar with the tectonic vocabulary they were asked to employ, the craftsmen had to be supplied with exact delineations of every profile and crocket, with the result that architects became what Eastlake, the first historian of Gothic Revivalism, admiringly calls 'artist-architects'; a type of designer who inevitably degenerated into an ornamentalist, concerned more with silhouettes and surfaces than with structures and plans.

The new emphasis on the value of chronology was even more disastrous than the concern for drawing. Today, this perversion still exists in the form of an undue emphasis on the importance of achieving 'modernity', and in a contemporary reluctance to enlarge old-fashioned existing buildings in conformity with the way they were originally built. In the mid-nineteenth century, it expressed itself by chronological accuracy with regard to the historical 'style' of new buildings, and by an enthusiastic campaign to destroy those 'anachronisms' which had accumulated in those genuine mediaeval buildings which still survived. At its best, this notion of chronological accuracy could perhaps be defended as an aspect of the ideal of 'consistency'; but the consistency was purely antiquarian, and had no tectonic value whatsoever. At the time it was known as 'synchronism' and its protagonists, such as Scott, insisted that all Gothic buildings should be 'Middle Pointed'. But as James Fergusson observed in 1862: 'the great lesson we have yet to learn before progress is again possible is that *Archaeology is not Architecture*. It is not even Art in any form, but a Science'. As a reaction against the triumphant criticisms of these architectural archaeologists (who were never happier than when condemning a pseudo-Gothic building because one of the mouldings was, when compared with the rest, a few years out of date), Eclecticism, which implied the deliberate disregard of chronological exactitude in the selection of tectonic elements, was put forward as an alternative doctrine; but this ideal, being diametrically opposed to that of Revivalism, will have to be discussed at a later stage.

The peak period of nationalistic Gothic Revivalism in England was 1857–9, when George Gilbert Scott delivered the official lectures at the Academy; but it only lasted a decade. It is probably fair to say that although churches continued to be built in neo-Gothic until well into the beginning of this century, the last great monument to the folly of the nationalistic Gothic Revival was the Law Courts in London, for which a limited competition was held in 1867. All eleven designs were Gothic (although one competitor submitted an alternative design in the Italian Revival manner); but such was the reaction which at this time was taking place that in an article published in *The Builder*, describing G. E. Street's winning design, the author commented that 'we can only anticipate that a building erected according to these designs, or to the principles and predilections that they involve, will be a deformity and an eyesore for all time'. In 1869, another article in *The Builder* asserted with remarkable prescience that 'if, as it appears, the large and costly building for the Courts of Law is again to be an antiquarianism, with canopied niches and shrines for saints eminent in the history of the bar, it is not unlikely that the reaction, inevitable as it is, against this exaggerated Mediaevalism, may assert itself to a degree unpleasant to the feelings of the architect even before his building is completed. We recommend our rising architects to look more to the future, less to the past. If more time were spent in considering what are the real building problems peculiar to modern times, and how to deal with them, less time in acquiring merely an archaeological knowledge of former buildings, we should probably build to more purpose, and to the more permanent use and enjoyment of those who will succeed us'.

The defects in the Law Courts had little to do directly with the pseudo-mediaeval detailing of silhouettes and surfaces. They arose from the neglect of the practical comforts of those who were to work in it; from the fact that the spaces were planned more with an eye to their scenic effect than to their workability. It was this neglect of functional planning which caused the Gothic Revival to fall into disrepute with those responsible for the construction of public buildings, and which brought about the various reactions which will be discussed in their proper place.

IO

Gothic Ecclesiology and Social Reform

If the ecclesiologists' dream of a Gothic Revival was more lasting, it was probably because, being mainly concerned with churches and the reform of the liturgy, the fulfilment of ideal planning problems formed an essential part of their schemes. These schemes were of course well leavened—or perhaps one should say ballasted—with romantic piety and romantic sociology, probably because the romantic attitude towards Gothic churches had been early awakened by the popular novelists of the eighteenth century. Mrs. Radcliffe had delighted her readers with descriptions of high vaulted aisles extending in twilight perspective, and dimly lit churches with monks and pilgrims crossing themselves, and passing soundlessly into the enshrouding gloom. 'The universal stillness of the place', she wrote in *The Italian* (1797), when describing her hero's reaction to the 'abbey of San Stefano'; 'the gleam of tapers from the high altar, and of lamps which gave a gloomy pomp to every shrine in the church—all these circumstances conspired to press a sacred awe upon his heart'. They pressed a similar sacred awe on the hearts of many other travellers to Italy, however unsympathetic they might be towards the religious beliefs of the local populace; but such sights were not to be seen in England until two events took place. The first of these events was the passing of the Catholic Emancipation Act in 1829, the second was the founding of the Oxford Movement in 1833.

A decade earlier, interest in Gothic architecture had already been stimulated by an Act of Parliament which provided a million pounds to be spent building churches in London and other parts of England. Politically, the Act of 1818 was intended by the government to provide for the spiritual needs of the new working-class suburbs, whose denizens might otherwise be tempted to indulge in the distressing atheistic excesses which had recently been witnessed in France. Architecturally, it resulted in the construction of a hundred and seventy-four churches in the 'Gothic' style. The preference for Gothic was motivated partly by the new romantic interests just mentioned, but mainly by the discovery that Gothic churches could be built more cheaply than Classical churches. It was soon evident, however, that the pursuit of cheapness conflicted with the interests of archaeology. Cheapness had been achieved by using cast iron for columns and tracery, and by making the walls of plastered brick. Thus the more extensively archaeological studies developed, the more violently was the objection raised that these churches were not true Gothic at all, but pitiful shams.

From this situation, there resulted one of the most important tenets of Gothic Revivalism, and of modern architecture in general, namely the idea that architecture is an ethical art, which is primarily concerned with the expression of truth. The notion of 'truthful expression' is primarily an aspect of the nineteenth century concern with structural integrity, and will therefore be dealt with under the heading of 'Rationalism'. But it also affected religious minds with the notion that architecture is intimately concerned with personal morality. 'The violations of truth' thundered John Ruskin in *The Seven Lamps of Architecture* (1849), 'which dishonour poetry and painting, are for the most part confined to the treatment of their subjects. But in architecture another and a less subtle, more contemptible violation of truth is possible; a direct falsity of assertion respecting the nature of material, or the quantity of labour. We may not be able to command good, or beautiful, or inventive architecture; but we *can* command an honest architecture. The meagreness of poverty may be pardoned, the sternness of utility respected; but what is there but scorn for the meanness of deception?'

At first this ethical viewpoint only turned men's minds towards the idea of truthful construction. But the effects of the Catholic Emancipation Act suggested also the importance of truthful planning, since the re-established Catholic worship occasioned a return to the internal arrangements for which mediaeval churches had originally been designed. It will be remembered that under the influence of the Puritans, all Anglican churches, whether new or mediaeval, had been designed as, or turned into, auditoria, with galleried pews arranged round a pulpit. Indeed, this arrangement was adopted in most of the churches built under the Act of 1818. But with the emancipation of the Catholics, the chancel again became the focal point of the church, and the altar the focal point of the chancel, whilst screens, statues, stained glass and liturgical ornaments, which for the last two centuries had merely been antiquarian curiosities, now became fundamental elements of worship in the contemporary English scene.

The man most responsible for drawing his fellow-countrymen's attention to the relationship between mediaeval church planning and liturgical usage was Augustus Welby Northmore Pugin, the son of Augustus Pugin, one of the leading delineators of Gothic architecture of the early nineteenth century. The elder Pugin, though he earned his living in England as a draftsman, was in fact a French nobleman exiled by the Revolution. It is thus not surprising that his son, though brought up a Protestant, should eventually have become converted to his father's ancestral religion, just as he was inspired by his father's love of Gothic forms. And so, with all the passionate enthusiasm of a convert, A. W. N. Pugin spent the rest of his short life aggressively clamouring for a return to a completely mediaeval way of life.

To this end, he published a number of brilliant monographs, the most famous being *Contrasts* (1836) and *The True Principles of Pointed or Christian Architecture* (1841). In *Contrasts*, he satirically compared the ugliness and confusion of modern cities with a romantic vision of the simple unified beauty of mediaeval towns. In *The True Principles of Pointed or Christian Architecture*, he attempted to show the logic upon which the whole Gothic system of design was based.

Most of the points he raised will be more appropriately dealt with under the heading of Structural Rationalism; but he also discussed the need for logical planning, claiming that Greek temples were utterly inapplicable to the purpose of Christian churches, and that 'the attempt is little short of madness when our country is literally covered with beautiful models of ecclesiastical structures of every dimension, *the architecture and arrangement of which have originated in their wants and purpose*'. He made the same point with reference to domestic architecture: 'The old English Catholic mansions were substantial appropriate edifices, suited by their scale and arrangement for the purposes of habitation. Each part of these buildings indicated its particular destination'. And he concluded this part of his book by stating his belief that all the inconsistencies of Classical architecture, and of bad pseudo-Gothic architecture, arose through the error of designing plans to suit elevations, instead of making elevations subservient to plans.

Pugin's proseletyzing zeal created too much antagonism amongst his Protestant compatriots for his ideas to be readily accepted, and powerful as his arguments were, they would probably have passed unheeded had it not been for the founding of the so-called Anglo-Catholic Movement in 1833. This Movement, which at the beginning was called the Oxford Movement, was started by a group of influential Protestant clergymen who were disturbed by the disruptive effects that Catholic Emancipation was likely to have on Anglicanism. Its immediate stimulus was a sermon by John Keble, given in St. Mary's church, Oxford, which was entitled 'National Apostasy', and was prompted by the government's suppression of ten Anglican bishoprics in Ireland. His general argument, as it subsequently developed, was to the effect that since Anglicanism could no longer depend on a Protestant parliament because of the rise of non-conformity and the repeal of the Test Act, it was unlikely (so he and his friends thought) that the Church of England would remain the official national religion, and it was therefore time for them to establish for themselves a new discipline and a new organization, and to reassert the doctrines which, so they considered, gave the Church of England certain divine prerogatives resulting from the Apostolic Succession.

The theological implications of these theories are irrelevant in the present context, although it is interesting to note the influence of 'the new awareness of history' on the theological ideals of the time. It is sufficient to say that the result of these theories was the adoption of a liturgy and ritual so mediaeval, so similar to that of Catholicism, that many of Pugin's notions of planning became applicable to Anglican religious needs.

The architectural programme of the Oxford Movement was put into effect by the Cambridge Camden Society, founded in 1839, and by its magazine, *The Ecclesiologist*, founded in 1841. Both were inspired by the ideal of what we would now call 'functionalism'; that is to say, they were not primarily concerned with promoting beautiful churches, but with creating churches which would efficiently serve the Anglo-Catholic requirements regarding ritual. Indeed, it can be convincingly argued that the Camden Society (or Ecclesiological Society, as it was later called) preferred a certain brutal ugliness to the more traditional notions of beauty, as may be seen in the most famous church of their most famous protégé, William Butterfield. 'There is here to be observed the germ of the same dread of beauty, not to say the same deliberate preference of ugliness, which so characterizes in fuller development the later paintings of Mr. Millais and his followers', *The Ecclesiologist* noted with satisfaction in a laudatory article published when All Saints', Margaret Street, London, was finally completed.

The fact is that, of the philosophical trinity: the True, the Beautiful and the Good, it was only with truth and goodness that these reformers were really concerned. It was not merely that the Camden Society believed that only a virtuous and devout architect could design a good church; it believed, as befitted a group of clergymen, that architecture was only good if it made people devout and virtuous. Even Ruskin, as pious as they, but more sensitive to beauty than most of the polemical writers of his age, quickly transformed his appeal for architectural integrity into a plea for social reform. In his earliest books on architecture, he had already cursed Classical architecture because it degraded workmen from the status of artists to that of drudges. The same dreadful defect, he claimed, was to be found in anything made mechanically, whether by casting or by machine. A large class of men had been formed, he wrote, whose constructional skill was merely brutish, as for example that of the 'navvies' then engaged on building the railways. Supposing, he continued, that the same sums of money had been employed in building beautiful houses and churches. 'We should have maintained the same number of men, not in driving wheelbarrows, but in a distinctly technical, if not intellectual employment; and those who were more intelligent among them would have been especially happy in that employment, as having room in it for the development of their fancy'. Similarly, he believed that gem-cutting was a soul-destroying task as compared with carving stone, and he believed that 'most women would prefer the pleasure of having built a church, or contributing to the adornment of a cathedral, to the pride of bearing a certain quantity of diamonds on their foreheads'. Even without knowing anything about Ruskin's distressing private life, one could hardly be surprised that the wife of a man who made such a statement caused their marriage to be annulled.

From 1860 onwards, Ruskin abandoned architectural criticism entirely and devoted himself to social reform, by lecturing and writing on industrial problems, education, morals and religion. Henceforth, for him, art became simply an incidental instrument to attaining a higher and more spiritual life, and if he judged works of art at all, it was simply as human actions having moral and intellectual qualities. For him, Gothic was the ideal style because he never doubted that every mediaeval mason was a superb artist. Indeed, one of the fascinating things about the most fervent Gothic Revivalists was their completely uncritical attitude towards the Middle Ages. Everything built between the eleventh and the sixteenth centuries, was, in their eyes, a masterpiece, however humble; and with pathetic loyalty, they expressed their unshakeable faith that all buildings could again be perfect if only society would return to a mediaeval way of living.

Ruskin's ideals were most actively promoted by William Morris, an early disciple, who also hated machinery, and who also sought to create an ideal society in which every man would be a creator of works of art. Morris, as a young man, had embarked on an architectural career in the office of G. E. Street, but had soon abandoned it to become an interior decorator. Thus neither he nor Ruskin were architects.

It may be wondered what can be the relevance to modern architecture of writings by men not primarily concerned with buildings. The relevance springs from the fact that the writings of both Ruskin and Morris, in the nineteenth century, embodied an idea which first appeared at the time of the French Revolution (in the writings and drawings of C. N. Ledoux), and which was to become of widespread importance in the twentieth century, namely the idea that architecture is essentially an instrument of social reform. This is what is really meant by the slogan popularized in the 1920s by Le Corbusier: 'the new spirit'—l'Esprit Nouveau. For example, in the first issue of the Revue Générale de l'Architecture which appeared after the liberal revolution of 1848, the editor described several projects for utilitarian buildings by remarking that 'architecture shows itself sensitive to the new spirit; for it is evident that the great instrument of all reform is first and foremost architecture'. Architecture, so the many followers of Ruskin and Morris claimed, may be beautiful, and it may be true, but it must above all be an instrument of goodness. Little wonder that a reaction against such an excessively puritanical doctrine soon took place, and that Oscar Wilde, wearing yellow satin knee-breeches and a green flower in his button-hole, proclaimed that for him, people were not good or bad but simply beautiful or ugly.

After the 1914–1918 war, there was a counter-reaction, especially in those countries that were defeated. As a result, we find a recrudescence of William Morris's socialistic ideal, which at its best was a determination to forge again the broken bonds between aesthetics and morality, still a powerful influence on architectural thought today. Meanwhile Rationalists, for the past two centuries, have had to contend with both radical aesthetes and radical moralists; with 'art for art's sake' and 'art for God's sake'. It will be seen in a later chapter how they met these opposing views, and at the same time put forward energetic ideals of their own.

11

Polychromy

To understand fully the ideals of architects in the mid-nineteenth century, particularly of Renaissance Revivalists and Gothic Revivalists, it is important to appreciate the influence of what was then called 'Architectural Polychromy', by which was meant the introduction of variegations into the exterior design of façades. The fact that the concern was with exteriors is important. There was nothing novel about polychromatic adornments *inside* buildings, and historians who have dealt indiscriminately with both interior and exterior coloration overlook the main issue at stake. What was new in the nineteenth century was the idea that the *exteriors* of buildings should all display colours of various hues, and whilst architects found justification for exterior polychromy by reference to many historical precedents (as befitted an age obsessed with historiography), it is fair to say that the philosophy of architectural polychromy, as enunciated in the nineteenth century, was specifically Victorian in character, and that it could never have existed as an architectural ideal in an earlier age.

For until about 1830, one fact was accepted unquestioningly by every Gothicist and Classicist, irrespective of their different allegiances; namely, that architecture was monochrome. Greek temples were considered as being built essentially of whitish marble, Gothic cathedrals as being built essentially of greyish stone. Variations of tone were accepted for structural reasons (for it was not unusual for the bases, walls and copings of a mediaeval cathedral to be constructed of masonry from different quarries, just as the main colonnade of the Louvre was built of at least three types of stone—Meudon, St. Leu and St. Cloud); but it had been theoretically assumed from the beginning of the sixteenth century that architecture was essentially a matter of *form*, which colour would tend to disrupt, and that a building only retained its visual integrity if it was roughly the same colour throughout. Even Italian Baroque architects, such as Bernini, Borromini and Guarini, seldom, if ever, used polychrome marbles on the exteriors of their buildings, whilst in France, that citadel of Classicism, exterior polychromy was only used in such exceptional circumstances as the garden pavilions at Versailles. It was

III

not until 1853 that any student at the French Academy in Rome thought of making a specific study of 'Polychrome Architecture', and that student, significantly enough, was Charles Garnier, who designed the colourful façades of the Paris Opera House in 1861.

One can imagine the shock, therefore, which followed the publication in 1829 of C. J. Hittorff's theory that exterior polychromy had not only been widely used by the ancient Greeks, but that it consisted of a garish mixture of reds, yellows, blues and greens. The announcement need not have caused the emotional disturbance it did, since traces of colour on the Athenian antiquities had already been noted by Stuart and Revett in the 1750s, and described by them in their famous book. But here they had confined their observations to incidental verbal descriptions, whereas Hittorff, after his examination of the temples at Selinus, made vivid polychromatic reconstructions which were rendered even more garish when later publicized by the crude techniques of lithographic reproduction current at the time.

In general, the Greek Revival architects tacitly ignored these discoveries, and continued designing monochrome temple façades for public buildings and private dwellings as if Hittorff's discoveries had never been announced. Even theorists like Alfred Bartholemew dismissed it as 'poly-gewgawdery', and described it simply as a German fad. They did this partly because of their conservative tastes, but mainly because Greek polychromy (being simply painted on the surface of the stone) was not very permanent, and however appropriate it might be in Attica and Sicily, it was certainly not appropriate further north. Moreover, the topic proved to be extremely controversial. Not only were there a number of archaeologists who denied Hittorff's conclusions by referring to the paucity of literary evidence for polychromy in Vitruvius and in ancient Greek texts; there were a number of enthusiastic amateurs, such as Gottfried Semper, who went to extremes, and claimed that every element of Greek architecture had been brilliantly painted, including the columns. Occasionally, controversialists on the same side contradicted one another, as for example when Semper claimed that the cella walls of the Hephaesteum in Athens had been blue, whereas Schaubert insisted that there was clear evidence that they had been red. Thus few Greek Revival buildings were ever coloured. Leo von Klenze tried to initiate a new fashion by applying colour to the circular Ionic temple built in the English Garden in Munich in 1833, and Theophilus Hansen used it extensively in the Athens Academy begun in 1859, but polychromy had little influence on the Greek Revival. It was mainly influential, for quite different reasons, with respect to the revivals of 'Renaissance' and 'Gothic'.

The Renaissance Revivalists' interest in colour was aroused by the fact that some of the most restrained Florentine architects of the fifteenth century, such as Brunelleschi, had used coloured faience roundels in the spandrels of their arcades, whilst the more ebullient Renaissance designers of northern Italy had loaded their façades with every variety of coloured marble, as may be seen in the Certosa at Pavia. As a result, we find César Daly reporting that in the 1830s, it was common for apartment buildings in Paris to be adorned with coloured marble panels surrounded by richly sculptured frames. But the interest of the Renaissance Revivalists, like that of the Gothic Revivalists, was less archaeological than practical. Firstly, those in England were trying to get away from what they considered to be the monotony of the standard stuccoed Georgian façades, and therefore sought greater variety. As G. E. Street observed, 'our buildings are, nine times out of ten, cold, colourless, insipid, academical studies, and our people have no conception of the necessity of obtaining rich colour, and no sufficient love of it when successfully obtained'. Secondly, they were seeking ways of counteracting the alarming effects of industrial soot. Whatever improvements in hygiene may have resulted from some products of the factories springing up in the newly industrialized towns, the effect of these factories themselves on the neighbouring architecture was disastrous, for their smoke covered every building with a coating of grime. The more rational architects therefore soon felt obliged to turn their attention to the possibility of facing their buildings (or constructing the façades of their buildings) with materials which were non-porous, and could be easily cleaned. For such reasons, therefore, polychrome terra-cotta adornments and glazed brickwork became fashionable, especially the latter, since there were, in most English industrial cities, many sound economic advantages in using brick.

Inevitably, those architects who were pursuing the twin goals of artistic excellence and historical accuracy turned their attention to Italy, for coloured exteriors had been popular there during the whole of the Middle Ages, as well as during the early stages of the Renaissance. Moreover, as Street pointed out, Italian Gothic architecture was essentially urban architecture, and was therefore a particularly appropriate subject of study in view of the problems they themselves then faced. As a result, two 'Italian Gothic' schools of polychromatic thought arose in addition to the Italian Renaissance school; one of these put its faith in what was called 'structural coloration' or 'sandwiching' (based on Pisan and Sienese prototypes); the other contended for a revival of Venetian Gothic architecture by means of marble veneers.

The leading architects of the 'structural coloration' school were essentially Rationalists. They believed that architectural form was necessarily structural form, and hence that effects of colour should result from the structural materials by which an edifice was actually built. Their ideas were best exemplified in the work of William Butterfield and G. E. Street, even though both these architects derived their original theories from the handbook of the opposing camp: Ruskin's *Seven Lamps of Architecture*. In this book, the virtues of polychromy were dogmatically propounded on the basis of a biological analogy with plants and animals, for according to Ruskin, colour in nature never followed form, but was arranged on an entirely different system. 'Colour is always arranged by God in simple or rude forms', he wrote in the chapter entitled 'The Lamp of Beauty', 'and it must therefore be best seen in them. I conclude then that all arrangements of colour, for its own sake, in graceful forms, are barbarous. . . . The stripes of a zebra do not follow the lines of its body or limbs, still less the spots of a leopard. I hold this then, for the first great principle of architectural colour: let it be visibly independent of form'. In practice, Ruskin advised limiting colour in buildings to irregular masses and zones, to spots of various shapes and dimensions, to chequers and to zig-zags. This technique is clearly visible on the external brick walls of Butterfield's church of All Saints', Margaret Street, London, and is doubtless one reason why Butterfield's love of ugliness appears so deliberate and systematic— 'a calculated assault on the sensuous qualities latent in the simplest building forms', to use John Summerson's phrase. Nineteenth century critics were more ribald in their appraisals, and described Butterfield's technique as 'the Streaky Bacon Style'.

Street's attitude to polychromy was completely different, especially after his visit to Italy in 1853. He also intended colour to be essentially decorative, but he envisaged it as being much more in harmony with the structural system, for, as he remarked at the beginning of his book, *Brick and Marble Architecture in the Middle Ages* (1855): 'I hold firmly the doctrine that no architect can properly neglect to avail himself of every improvement in construction which the growing intelligence of this mechanical age can afford him'. For Street, therefore, the Pisan method of laying alternate courses of differently coloured natural stone or brickwork was the best, and he asserted that the Venetian method of veneering marble on to a rough brick wall was 'rather likely to be destructive of good architecture, because it was sure to end in an entire concealment of the real construction of the work'.

But this, it became clear, was precisely what Ruskin wanted. 'The science of inner construction is to be abandoned', he announced in *The Stones of Venice* (1851), and he now contended that 'the school of incrusted architecture' was the only one in which perfect and permanent chromatic decoration was possible. 'Look upon every piece of marble as a cake of very hard colour, of which a certain portion is to be ground down or cut off, to paint the wall with', he informed the architectural profession. Brickwork, he claimed, was necessarily an inferior material, and must therefore be clothed with the brightness of a protective skin of marble, just as the body of an animal was protected by its scales. Later, abandoning his biological analogies in favour of a yet more extravagant parallel, he asserted that a brick building faced with marble was like a man clothed in armour, in that no one would ever claim to be deceived by the latter on discovering that the man was not made of solid steel!

For Ruskin, architecture had become, in fact, a kind of jewellery, and he contended that columns could appropriately be built independently of the construction (as they were on the façade of St. Mark's, Venice) 'exactly in proportion to the importance which the shaft assumes as a large jewel'. Jasper, porphyry, serpentine, lapis lazuli and alabaster were names dearer to him now than all the building stones of northern Europe, and they occur in his writings on Venetian architecture with the same lyricism and sensuality that Oscar Wilde was later to use when describing jewellery in *The Picture of Dorian Gray*. It was due to Ruskin's influence that so many marble columns were used in the Oxford Museum, although here they had a didactic significance, in that each represented a different geological specimen of scientific interest.

The extent to which Ruskin's theories were followed is not so easy to appreciate nowadays, when so many commerical buildings of the 1850s have been demolished. But descriptions of buildings designed in this era tell us a lot about the changes brought about in the London scene due to the impact of his ideas. For example, the façade of the Crown Life Insurance Company's office, built in Bridge Street by his protégés Deane and Woodward (the architects of the Oxford Museum) was built of Portland stone, Forest of Dean stone, Mansfield stone, Warwick stone, red and grey granite and Sicilian marbles. 'The design', wrote the editor of *The Builder*, 'is commonly described as Venetian Gothic, and doubtless many of its ornamental details bear resemblance in character to the Gothic; but the Byzantine and Saracenic features are so prominent that the whole effect is very different from that of Gothic, to an English eye'. It bordered in fact on Eclecticism, a subject to be discussed in a later chapter.

Oddly enough, Ruskin's basic theories became really important after 1890, when he himself was in his dotage, and when building methods were of a type of which he himself would have violently disapproved. For it will be perceived that although the fallacy of Ruskin's reasoning lay in its assumption that bare structural brick walling must necessarily be ugly, it was soon apparent, with the introduction, in the late 1880s, of structural steelwork, that this new material necessitated some kind of veneer in order to make it fireproof. Thus the theoretical situation was radically altered, and even the most fervent Rationalists now adopted Ruskin's ideals. Many of these architects designed their veneers simply as simulated forms of load-bearing masonry; but others, such as Louis Sullivan, invented a type of terra-cotta panel which, in its appropriateness as well as its beautiful and original detailing, showed the real applicability of Ruskin's notions.

Louis Sullivan has been given a great deal of importance in recent books on modern architecture (mainly because he was the teacher of Frank Lloyd Wright), and there are few writers on the subject who have not regarded him as one of the great pioneers of contemporary design. Yet an examination of his actual buildings would suggest that it is as the culminator of Ruskinism that his achievement is most solidly founded. He had, as Frank Lloyd Wright observed in *Genius and Mobocracy*, no structural sense of the nature of materials, which were simply valued by him for the ornamental possibilities of their surfaces. His designs for what some authors have called his 'skyscrapers' (by which they mean his nine-storey and twelve-storey office buildings at St. Louis and Buffalo) contributed little to the technology or even to the aesthetics of twentieth century skyscraper design, since they were not free-standing blocks, but had U-shaped plans and fair faces on only two sides. Moreover, the buildings he designed before 1890 were undistinguished, even in the dreary age for which they were built. Sullivan (especially after Wright began to work for him) showed his genius especially as an ornamentalist, or as what would today be called a 'stylist'—that is to say, a man who can put an attractive sheath around someone else's structural frame. If he bequeathed anything to posterity apart from his own ornament, it is to be found only in the polychromatic veneers on Frank Lloyd Wright's early domestic architecture, such as the Coonley house. But the twentieth century has proved not to be an age of ornament, and ornament, it will be perceived, was the essence of Ruskin's theory of architecture, just as it was the basis of all the controversies regarding the revival of the historic 'styles'.

12

Eclecticism

The various aspects of Revivalism so far dealt with have all implied two alternative attitudes towards the past: first, the attitude of those idealists who, passionately espousing one particular period of architectural history, whether Roman, Greek, Renaissance or Gothic, claimed that it was only by returning to this pure source of inspiration that a good contemporary architecture could be created; secondly, the attitude of the many cynics whose ideals, if they had any, were opportunist, and who were usually guilty of what theologians would call 'indifferentism' (that is to say, they contended that all styles were of equal value, and that the whole notion of stylistic integrity or stylistic tradition was an illusion). These latter architects felt free to turn their hands from one historic style to another according to the circumstances, or the wishes of their clients. Sometimes the circumstances undoubtedly justified such an attitude, as for example when William Wilkins, a confirmed Greek Revivalist, built a Gothic porch for King's College, Cambridge, so that it would harmonize with the chapel. Similarly, we have already seen that Charles Barry built a Gothic Parliament Building to harmonize with Gothic monuments nearby. Usually, however, indifferentism was, at its best, an expression of uncommitted romanticism, and at its worst a matter of capitalizing on a client's whims.

There was however another possible attitude towards the past which we may call Eclecticism, and which became particularly prevalent in the second half of the nineteenth century. Eclecticism is an unfortunate word to have to use, because it has been endowed with so many contradictory meanings, most of which are pejorative. For G. E. Street and Robert Kerr, as for many people today, it was understood as a synonym for what has just been termed Indifferentism. For the Camden Society it meant the remodelling of a mediaeval church in whichever of the old styles was prevalent there, as opposed to rebuilding the entire church in the 'best' style, that is to say of the late thirteenth century. To most theorists of the nineteenth century, however, Eclecticism was understood to mean something far more sensible, and far more in harmony with Diderot's definition of Eclecticism (quoted in the introduction to this book).

The nineteenth century notion of Eclecticism first became current in France in the 1830s, when it was used by the French philosopher Victor Cousin to mean a composite system of thought made up of views selected (ἐκλέγω) from various other systems. This is its proper meaning. The Eclectics were in fact claiming quite rationally that no one should accept blindly from the past the legacy of a single philosophical system (or of a single architectural system) to the exclusion of all others, but that each should decide rationally and independently what philosophical facts (or architectural elements) used in the past were appropriate to the present and then recognize and respect them in whatever context they might appear.

According to Victor Cousin's lectures (eventually published under the title *The True, the Beautiful and the Good* in 1853), Eclecticism was not an attempt to create a completely new system; it was simply the inevitable result, in an age dominated by historicism, of studying the history of philosophy, in that it recognized that a number of facts emphasized in different historical periods were not only true in themselves, but, when removed from their original contexts of conflicting philosophical systems, and reassembled, constituted a coherent system of thought. 'These facts thus become', he wrote, 'a living system'.

The significance of Victor Cousin's search for a living system of philosophy was that it coincided with the leading architects' search for a 'living architecture' as a way out of the impasse of stylistic copying. His philosophy thus suggested to them the possibility of selecting tectonic elements from every style, and re-amalgamating them according to contemporary needs. The system was more rational than imitations based on archaeological and hence chronological accuracy, yet it had the advantage of fitting in perfectly with historiographic tastes. It could therefore be adopted without doing violence to the ideas current at the time.

It is not certain when the new idea first began to emerge as an important intellectual force. As early as 1740, Pierre de Vigny, who had been involved with the restoration of a number of mediaeval buildings, had claimed that 'since genius must work in complete freedom, it should take over and make use of what is best in each style'. Payne Knight, in his *Analytical Inquiry into the Principles of Taste* (1805) had observed that 'in the pictures of Claude and Gaspar, we perpetually see a mixture of Grecian and Gothic architecture employed with the happiest effect in the same building', and he went on to urge that this was the 'best style of architecture for irregular and picturesque houses'. Moreover, Renaissance Revivalism had always been a type of Eclecticism (even though its practitioners did not necessarily recognize the fact) since fifteenth century Florentine architecture had mixed antique, Byzantine and Carolingian elements with marked freedom, just as sixteenth century French and English architecture mixed Classical elements with Gothic. Indeed, the historiographic predilections of the age made it inevitable that when Eclecticism was put forward as a positive philosophy, the less thoughtful architects of the period should simply regard it as a new excuse for the revival of the more hybrid 'styles' already in vogue.

Perhaps the first specific enunciation of an eclectic theory of architecture is to be found in Thomas Hope's *An Historical Essay on Architecture* (1835). In the final paragraph of this book, Hope complains of the variety of 'styles' used in England, and then continues with a sentence which, being as eloquent as it is involved, deserves to be quoted in full: 'No one seems yet to have conceived the smallest wish or idea of only borrowing of every former style of architecture whatever it might present of useful or ornamental, of scientific or tasteful, of adding thereto whatever other new dispositions or forms might afford conveniences or elegancies not yet possessed, of making the new discoveries, the new conquests, of natural productions unknown to former ages, the models of new imitations more beautiful and more varied; and thus of composing an architecture which, born in our country, grown on our soil, and in harmony with our climate, institutions and habits, at once elegant, appropriate and original, should truly deserve the appellation of "our own" '.

It was to be ten years before the same theme was publicized again, this time by the editor of *The Builder*. In a leading article lamenting that the world had never beheld so unsatisfactory a state of architecture as that which then existed, he claimed that the whole of Europe seemed bent on producing structures which cheated an observer into believing he was confronted with the works of another century. There was, he said (echoing Hope's phrase) no style at the time which they could call their own. He therefore proposed a remedy which was in fact the doctrine of Eclecticism. 'Assuming', he said, 'that the objects and destination of a building are provided for, an original style, characteristic of the age, might be provided by a complete investigation of every style of architecture, and the adaptation of all beautiful features which do not militate with each other and with the actual requirements of the building'.

The editor of *The Builder* was not at this time a consistent or reliable guide, since he was never sure in his own mind whether he was proposing the combination of appropriate elements from all the 'styles', or simply the adoption of that historical 'style' which provided the greatest latitude (such as the 'Renaissance Style'). Moreover, he lacked the perspicacity of the later French Eclectics in that he was clearly under the delusion that an original style could be created by combining tectonic elements invented at different dates. This view was similarly expressed in the discourse pronounced by T. L. Donaldson when he became professor of architecture at University College, London, in 1842. 'We are wandering in a labyrinth of experiment', he explained, 'and trying by an amalgamation of certain features in this or that style of each and every period and country to form a homogeneous whole with some distinctive character of its own, for the purpose of working it out into its fullest development, and thus creating a new and peculiar style'. It is therefore probably fair to say that the first serious call for an Eclectic architecture, certainly the first to be made by actually using the term, was a result of Victor Cousin's influence, and first occurred in the periodicals published in France.

Cousin's lectures at the Sorbonne on 'The True, the Beautiful and the Good' had of course attracted a good deal of attention in Paris even before they were published in his book, and it seems reasonable to suppose that the French Classical Rationalists' adoption of the slogan 'The True, the Beautiful and the Useful' in the 1840s was simply an echo of Cousin's title. But in 1853, the year Cousin's book was published, Eclecticism was put forward seriously by the editor of the *Revue Générale de l'Architecture* as a means of initially overcoming the problems of conflicting styles. Eclecticism, he wrote (in an article later translated into English and published with evident approval by *The Builder*) could certainly not create a new art, but it could at least be a useful transition from Revivalism to the new architecture of the future. As yet, creative artists were limited to heterogeneous designs, because no single principle animated their endeavours. This was necessarily so, because they were part of a society which itself did not as yet have any universally recognized principles. Thus both the architect and the community proceeded towards the future weighed down by a confused mass of elements borrowed from all earlier societies. Admittedly, the confusion which would result from an eclectic amalgamation of all the 'styles' was itself vicious; but it was one of the necessary conditions for the progress of architecture. In any well designed contemporary building, diverse and essentially modern elements would have to be combined with fragments from the past, but in so doing they would exercise a salutary action which would each day become more and more evident. Though the resulting confusion of forms would be bad in itself (in the sense that each particular building would thereby be defective), from the point of view of research, of experimentation, and of the progressive development which would result, it would be beneficial. 'In the architecture of the future', he concluded, 'we shall have arches, vaults, beams, pillars and columns, as in ancient architectures, but we shall also have an aesthetic principle which will bear the same relationship to past principles as a locomotive bears to a stage coach'.

One cannot help but be struck by the extraordinary humility of the theorists of this age, who had such a keen sense of the inadequacy of their own architecture. They regarded the study of history as a guide to the future, but they were ashamed of the results of their own endeavours, and were baffled by the direction which the new technology would take. From the last quoted remark it will be perceived that whilst the writer of this article, like all the leading architectural theorists of the time, was hoping for, and speculating upon, new constructional developments, he suffered from the disadvantage of being unable to prophesy accurately the kinds of tectonic form that the new technology would produce. He thus had to content himself with the useful but purely negative task of combating the baneful influence of the archaeologists. In this he was eminently successful. He distracted the public's attention from criticisms based on antiquarian criteria, and reduced his fellow architects' concern with archaeological problems of form and 'style', thereby allowing more attention to be paid to the many practical problems created by the needs and opportunities of the age. But the architects could not suddenly abandon all interest in ancient monuments; they simply ceased, according to the editor of the *Revue Générale de l'Architecture*, to try to obtain from them absolute rules for the present and the future. Moreover, to avoid degrading architecture to what he called the 'mere craft of building', he considered it necessary that there should still be some concern with questions of form and beauty. Since the lack of a new style obliged architects to practise Eclecticism (that is to say, to make a free use of the entire past), he decided to continue his series of historical studies, with a view to providing what he called *motifs*, or historic elements which could be incorporated into modern buildings whenever they were appropriate. At the same time he inaugurated the important practice of illustrating new buildings in his magazine; an innovation which will not seem to us particularly perspicacious, but which was nevertheless something of a novelty for the age.

In England, the reaction against pure Revivalism in favour of Eclecticism was provoked less by French theorists than by the competition for a new Foreign Office held in 1857. The story of this extraordinary scandal, known at the time as 'The Battle of the Styles', has been told in detail and with considerable wit by Kenneth Clark in *The Gothic Revival*, so there is no need to do more than summarize it here. Briefly, it may be said that the competition, for which there were two hundred and eighteen entries, was won by Coe and Hofland in the 'Renaissance Style', with George Gilbert Scott, the protagonist of the Gothic Revivalists, gaining third place; but so energetically did Scott argue (by means of parliamentary lobbying and letters to the newspapers) the merits of Gothic, that he persuaded the Minister of Works to override the jury's decision, and to promote his own scheme to first place.

Had the matter rested there, the results, as far as the history of architectural ideas is concerned, would have had no special importance; but it so happened that there was also a powerful 'Classical' lobby (consisting of such distinguished architects as Smirke, Barry and Cockerell, and including several members of Parliament such as Sir William Tite) who refused to accept defeat, and who went as a deputation to the Prime Minister. The Prime Minister, Lord Palmerston, was, fortunately for them, a confirmed Classicist. He therefore steadfastly refused to allow Scott to build a 'Gothic' building, even though he eventually accepted Scott's right to the commission he had so adroitly purloined. Not that Palmerston had any predilection for architectural controversy; indeed, his nonchalant attitude towards the finer ethical points of stylistic discrimination must have made both parties in the controversy wince. 'It is quite manifest', he announced to a deputation of Gothic Revivalists, 'that a man of Mr. Scott's ability can put any face he pleases to a given ground plan. The course I propose is this: to take a sum that will be sufficient for the foundation, and to request Mr. Scott in the meanwhile to devise some elevation that shall be in a different style, more cheap, more light, more cheerful, and better adapted to the purpose of the building'; in other words: Renaissance Revival.

This was of course an excellent opportunity for Scott to figure as a martyr to the cause he so volubly espoused, for the obvious course for him to take was to resign his dubiously acquired commission. But the temptation to pocket the fees was too much for him, and so he tamely acceded to the Prime Minister's demands, employing Digby Wyatt to do the Renaissance detailing. Doubtless it was this fiasco which eventually destroyed what little public faith existed in the claims of the Revivalists, and allowed Eclecticism to assert itself as the only viable doctrine which could be accepted in the circumstances of the time.

Eclecticism was known in England as the 'Queen Anne Revival' because it derived its historical justification from a period in English history when Eclecticism had flourished naturally as the unsophisticated expression of a sort of hybrid Classicism. The idea of this Revival seems to have been first put forward in 1861, and the credit for its adoption must be attributed to a former devotee of the Gothic Revival, the Reverend J. L. Petit. Petit seems to have become disillusioned by the Gothic Revival as early as 1856, for in that year he became involved in a controversy with Scott, claiming that though he once thought the revival of a living Gothic architecture possible, the sight of recent examples had convinced him that 'the attempt to revive the Gothic style would not be successful, since it tends rather to mere conformity with mediaeval types, than to the development of mediaeval principles'. But it was not until 1861, at a lecture given at the Architectural Exhibition, that he first suggested that the right approach was that of Eclecticism, and he told his audience that if they were to look at the best monumental buildings of Queen Anne's reign, they would see that these were well designed because they were simply vernacular buildings plus ornamentation of a very appropriate kind. They harmonized with the character of the houses men built when they built without reference to style, and when they were guided solely by consideration of their own requirements, the state of society, climate and materials. It was thus a style which was perfectly suited to the wants of their own day, 'expressive, or capable of being made expressive of the spirit of the age; and sufficiently comprehensive to embrace both vernacular and monumental works, and that large class which partakes of both characters'.

The significance of this proposal, as far as subsequent developments were to be concerned, was twofold. First, it deliberately broke through the archaeological barrier which in England had separated architecture from life for nearly a century, and substituted the idea of selecting architectural forms on the basis of their appropriateness, according to the designer's unfettered choice. Secondly, it introduced the idea that 'vernacular' forms should constitute the basis of all architectural design. The Queen Anne period was taken as a suitable historical precedent because many of the buildings constructed then were characterized by what has been called 'artisan mannerism'; an unsophisticated mixing of various tectonic and decorative elements without that antiquarian pedantry which in the following reign so often typified the architecture of Palladianism. Moreover, the Revival itself went even further. It often employed motifs that were not eighteenth century at all but more strictly Jacobean. In other words, the 'Queen Anne Style' in England was really the equivalent of the early 'Louis XIII Style' in France, when Renaissance decorative motifs were applied undogmatically to freely planned compositions without strict reference to antique prototypes or rules.

The most revolutionary feature of Petit's theory was the introduction of the notion that the basis of a living architecture was 'our ordinary or vernacular architecture' (a notion he may well have derived from Scott's *Remarks on Gothic Architecture* of 1858, where the relationship between 'vernacular domestic architecture' and the ecclesiastical architecture of the thirteenth century was fully discussed). Indeed, it would be no exaggeration to say that this has been one of the most potent concepts to be put forward during the last hundred years. In the first place, it undermined the old idea that architecture was essentially something to do with temples and churches, by giving minor domestic architecture a predominant influence in architectural theory. In the second place, it challenged the pernicious Italian Renaissance doctrine—introduced into architectural education in 1806 with the founding of the French École des Beaux-Arts—that architecture was essentially one of the three arts of design; for by insisting upon the analogy between architecture and speech (an analogy which will be discussed in detail later), it helped separate the theory of architecture from that of sculpture and painting— arts in which a vocabulary of standardized elements plays no part. In other words, it sought to establish the doctrine that just as speech is composed by selecting from a vocabulary of naturally evolved words, so architecture should be composed by selecting from a vocabulary of naturally evolved tectonic elements, all established by purely practical criteria, and articulated in accordance with the requirements of functional needs.

It will thus be seen that the problems which occupied the minds of the more thoughtful architectural theorists of the 1860s were concerned more with the nature of the structures to be ornamented, rather than with the problem of ornamentation in itself. Yet the fact that traditional vernacular architecture was in fact moribund, and that no new structural systems were created until the development of the steel and reinforced concrete frame in the late 1880s (despite many gallant attempts to create a new universal architecture of iron) meant that, for the practising architect, the main emphasis was still inevitably placed on ornamentation. Thus in any study of nineteenth century architectural ideals, ornamentation must necessarily be a major concern.

★   ★   ★

The mid-nineteenth century's attitude towards ornament is of considerable interest, especially in view of the reaction against ornament which occurred about forty years ago. The Victorian fondness for it was to some extent itself a reaction against the exaggerated plainness which had affected late eighteenth century and early nineteenth century buildings (and which was associated, in France and America especially, with the idea of republican virtue); but it was mainly the result of an attitude of mind which saw ornament as what we would now call a 'status symbol'. In other words, it was not only a symbol of the status which the middle classes had actually achieved, but of the status which each citizen wished his neighbours to think he had achieved. 'We want to seem what we are not', wrote Gustave Planche in 1857, as he criticized the preference for cheap reproductions rather than for appropriately designed utilitarian objects made by machine.

Ornament has, of course, always been symbolic, since from the sixteenth to the eighteenth century it relied for most of its significance on Classical mythological allusions. But at that time it was also the prerogative of the rich, so it was inevitable that as the Industrial Revolution extended the fruits of wealth to all classes of society from 1830 onwards, the newly enriched middle classes (whose tastes had never had the benefit of an aristocratic education) unconsciously aped the newly rich of earlier ages. They no longer prized the simplicity of the older nobility's furniture and silverware, but sought instead facsimiles of the florid metalwork and upholstery which had been favoured by the newly enriched Renaissance princes of the sixteenth century. This taste, which César Daly called '*le besoin de luxe et de l'éclat*', was most clearly seen in the objects exhibited at the 'Exposition de l'Industrie Française' in 1834 and at the Great Exhibition of 1851; yet although Owen Jones criticized the latter objects as 'vagaries of the vilest taste, ugliness and incongruity', he considered ornament itself to be a natural result of cultural evolution. As he remarked in his *Grammar of Ornament* (1856): 'ornament must necessarily increase with all peoples in the ratio of the progress of civilisation'. Similarly, Gottfried Semper, in *Uber Baustile* (1869), remarked that 'the striving for individuality tends to express itself in adornment, for by adorning anything, be it alive or inanimate, I bestow upon it the right of individual life'. Even the editor of *The Builder* (who, like Owen Jones, deplored the decline in taste, and lamented the popularity of cast ornamentation in the 1850s) had to admit that 'you cannot, if you would, put out the desire for ornament, which is part of the natural yearning after pleasure'.

In architecture, the responsibility for giving excessive emphasis to the importance of ornament can be attributed largely to the archaeologists, since they had noticed that in all architectures of the past, it had been ornament, and ornament alone, which had allowed a building to be accurately dated. But ecclesiologists also bore some responsibility in this matter since they regarded the ornamentation of churches as an act of devotion—what Ruskin called 'the Lamp of Sacrifice'. Ornamentation, according to Ruskin, was the principal part of architecture, in that the highest nobility of a building did not consist in its being well built, but in its being nobly sculptured or painted. 'This is always', he stated (with uncommon insight, for his views were not as widely shared as is sometimes supposed) 'considered one of my most heretical propositions'. Yet even James Fergusson, the leading English Rationalist of his day, and an opponent of Ruskin's views, defined architecture in his *History of Architecture* as 'nothing more or less than the art of ornamental and ornamented construction'. Thus he, like most practising architects of his generation, considered that ornamentation was the main difference between architecture and mere building, just as it was, in his opinion, the main difference between a gentleman's carriage and a brewer's dray.

As will be seen later, Fergusson and the other Rationalists appreciated better than any of their contemporaries the true importance of structure as a formative influence on architectural design. But their belief that architecture must be ornamented, and that the main defect of civil engineering was that it 'lacked artistic treatment', occasionally led them to give ornament more attention than it deserved. Sometimes this resulted, paradoxically, in complete cynicism, as may be seen from the lecture entitled 'The Architecturesque', delivered to the Royal Institute of British Architects in 1869 by Robert Kerr, one of the founders of the Architectural Association, and professor of building construction at King's College, London. Architecture, he sarcastically remarked, was obviously just a dress by which the artist's pencil, like a magician's wand, transformed a structure from a dull lifeless piece of building into something eloquent. It ought therefore more fittingly to be called the Architecturesque. This dress was constituted primarily by ornament, the desire for which, more than anything else, evidently separated the intelligence of man from that of the lower animals, and urged him to strive after perpetual novelty. What people had been in the habit of calling the principles of architectural design were, he continued, simply the principles of architecturesque treatment. Good architecture was true architecturesque, bad architecture was spurious architecturesque, and the means of obtaining both were fourfold: structure ornamentalized (or rendered in itself ornamental), ornament structuralized (or rendered in itself structural), structure ornamented, and ornament constructed.

Without commenting here on the implications of these four categories (and any readers who regard them as quaintly old-fashioned may care to note the following remark by Bruno Zevi, quoted by Colin Faber in *Candela: The Shell Builder* (1963) p. 171: 'We have strong reservations about "plastic structuralism", but none about "structuralized plasticism" ') there are one or two points which should be clarified regarding the attitude of the more enlightened nineteenth century critics towards the contemporary concern for ornament. Firstly, it should be realized that even apart from those puritanical Greek Revival extremists, such as the American sculptor Horatio Greenough, who deplored all ornament except that to be found on Periclean temples, there were many writers who criticized the bad taste of the age. This taste was more open to criticism as regards what was then called 'decorative art' (that is to say household furnishings) than architecture, since architectural ornament, being based mainly on historical precedent, was more conservative in its inspiration, and relied more on imitation than inventiveness. But even the excess of architectural ornament was occasionally criticized at the time. In 1864, Professor George Aitchison told the Royal Institute of British Architects that even the most unobservant eye must have remarked that ornament was looked on either as an advertisement, or as a humouring of the prejudices of the vulgar. 'I think a purity of outline and elegance of proportion, with an almost total absence of ornament, might gradually be made to pervade everything, from our buildings to our teaspoons', he concluded, and told that same body in 1875 that if ever they were to have an architecture of their own age, they must endeavour to look less at absolute ornament than at general gracefulness of form. Similarly, the editor of *The Builder* asserted in 1866 that what was then most required was, after the extinction of the smoke nuisance, 'a moderation in the use of ornament'.

Secondly, it should be noted that the great defect of the nineteenth century was not so much the use of ornament itself as the total neglect of what the earlier French Classical theorists had called *convenance* and *bienséance*: terms which may be translated as 'suitability' and 'decorum'. In the seventeenth and eighteenth centuries, as in all the great ages of architecture, ornamentation was applied only to the more important buildings, and was then designed according to a carefully limited system of symbols. Even Ruskin, who believed in ornamentation for its own sake more than any other Victorian, contended that 'there is a general law, of particular importance to the age in which we live, namely not to decorate things belonging to purposes of active and occupied life'. 'Wherever you can rest, there decorate; where rest is forbidden, so is beauty; you must not mix ornament with business', he added, deploring the current enthusiasm for decorating railway stations.

Thirdly, it must be understood that the nineteenth century's excessive love of decoration had virtually nothing to do with the use of machinery. It is sometimes assumed today that ornamentation degenerated and became improper only because it was machine-made. On the contrary, most nineteenth century ornament was either hand-carved or cast: both processes of the greatest antiquity and respectability. Admittedly a wood-carving machine was used to rough out the interior ornamentation of the Palace of Westminster, and five such machines were shown at the Great Exhibition of 1851; but mechanical equipment for creating ornament was as rare in the nineteenth century as it is today, and this must necessarily be so, because of the nature of the task to be performed. The fault of nineteenth century ornamentalists was not that their work was machine-made, but that it was applied indiscriminately, and it was this which caused a reaction against all 'applied ornament' in the twentieth century. It would nevertheless be true to say that the ornamentation of surfaces eventually became obsolete because it does not accord with the mechanical techniques of fabrication characteristic of the new age.

We may appropriately ask ourselves, however, whether in fact nineteenth century excesses caused the abolition of ornament, or whether ornament has simply been transmuted into a new guise. In 1908, Adolf Loos published a diatribe against ornament entitled *Ornament and Crime*, and it is usual to consider that this article was not only responsible for the plainness of architectural surfaces which dated from this era, but was also responsible for the abolition of architectural ornament itself. Undoubtedly the intricate surface patterns which were so popular a feature of late nineteenth century buildings disappeared shortly after Loos's article was published, just as detailing disappeared from painting and sculpture at the same epoch. But it may be argued that a new type of ornament was created, this time not as something applied to surfaces, but as a basic constituent of architectural compositions themselves.

The essence of architectural ornament, as we have seen, was that it was symbolic. It might be the owner's power, or the purpose which the building served, that needed to be symbolized, but if so, only ornament could indicate the possession of that power, or what the building's purpose was. But such symbolism is precisely the aim of many of the monumental compositional forms which today 'express' the status of the owners or the function the buildings are designed to fulfil. The difference between architecture and plain, honest, straightforward building is thus still mainly a matter of arbitrary shapes, whether it be (to use Robert Kerr's phrase) ornament structuralized or ornament constructed.

This fact seems to have been clearly recognized by Walter Gropius when he wrote in *The New Architecture and the Bauhaus* (1935) that the ultimate goal of the new architecture was 'the composite but inseparable work of art, in which the old dividing line between monumental and decorative elements will have disappeared for ever'. Ornament has not ceased to exist; it has merely been merged imperceptibly into structure. Thus the changes we have witnessed during the last forty years are not due to the fact that sculpture has disappeared from architecture; they are due to the fact that architecture has become a form of abstract sculpture. This should be clearly recognized when we study and criticize the ideals of the nineteenth century; for we still have to face the problem of distinguishing the moment when plain, honest, straightforward building becomes architecture, and the choice as to whether we ornament structures, construct ornament, or seek an alternative which has never yet been discovered, is still for us to decide.

13

The Demand for a New Architecture

O ne of the most curious and far-reaching phenomena of the mid-nineteenth century was the insistent and widespread demand for a new architecture, which reached its climax about 1853. After that date, the idea became dormant for half a century, mainly because it had by then become apparent that every argument had been expended without a new architecture seeming any nearer; for in point of fact, it was impossible for a truly new universal architecture to establish itself before the invention of new structural systems, and this only occurred in the 1890s, with the commercial development of steel and reinforced concrete frames. Why then, was a new architecture so strenuously demanded nearly half a century too soon, when there was no immediate probability of its being produced? Was it because of the development of new or cheaper constructional methods? Was it because of the need for new types of buildings? Was it because of the public's craving for originality? Was it because of the dissatisfaction of individual clients? Or was it for quite abstract reasons which had significance only for architects and the architectural critics themselves?

Before discussing these questions it may be as well to document more precisely the origins and the development of the controversy. We have seen that Thomas Hope was demanding a 'contemporary' architecture as early as 1835, and it is evident from an article in the second volume of the *Revue Générale de l'Architecture* that controversy on this topic was already common in France by 1841. In 1842 T. L. Donaldson of London University, in his inaugural address as first professor of architecture, criticized the current situation and asserted that 'a recurrence to first principles was never more essential'. The next year, in the first issue of *The Builder*, architectural students were informed that Greek, Gothic and all the other 'styles' were defunct, and that there were already signs of a new era. 'From the workshop, the mine and the laboratory', the article continued, 'must proceed the new spirit, the new genius of structure, which our young architects are to clothe with befitting grace and ornament'. In 1847, F. W. von Horn published his *System eines Neugermanischen Baustils*, in which he remarked on the general desire which had arisen for a new style of architecture which, conforming to the demands of construction as well as of taste, should perfectly satisfy the wants of the present time. In that same year, a paper was read to the Architectural Association entitled 'On a new Style in Architecture', in which the question was asked: 'are we to have an architecture of our own period, a distinct, individual, palpable style of the nineteenth century?' In 1848, an article (entitled 'Modern Architecture should meet Modern Requirements') was published in *The Builder* expressing the hope that the younger generation of architects would produce, however scantily, 'the first germs of future style'. In 1849, the *Revue Générale de l'Architecture*, in a leading article entitled 'Architecture of the Future', demanded 'a new architecture, a new style', which would bring them out of the sterility and servility of copying. 'This', the author continued, 'is what we are all asking for, this is what the public expects'. In the same year James Fergusson, in his book entitled *A Historical Inquiry into the True Principles of Beauty in Art, more Especially with reference to Architecture*, announced that in order to restore architecture's progressive vitality, it was essential to give up all imitations of past styles, and to start at once with the determination to surpass all that had been done before.

Examples of this sort of statement could be multiplied almost indefinitely, and in fact several more will be cited in due course. Sufficient to say here that despite sporadic excursions into the theme after 1854, speculation on this matter was largely abandoned by the more practically-minded theorists in favour of Eclecticism. This, as has already been shown in the preceding chapter, was expounded systematically by the *Revue Générale de l'Architecture* in 1853, and by the editor of *The Builder*, in translation, in 1855.

Were the demands for a new architecture motivated by the development of new or cheaper constructional methods? The answer is that although they were indeed inspired by faith in the rapid developments of cast iron construction, this faith proved at the time illusory, and there were in fact few practising architects, if any, who followed the lead of amateurs like Jobard and Pickett, and demanded an architecture made exclusively of cast iron and glass.

Were these demands motivated by the need for new building types? Indeed they might well have been, but it is a curious fact that few theorists of the time suspected that new planning requirements could or should produce a new architecture. Today it is obvious that pseudo-Gothic hotels, or pseudo-Greek banks and museums, constitute an essentially nineteenth century building type simply because they *are* hotels, banks, museums, etc.; but the majority of architectural critics of that time found little consolation or satisfaction in the thought that their society was creating compositions appropriate to the era. Unlike the editor of *The Builder*, they saw no theoretical relevance in the fact that labourers' model cottages, railroad stations, viaducts, lunatic asylums, prisons, workhouses, public baths, banks and suburban residences were 'for the most part genuine expressions of the wants and views of the day'. Similarly, they derived no comfort from the contemplation of public markets,

I

factories and warehouses, or the thought, expressed by the editor of the *Revue Générale de l'Architecture*, that 'the need to satisfy these new requirements has frequently led to lines, forms, and proportions which have no place in our architectonic alphabet'. Yet even Repton, as early as 1803, had remarked that though his contemporaries professed to copy models of past eras, they were adding improvements and conveniences which modern wants suggested to them, and that thus, in later ages the dates of their buildings would never be confounded.

Were the demands for a new architecture motivated by the public's craving for originality? Undoubtedly to some extent they were, since the craving for novelty had, as we have already seen, been fostered since the middle of the eighteenth century. Indeed, it has proved one of the most consistent characteristics of the modern age, especially in the manufacturing industries, where vast sums of money are expended annually to encourage people to buy new versions of standard artifacts in each successive year. As early as 1737 Jacques-François Blondel had deplored 'the spirit of novelty which reigns in the public'. In 1872, in a leading article entitled 'Originality', *The Builder* complained that a pathetic cry was then being raised, 'like a voice crying in the desert' for originality in architecture, and that this same demand was being made in other quarters, notably in literature. But the same writer perspicaciously observed that by 'originality' people usually meant eccentricity, since a column designed upside-down would undoubtedly be original in this sense of the word. Moreover, this was usually the type of originality produced.

The first textbook to publish a comprehensive international survey of historical monuments drawn to the same scale (namely Durand's *Recueil* of 1800) had actually been entitled 'A Collection and Parallel of Buildings of every Type, ancient and modern, remarkable by their Beauty, Size and *Singularity*'. Nevertheless, the most convincing demands for a new architecture were usually voiced by opponents of originality for its own sake. Propagandists like James Fergusson went out of their way to draw their theories from the gradual and rational evolution of Classical and mediaeval forms. Contemporary oriental architecture was praised by him because it was still continuing to evolve in accordance with an unbroken tradition. What Fergusson and his fellow Rationalists wanted was not arbitrary change, nor novelty for its own sake, but a change corresponding to the social and technological changes then newly brought into being in contemporary civilization; and although there were undoubtedly architects who did prize novelty for its own sake, this charge cannot be levelled against those theorists who most cogently demanded a new architecture at this time.

Were the demands for a new architecture motivated by the dissatisfaction of individual clients? On the contrary, the clients were the last people to demand a change, and the dissatisfaction stemmed almost entirely from the architectural historians and journalists who, for reasons which will be duly analysed, were unable to cope taxonomically with the imitative styles (or 'monkey styles' as Greenough and Fergusson called them) with which architects seemed so unaccountably content. Architectural critics, such as the editor of *The Builder*, might well have considered the state of architecture in 1847 to be a reproach to the age, but Professor Donaldson, four years later, felt called upon to remark to the Architectural Association that English architects were being treated unjustly, in that 'the present tone of criticism is to depreciate all modern works of architecture'. By 1858 even the editor of *The Builder* himself was beginning to feel that the harshness of current architectural criticism was having the very opposite effect to that which he desired, and put forward the view that architectural progress was 'impeded as much through the too frequent and unjust depreciation of such as would be advancing in their tendency as it suffers from the perpetration of works absolutely bad'. By 1872 he had reached a state of complete despair, for he then wrote that if there was one subject more than another with respect to which doubt, difference and contradictory opinions seemed to be the order of the day, it was the still vexed question as to the form, the nature and the degree of the purely artistic element which was possible in modern architecture. This, he said, was a question which, in some of its more recent forms, resolved itself almost into the enquiry whether there was any such thing as architecture possible in the present day, and whether there was anything comparable in importance and in beauty to the architectural remains of the past.

The inferiority complex implied by this last remark was mainly due to two curious delusions: firstly, that everything built in earlier epochs was beyond reproach, and secondly, that if the architects of ancient Greece or the Middle Ages could be reborn, they would have no difficulty in solving the current problem of creating original, apt and beautiful buildings. There were admittedly some writers, such as Fergusson, who dismissed as 'twaddle' the contention that the Classical and mediaeval eras were perfect; but his was a minority view. 'Suppose', wrote Viollet-le-Duc in his *Dictionnaire*, 'that an architect of the twelfth or thirteenth century were to return among us, and that he were to be initiated into our modern ideas; if one put at his disposal the perfections of modern industry, he would not build an edifice of the time of Philip Augustus or St. Louis, because this would be to falsify the first law of art, which is to conform to the needs and customs of the times'. He would, the reader is presumably intended to conclude, have had no difficulty in designing a new architecture appropriate to the new age. Similarly, those who heard James Picton talking to the Royal Institute of British Architects on structural ironwork in 1880 were assured that if iron had been available to the ancient Greeks or the mediaeval masons, 'the genius which designed the Parthenon or that which soared aloft in the nave of Amiens or the choir at Le Mans would have been equally successful in the design of a metallic structure'.

It may unhesitatingly be asserted that the demand for a new architecture arose almost entirely from the fact that architectural historians were dominated by one notion, and one notion only; namely, that a modern building was essentially a collection of potential antiquarian fragments which one day would be rediscovered, and studied by future historians with a view to determining the social history of the Victorian age. This belief was strongly reinforced by the current scientific researches into comparative anatomy (as the demands for 'comparative anatomies of architecture' by César Daly and Viollet-le-Duc, and as the title of Banister Fletcher's *History of Architecture by the Comparative Method* make plain); for historians like Fergusson insisted that since it was possible for them, whenever they found traces of the plan of an ancient edifice, or discovered a few *disjecta membra* of its details or ornaments, to at once reason on and reconstruct the original building with certainty (just as an anatomist could reconstruct the whole form of an extinct animal on the evidence of a few vertebrae or teeth), so it should be possible for architects of a future age to do the same thing with contemporary architecture. They argued that just as a fossil or a bone allowed a geologist to discover the habits of an animal on which no living eye had ever rested, so 'any true style of art enables the archaeologist to tell from a few fragments in what century the building to which it belonged was erected'. The challenge which Fergusson and his fellow critics thus offered the architectural profession was quite explicit. They did not in fact ask for an architecture which would simply be acceptable to the new age; they demanded a vocabulary of ornamental and tectonic details which would be taxonomically identifiable whenever fragments were unearthed at some future date. It was in vain that more moderate critics, including the architects themselves, suggested that an evolution might well be apparent to future generations, even though it was proceeding too slowly to be noticed by those living at the time. It was in vain that the editor of *The Builder*, in 1847, asserted that he was not amongst those who looked for great and sudden changes in style; that he did not expect to find architects employing details never before met with, or producing at once, 'as with the blow of harlequin's wand in a pantomime', a building altogether different from others already erected. It was in vain that he expressed his doubts as to 'whether the changes of style in Gothic architecture appeared as great and important whilst in progress as they do to us', or suggested that the violence of contemporary criticism was due to the fact that the critics were not trained architects but laymen. The historians would not rest until architects had complied with their demands.

The demand for a contemporary style was not of course confined to architecture, but also extended to literature, so it was very much in character with the artistic temper of the age. Victor Hugo, for example, had declared that there could only exist one literature for each epoch, just as there could only exist one form of society, and that earlier literatures, whilst they had left 'immortal monuments' to posterity, had been obliged to disappear with the generations whose social customs and political ambitions they had expressed. The genius of the nineteenth century might well prove, he thought, to be as fine as that of more illustrious epochs; but it could not be the same, and it was not within the power of contemporary writers to resuscitate a bygone literature, any more than it was possible for a gardener to replace fallen leaves on spring branches.

The same theme was expressed by André Chénier. 'Everything has changed for us', he wrote in his poem entitled *l'Invention*, written in about 1820: 'habits, customs, sciences; why then must we so painfully strive to live in the past, refusing to see what is close to us?' And in words which were to be later so closely paraphrased unconsciously by Viollet-le-Duc, he asked whether Homer and Virgil would have scorned the fruitful riches of modern knowledge if they had lived in the nineteenth century, and sung their songs in the present day. At the same time there were other writers who thought that poets should not so much express their age as be, in Lamennais' words, 'the prophets of the progress of society'. We thus find already established that distinction which still bedevils the theory of art, namely the distinction between 'contemporary artists' and '*avant garde* artists'.

All the creative artists of the era were dominated by two conflicting schools, each of which paradoxically stemmed from the same attitude towards history. The Revivalists were dominated by their awareness of the legacy of history. The anti-Revivalists were dominated by their awareness of the evolutionary nature of history. Fortunate indeed were those romantic writers who were able to display both qualities in their work, as in some of Victor Hugo's historical novels. Yet those who demanded a new architecture denied the possibility of reconciling the two points of view, and it was in vain that practising architects asserted that they were reinterpreting ancient idioms in modern themes (just as the novelists were narrating ancient themes in modern language). For the anti-Revivalists were not interested in themes; they were only concerned with language. Moreover, they saw progress as an indivisible totality, and, under the influence of the rapid cumulative improvements in the mechanical arts, were convinced that the fine arts should follow suit at a similar speed.

Admittedly, the more thoughtful theorists perceived the error of assuming exact analogies between the mechanical arts and the fine arts, for as has already been pointed out, it had long been known that the fine arts did not obey cumulative laws of progress, like science and industry. Thus, throughout the eighteenth century, it was generally held that since nature was not progressive (but changed by cycles), and since the fine arts were based on nature, then the fine arts must also be cyclic rather than evolutionary; a view put forward as early as the sixteenth century by Vasari. In 1817, Hazlitt pointed out that whilst the sciences advanced by accumulated effort and research, art depended on individual genius and an incommunicable power; in 1850, Victor de Laprade asserted, like Hazlitt and Victor Hugo, that art does not progress gradually like science, but can attain perfection very rapidly. In keeping with this line of thought, therefore, the editor of the *Revue Générale de l'Architecture* divided the architectural drawings of the salon of 1844 into three categories: studies of pure construction, planning studies, and drawings of ancient monuments, the latter described as being conceived 'with a view to the progress of art properly so called'. Yet such distinctions were in practice disregarded and for good reason. Architecture, unlike the other arts, is a science as well as an art; thus it can fairly be argued that since technology has developed rapidly in the last two centuries, so should architecture. Critics therefore continued to deplore the fact that architecture was the only branch of human ingenuity in the nineteenth century which remained an exception to this general rule. In 1849, the *Revue Générale de l'Architecture* published an allegorical drawing showing Minerva, the goddess of the arts, riding a locomotive labelled 'Progress', beneath which was the caption: 'Respect for the Past, Liberty in the Present, Faith in the Future'. The railways were the favourite symbol of the progress of the age, for what could be more striking than the difference between a locomotive and a horse? The trouble was to decide how a comparable difference could be fairly introduced into the appearance of buildings.

The most logical step seemed to be to seek inspiration from the example being set by inventors, engineers, and scientists. Indeed, it is a characteristic of the age that the architectural periodicals were not then fashion magazines, as they so often are today, but made it their policy simply to explore the applicability of new technological methods to architectural design. It was for this reason that they were so much more concerned with disseminating scientific knowledge than with publicizing current buildings. The first issue of the *Revue Générale de l'Architecture* announced that the editor's intention was to demonstrate to architects and engineers the close correlation which existed between science and art (two aspects of truth which, he claimed, must necessarily be in accordance with each other as two logical consequences of the same principle). Each issue of his magazine would therefore consist of four parts: history, theory, practice and miscellanies, the latter to include any new developments in the sciences of construction not specifically architectural. But unfortunately, the more ardent promoters of the idea of a new architecture were not content simply to exercise their intellects in adapting current innovations in civil engineering to architecture. They sought to extract a new architectural theory by *analogies* with engineering, and these involved them in three fallacies. The first was based on the fact that invention seemed an essential aspect of engineering progress, the second was based on the fact that experimentation seemed an essential prerequisite for invention, and the third was based on the fact that engineering invention necessarily seemed to involve the production of new forms.

The notion that invention is an essential aspect of engineering was only too plausible at a time when being an inventor was a profession in itself. Ingenious mechanics in those days studied invention as young men today study salesmanship; for just as today, it does not matter whether or not a shop assistant knows anything about the goods he is selling provided he has mastered the technique of persuading customers to buy them, so in the nineteenth century one only had to learn how to invent in order to invent anything. The career of Thomas Alva Edison (who, with no formal education, took out over a thousand patents in fifty years, ranging from dictaphones to concrete houses) is perhaps the most striking example of the nine-teenth century's ideal of *uomo universale*; but there were many others like him. James Bogardus, whose fame rests mainly on his invention of prefabricated cast iron buildings, was trained as a watchmaker, and also invented a new kind of pencil, an engraving machine and a deep-sea sounding apparatus. François Coignet, one of the pioneers of modern concrete, was a chemical engineer. Frederick Ransome, another pioneer of modern concrete, worked for a firm which manufactured farm machinery. The idea thus gained credence that a new architecture was essentially something that needed only an inventor to invent it, and arguments such as those advanced by César Daly, to the effect that architecture was an art which evolved slowly and imperceptibly in accordance with changes in society, seemed quite out of place in that impetuous age.

Perhaps the most ingenious inventors of this group were William Vose Pickett and his disciple, Jean-Baptiste Jobard. Two occurrences seem to have combined to give Pickett his inspiration as to how to bring a new architecture into existence. The first, he informs us, was a visit to some caverns in Derbyshire, where the stalactites suggested to him the idea of a new architecture of curves. The second, about which he is rather reticent, was the publication, in 1842, of Ambrose Poynter's prize-winning essay entitled *On the Effects which should result to Archi-tectural Taste, with regard to Arrangement and Design, from the general introduction of Iron in the construction of Buildings.* Poynter had not considered that there was any logical way in which iron could radically modify traditional forms, but Pickett insisted that iron, being cast, was not suited to sharp angles, and by combining the two ideas, proposed a 'Metallurgic Architecture' of plastic shapes, which he patented on May 7th, 1844. Despite the name, he did not confine this architecture to metal construction, but considered all manufactured materials, such as papier-mâché, as appropriate for the application of his theory.

Two analogies were used to support his proposals. Firstly, as evidence of the perfect and satisfactory applicability of metals to 'numerous synonymous purposes', he instanced bridge-building and ship-building. Secondly, as evidence of the logic of curved structural forms, he instanced 'organic nature in general'. In the human skeleton, he observed, the rounded or undulating line is generally predominant, just as in the composition of flowers, the curved line is also predominant, although counterbalanced by the introduction of straight lines in the *stamina* and stems. These curved forms can be justified on structural grounds, since the variations in the thickness of, say, the leg-bones of animals, clearly correspond to the variations in stress to be resisted, and he noted that animal bones invariably swell out wherever there is a joint. The same principle was observed by engineers in designing the components of machinery, such as piston-rods, so why not also in architecture?

The incidence of both straight and curved lines in plants was used by Pickett to justify similar juxtapositions in his New Architecture, since he saw that it was inevitable that certain elements, such as floors, would have to be designed as flat surfaces; but he objected to any angular junctions or sharp corners, and envisaged an angle-less architecture composed predominantly of curves. He foresaw that this would mean rejecting all the traditional canons of proportion, but again he could justify his theory by analogy with natural organisms. The existence of proportion in the productions of organic nature, he explained, could not be ascertained by measurement or calculation, but could only be perceived intuitively. It therefore followed that a similar condition applied to an architecture modelled on nature, in that the proportions of a building designed in this manner could only be adjusted in the way a sculptor gave beauty to a statue, i.e. 'through the mental operation of feeling and judgement in the artist'.

In addition to his general notion of plasticity, Pickett put forward several other ideas which seem to have anticipated the architecture of a later age. Firstly, he proposed that instead of supporting roofs on a series of columns, they should be designed according to a system analogous to the suspension bridge. In its most modest form, the system he envisaged merely involved the substitution of suspended canopies for colonnaded porticos, as in the design he submitted to the Commissioners of Works for the modification of Nash's Regent Street Quadrant in 1848. But he also envisaged the spanning of vast halls, such as auditoria and churches, with suspended roofs, and considered that the recently completed suspension bridge at Charing Cross, with a span of 700 ft., was 'perfectly analogous to a roof'. In applying the principle of suspension, he explained, it would be sufficient merely to provide an efficient skeleton frame on which to rest the roof, and from which to hang the chains. The enclosing walls might then be as slight and thin as the general purposes of shelter and comfort would permit. This system should not, he said, be concealed, as so often happened with structural ironwork, since being the simple expression of a basic principle of metallic construction, it must inevitably be in perfect harmony with the rest of the building. The skeleton frame would give singularly beautiful effects of light and shade round the outer circumference of the building, and a fine sky-line would be produced by the pinnacles with their suspended chains. He submitted a project incorporating this principle for the Army and Navy Club Competition of 1847, but his only reward was a derisive paragraph from the editor of *The Builder*, who published an article reviewing all the schemes.

Secondly, he envisaged the introduction of built-in furniture. The hollow walls of his metal-framed houses could be used, he said, for the purposes of storage usually fulfilled by wardrobes, cabinets, and other heavy or cumbrous pieces of furniture, which mar the architectural effect of an apartment, harbour dust, occasion trouble with the carpeting, stand in the way, increase the cost of housekeeping, and 'constitute the class of furniture most difficult to reconcile with architectural proportions and arrangements'. Could their presence be dispensed with in houses, he continued, the difficulties of making furniture harmonize with the general design of interiors would be in a great measure overcome. 'Modern buildings', he complained, 'instead of following the example of nature, and causing beauty to issue out of each and every utility, have renounced the offered conveniences, rather than call in the aid of taste and invention to the accomplishment of the latter result'.

Pickett also proposed the use of pierced metal screens, suspended a short distance in front of the façades of buildings in a manner which sounds curiously descriptive of the currently fashionable metal *brises-soleil*. He thought of these elements as mainly decorative, arguing that since the characteristic ornament of masonry architecture consisted of forms carved in relief out of the solid structural mass, the 'extraneous or decorative features' of his New Architecture should consist of delicately pierced plates secured by rods in advance of the wall. These, in addition to being ornamental in themselves, would cast shadows on to the surfaces of the hollow metal walls to which they were attached. But he also envisaged them as performing a functional service. 'The utility it is intended to serve', he wrote, 'is that of a sun-shade, it being an external appendage to heads of windows exposed to strong light and sunshine. Being composed of interstitial or transparent metal-work with an inner lining of brass gauze, it is eminently calculated to check the force of the sun's rays, without excluding the light during dull weather'. It was, he claimed, equally suited to public as well as private edifices, since while serving a similar use, it would impart a bold and imposing effect to the external façade, and at the same time exhibit decorative effects of light and shade inside the building.

Pickett marshalled every argument which might serve to persuade his readers and his audiences, and he did not fail to explain that the forms he recommended could be justified on practical grounds, with respect to the technique of casting metals. But whilst urging the adoption of his proposals by appeals to structural rationalism, he had none of the fastidious distaste for shams evinced by most of his contemporaries. Indeed, it is his brazen disregard for the sacred nineteenth century Rationalist principle of the primacy of structure as the determinant of architectural form which distinguishes him from the other theorists of the period, and relates him so closely to the creators and successors of Art Nouveau. 'In the practice of this Architecture', he proclaimed, with even more italics than usual, 'there will of course be no more *necessity* for the employment of *iron* in the construction of the walls of edifices, than there is for the use of *stone* for the like purposes of other Architectures; brick, bitumen, and various species of cement being equally available as substitutes for either. But while (in the practices of pre-existent Architecture) *cemented walls* are required to be cut or marked out in straight lines, to represent the effects of blocks of stone in masonry, so likewise whenever similar substances are made use of in *this art*, it will be equally necessary to employ them in such a manner as that *they* also shall represent the external effects of a principle of construction, consistent with the forms and general purpose of this art, and adopted to the native properties of *iron*.'

It is not perhaps immediately apparent why Pickett's ideas should have taken so long to be accepted, in view of the fact that all his main proposals have been put into effect during the last sixty years. But he had, alas, one grave deficiency which proved an insuperable barrier to the propagation of his schemes. He was unable to draw. In the preface to his book, he made a pathetic appeal to 'any artist who might find himself prompted by the impulses of genius to produce illustrations of the system', but presumably none was forthcoming, for no illustrations were included in his published descriptions, and only vague sketches accompanied his patent, and the advertisements he handed round. He thus had to rely on the impassioned imagery of the written word. In 1845 he published, with the tardily acknowledged assistance of his sister Elizabeth, a 144-page book entitled *A New System of Architecture*, and for the next four years he tried to promote his ideas by means of articles in the *Athenaeum* (No. 867), the *Fine Arts Journal* (vol. i, nos. 15–26) and the *Westminster and Foreign Quarterly Review* (April 1849); by lectures to such organizations as the Society of Arts and the Brighton Literary and Scientific Institution; and by addresses to the Prince Consort, the President of the Board of Trade, the Royal Institute of British Architects, the Royal Commission of Fine Arts, the Royal Society, the Royal Academy and the King of the French. The Academy Professor (C. R. Cockerell) suavely replied to one of his letters by saying that whilst he rejoiced in the acquaintance and polite regard of a mind of Pickett's deep quality, he could not but observe that 'with the accustomed warmth of genius and originality, you have treated the subject with an enthusiasm that few readers will acquiesce in; for you term that a discovery which is an improved and enlarged view of what has been going on in Europe for some time . . . Where shall I send your precious manuscript, being unwilling to consign it to the post?'. The Prince Consort's secretary's reply was less devious, and simply stated that 'from the investigation which his Royal Highness has made on the subject of your invention, he regrets to say that *he does not consider it of any value and importance*, and will therefore *not trouble* you to send any model for his inspection'. But Pickett's ideals were not entirely without influence, since it seems reasonable to suppose that Jean-Baptiste Jobard, the director of the Belgian Industrial Museum, got his much-publicized idea of a 'Metallurgic Architecture' from Pickett's book, and it may even be possible that the latter's *New System of Architecture* was thus the direct inspiration, and not merely a prefiguration, of Belgian Art Nouveau.

Jobard's main contribution was the suggestion that the iron should be combined with glass, and in an article published in the *Revue Générale de l'Architecture* in 1849, he contended that glass was called upon to play a particularly important role in metallic architecture. Yet instead of envisaging large sheets of glass, he evidently considered that it would be used in a pseudo-Gothic manner as an infilling for cast-iron tracery, and the first real anticipation of contemporary methods of combining metal and glass is undoubtedly the Crystal Palace, which James Fergusson perspicaciously hailed as the precursor of the 'Ferro-Vitreous Art'.

However, this chapter is not so much concerned with the technological developments which eventually created a new architecture as with the philosophical bases on which the demand for such an architecture rested. It will be appropriate there-fore to turn now to consider the notion that experimentation is an essential pre-requisite for invention; a notion which gave rise to the theory, still very popular today, that we live in a period of perpetual artistic primitiveness. This was noticed as early as 1855, for in *The Builder* of that year it was remarked that 'in endeavour-ing to fix some distinctive characteristic of the age—after rejecting the ordinary one as asserted, namely, the prevalence merely of contemporaneous "styles"—we found that no other period had practised so much the experimental system'. Similarly, many critics today still consider that every good architectural design must necessarily be an anticipation of something that not even the future will ever determine, and there is at times something almost ludicrous in the determination to be archaic and to stay archaic decade after decade. 'Paestum is beautiful to me because it is less beautiful than the Parthenon', Louis Kahn recently asserted; 'Paestum is dumpy, it has unsure, scared proportions, but it is infinitely more beautiful to me because to me it represents the beginning of architecture. It is a time when the walls parted and the columns became and when music entered architecture. It was a beautiful time *and we are still living in it*'. Now few practising architects of the nineteenth century believed that they were living in an archaic time; nor did their clients want archaic buildings. On the contrary, in that optimistic and otherwise complacent age, men were all artlessly delighted by the superiority of their own society as compared with those of preceding civilizations. The fact that this artless complacency has now vanished is a tribute to the influence of men such as Fergusson. Experimentation has now come to occupy the most prominent place in the curricula of our architectural schools, whilst cynics might well argue that the architectural pioneers whose more radical projects have proved most impractical are the ones whose reputations have achieved the highest fame.

The notion that invention must necessarily produce new forms was of course the most vital aspect of the analogy, since it was essentially new forms that the architectural historians were demanding. The fact that architects persistently and obtusely failed to create any new forms, as the engineers were doing, thus struck the historians as particularly exasperating. 'Of those arts which in this country have been cultivated on the most common-sense principles, and consequently which have been most essentially progressive, there is none more remarkable than that of Civil Engineering', asserted Fergusson, and he suggested that all architects needed to do was to apply the same common-sense principles to their own work. Yet when specifically challenged as to what he proposed to substitute for Grecian pillars, Gothic pinnacles and all the other antique and mediaeval paraphernalia which then made up the stock in trade of an architect, he had to confess that he 'did not know'. He tried to evade the issue by retorting that no ship-builder could tell what ships would look like a hundred years hence; but the architects were not asking him to prophesy what buildings would look like in the following century; they were asking him to tell them what buildings should look like there and then. Fergusson was not however abashed, and in the third volume of his *History of Architecture* (1862) he continued to assert that if the idea of introducing a new style had taken possession of the public mind at the same time as it adopted mediaeval Revivalism, architects would by that time have created a style worthy of the nineteenth century, and the public would have laughed in astonishment at any man who would have then proposed to erect a church or any other building after the pattern of the Middle Ages.

In addition to the idea of progress, another ideal which stimulated the architectural speculations of the time was that of liberty, with which must be associated the ideal of reform. This was an age which was distinguished by the suppression of the slave trade, and transformed politically by revolutions and changes in parliamentary representation. Thus when Thomas Babington Macaulay, speaking in favour of the first Reform Bill, asserted that 'a representative system, framed to suit the England of the thirteenth century, did not suit the England of the nineteenth century', he was simply anticipating what architectural critics would soon be saying about the Gothic Revival. Similarly, phrases like 'the slavery of past styles' awakened very potent moral ideas in the minds of those then subjected to appeals for a new architecture, and many of the remedies proposed were actually based on the notion of artistic liberty. This was particularly so with respect to the violent criticisms with which the French École des Beaux-Arts was assailed during this period. After remarking in the *Revue Générale de l'Architecture* of 1847 (with reference to one of the school's programmes for a church) that the style of all modern architecture would be much nearer solution if only the question of a modern style of ecclesiastical architecture could be resolved, the editor asserted that 'every artist should be left free to consult his own nature, his own powers and the feelings of the public', and that following Molière's example, an artist should take whatever was worth taking wherever he could find it. This latter remark was of course an appeal for Eclecticism, which most of those who clamoured for a new architecture eventually accepted as the only kind of freedom possible, once it was obvious that no radically new architecture would be immediately forthcoming.

In the following year, the *Revue Générale de l'Architecture* published an article entitled 'Artistic Liberty', which contained a list of architects who were considered by the editor to be propagating 'the true principles of liberty and progress'. Its main interest lies in the fact that the men listed—Labrouste, Duban, Constant-Dufeux and Reynaud—were all teachers, the first three being in charge of studios at the École des Beaux-Arts, the latter being professor of architecture at the École Polytechnique. It will be opportune, therefore, to discuss here the impact of the demand for a new architecture on nineteenth century architectural education, since in more recent years it has been in the architectural schools that the mystical appeal of architectural reform has exercised its greatest force.

In England and America there were virtually no schools of architecture, whilst in Germany architectural instruction was based on the model of the French École Polytechnique. It is thus fair to say that in France we find the character of the formal architectural education of the age. This character was dominated by the traditions of the École des Beaux-Arts, a lineal descendant of the pre-revolutionary Royal Academy school (though with a number of important modifications which will be discussed later). In the first half of the nineteenth century, no architectural history was taught in the school (despite the appointment of a professor for this purpose) because the Academicians, being Classicists to a man, considered that comparative studies of the architectures of the past were not educationally profitable. In this they may well have been right; but as a result of agitation and criticism by anglophile architectural magazines, courses in history were eventually given, and as soon as this happened, a dilemma made itself apparent; namely, how to define the distinction between architectural history and architectural theory.

The importance of this distinction cannot be over-emphasized, since the very validity of the notion of a theory of architecture is now hotly debated. Essentially, the distinction is this: that the theory of architecture is concerned with everything pertaining to the way people actually build in the present, whereas the history of architecture is concerned with the way people used to build in the past; but the distinction between the two was by no means easy to determine in the nineteenth century, and it is still not easy to determine, judging from the material included in Sigfried Giedion's *Space, Time and Architecture*. In the nineteenth century, the dilemma arose from two causes; firstly, from the fact that even the best theorists, under the influence of historiography, spent their time studying the past in order to try to extract from it a valid body of principles applicable to the present; secondly, from the fact that by a misplaced sense of decorum, they considered themselves prevented from discussing the work of architects who were still alive.

The history of the changing attitudes towards architectural theory during the last two centuries is of unusual interest. Before 1750, as we have seen, there was no possibility of a conflict between architectural theory and architectural history, since architectural history did not properly speaking exist, the virtues of Classicism were unquestioned, and every study of an antique or early renaissance monument was thus related to the theory of current design. The first awareness of any conflict between the two notions seems to occur in Leroy's study of the Athenian antiquities (1758), when, faced with the dilemma of dealing with a kind of Classicism that did not fit into the current architectural traditions, he decided, as has already been mentioned, to divide his book into two parts: one dealing with the subject 'from the point of view of history', the other dealing with it 'from the point of view of architecture'.

Within a century, the history of architecture had almost entirely supplanted the theory of architecture, and although there were occasionally perspicacious teachers, such as Léonce Reynaud, who perceived that what students needed most was a study of current building technology, most treatises on architecture were, like

Gaudet's famous *Eléments et Théorie de l'Architecture*, simply historical studies arranged according to building types. Moreover, whereas J. F. Blondel's history of architecture (forming the first part of his *Architecture Française* (1752)) continued up to his own day, as did that written by Elmes in 1821, few of the mid-nineteenth century histories of architecture went beyond 1750, whilst some of them stopped as early as 1500, the date when, according to Fergusson and other Rationalists, true architectural evolution ceased. Admittedly Fergusson eventually added a third volume to his general *History of Architecture* of 1855, and covered the period from 1500 to his own day: but this was so that he could make a critical attack on current trends. In his introduction to the third volume, he remarked that whereas the styles of architecture described in the previous two volumes were what he called 'the True Styles', those that remained to be examined were 'the Copying or Imitative Styles', which lacked truth, intellectual value, and all ethnographic significance. They were thus worthy of study only in so far as the reader could speculate as to why architecture had arrived at its current parlous condition.

The effect of all this was to obscure two more fundamental dilemmas inherent in the demand for a new architecture. The first of these concerned the distinction between a new architecture and a true architecture; the second concerned the distinction between a contemporary architecture and a future architecture. Since neither of these distinctions has yet been satisfactorily resolved, it is worth commenting on them in some detail.

Historians like Fergusson (and he was to some extent a pioneer in this matter) considered that the essential purpose of architectural history was to derive a valid contemporary theory of architecture from the study of the past. As the history of architecture had been written by earlier authors, it had been little more than a series of technical archaeological descriptions of buildings arranged chronologically, without much attempt to elaborate any general theory of art. But the true aim of architectural history, according to Fergusson, was to study buildings with reference to the future creation of a new style. Fergusson was aware that architects before 1500 had not been primarily concerned with either the past or the future, but only with the present. Hence he was convinced that their buildings, like the current buildings of the Chinese and Hindus, were a natural and inevitable outcome of the social structures within which they were produced. It was this natural process that he wanted contemporary architects to imitate. But he found himself, on the one hand, denying that the current architectural expression of his own society could possibly be a true architecture (simply because it was not a new architecture), and on the other hand denying that current architecture was genuinely contemporary, because it gave no indication of the forms which future generations would create.

The result of such paradoxical contradictions was simply to create a sense of acute self-consciousness among architects, who were henceforth unable to design any forms naturally because they were watching themselves create. Fergusson never seems to have realized that the sole reason why architecture evolved naturally before 1500 was because the architects of those days were unaware of the process of evolution. Once architects became aware of the historical process by which evolution took place, their architecture was as incapable of evolving naturally as they themselves would have been incapable of eating naturally by following a text-book explanation of the movements of the epiglottis. It was in vain that J. P. Seddon, in 1850, urged architects to pay no attention to styles, but to leave all classification to posterity. It was in vain that clients, such as those described by Robert Kerr in *The English Gentleman's House* (1864), demanded 'no style at all but the comfortable style, if there be one'. Even if architects had approved this attitude, they could have done nothing about it, since the involuntary impact of historiography was too strong to be suppressed.

Fergusson's confusion between a true architecture and a new architecture was the less serious of his two dilemmas, since it could convincingly be resolved by asserting, very properly, that few architects of the time were seriously trying to relate their buildings to the current state of society and technology, and that they were on the contrary 'slaves to archaeology'; abusing the public's confidence by fobbing it off with obsolete survivals from the past. But the confusion between contemporary architecture and the notion of an architecture of the future was more serious. It is evident that any proposed architectural reform must, because of the time necessary for it to achieve fruition, imply a benefit to accrue in the future rather than one to be enjoyed in the present; but there were those whose passion for the cause of a new architecture tempted them to create deliberate and unnatural changes in society and technology so that architecture would be bound to change in conformity with them.

Evidently, no one would or could quarrel with those who have tried to improve the conditions of life of their fellow human beings, or with those who have carried out enterprising research into new building techniques. On the contrary, they have deserved and received our deepest respect. But in the last hundred years we have witnessed eccentric projects for Futurist dwellings, and seen elaborate publicity used to promote new synthetic materials, all of which suggest that architectural changes are not always based on profound sociological studies, or on extensive tectonic research, but, on the contrary, are based on artificial and arbitrary concepts deliberately devised for the express purpose of creating new architectural forms for their own sake.

We thus find, in the nineteenth century demand for a new architecture, as in all revolutionary movements, that the moderates were pushed aside by the extremists, and that the appeals of such men as César Daly, who deprecated the notion that a new architecture could be created by spontaneous generation, were impatiently thrust aside by men with more radical views. Yet despite the publicity given to the latter, the sensible attitude of César Daly undoubtedly corresponded to the point of view of most practising architects. In 1849, the Royal Institute of British

Architects made a public appeal to its members regarding the current aspiration to discover new architectural forms, pointing out that it could only be by a thorough appreciation of the actual state of science, and by a thorough knowledge of the requirements of the present day, that there could be any hope of creating and maturing ideas which would leave their mark on the architecture of the epoch. The more radical theorists clamouring for a new architecture were not practising architects, so that, being unable to draw, they were condemned to the frustration of waiting for others to put their hopes into tangible shape. Probably the only historian to make any intelligible suggestions was Fergusson, who in criticizing the design accepted for the British Museum, suggested that it would have been better modelled on the latest and most progressive example of industrial architecture: namely, a flax mill recently constructed in Leeds, in which two acres of floor were roofed by an ingenious series of standardized brick domes supported on widely spaced iron columns. But just as Marshall's Flax Mill was walled externally with a replica of an Egyptian temple (though Fergusson does not allude to this fact), so Fergusson had in fact few useful suggestions to make concerning the exterior of the British Museum, despite his biting criticism of Smirke's façade. Yet it was the design of façades that most troubled the radical critics of the time, for even the most gruesome expressions of Revivalism, such as the Oxford Museum, or the Walhalla at Ratisbon, often contained quite advanced structural features internally, such as open metal roofs.

Fergusson was one of the many controversialists who wrote long and violent criticisms of Street's design for the new Law Courts; but when it came to making alternative proposals, he had nothing more stimulating to suggest than that the window heads should have been semicircular rather than pointed. Seventeen years earlier, he had been involved in a similar controversy with Scott, but apart from referring his readers to the Crystal Palace, as an example of progressive building, he could think of no specific illustrations of his principles, and contented himself with enunciating three aphorisms: firstly, that an architect's principal duty was to design a building wholly and solely for the purposes for which it was to be used; secondly, that he should construct it with reference to the best materials available; and thirdly, that he should ornament it appropriately and elegantly without any reference to any style. No wonder that Scott was able to retaliate with such telling effect. If, he remarked sarcastically, the gentlemen who loaded the pages of *The Builder* with their protests against copyism were to spend even a portion of their spare time in endeavouring to invent or discover that new style which was their ideal panacea for architecture, they might be doing a real service to art. 'The real question is simply this', he wrote: 'As we are called upon to progress, and admit the propriety of the call, what is to be the starting point from which our progression is to commence? All we at present know is that our opponents have decided that we are wrong, but this discussion will produce only perplexity unless they tell us clearly and specifically what is right. When we ask for the practical working out of what our opponents are so fond of urging, the result is absolutely nil!' As Robert Kerr so justly remarked when criticizing Fergusson in 1868 at a meeting of the Royal Institute of British Architects, his architectural ideas were too superficial, and this was because it was impossible for any man who had not passed through the drudgery of practical architectural business, and the design of practical buildings, to understand adequately the elementary principles on which architectural design ought to be based.

There were of course attempts at this time on the part of architects themselves to design a new architecture. In 1850 Robert Kerr showed a design for a public building at the Architectural Exhibition, in which the structure was simply a series of colonnades filled in with single large sheets of plate glass. In the following year, the Munich Academy of Arts offered a prize of four thousand florins to anyone who could design an educational building in a new style of architecture. Even the École des Beaux-Arts insisted in one of its programmes (in 1847) that the design (in this case for a sacristy to be added to a thirteenth century church) was 'to leave no doubt as to the epoch in which the new structure was built'. But usually 'originality' was of the kind described by Sir Arthur Blomfield, president of the Architectural Association, when he remarked that every young architect seemed to think himself bound to out-do everyone else in broken-backed windows or oddly shaped rooms. To Blomfield, the very mention of a 'Victorian Style' was, he said, enough to make his heart sink, and to make him tremble for the prospects of art. Such a thing as the creation of a new style would, he thought, be so complete a falsification of all history and all analogy that he advised his audience to disabuse their minds of any such expectation. In architecture, at least, if nothing else, the development theory was the true one, and that development would have to be gradual, and, to a certain extent, almost unconscious. Any attempt to force the natural development of architecture by a morbid straining after originality would, he felt sure, have the most disastrous results.

The strivings of the historians to evolve a new architecture by analogy with earlier architectures thus seemed to have failed; but their failure had at least one important result. It forced theorists to study the heuristic possibilities of other kinds of analogy. Now it may well be argued, despite the nineteenth century's lack of success, that analogies with other buildings will always be the surest kind of analogy for architectural theorists to pursue. Conversely, it can be argued that the less affinity existing between two objects or disciplines from which analogies are drawn, the greater the possibility of error. For as Arnold Toynbee has pointed out, the weakness of analogy as a method of thought seems to lie in the nature of most of the phenomena to which it is applied, since the possibility of error always arises when the entities between which one is drawing an analogy are not mathematical abstractions but are observed phenomena. Two or more phenomena may have facets which do in fact genuinely correspond with each other; but we may fall into error by failing to abstract the genuinely corresponding features precisely, or by making the unwarrantable assumption that an analogy which holds good just for these facets is also applicable to the phenomena in their entirety.

Analogies with past architectures proved a failure, not because of any of the errors indicated by Toynbee, but because of the over-sensitive historical consciousness of the age, which caused such analogies to degenerate into archaeological mimicry. Therefore the only kinds of analogy left were what we may call 'functional analogies': analogies with living organisms, machines, and bodily functions, such as human taste and speech. It is clear that these analogies were not an ideal in themselves; but Functionalism was, and this eventually became the most important ideal of modern architecture. It is with these various functional analogies that the next four chapters will be concerned.

Part Three

FUNCTIONALISM

14

The Biological Analogy

The origins of the biological analogy, like so many ideas which have influenced modern architectural doctrines, can also be traced to about the year 1750. At that time, two epoch-making scientific books were published: Linnaeus' *Species Plantarum* (1753), in which the entire vegetable kingdom was classified binominally according to the disposition of the female reproductive organs, or 'styles', and Buffon's *Histoire Naturelle* (1749), a vast compendium which attempted to incorporate all biological phenomena into a general interpretation of the laws governing the universe. Linnaeus' work does not immediately concern this present enquiry, although it is probably not without significance that his mania for classification so closely paralleled the awakening archaeological obsession of the age. Buffon's views, however, are of considerable relevance, since he disagreed both with Linnaeus' immutable species, and with his whole doctrine of classification by arbitrarily chosen characteristics. On the contrary, he believed that this kind of compilation obscured the fact that all species must have derived from a single type, and, supporting his views on this subject both by the evidence of fossil shells, and by reference to mammoths recently discovered in Siberia (which he refers to as 'ancient Monuments'), he put forward a philosophy of creation in which the idea of evolution was expressed clearly for the first time.

In so far as his system relates to biological ideas used later by architectural theorists, there are two features which deserve mention. The first is that, in hitting upon the idea of evolution, he saw it as essentially a process of degeneration, not of improvement, since his religious beliefs (or his respect for those held by his contemporaries) prevented him from assigning the evolutionary process to any but the lower animals. On the other hand he was the first scientist to distinguish correctly between the 'vegetative' and specifically 'animal' parts of animals, whereby an animal may be regarded simply as a vegetable organism endowed with the power of moving from place to place. Thus 'organic life' has come to mean, for architectural theorists at least, the sum of the functions of the 'vegetative' class; for all living organisms, whether plants or animals, possess them to a more or less marked degree.

FUNCTIONALISM

The scientist who first gave classical expression to this meaning of 'organic' was Xavier Bichat, whose *Physiological Researches on Life and Death* was published in 1800. Until then it was normal, especially in view of the humanistic culture of the age, for the biological analogy to refer to animals rather than plants. Lord Kames, for example, who disliked symmetry in gardens, contended nevertheless that 'in organized bodies comprehended under one view, nature studies regularity, which for the same reason, ought to be studied in architecture'. At the beginning of the nineteenth century, however, 'organic' came to be regarded less as a quality of 'life which moves' than of life rooted to a particular spot. It was thus the asymmetry of plants and viscera, rather than the symmetry of animal skeletons, which came to be accepted as characteristic of organic structures, whereby biology could still be adduced to support the architectural fashions of the age.

The most important enunciations of evolutionary theory at this time were those published by Lamarck. Lamarck was essentially a botanist of the school of Buffon, but when, at the age of fifty, he was appointed professor of Zoology by the National Convention without any previous experience at all, he was obliged to transfer his attention to the study of anatomy. As a result of this combination of disciplines, he was eventually led to conclude that living forms had not evolved retrogressively, as Buffon had believed, but progressively. This change of attitude was only to be expected. Buffon, living in the age of Rousseau, and at a time when the Book of Genesis was literally accepted, naturally favoured a hypothesis implying a Fall from perfection. Lamarck, in the age of Revolution, and at a time when the idea of Progress was literally accepted, naturally favoured a contrary view. It detracts nothing from the brilliant originality of either theory to assert that they were both very much in the spirit of the age.

Similarly, it was not entirely strange that Lamarck should suggest that evolution was due to environment. The importance of this influence on art, law and society had already been emphasized by Winckelmann, Montesquieu and de Goguet respectively, although they did not, as far as I know, go so far as to say that it actually caused evolution direct. This, however, was the essence of Lamarck's revolutionary argument. 'It is not', he wrote, 'the organs—that is to say, the form and character of the animal's bodily parts—which have given rise to its habits and peculiar properties, but, on the contrary, it is its habits and manner of life and the conditions in which its ancestors lived that has in the course of time fashioned its bodily form, its organs and its qualities'.

The word 'biology', or science of life, was invented by Lamarck in about 1800; at the same time, the word 'morphology', or science of form, was invented by Goethe, who in his own day was as famous as a scientist as he was as a poet. Being a poet, however, he understood the term morphology in a much wider sense than we do today (when the subjects of its study are confined to the comparison and relationships of living structures and their development), and included non-living forms such as rocks. This, as we shall see, was to be another element of confusion in the biological analogy, in that from its inception, there was uncertainty as to whether morphology was concerned with structures which live, or with structures which grow. Félix Vicq d'Azyr, for example, at the end of the eighteenth century, had rejected the old comparison between the growth of organisms and the growth of crystals, contending that crystals are mathematically regular in shape and homogeneous in structure, whereas organisms are of rounded shapes and complex composition. On the other hand Jacob Schleiden, fifty years later, considered that life was nothing more or less than a 'form-building force', and he considered the growth of crystals and organisms to belong to the same category of phenomena. As late as 1898, Herbert Spencer could still assert that the growth of crystals and organisms was 'an essentially similar process'. Since it was Spencer's biological works which mainly influenced Frank Lloyd Wright, the possible effects of this ambiguity will be obvious.

Moreover, as soon as the new science of morphology was established, and pursued methodically by the study of comparative anatomy, two dilemmas in the interpretation of the facts at once made themselves apparent: does form follow function, or does function follow form? To the layman, the conundrum might appear as futile and as insoluble as the problem of the chicken and the egg, but to those familiar with modern architectural theories its importance will need no justification. Amongst biologists, the distinction was considered sufficiently important to perpetuate a bitter quarrel for half a century, the leader of the 'form follows function' school being Georges Cuvier, the leader of the opposing faction being Geoffroy Saint-Hilaire. Cuvier (who was incidentally a friend of the architect A. T. Brogniart, and obtained his assistance in examining fossilized building stones) stated that every modification of a function entailed the modification of an organ. Geoffroy Saint-Hilaire protested against arguing from function to structure as an 'abuse of final causes'. The controversy might well have continued indefinitely had it not been that advances in cell-theory distracted attention from morphology, by causing organisms to be seen no longer as cleverly constructed mechanisms, but simply as an aggregate of cells. Perfection of the microscope, in fact, made scientists more interested in the trees than in the wood.

In the event, when the biological analogy was first seriously applied to art theory, the delicate topic of 'form versus function' was avoided completely, since interest was concentrated on the way forms grow, rather than on the way they work. From the time aesthetics became associated with psychology in the middle of the eighteenth century, philosophers had been trying to explain how inspiration (or 'genius' as it was sometimes called) grew in the human mind. Buffon himself, in his speech on *Style* to the Académie Française (1753) was perhaps the first to hint at a biological analogy when he remarked that 'the human mind can create nothing, and only produces after having been fertilized by experience and meditation, in that its perceptions are the germs of its products'. Later Young, in his *Conjectures on Original Composition* (1759), stated that 'an original may be said to be of a vegetable nature; it rises spontaneously from the vital root of genius; it grows, it is not made'. But it was left to Samuel Taylor Coleridge to express the idea as a complete artistic theory, and bring the biological analogy to the attention of the English-speaking world.

There seems little doubt that Coleridge derived his ideas from Germany, where he had studied in his youth, and where such ideas had long been in circulation. Young's *Conjectures*, though virtually ignored in England, had been twice translated into German within two years of its publication, and had become an important part of the gospel of Storm and Stress. J. G. Herder, in his essay *On the Knowing and Feeling of the Human Soul* (1778), had used plants as an analogy for the development of art forms from the soil of their own time and place. Goethe, in his famous early essay on German architecture, had described Gothic as the organic product of growth in the mind of genius. But Coleridge, who was himself an amateur biologist, not merely translated these views into English; he organized the attack against the whole 'Mechanico-Corpuscular' philosophy of creation. 'The form is mechanic', he wrote, 'when on any given material we impress a predetermined form, as when to a mass of wet clay we give whatever shape we wish it to retain when hardened. The organic form, on the other hand, is innate, it shapes as it develops itself from within, and the fullness of its development is one and the same with the perfection of its outward form'. This may be compared with Frank Lloyd Wright's remark in his essay entitled 'In the Cause of Architecture' (1914): 'By organic architecture I mean an architecture that develops from within outward in harmony with the conditions of its being as distinguished from one that is applied from without'.

Several criticisms relevant to the present enquiry may be made concerning Coleridge's views. One is that the process of artistic creation is explained by him as virtually an unwilled and unconscious process of mind. The second is that however violently he might attack the 'mechanical' theory, it has been frequently used by biologists to explain how living organisms actually work. It was not only early philosophers such as Descartes who regarded the animal body as a machine. One of the most famous of Cuvier's disciples, Henri Milne-Edwards, stated that he had 'tried to grasp the manner in which organic forms might have been invented by comparing and studying living things as if they were machines created by the industry of man'. Finally, it is worth noting that no explanation of morphological development was more mechanistic than Darwin's theory of 'Natural Selection'.

It has already been pointed out that by 1859 there was nothing novel in the idea of evolution as applied to the theory of life, even though the term 'evolution' was not used in this sense until 1831. This is equally true with regard to the theory of architecture. The Classical architects of the early eighteenth century believed implicitly in evolution, since they believed that the moderns had improved on the Romans, just as the Romans improved on the Greeks. Even mid-nineteenth century writers on architecture such as Fergusson, who specifically criticized Lamarck's theories, believed in architectural evolution because they believed in Progress. For biologists the novelty of Darwin's theory was that it attributed evolution to a selection of *existing* forms (or, to put it another way, the elimination of obsolescent forms) by Nature herself. It thus inevitably weighed the balance in favour of the 'function follows form' school by presupposing that the forms existed in the first place. Lamarck had claimed that a change in environment actually modifies the form of animals, and that these changes are transmitted by heredity. Darwin claimed on the contrary that the changes were arbitrary and accidental, and that species changed only because the unfunctional forms never survived. He compared the action of natural selection to that of a man building a house from field stones of various shapes. The shapes of these stones, he said, would be due to definite causes, but the uses to which the stones were put in the building would not be explicable by those causes. Yet as Charles Singer has pointed out, when a man builds a house, there is the intervention of a definite purpose, directed towards a fixed end and governed by a clearly conceived idea. 'The builder in the proper sense of the word *selects*. But the acts of selection—mental events in the builder's mind—have no relation to the "causes" which produced the stones. They cannot therefore be compared with the action of Natural Selection.' Architectural theorists who are guilty of similarly inexact analogies between building and botany may find consolation in the thought that a classic precedent was furnished by the Master himself.

If in fact we look at those phenomena which scientists consider as biological, we shall see that the number of exact parallels which can be drawn is slight. Vicq d'Azyr classified organic functions into nine categories: digestion, nutrition, circulation, respiration, secretion, ossification, generation, irritability and sensibility, and of these, only circulation would seem to have any analogy with the function of buildings. Similarly, if we examine morphological systems of classification, whether it be the Linnaean system (based on one selected feature), Cuvier's system (based on total structure related to inner parts), or the system of von Baer (based on what he called the 'spatial relationship' of organic elements, i.e. radial, longitudinal, massive and vertebrate), there seems little even remotely suggestive of buildings and the way they are designed. It would seem as if the analogy must always be general and poetic, and in fact the features held in common seem limited to four: the relationship of organisms to their environment, the correlation between organs, the relationship of form to function, and the principle of vitality itself.

The most comprehensible analogy concerns the influence of environment on design, an idea which undoubtedly derived its main stimulus from Darwin, although it first emerged as a biological theory in the work of Alexander von Humboldt. Von Humboldt opposed the academic methods of Linnaeus, and suggested that plants should be classified according to the climates in which they were found, rather than according to inherent characters determinable in a museum. Being of a romantic and aesthetic disposition, he sought a system of classification through the impression made by landscapes when simply looked at by the ordinary observer. Contending that each latitude possesses its own characteristic natural physiognomy, he eventually differentiated between certain vegetable types according to the impression given of their form as a whole. He was very interested in architecture and described in detail the pre-Columbian buildings he found in Central America. He nowhere seems to have suggested, however, that the design of buildings had much relationship with topography and vegetation, although he thought that pyramids were best suited to mountainous ground. Only in the sphere of engineering did he exert any influence on construction, in that his description of Peruvian suspension bridges is known to have suggested modern experiments in this field.

Darwin naturally took von Humboldt's doctrine considerably further by contending that Nature had *selected* those forms which were most suitable for the environments in which they were situated, but he offered no suggestion as to how Nature created such forms in the first place. He had in fact no training and probably little interest in pure morphology, and in so far as his work affected morphological studies, it was to cause the public to regard organisms *historically*. In his first draft of the *Origin of Species*, written in 1842, he remarked that 'we must look at every complicated mechanism and instinct as the summary of a long history of useful contrivances much like a work of art'. Whether or not he actually regarded the history of architecture as analogous with natural selection, I do not know. But there can be little doubt that so far as his biological theory of the relationship of form to environment is concerned, the relevance of Darwinism to architecture has tended to decrease. Improvements in air-conditioning equipment are making architectural form increasingly independent of climatic considerations. Plate-glass walls are as fashionable in Canada as they are in more temperate climates, whilst traditional Japanese frame construction is more frequently emulated outside than inside Japan. Only in districts where distinctive local materials can be used for domestic architecture is there any likelihood of regional characteristics influencing form, and even in newly developed areas where the example has been set, such as Arizona, there seems little evidence of a desire to carry the movement very far.

As regards the 'correlation between organs' (which one might perhaps compare with the relationship between the parts of a building), the fact was first enunciated as a biological principle by Vicq d'Azyr, who pointed out that a certain shape of tooth presupposes a certain type of structure in the extremities and the digestive canal, because the animal's bodily parts are adapted to its way of living. This idea was taken even further by Cuvier, who, from small fossil fragments, showed how one could reconstruct extinct animals by a sequence of deductions based on the interdependence of each organic part. Yet in so far as this discovery relates to architectural theory, it suggests merely a curious parallel with the Renaissance theory of modular proportions, whereby, as the Humanists had observed, the proportions of the human body are so standardized that if one were to find the finger of an antique statue, it would be possible, theoretically, to re-construct the whole (a fact enthusiastically seized upon by the great forgers of the age).

In general, the only major biological fact which seems directly analogous to modern architecture concerns the relationship of form to function; but as we have seen, the theory that form follows function was hotly contested by those who believed that function follows form. It is curious to note that this dilemma was specifically pointed out by Herbert Spencer, from whose writing (so Frank Lloyd Wright tells us) Louis Sullivan derived many, if not all, his biological ideas. However, since nobody has ever denied the obvious fact that form and function are in some way related, it is worth considering how this relationship does fit in with a theory of architectural design.

In case it should be objected that such a topic is less a part of the 'Organic' theory than of the 'Functional' theory, it is opportune to suggest that whereas in the functional analogy, the relationship between form and function is considered as necessary to *beauty*, in the biological analogy, it is considered as necessary to *life*. Historians are generally agreed that credit for this new interpretation must be given, as far as architectural theory is concerned, to Louis Sullivan, although it may be noted that he never expressed it or applied it until after he had met Wright. It had been foreshadowed as early as 1855 by Baudelaire, who, perhaps with von Humboldt in mind, suggested that the best critics were those who had travelled alone through forests and prairies, contemplating, dissecting and writing; 'they know', he wrote, 'the admirable, inevitable relationship between form and function'. Similarly Viollet-le-Duc, like Ruskin before him, drew attention to the way mediaeval sculptors had studied the morphology of vegetation, and how they understood that the contours of plants 'always express a function, or submit themselves to the necessities of the organisms'. He did not, however, draw any major philosophical conclusions from this observation, except to say that the masons 'sought to bring out in the structures of their buildings those qualities they found in vegetation'. The French Rationalists were in fact more interested in the idea that form follows structure (which they found quite intelligible without the use of elaborate analogies), so that there can be little doubt that it was Sullivan who first made biological analogies the foundation of a total architectural creed.

Despite his period of study in France, Sullivan seems to have derived little inspiration from Viollet-le-Duc's theories, since his main interest was in composition rather than in construction (which he left to Adler). Yet following the anti-academic fashion of his age, he objected to the term 'composition', although in the circumstances it is difficult to see why. Since 'decomposition' is the chief characteristic of organisms which are dead, it might reasonably be inferred that 'composition' is the chief characteristic of organisms which are living. But, like so many theorists who have found the biological analogy stimulating, he never really pursued it very deeply, and made little distinction as to whether it referred to the object created or the process of design. Whilst some of his writings suggest a Lamarckian interpretation of evolution (as when he wrote that 'it was not simply a matter of form expressing function; the vital idea was that the function *created* or organized its form'), most of them suggest the Coleridgean analogy between biology and poetic vision. It is perhaps significant that his first enunciation of an architectural doctrine—the address on *Inspiration* given to the Western Association of Architects' Convention—was in the form of a long poem intelligible only to three other people in the room.

In the present century the biological analogy has been associated primarily with Frank Lloyd Wright, into whose young hands Sullivan enthusiastically transmitted his copy of Spencer's biological works. What Wright has meant by 'Organic Architecture' has not always been clear; Sigfried Giedion even goes so far as to contend (with good justification) that he was unable to explain the term himself. The difficulty is that for Wright it meant so much: crystalline plan forms, the possibility of growth by asymmetrical addition, the relationship of composition to site and client, the use of local materials, the individuality of every created thing, the need for every artist to endow his work with the integrity of his innermost being, and so on. But primarily it meant for him a *living* architecture; an architecture in which useless forms were sloughed off as part of the process of a nation's growth, and in which every composition, every element and every detail was deliberately shaped for the job it had to perform. With this interpretation no one can take exception, and perhaps the safest thing to say of the Biological Analogy is that it is simply a more poetic expression of Perret's ideal of *L'Architecture Vivante*.

It is now a century since the *Revue Générale de l'Architecture* launched the slogan 'Organic Architecture' in this sense, although at the time it proved premature. 'We have named it Organic', wrote the editor in 1863, 'because it is, in relationship to the Historic and Eclectic Schools, what the organized life of animals and vegetables is in relationship to the unorganized existence of the rocks which form the substratum of the world'. Since then, many developments have occurred in biological theory, and many in architectural practice. Occasionally, some of the former can be paralleled with some of the latter. Claude Bernard's discoveries concerning the way the body adapts itself to changing conditions (or vaso-motor mechanism) suggest clear parallels with the flexibility of modern planning. Similarly Milne-Edwards' law of economy, which states that nature does not always create a new organ for a new function, but often adapts undifferentiated parts to special functions, or even converts to other uses organs already specialized, suggests many interesting parallels in this present age of standardized forms. Most important of all, Wilhelm Roux's discovery that the blood-vascular system is largely determined by direct adaptation to functional requirements demonstrates that form does occasionally follow function after all. But in general, detailed analogies are as dangerous now as when the slogan was first formulated, and apart from holding that architecture must be a living art, we cannot go much deeper into the mystery of life than when the *Origin of Species* was first given to an astonished and excited world. Nature has given us examples of how to reject forms only appropriate to earlier cultures; but the study of plants and animals can do little to help us evolve forms appropriate to conditions today.

Within the last few years, however, one surprising change has occurred in the philosophy of architecture which provides a curiously apposite termination to a study of the biological analogy. The nineteenth century's naïve faith in evolutionary progress is now being seriously challenged, and a suspicion has arisen that Buffon's approach may not have been entirely wrong. This does not of course mean that optimism has given place to pessimism, but simply that we no longer accept, like the followers of Darwin, the idea that every change must be for the best. According to Geoffrey Scott, the great harm done by the biological analogy was that it substituted the criteria of evolution for the criteria of aesthetic judgement, whereby architectural historians were no longer concerned with whether a building was good or bad, but simply how it was to be classified chronologically. Recently however it has become clear, in both Europe and America, that the leading architectural periodicals are no longer content merely to divide all new buildings into the two categories: 'evolutionary' and 'vestigial', and leave it at that; they are subjecting contemporary architecture to systematic criticism in order to determine how improvements can best be brought about.

This of course is the very opposite of natural selection, but it has become necessary because we can no longer afford to regard every new 'contemporary' building as automatically an advance on the rest. In the early years of the International Style, there was much to be said for accepting every manifestation of the new spirit uncritically, since premature disparagement might have stunted its early growth. Today, when the functional forms evolved by the leading modern architects are so widely accepted, there is obvious danger of their misuse, and nothing can better serve the advancement of architecture than that examples of this should be publicly singled out.

An even more cogent reason for the new critical attitude is that, just as biologists have become very conscious of 'biotic' environment (i.e. the influence of free organisms on each other), so we are becoming much more aware that 'environment' does not only comprise natural scenery, but also the accumulated legacy of the buildings in our towns. Not long ago it could automatically be assumed by an *avant-garde* architect that any building bordering a city site must be 'beaux-arts', and hence unworthy to be taken into consideration. At best he regarded them as a 'foil', by which he meant that whatever shape his own building might take, it would produce a striking contrast with all the buildings nearby. Neither view has much justification today. The urban scene, especially in America, is in many districts predominantly 'contemporary', so that modern architecture has no longer an excuse for ignoring its neighbours. On the other hand, with the general acceptance of Functionalism, there is no need to perpetuate the early revolutionaries' aggressive disdain for the so-called 'beaux-arts' styles. Such buildings, when juxtaposed against our own, bear gratifying testimony to the victory of the fittest, but they also carry the awful warning that, in architecture, it is not necessarily only the Fittest which Survive.

15

The Mechanical Analogy

O f the various analogies used in the last century to clarify the principles of a new architecture, probably the only one to equal in importance the biological analogy has been the analogy between buildings and machines. Historically, it may even be said to take precedence, especially if we extend its meaning to include the more general thesis that functional efficiency is a kind of beauty; for, as Edward de Zurko has shown in his *Origins of Functionalist Theory*, the idea of relating beauty to the simpler aspects of mechanical utility goes back to remote antiquity, whilst the idea of using machines as functional analogies was itself applied to physics, politics and economics long before it was applied to architecture.

We have already seen how, at the beginning of the nineteenth century, Henri Milne-Edwards tried to grasp the way organic forms developed by studying them as if they were machines. But in the middle of the eighteenth century, the affinities between organisms and machines were considered more notable for their disparities than for their similarities. Hogarth, for example, in his *Analysis of Beauty* (1753) remarked that the beauty of a clock mechanism was as nothing compared with the beauty of the human body, and in criticizing Harrison's marine chronometer in this respect, he observed that 'if a machine for this purpose had been nature's work, the whole and every individual part would have had exquisite beauty of form without danger of destroying the exquisiteness of its motion, even as if ornament had been the sole aim'. It was not until the middle of the nineteenth century, when the demand for a new architecture became insistent, and when more grandiose types of machines had been invented, that the mechanical analogy was used in an attempt to solve problems of architectural theory. By the end of the century, only very special and esoteric groups, such as those which supported the theory of 'Art for Art's sake', dared publicly support the view that purely utilitarian objects were necessarily ugly.

Today, we are mainly familiar with the mechanical analogy as expressed by Le Corbusier in *Towards a New Architecture*; but his *exposé* has a long and distinguished ancestry, so it will probably be best to start with the man who perhaps originated the idea, namely Horatio Greenough. Greenough was a strange person to be an architectural theorist, since he was really a sculptor, and his fame rests mainly on the fact that he persuaded the United States Government to buy his partially nude statue of George Washington. The idea of exhibiting a nude statue of a contemporary statesman was doubtless less strange in the era of the Greek Revival than it would seem today. Canova had carved a statue of Napoleon in the nude, and Greenough expressedly stated that he had depicted Washington naked to the waist so that he would not be dated by clothes. Thus his obsession with the stylistic disadvantages of exterior coverings may explain his impatience with the artificiality of contemporary architectural ornament. It certainly explains why he admired the mechanical perfection of the American trotting wagon, and why he urged architects to study the uncomplicated outlines of ocean-going ships. 'I would fain beg any architect who allows fashion to invade the domain of principles to compare the American vehicles and ships with those of England, and he will see that the mechanics of the United States have already outstripped the artists', he wrote somewhat chauvinistically, in an undated article on 'Structure and Organization'. Similarly, in his essay entitled 'American Architecture' (1843), he wrote: 'could we carry into our civil architecture the responsibilities that weigh upon our shipbuilding, we should ere long have edifices as superior to the Parthenon as a modern battleship is superior to the galleys of the Argonauts. Instead of forcing the functions of every sort of building into one general form, and adopting an outward shape without reference to the inner distribution, let us begin from the heart and work outwards'.

Now it will be immediately perceived that this ostensibly plausible argument contains two sophisms. Firstly, it draws unwarranted conclusions from what Greenough calls the 'responsibilities that weigh upon ship-builders'; secondly, it implies that in ship-building, a good design 'begins from the heart and works outwards'. 'Could our blunders on terra firma be put to the same dread test that those of ship-builders are', he exclaimed, 'little would be now left to say on this subject'. But the very fact that there has been so much to say on the subject of architectural design demonstrates the fact that the laws of stability affecting buildings are far less stringent than those affecting ships, and thus the former allow far greater scope for arbitrary variations. Similarly, whether or not a building should be planned from the inside outwards, this is certainly not the sequence observed when designing a ship, for here the shape of the hull is of paramount importance, and the internal partitions are fitted in as best they may. If anything, therefore, the ship analogy points to exactly the opposite conclusions drawn from it by Greenough; not that this has stopped later theorists from trying to reconcile these various conflicting ideas in exactly the same way.

Greenough's writings may well have been known to James Fergusson, for he, like Greenough, refers to Revivalist architecture as 'the Monkey Styles'. But whether or not he absorbed Greenough's ideas, or deduced the mechanical analogy for himself, he certainly made the most of it, and elaborated in even greater detail upon the similarities between the ideals of mechanics and ship-builders, and the ideals which architects ought to possess. When discussing the system by which mediaeval architects had achieved a truly rational architecture, he remarked that it was the same system as that perseveringly followed by every industry and science in his own day. 'In our manufacture of steam-engines, in our cotton spinning and weaving machinery, in our agriculture, and, in short, in everything that is creditable to us, we have followed the same path', he exclaimed in his *Historical Inquiry* (1849). He also asked his readers to take, as an example, the history of ship-building, which he traced from the time of William the Conqueror to 'the last 120-gun ship launched from our dockyards'.

Yet here Fergusson introduced an additional sophism into the argument; this time the error of assuming that scientific evolution and artistic evolution follow the same laws. Fergusson himself was astute enough to perceive this dilemma, and honest enough to comment on it, though at first he only admitted it hesitantly, and simply confessed that other people might not find all ships to be objects of beauty, even though they were so to him. Nevertheless, he admitted that since most ships were designed for purely utilitarian purposes, they must be 'classed among the objects of useful art'. But, he continued, one only needed to formulate mentally the distinction between a cotton factory and a nobleman's palace, and then to compare the difference between a merchant ship and a pleasure yacht, to perceive that if a palace is entitled to be considered an object of fine art, then so must the yacht be for the same reason. By 1862, however (when he published the third volume of his *History of Architecture*), he felt bound to carry this sophistical argument to its inevitably inane conclusion. The comparison between ship-building and cathedral-building came to a halt, he said, because 'ship-building never became a purely fine art', whereas architecture did. The difference was thus, he thought, one of aim, for had architecture never progressed beyond the limits of house-building, it would, in his view, have been no nearer a fine art than merchant ship-building, since palaces would only have been magnificent dwelling places. Yet men of all ages had sought to erect houses more dignified and stately than those designed for their personal use, and it was only when architects threw aside all shadows of utilitarianism, and launched boldly forth in search of the beautiful and the sublime, that building became a truly fine art. 'If', he therefore concluded, in one of the finest passages in his book, 'we could imagine any nation ever to construct ships of God, or to worship on the bosom of the ocean, ships might easily be made such objects of beauty that the cathedral could hardly compete with them'. But this was clearly the complete negation of the analogy he had urged in his *Historical Inquiry*, and thus the validity of the argument was completely overthrown.

Nevertheless, Fergusson's speculations made one very useful contribution to the study of the problem. They drew attention to the influences resulting from anonymous collaboration in the progressive accumulation of technical knowledge. The importance of collaboration has been greatly insisted upon by Walter Gropius with reference to the philosophy of the Bauhaus, so that it will need no recommendation here. But credit should be given to Fergusson for having been one of the first to see that this was the clue to the mechanical improvements of his age. In the development of a modern ship, he wrote, 'millions of brains of all calibres' had been involved, so that nobody either knew or cared who did it, any more than they knew or should care who built the great mediaeval cathedrals. This same conclusion (though without the same mechanistic reasoning) was reached by Viollet-le-Duc in the preface to his *Dictionnaire*. 'The life of a man is not long enough to allow any architect to absorb the totality of a task which is both intellectual and material', he wrote; 'an architect can only form part of a whole; he begins what others will finish, or finishes what others have begun, but he cannot work in isolation, for his work is not his own personal achievement, like a painting or a poem'.

Since Viollet-le-Duc was the leading nineteenth century apostle of Gothic Rationalism, he relied less on analogies than on common-sense arguments derived from the study of the structures of the past. But in so far as he used analogies, he favoured machines, especially ships and locomotives. In this he may well have been influenced by Fergusson or by his own patron, Prosper Merimée, who complained in newspaper articles that architects were, so to speak, 'designing steam-boats on the models of antique galleys'. Moreover, the analogy between Gothic architecture and machinery had long been quite common, for as early as 1804, Friedrich von Schlegel had compared Strasbourg cathedral with the mechanism of a watch. It is not surprising, therefore, that when Viollet-le-Duc came to expound his own theories in his lecture course (*Entretiens sur l'Architecture*, 1863), and argued that contemporary public buildings lacked style because architects were trying to ally the forms left by tradition with needs which were no longer in harmony with those traditions, he should have referred specifically to machines and ships. 'Naval architects and mechanical engineers do not, when they make a ship or a locomotive, seek to recall the forms of a sailing ship of Louis XIV's time or those of a stage coach', he wrote; 'they obey blindly the new principles given to them, and produce works which possess their own character and their own style, in the sense that everyone can see that they indicate a destination which is quite precise'. Hence, he explained, a locomotive had a physiognomy which made it a distinct created thing, in that its exterior form was the expression of its potentialities.

The sound common sense of these remarks is evident enough; yet the reference to a 'precise destination', and the notion of the 'expression of potentialities' betrays the presence of yet more fallacious comparisons between architecture and machines. Firstly, it is quite clear that one of the principal differences between machines and buildings is that buildings do not have the same sort of precise destination as machines; for an automobile is an object with a single function: to travel. The more precise a machine's destination, the more beautiful it is, as can easily be seen by comparing a machine which has some single overriding purpose (like a supersonic projectile) with a machine which manipulates objects in a sequence of complex operations (like a packaging machine). Now this argument cannot hold with respect to architecture. The notion that every building *should* have a precise destination is of course very old, for even in the mid-eighteenth century, J. F. Blondel was troubled by the fact that the designs submitted for the completion of the Louvre were so different in character, and argued that if every architect had designed his submission rationally, there would have been only very slight disparities between them. Today, the disparities in the character of designs submitted for the same competition are even greater, and one would have to be very naïve to believe that the architectural expression of function will ever be reduced unequivocally to forms generally accepted as inevitable by the entire architectural profession.

Viollet-le-Duc's other fallacy was to some extent shared by Greenough, since the latter defined beauty as 'the promise of function'. The promise or potentiality of function is certainly a distinctive and fundamental characteristic of living organisms or of machines when they are at rest, for the simple reason that living organisms and machines are designed either to move or to have moving parts. What, however, is the quality of a building which corresponds to the beauty of potential movement? How does one distinguish between the beauty of a machine's movement and the beauty of the machine itself?

Viollet-le-Duc admitted that many people regarded locomotives as ugly, even though he himself found something to be admired in their 'brutal energy'. But whether we regard machines as beautiful, or as possessing other aesthetic qualities, it will be apparent that the mechanical analogy shares with the biological analogy the same basic disadvantage when applied to architectural theory, in that form and movement are inseparably combined. Just as some biologists argue that no living body can be separated into separate entities, even for puposes of study (since they are no longer organisms once they are dissected); just as it can be argued that the theoretical distinction between anatomy and physiology is false, since a heart can only be a heart that beats; so it can be argued that a machine is essentially the physical embodiment of a process which occurs in time. Once the machine stops moving it has no meaning except as *potentially* something that moves, and once it is incapable of movement it is either a bad machine or one that has broken down. Viollet-le-Duc perceived this, but he did not, like Auguste Perret, perceive that this was a clue to the whole difference between character and style. 'A locomotive', remarked Perret, 'merely has character; the Parthenon has both character and style. In a few years, the most beautiful locomotive of today will be merely a mass of scrap metal; the Parthenon will sing for ever'. This argument does not take into account the motives of those who treasure old automobiles; yet even Fergusson had remarked in his *Historical Inquiry* that 'if fifty years hence one of our most perfect locomotives exists, it can only be in a museum of mechanical curiosities to be stared at and laughed at'. He failed to draw the obvious conclusion from this observation, even though he wrote an entire history of architecture intended to illustrate the enduring qualities of the buildings of the past.

The next ardent supporter of the mechanical analogy to follow in this line of succession was Anatole de Baudot, Viollet-le-Duc's enthusiastic disciple. Like Viollet-le-Duc, de Baudot's professional career was mainly concerned with the repair of historical monuments, but he also publicly speculated, by means of lectures and magazine articles, on the nature of contemporary architecture, and asserted, like Viollet-le-Duc, that modern society did not need a new style so much as a style which, in the mediaeval tradition, could take advantage of the technical improvements of the age. 'Do we not have one of the most useful and interesting examples in the new expressions of terrestrial and marine vehicles?' he asked sententiously in his lecture course entitled *Architecture, Past and Present*, published posthumously in 1916. 'Have these been given the forms of carriages or ships of the time of Louis XIV? Not at all; the inter-relationships and appearances were deduced from scientific and industrial data. Why therefore are fixed shelters, that is to say, buildings, not designed in a similar way?' Once again, the argument is good as far as it goes, but if taken any further results in all sorts of inconsistencies. For example, admittedly the railway carriages of de Baudot's day were different from the carriages used in the reign of Louis XIV. But then the wheeled carriages of the reign of Louis XIV were also vastly different from the chariots used by the Romans, whereas the architectural elements at Versailles and those of Hadrian's villa were basically the same. Moreover, the similarities between the two palaces were not illogical, since both were built of the same materials and fulfilled similar physical and emotional requirements. The mechanical analogy was in fact only valid when new materials or new functions were involved, and it is to de Baudot's credit that he was the first architect to design a church in reinforced concrete: his famous church of St. Jean-de-Montmartre, Paris.

It will by now be clear, therefore, why the publication of Le Corbusier's *l'Esprit Nouveau* articles in book form was greeted at the time as simply a rehash of de Baudot's well-worn ideas. There were of course obvious differences in approach; for example, Le Corbusier did not like Gothic architecture, since for him a mediaeval cathedral, not being fundamentally based on spheres, cones and cylinders, was obviously 'not very beautiful'. Hence, unlike de Baudot, he based his theory of design on the monumental prototypes of ancient Greece and Rome. The only novelty of his analogical approach seemed to be his inclusion of aeroplanes and automobiles in addition to ships, and it is not therefore surprising that in a review published in the February 1924 issue of *l'Architecte*, Pol Abraham observed caustically that 'the admirable preface which de Baudot wrote for his book *Architecture, Past and Present* contains explicitly, though undoubtedly in less extravagant language, the essence of Le Corbusier's articles published in *l'Esprit Nouveau*'.

Every student of modern architecture will be, or ought to be, familiar with the text of Le Corbusier's famous book, so there is no need to describe the relevant chapters in detail. They merit close analysis, since there can be little doubt that those who studied *Towards a New Architecture* when it was first published were primarily influenced by the numerous photographs of ships, aeroplanes and automobiles, and that it was this book which popularized the mechanical analogy in the English-speaking world. Many readers concluded that the lesson they were being asked to learn was simply the theory that functional forms are beautiful. But this is not in fact the message of the text. The text specifically states that 'when a thing responds to a need it is not beautiful', and that though a chair is a machine for sitting in (just as a house is a machine for living in) a chair is in no way a work of art; for true art consists only of 'pure art—a concentrated thing free from all utilitarian motives'; that is to say, painting, literature and music. Nevertheless, it is made clear that ships, aeroplanes and automobiles have certain lessons for the architect, since in a scientific age the perfection and harmony seen in the Parthenon can only correspond with 'sensations of a mechanical kind'. Thus the Greek temple is related by its standardization to the large machines with which we are so familiar, and the lesson of the machine is thus reduced to three generalizations: firstly, that a well-stated problem naturally finds its solution; secondly, that since all men have the same biological organization, they all have the same basic needs; and thirdly, that architecture, like machinery, should be a product of competitive selection applied to standards which, in turn, should be determined by logical analysis and experimentation.

How then does Le Corbusier solve the recurrent dilemma of reconciling the notion of architecture as a science with the notion of architecture as an art? There is some confusion in his pronouncements on this topic, for in one place he writes that architecture can be found in the telephone as well as in the Parthenon, and that 'our engineers produce architecture, for they employ a mathematical calculation which derives from natural law', whereas elsewhere (and this is the essence of his argument), he asserts that the engineer's aesthetic and the architect's aesthetic are two things that are basically distinct. Whereas the engineer, he writes, inspired by the laws of economy, achieves only harmony, the architect, by his arrangement of forms, realizes an order which is a pure creation of the spirit; that is to say, the latter alone produces true beauty. In the Parthenon, 'the engineer is effaced and the sculptor comes to life', and in several other passages he emphasizes the essentially sculptural quality of the architect's art.

Nevertheless, despite such statements, Le Corbusier's name is frequently identified with 'Functionalism', and J. E. Barton, in *Purpose and Admiration* (1932), asserted that the vogue for the word 'Functionalism' was largely inspired by Le Corbusier's writings and work. The reason for this confusion is probably to be found, not in the actual text of Le Corbusier's book, but in the preface provided by Frederick Etchells for his translation of the English edition. In modern mechanical engineering, Etchells wrote, forms were developed mainly in accordance with function; yet although the designer or inventor probably did not concern himself directly with what the final appearance would be, he had a natural sub-conscious instinct for order, and thus it was 'difficult for him to avoid plastically good results'. Hence for Etchells, the originality of Le Corbusier's book is that it makes the reader see the Parthenon or St. Peter's, Rome, as a man might look at an automobile, whereby 'these buildings, studied in their functional and plastic aspects, emerge in a new guise'.

Few readers today would draw such a conclusion from *Towards a New Archi-tecture*, having in the meantime witnessed the creation of Notre-Dame du Haut at Ronchamp; but there is no doubt that Le Corbusier's slogan: 'a house is a machine for living in' exercised a powerful influence on the twentieth century's natural desire to adopt mechanical analogies, for, as P. W. Bridgeman remarked in *The Logic of Modern Physics*: 'many will discover in themselves a longing for mechanical explanation which has all the tenacity of original sin'.

There is no need to list further the pitfalls of the mechanical analogy, or to emphasize the dangers of comparing objects which are motionless with objects whose essential purpose is to move. But it may be appropriate to conclude by mentioning one of the more disastrous consequences of this analogy, since its gravity seems to be increasing; namely, the fact that buildings so often tend to be treated as isolated objects, set arbitrarily in the landscape or city, rather than as part of the environment in which they are placed. One great advantage of the biological analogy was that it laid particular emphasis on the importance of environment, since clearly all living organisms depend on environments for their existence, and constitute in themselves environments which influence other organisms nearby. But the mechanical analogy unwittingly lent support to exactly the opposite conclusions. Ships, aeroplanes and automobiles are not designed for precise localities, nor are they designed with a view to the specific spatial relation-ships between one another; and it is this which has undoubtedly increased the tendency to design every building as if it were an isolated object in space. Moreover, we are now only too familiar with the way in which industrial designers envelop mechanisms, in arbitrary enclosures, the resultant appearance being paradoxically the very opposite of what the nineteenth century theorists visualized when they drew attention to the functional appearance of modern machines. It is for these reasons that the mechanical analogy never provided a coherent solution to the problem of creating a new and rational vocabulary of standardized machine-made architectural forms which would harmonize with their surroundings, and with each other, as well as with the modern age.

16

The Gastronomic Analogy

In a lecture on 'The Principles of Design in Architecture', given on December 9th, 1862, to the cadets of the School of Military Engineering at Chatham, James Fergusson explained to his astonished audience that the process by which a hut to shelter an image is refined into a temple, or a meeting house into a cathedral, is the same as that which refines a boiled neck of mutton into *côtelettes à l' Impériale* or a grilled fowl into *poulet à la Marengo*. 'So essentially is this the case', he continued, 'that if you wish to acquire a knowledge of the true principles of design in architecture you will do better to study the works of Soyer or Mrs. Glass than any or all the writers on architecture from Vitruvius to Pugin.'

No other architectural theorist, either before or since, seems to have used this analogy; a very curious fact when one considers the general cultural significance attached to the word 'taste'. 'Taste', as early dictionaries make clear, meant originally only 'the sensation excited in certain organs of the mouth', and its metaphorical adoption in the seventeenth and eighteenth centuries as the standard term for what we now call 'aesthetics' implies a clear recognition of the importance of this faculty as a key to understanding the nature of human discernment. As Addison pointed out in *The Spectator* of June 19th, 1711, 'we may be sure this metaphor would not have been so general in all tongues, had there not been a very great conformity between mental taste and that sensitive taste which gives us a relish of every different flavour that affects the palate'. Yet few of the various treatises on aesthetics published in the second half of the century even discuss this parallel, and the most exhaustive of them, namely the *Essay on Taste* published by Archibald Alison in 1790, does not mention food and drink at all.

One reason for this curious omission (apart from another, more important reason, which will be discussed later) may be that gastronomy was then in its infancy. Until the end of Louis XIV's reign, eating habits were extremely coarse, and it was not until the middle of the eighteenth century that modern refinements in cooking were widely adopted. The word 'gastronomy' itself was not introduced into the French language until about 1800, and we are told by Brillat-Savarin, the first modern writer on the subject, that even in 1825 it was still sufficiently novel to bring 'a smile of hilarity to all countenances'. The general appreciation of fine cooking was due mainly to the establishment of restaurants, the first of which was founded in Paris in 1770, and it was not until the Napoleonic era that these had multiplied sufficiently to give French cooking its universal and popular prestige. But it is still difficult to explain why the analogy between architecture and fine cooking should have been so persistently neglected during the last century, considering the urge experienced by so many architectural theorists to justify their ideas analogically with reference to other sciences and creative arts.

There is no doubt that if one wishes to demonstrate the distinction between architecture and plain, ordinary, straightforward building (and this is clearly what Fergusson was trying to do), the distinction between gastronomy and plain, ordinary, straightforward cooking possesses many close similarities not displayed by music, literature, biology, mechanical engineering, or any of the other arts or sciences with which architecture has so often been compared. Firstly, it is concerned, as Brillat-Savarin observed, with the conservation of mankind, and is thus, unlike the other arts, a necessity rather than a luxury. Secondly, unlike all those analogies just listed, it concerns something which is both a science and an art. Scientifically, gastronomy demands the combination of a number of prepared materials of known strength, arranged according to an ideal sequence or plan, the efficacy of which can be analysed and tested. Artistically, it goes far beyond the dictates of scientific analysis, for gastronomy, like architecture, requires intuition, imagination, enthusiasm, and an immense amount of organizational skill. Gastronomy is also more expensive than plain, honest, straightforward cooking, since it usually involves lengthier preparation and richer ingredients. It seems reasonable to suppose that there may also be other, more subtle, similarities between gastronomy and architecture, and that these may help us to visualize what the essential virtues of architecture ought to be.

Perhaps the most instructive way to seek out these similarities is to compare gastronomy and modern architecture in the age in which they both originated, namely the mid-eighteenth century, and then compare them as they are today. This first era, according to John Steegman, can only be fittingly described as the era of the Rule of Taste. This title is most appropriate, he says, because it implies a régime in which taste—the only word expressing both an immutable quality of discernment, criticism and perception, and an active sensitivity to temporary fashions—is paramount, and a time when fashions in taste are governed by universally acknowledged rules. These rules were not in fact very easy to determine, but there is no doubt that the leading architectural theorists of the period were constantly trying to formulate them, and that they did this by studying not only the buildings of antiquity, but the best buildings of their own day. The first regular meeting of the French Academy of Architecture began its discussion in 1672 with the question: 'What is good taste?', and although the problem was never satisfactorily resolved, it was generally agreed that 'the true rule for recognizing things which display good taste is to consider what has always been most pleasing to intelligent persons, whose merits are known by their works or their writings'. In other words, the supreme rule of the Classical artist was that his work should please.

This desire to please was also, and still is, the principal aim of a good chef, but it is doubtful whether it is the aim of all the leading painters, sculptors and architects today. For whereas a good chef is concerned only with the whims of his clientele and the appreciation which his artistry will receive, artists like Henry Moore boast their refusal to fulfil commissions requested by connoisseurs they respect. A good chef does not, after competitions, write abusively of experts who prefer some other artist's work. He does not feel that he is prostituting his art by creating something which resembles a work created two centuries before. If ever he says to a client: 'take it or leave it' (and there are ways of saying this in French with considerable force), it is only when he realizes that his client has no standards of taste, not simply because the person's tastes differ from his own. On the contrary, it is in the vicarious adaptation of his own tastes to each different customer's appetite that his supreme artistry resides; hence his art is always essentially human, because it keeps in the closest contact with the subtly varying moods of mankind.

Today, taste is no longer synonymous with aesthetics, because the modern theoretical approach to art takes no account of the public at all. The eighteenth century philosophers, though fully aware of the distinction between what they called 'active taste' and 'passive taste', were essentially concerned with the latter, i.e. with art from the point of view of an observer's reactions. Today, however, as a result of the influence of Benedetto Croce, aesthetic theories are usually only concerned with the act of artistic creativity itself. Art is considered to be essentially a form of expression, and it is now irrelevant to enquire whether or not it gives pleasure, since this is not its aim. It is as if an omelette were judged simply by the genuineness of the chef's passionate urge to go around breaking eggs.

The architectural theorists of the mid-eighteenth century tried to establish Classical recipes for good architecture in much the same way as the chefs of that period were trying to establish Classical recipes for *haute cuisine*, and the criterion of both was that the results should be widely enjoyed. Not just enjoyed by other architects and other chefs, or by the editors of the *Almanach des Gourmets* and *l'Architecture Française*, but by all persons of cultivated taste. Now this very word 'cultivated' implies that taste can not only be trained, but should be trained according to certain universally accepted standards. If those who teach the arts do not believe in such standards, or if they claim that they are still searching for such standards, it is clear that whatever the merits of their instruction, they are concerned essentially with fashion, not with taste.

The standards of gastronomy have remained unchanged for two centuries and are uncontested. The standards of architecture might also be uncontested if romantic influences had not, for two centuries, vitiated its theoretical basis, and spread the germs of its debilitating criteria like phylloxera throughout the Western world. It is no coincidence that Anglo-Saxon cooking is proverbially bad, for bad food and bad architecture both derive from the same philosophical disease.

This disease is, quite simply, Romanticism, or the refusal to accept the fact that, in the highest art, sensation must be subordinate to reason. For two centuries, Western art has been divisible into two antagonistic categories, which may be described either as romantic versus classical, or emotional versus rational. Now the essential nature of the revolution which took place in French cooking in the mid-eighteenth century was that the coarse and purely sensual methods of Roman, Mediaeval and Renaissance eating were *rationalized*. 'Gastronomy', explained Brillat-Savarin, the father of the new art, 'is the rationalized knowledge of everything which relates to man in so far as he nourishes himself'. 'Only intelligent men', he continued, 'honour fine food, because the others are not capable of an operation which consists in a sequence of appreciation and judgements'.

In conformity with Brillat-Savarin's philosophy, the leading French architectural theorist of the mid-eighteenth century, namely J. F. Blondel, similarly defined taste as 'the fruit of reasoning', and added, in words which almost paraphrase Diderot's definition of a true philosopher, that 'taste founded on reason accepts neither ready-made systems nor the authority of private opinions'. But in England at this time, the writers on Taste were already rejecting Classicism in favour of Romanticism, and it is doubtless mainly for this reason that Alison, in his *Essay on Taste*, did not mention food at all, since gastronomy clearly did not fit into the romantic aesthetic theory of 'the association of ideas'.

According to this theory, it will be remembered, man's awareness of the beauty of proportions is due entirely to a mental association of the relationship between form and function, and the appreciation of the beauty of buildings is due entirely to the stimulus given man's imagination by (in the case of Gothic Revival, Greek Revival or Classical designs) the evocation of the lost glories of the Middle Ages, Greece or Rome. Today, we also seem to consider that architectural beauty is based on the idea of Functionalism and romantic associations, although nowadays we romanticize the future, rather than the past. In both instances architectural appreciation, being subjective, is primarily governed by fashion, which to the Classical theorist was 'the tyrant of taste'. 'Taste, once acquired, should exclude every kind of fashion from architecture as so many obstacles to its progress', J. F. Blondel told his students two centuries ago, and went on to criticize young architects for neglecting sound principles in favour of new inventions, which must inevitably be superseded by other novelties in their turn.

Novel recipes for preparing food are, of course, frequently invented, but the old recipes still retain the same authority and prestige which they had before, because they are, literally, what Frank Lloyd Wright called 'in the nature of materials', and thus their aesthetic properties never become stale. The recipes in Viard's *Cuisinier*

Royal (a book already printed in ten separate editions by 1820) are all to be found in the latest edition of *L'Art Culinaire Français*, and the latter only supersedes the former because in the latter, there are three thousand recipes more. In gastronomy, there is no prestige attached to novelty *per se*, and nobody asks a chef if he can be guaranteed always to provide something 'contemporary'. Nor would any gastronome ever refuse *filets de volaille à la Bellevue* simply because they were invented by Madame de Pompadour, or angrily ask why he was not getting the latest recipe from the *Ladies' Home Journal* instead. In cooking, as in any art which really flourishes, the only values recognized are those concerned with degrees of excellence, and the decline in architecture occurred when architects forgot this, and started worrying about whether they were being 'contemporary' or 'reactionary', instead of whether their work was good or bad.

There are several factors which encourage this attitude, but there is one which is particularly obvious, namely the fact that whereas the eighteenth century recognized the rarity of a creative artist, the twentieth century, convinced of the operation of some universal law which equates supply and demand, and deluded by a combined faith in the virtues of a college education, and an equally solid faith (fostered by exhibitions of Action Painting and juvenile art) in the virtues of no artistic education at all, is convinced that everyone is potentially some kind of an artistic genius, and that anyone can become a creative architect once he can use a set-square and pass technical examinations. Yet it must be obvious that in architecture, as also in gastronomy, drama, and music, there are two kinds of artist; those rare spirits who can create original compositions, and those, less gifted, whose vocation is to adapt, interpret or assist.

Creative genius is in fact extremely rare in all the arts, but it is demonstrably rare in gastronomy, drama and music because it is the general public, rather than a few *avant-garde* connoisseurs or magazine editors, which decides whether the artist's originality is worth anything or not. Any contemporary musician can get his compositions broadcast, but with rare exceptions, the only public auditorium in which he has a chance of hearing his work twice is, according to the late Sir Thomas Beecham, the Albert Hall in London (the echo of which has long been notorious). Theatre-goers and music-lovers, as well as gourmets, know from hard experience that even the most favourable conjunction of circumstances rarely produces more than half-a-dozen original geniuses in each generation, however generously they may be subsidized by the Ford Foundation or the Fulbright Fund. Most artists are condemned by Fate, whatever their ambitions, to be executants who adapt and re-interpret (with greater or lesser sensitivity and appropriateness) the basic ideas created by someone else; yet all young architects regard themselves as creative artists, because our whole system of architectural education is specifically organized to give them this idea.

In English, the word 'chef' is synonymous with 'cook', but this title, like that of 'architect', should belong by right to those who have not only fully mastered every known aspect of their art, but were endowed at birth with the divine gift of the Muse. 'On devient cuisinier, mais on naît rôtisseur', wrote Brillat-Savarin, in Aphorism No. XV. 'On devient ingénieur, mais on naît architecte', wrote Auguste Perret a century later, and listed it as Aphorism No. I.

17

The Linguistic Analogy

The analogy between architecture and language has been less popular in recent years than it was from the middle of the eighteenth century to the middle of the nineteenth century, probably because it lacks the scientific glamour possessed by analogies with living organisms and machines. Yet in view of the importance now given to the linguistic analogy in the interpretation of the other Fine Arts, this neglect must necessarily occasion some surprise. For ever since Benedetto Croce rehabilitated the philosophy of the mid-eighteenth century historian Giambattista Vico by asserting that all art is a type of language, it has been customary for writers on aesthetics, such as R. G. Collingwood, to regard all arts as essentially something to do with 'expression'. Hence art has come to be regarded as a kind of eloquence, whereby its virtue is not in the form produced so much as in the emotion which produces it; not in the object created but in the intensity and sincerity by which expression is achieved.

An attempt was recently made, in a book entitled *Art and the Nature of Architecture*, by Bruce Allsopp, to interpret Collingwood's theory of aesthetics in terms of architecture; but it seems fair to say that the very fact that Collingwood avoided all mention of architecture in his *Philosophy of Art* demonstrates that, for him, architecture could be related only with the greatest difficulty to the other arts when defined in such terms. It might even be claimed that Collingwood asserted negatively, by his omissions, that the theory of architecture is not compatible with the theory of painting, sculpture, ballet, and the other arts. Nevertheless, whether or not architecture is analagous to painting and sculpture, there are, quite apart from the theories of Benedetto Croce and his followers, certain aspects of literature which show a close parallel with architecture, whereby the linguistic analogy has proved a useful catalyst in the formulation of certain architectural ideas.

Language, after all, has one great advantage over the biological and mechanical analogies, in that neither of the latter tells us anything about human emotions or the way these emotions are experienced. They undoubtedly give architectural theorists many clues about the nature of structure and function; but they are useless when it comes to solving the aesthetic problems which constitute, and always have constituted, the main dilemma of the modern age. Language, on the other hand, unlike biology and mechanical engineering, but like architecture, is both functional *and* emotional. It has a basic functional purpose, which is to fulfil the needs of communication; but in fulfilling this need it can be made to attain an emotional power which raises language to the ranks of the Fine Arts.

Vague analogies between architecture and literature can be found in the seventeenth century, as for example in the preface to Perrault's edition of Vitruvius (1685), but the first serious attempt to relate the two ideas philosophically seems to be in Charles Batteux's *The Fine Arts reduced to a single Principle* (1747). Batteux does not devote much time to discussing architecture in his book; but his very reason for specifically excluding it from a theoretical study devoted to music, painting, sculpture and ballet is extremely pertinent to the present enquiry; for since the time of the Renaissance, Italian theorists had automatically listed architecture, painting and sculpture as the three sister 'arts of design'. According to Batteux, however, architecture only deserved an honorary place among the Fine Arts, for in his view the purpose of the Fine Arts was simply to give pleasure, whilst the purpose of architecture was more comparable to that of eloquence, in that it had to be useful as well as to please.

It is not surprising that the relationship between architecture and language should be particularly noted in France, since the architects there, following the mediaeval tradition whereby an architect was essentially a man versed in the craft of building, had never professed solidarity with the painters and sculptors. This was why, before the French Revolution, the Academy of Architecture was a quite distinct organization, and why it was only in the nineteenth century that architecture was merged into an Academy of Fine Arts.

In the eighteenth century, French uses of the linguistic analogy do not seem to have been numerous, but those recorded are sufficiently explicit to imply that it was generally congenial to the age. For example, Germain Boffrand, who in his *Book on Architecture* (1745) extracted a whole theory of architecture from Horace's *Ars Poetica*, remarked that 'the profiles of mouldings and the other parts which compose a building are to architecture what words are to speech'. Similarly, Quatremère de Quincy, in a prize essay he wrote on Egyptian architecture in 1785 for the Academy of Inscriptions, contended that the invention of architecture should be compared with the invention of language, in the sense that neither could be attributed to a single person, but both were the attributes of mankind. As far back as the 1750s, J. F. Blondel, who on several occasions compared architecture with literature in his lecture courses, specifically discussed the similarities between architecture and poetry, but his remarks will be more appropriately quoted when dealing with the various ways in which the analogy was applied.

In the first half of the nineteenth century, the analogy seems to have been especially popular. James Elmes, in his *Lectures in Architecture* (1821), remarked that there were two methods by which a race could imitate the architecture of another country; one true, the other false. 'The true mode is less an imitation than an adoption, and consists in receiving as an alphabet, in their entire shape, the system, the rules and the taste of a style of architecture'. Later, like Quatremère de Quincy (from whom he probably obtained the idea), he tried to show that there was a connecting link between the several countries that had given the same stylistic character to their architecture, and that this connection was 'not unlike the philological connection of languages with their roots and parent stock'. Inevitably, such arguments based on the new science of comparative philology were used by conscientious Revivalists who were seriously trying to create a new architecture on the foundations of the past. Thus William Burges, in a lecture given to the Architectural Association in 1867, announced that 'at the present time, we are seeking for an architectural language suited to our times, but we ought not to be disappointed that we do not get it in a single year, since almost every language can be traced back to a parent stock, and so with our new architecture'. Hence he recommended the study of thirteenth century French architecture as the surest means of creating a new British architecture in conformity with structural traditions and climatic needs.

The linguistic analogy became particularly popular with the rise of the architectural magazines. The first issue of *The Builder* (1843) contained a letter to the editor which remarked on the difficulties of creating a new style of architecture, and asserted that style in building appeared to have in its rise and progress a great similarity to language. The language of rude nations was (so the author insisted, despite, one would have thought, clear evidence to the contrary) plain, simple and unadorned, and it only acquired beauty, harmony and splendour with the advance of civilization. From this statement, he concluded that 'it would be as difficult to invent a new and complete style of architecture as to produce a new and independent language'. A new architecture, in other words, could only develop gradually with time.

Two years later, the editor of the *Revue Générale de l'Architecture* used a similar analogy to urge the contrary view. He considered that the civilization of his own day had a character which distinguished it clearly from those of preceding epochs, and that it was up to modern artists, using their right of free creativity, to seek the forms of a 'new architectonic language' suited to modern times, as compared with the 'architectonic alphabet' of the past. The use of the term 'architectonic alphabet' also occurs in another of his editorials, written immediately after the revolution of 1848, as a justification for artistic freedom. In 1853, he was again observing that 'a new style is a new language'—on this occasion to excuse the 'stuttering and mistakes' which any new architecture must, he thought, be guilty of. The last really eloquent use of the analogy by an architectural journalist is probably Montgomery Schuyler's essay on 'Modern Architecture', published in the

Architectural Record in 1894. The literature of every modern nation, he wrote, was an image of the mind and spirit of that nation; yet in contrast to this, the architecture of every modern nation was coming more and more to lose its distinctiveness, and to resemble the fashions of Paris, like modern dress. This had not always been so. Mediaeval architecture told us more of mediaeval life than all the other documents of that life, to such an extent that it was only from mediaeval monuments that modern men could succeed in penetrating the spirit of the Middle Ages. It thus seemed to him that if contemporary architects were to follow the analogy between architecture and literature, it might lead to a comprehension of the very different state of the two arts. It seemed obvious to him that modern literature was an exact reflection of modern civilization, for if a fault were found with a country's literature, no one suggested that it could be remedied by the introduction of different technical methods. If one particular literature were found to be pedantic, another frivolous and another dull, critics would without hesitation impute these defects to national traits. Thus the notion that any modern literature was not a complete expression of the national life would no more occur to anyone than the notion that any modern architecture *was* such an expression.

It should not be concluded from these quotations and references that all the leading theorists who mentioned the analogy were in favour of it. Léonce Reynaud, in the essay on 'style' which occurs in his *Treatise on Architecture* (1850) concluded that the differences were greater than the similarities. Architecture did not, he thought, permit the same clarity of expression as language; nor had it given rise to the same diversities which were to be found in vernacular speech, or in the changes resulting from the evolution of tongues during the past. Moreover, elementary tectonic forms 'which are to architecture what words are to speech', were not arbitrary, as in language, but derived from permanent, universal, scientific laws. Nevertheless, he described the style of each era as constituting 'a sort of distinct idiom; the words and laws of language', and compared the style of individual architects to that of writers 'who use the language of their own era to express their thoughts'. Similarly, he used the linguistic analogy as a justification for condemning Eclecticism, claiming that between all the parts of a single architectural style there is an intimate correlation comparable to that which exists between words of the same language.

James Fergusson also rejected the linguistic analogy at first. In his *Historical Inquiry*, he had divided the arts into three main categories: technic, aesthetic and phonetic, and he therefore dismissed the idea that architecture could have anything in common with the phonetic arts, since according to his definition of architecture, it was purely a combination of the technic (constructional) and aesthetic (ornamental). 'Architecture imitates nothing, illustrates nothing, tells no tale', he wrote; 'it barely manages to express an emotion of joy or sorrow with the same distinctness with which they can be expressed by the unphonetic brutes'. Admittedly, he added, a building might become phonetic by the addition of sculpture and painting; but it was important not to confuse the two modes of utterance, since the eloquence was in the last named arts, not in the technic.

Even those who favoured the linguistic analogy did not necessarily draw logical conclusions from it. The most striking example of this is Professor Donaldson's use of the analogy as an excuse for Indifferentism. Style in architecture, he announced, in a discourse at University College, London, in 1842, could be compared to languages in literature. There was no style, as there was no language, which had not its peculiar beauties, its individual fitness and power; there was not one that could be safely rejected. Each enshrined a principle that an architect could appropriately apply in some emergency. 'And as the traveller', he continued, 'who is master of several languages finds himself at home and at ease among the people with whose language he is familiar, so the architect who can command the majesty of the Classic styles, the sublimity of Gothic, the grace of the Revival or the brilliant fancies of Arabic is the more fitted for the emergencies of his difficult career'.

The paralogism inherent in this argument will be only too obvious. The correct conclusion to be drawn from the premises as stated by Donaldson is surely that just as a traveller to Arabia is better equipped for his travels if he can speak Arabic, so a foreign architect commissioned to construct a building in Arabia is likely to produce a more competent design if he is familiar with Arabian architectural traditions. As William Hosking, Professor at King's College, London, remarked by way of a rejoinder: 'In truth, each particular style may be considered as a distinct and peculiar language; and as in the case of a language, before a man can compose in it he must not only learn to speak and to read it, but to think in it. Where is the architect who can use with truth and freedom all the various styles of architecture?' Donaldson thus perversely changed the whole meaning of the linguistic analogy as it was understood by his contemporaries. For them, a true architecture could only be created on the assumption that it would be the natural, unquestioned mode of expression, and it was in this light that so many grasped at the analogy as a way of leading them out of the dilemma of stylistic Revivalism to which Donaldson was inviting them to return.

A similar sophism is to be detected even in the writings of such an astute polemicist as César Daly. In the 1860s, when trying to justify his publication of historical 'fragments' in the *Revue Générale de l'Architecture*, he asserted that architecture was a language which had undergone as many revolutions and radical transformations as its history presented distinct styles. Thus an architect who had only studied one style of architecture was like a Frenchman who knew no Latin; that is to say, by occupying himself with one single style, he could know it only very incompletely.

Both Daly and Donaldson thus disregarded the principal virtue of the analogy, which is that all spoken languages are based on what is usually called a vernacular, that is to say, an indigenous manner of speech which is not self-consciously foreign or of learned formation, but is natural, spontaneous and uninhibited. As Auguste

Perret was later to say, 'Construction is the architect's mother tongue; an architect is a poet who thinks and speaks in construction'. The influence of this notion has already been discussed with reference to the 'Queen Anne Revival' in England, but in that context the analogical significance of the word 'vernacular' was not particularly stressed. Nor were the origins of the word dealt with; yet it is significant that the notion first appeared in literary criticism in the mid-eighteenth century as a result of the study of Shakespeare. Dr. Johnson, for example, pointed out in 1765, with reference to Shakespeare's comic characters, that if there was a style which never became obsolete, it was to be found in the common social intercourse of life 'among those who speak only to be understood, without ambition of elegance'. By the beginning of the nineteenth century, even the most elegant poets had abandoned the artificial phraseology of the Augustan age in favour of vernacular expression, for, as Wordsworth remarked, 'the poet thinks and feels in the spirit of human passions; how then can his language differ in any material degree from that of all other men who feel vividly and see clearly?'

The cult of the vernacular was occasionally an excuse merely for coarseness of expression. But in its noblest interpretation, it was the surest guide to an understanding of the difference between architecture and good, plain, honest, straightforward building. Thus when G. G. Scott talked about 'vernacular domestic architecture' in his *Remarks on Gothic Architecture* (1858), or when J. L. Petit lectured in 1861 on the lessons to be learnt from the 'simple vernacular buildings' of Queen Anne's reign, they were using the linguistic analogy in its most plausible way, since they were suggesting that all good architecture is basically a natural, indigenous, spontaneous and unaffected way of building, whatever else it may be besides. The main problem in the nineteenth century was less to decide what distinguished architecture from vernacular building than what, in fact, were the tectonic qualities which most aptly corresponded to the linguistic idea of a vernacular. Most of the theorists thought in terms of regional domestic architecture, little realizing that regional architecture was being killed by the impact of the Industrial Revolution. Certainly, there were few theorists as perspicacious as James Fergusson, who perceived that the modern equivalent of mediaeval vernacular construction was to be found in the latest works of the civil engineers, and it is significant that although he at first disapproved of any parallels between architecture and speech, he was nevertheless astute enough to observe in his *History of Architecture* (1855) that good engineering was absolutely indispensable to a satisfactory architectural effect of any kind, since 'the one is the prose, the other is the poetry of the art of building'.

In recent years, the demand for a new 'vernacular' architecture, though decried by John Summerson as simply a confession of ignorance as to the nature of 'vernacular' architecture in the past, nevertheless has had eloquent supporters. As recently as 1959, J. M. Richards, in *The Functional Tradition in Early Industrial Buildings*, asserted that no art can remain for ever in a state of revolution, and that

178

we now need to create a vernacular language. Earlier, in his *Introduction to Modern Architecture*, he referred frequently to the merits of Georgian vernacular architecture, where 'the architect's imagination and his artistic sense were exercised within the limits set by a universal architectural language', and where great architects could work 'in a language everyone understood'. For him, the task of the modern architect was 'to go back, in a sense, and pick up the threads of a common architectural language at the point where they became unrecognizably entangled by the break-up of eighteenth century society'.

Another useful aspect of the linguistic analogy concerns the distinction between vocabulary and composition. Just as building elements may be described, in J. M. Richards's phrase, as 'the words, as it were, that form our architectural language', so the term 'composition', though now unfashionable in architectural circles, can be used to indicate the means of assembling those elements into an architectural whole. At one time the word 'composition' was used to indicate the imaginative creative act implied by all works of art, particularly paintings, and theorists like Leonardo da Vinci used it to denote the pictorial grouping of human figures. It has certainly been used by architectural theorists since the eighteenth century, though it was left to Julien Guadet to expound its traditional meaning precisely. In his *Eléments et Théorie de l'Architecture* (comprising lectures given from 1894 onwards) he was at pains to distinguish between 'composition' (by which he meant the conception of the total building) and 'study' (by which he meant the proportioning and refinement of its parts). The term 'composition' is clearly more applicable to architecture and music than to sculpture and painting, for it is only in the first two that a work of art is composed of standardized elements. As J. N. L. Durand remarked in his *Summary of Lectures given at the École Polytechnique* (1802), 'the elements are to architecture what words are to speech, what notes are to music, and without a perfect knowledge of which it is impossible to proceed further'.

The influence of the notion of composition on the architecture of the last two hundred years will be more appropriately dealt with in relationship to ideals of planning current since 1750. But mention can be made here of various analogical notions popularly related to the idea, such as the notion of a grammar of design, the notion of a distinction between vocabulary and syntax, and the notion that ornamentation in architecture is like ornamentation in poetry, i.e. something distinguishable from the basic structural form.

The term 'grammar of design' was first popularized by Charles Blanc in his book entitled *A Historical Grammar of the Arts of Drawing* (the short French title of which was *Grammaire des Arts du Dessin*), published in 1867. But like Owen Jones in his earlier *Grammar of Ornament*, he did not pursue the analogy into the text, and assumed, presumably, that the significance of the title would be self-evident without further comment. Nor did he succumb to the temptations, so glibly indulged in by later writers such as Trystan Edwards, of erecting a whole 'theory of architecture' on notions such as 'punctuation', 'inflection', and so on. Admittedly, in one place he spoke of 'the language of architecture', but in general, he left it to the reader to deduce the notion that in architecture, as in literature, there is a distinction between vocabulary and syntax—between the correct use of elemental units and the correct way these are joined together. Of course, in Charles Blanc's day there were recognized rules of grammar which no educated person dared break, just as there was an authoritative dictionary which laid down the meanings to be attached to words. Today, the most fashionable poets have abandoned the rules of grammar, just as lexicographers have abandoned the notion that words have a 'correct' usage which may differ from their common usage. Hence the notion of a grammar of design is no longer as popular as it was a century ago, even though it might be argued that, with the recent increase in the standardization of building components, the analogy might prove more fruitful than ever before.

The first use to be made of an analogy between poetic ornament and architectural ornament seems to have been in a speech delivered by Fénélon to the French Academy of Literature in 1693, when he cited bad architecture as an illustration of what he considered defective in bad oratory. 'The boldest and most ornate works of Gothic are not the best', he declared to his fellow academicians; 'for one must never allow into a building any element destined solely for ornament, but rather turn to ornament all the parts necessary for its support'.

The first use of the same analogy by an architect seems to be J. F. Blondel's assertion that 'architecture is like literature; the simple style is preferable to an inflated style, since one only weakens a great idea by trying to raise it up with pompous words'. Elsewhere in his lecture course, he had touched on the same theme with specific reference to ornament: 'Architecture is like poetry; all ornament which is only ornament is excessive. Architecture, by the beauty of its proportions and the choice of its arrangement is sufficient unto itself'.

This comparison between architecture and poetry was of course the inevitable counterpart of the analogical comparison between building and vernacular speech, in that both were used to explain the distinction between architecture and plain, straightforward construction. The twin notion which its advocates wished to convey was that architecture does not differ from plain building by the use of special elements, any more than poetry differs from common speech by the use of a special vocabulary; the differences lie in the fact that the common elements are arranged in a particularly felicitous and emotionally life-enhancing way. Poetry, they argued, differs from plain speech only by being more ordered, more rhythmic, more disciplined, more regularly proportioned and more concise. In drama, poetry is the means used to express character, for as Lascelles Abercrombie has observed, Shakespeare's poetic art is essentially the art of irresistibly impressing on our minds the character of those who speak. Hence it will be understood why, in the mid-eighteenth century, prose was thought to differ from poetry only by being unenhanced and less refined, and why, at a time when the word 'style' meant precisely the type of expression appropriate to a literary composition, architectural theorists tended to describe architectural style analogically as poetry. 'Style', wrote J. F. Blondel, 'is, in a figurative sense, the poetry of architecture; a colouring which contributes towards rendering all an architect's compositions really interesting. Hence it is the style suitable to different subjects which leads to infinite variety in different buildings of the same type or in buildings of different types. In a word, style, in this sense, is like that of eloquence'. Needless to say, his two pupils Boullée and Ledoux, the exponents of *architecture parlante*, were equally taken with the analogy. 'The poetry of architecture is acquired by giving monuments their proper character', exclaimed Boullée in his *Treatise*. Similarly Ledoux asserted that 'architecture is to masonry what poetry is to literature; it is the dramatic enthusiasm of the craft'.

The linguistic analogy, then, was essentially a means of explaining how artistic expression could be achieved by limiting components to purely utilitarian elements, which might then be refined or decorated as decorum demanded. In an age which accepted architectural beauty as essentially a matter of proportion; which agreed with Alberti's definition of ornament as simply an added brightness; which could still regard traditional craftsmanship as the basis of vernacular construction; the linguistic analogy was a salutary guide to achieving fine buildings in harmony with the age and with each other. When, in the middle of the nineteenth century, Classical theory was finally abandoned; when traditional craftsmanship diminished through the more extensive use of mass-produced components; when poetry became the spontaneous outpouring of intimate personal sentiments rather than the austere ennoblement of universal themes; then the analogy no longer served as a guide to the creation of a new architecture in the sense of creating a universal, natural tectonic language, but rather encouraged personal expression at the expense of environmental harmony. This was the age when Wordsworth claimed that 'poetry is the spontaneous overflow of powerful feelings'. This was the age when anything in poetry corresponding to the architectural notion of function was regarded as superfluous, and when a literary plot was, as J. S. Mill put it, 'a necessary evil'. This was the age when poetry was regarded as a soliloquy (which, as Professor Martinet has pointed out in *A Functional View of Language*, is the complete negation of language); when it was claimed that if the poet's act of utterance was other than an end in itself, it ceased to be poetry, but became mere eloquence. According to Shelley, a poet was a nightingale who sat in darkness and sang to cheer his own solitude with sweet sounds. How then could the linguistic analogy hope to inspire the creation of a new architecture in harmony with the new world, if poets were becoming more and more unsociable, introspective and withdrawn into themselves?

It may thus be said, in conclusion, that however heuristically successful analogies might be in scientific investigation, they generally proved misleading and disappointing to the architectural theorists of the nineteenth century, since in fact the only way to reason cogently about architecture is by reference to structures which have actually been built. It was for this reason that the most powerful impulsion came, not from analogical theorizing with respect to other arts and sciences, or from studying the buildings of the remote past, but from studying the work of those men who were creating new types of structure in the era in which all this speculation occurred, namely the work of civil and military engineers. It is thus with the ideas of structural engineers, and with those of that whole group of architectural theorists who may be classified as 'Rationalists', that the next three chapters will be concerned.

Part Four

RATIONALISM

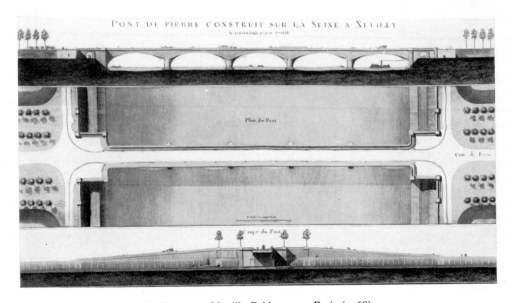

R. Perronet: Neuilly Bridge, near Paris (1768)

THE INFLUENCE OF ENGINEERS

Illustrating the new importance of mathematical studies in constructional design

XVII

Calver Cotton Mill, Curbar (1785)

RATIONALISM

Illustrating the basis of Rationalism: straight-forward building unadorned except when the needs of decorum demanded ornament

XVIII

C. Barry: Lord Ellesmere's mansion (Bridgewater House) London (1849)

RATIONALISM

*Illustrating the basis of Rationalism: straight-forward building, suitably
adorned when the needs of decorum demanded ornament*

XIX

L. von Klenze: The Picture Gallery (Pinakothek) Munich (1826)

RATIONALISM

*Illustrating how Renaissance motifs were often employed by architects
needing adaptable forms for new building types*

XX

18

The Influence of Civil and Military Engineers

Amongst the many influential events which took place around 1750, few exercised such a profound change on architectural theory as the establishment of civil and military engineering as distinct and separate disciplines. For as Hans Straub has rightly remarked in his *History of Civil Engineering*: 'it was during the second half of the eighteenth century that the science of engineering proper came into existence, and with it the modern civil engineer who based his designs on scientific calculation'. Specifically, the change occurred with the establishment of a school of civil engineering (usually referred to as the École des Ponts et Chaussées) in Paris in 1747, and of a school of military engineering at Mezières in 1748. Naturally the transition after these dates was quite gradual. Not only did architects continue to design works of civil engineering for many years, but it was quite common, even at the beginning of the nineteenth century, for civil engineers like Gauthey and Telford to design churches. Nevertheless it can be asserted that about 1750 a division took place between the two professions.

Before 1750 no one would have questioned the advisability of appointing architects to design bridges, or suggested that the design of bridges was the responsibility of any other type of person. Palladio had included designs for bridges in his *Four Books of Architecture*. The elder Blondel designed a bridge at Saintes on unusually complicated foundations, and discoursed upon bridge design in the lectures he gave at the Academy of Architecture's school in 1672. The Academy itself devoted most of its sessions in 1684 and 1685 to problems of bridge design, prompted no doubt by the current project for building an aqueduct at Maintenon. Thus it was an architect, Jacques Gabriel (a former assistant of Jules-Hardouin Mansart), who was appointed chief engineer of the French Department of Bridges and Roads in 1716, in which capacity he built a bridge over the Loire at Blois. His successor was Germain Boffrand (another pupil of Jules-Hardouin Mansart) who, though famous mainly for the brilliance of his rococo interiors, also distinguished himself by designing important bridges, such as those at Nantes and Sens.

The reason architects could adequately fulfil official posts as chief engineers (or *'premiers ingénieurs et inspecteurs généraux des ponts et chaussées'* as they were officially called) was due to the fact that before 1750, the design of bridges was considered as simply an extension of the problem of masonry vaulting, or stereotomy. Hence little distinction was then seen to exist between the two, except as regards minor problems of assembly, and minor difficulties resulting from occasional slight increases in the spans. Admittedly the problems of bridge design involved complications not usually met with in the design of ordinary vaulting, such as those resulting from the effects of heavy live loads, and from various problems in hydraulics. But in an age when bridge spans seldom needed to exceed eighty feet, the problems of stereotomy and the problems of erecting and removing formwork were very similar to those which occurred in ordinary public buildings, and this was particularly so in France, where the leading architects were not aristocratic amateurs, as in England, or painters and sculptors, as in Italy, but were trained in the art of masonry construction in accordance with a tradition going back to the Middle Ages.

The establishment of civil engineering as a separate profession was almost entirely due to Rodolphe Perronet, the first director of the École des Ponts et Chaussées, and the chief engineer of the Department of Bridges and Roads from 1764 until his death in 1794. As a young man, he had joined the Corps of Military Engineers, but the sudden death of his father caused him to renounce this career temporarily, and to become an architect, working for Jean Beausire, a member of the Academy and architect to the city of Paris. In 1745, however, at the age of thirty-seven, he transferred to the Department of Bridges and Roads, and it was here that he showed that genius which was to make him a pioneer in the history of civil engineering. He not only organized a proper school of civil engineering out of what until then had been the headquarters drawing office, but seems to have been the first to perceive that, when designing spans of unusual length or flatness, it was not enough simply to estimate dimensions by rule of thumb, but that calculations needed to be made based on the principles of mechanics and the strength of materials.

His most famous bridge was that spanning the Seine at Neuilly, built between 1768 and 1772: the first bridge in which the formwork was designed on scientific principles and in which the size of the piers was calculated accurately according to the loads to be carried. In other words, unlike earlier bridges, in which no account was taken either of the thickness of the vault or the height of the piers, and in which the width of such piers was assessed simply as a fifth of the spans butting against them, the piers of the Pont de Neuilly were calculated so precisely that they could be reduced to one tenth. Not that such refinements were to become really important until the development of iron bridges in the following century; for as Thomas Telford remarked, in small masonry bridges a designer could take whatever curve appeared most beautiful or useful, and by so adjusting the joints, throw the ultimate pressure in whatever direction he thought most conducive to the structure's strength. But as bridges became larger in span, and as materials more resistant to tension came to be employed, the use of mathematics, and the analysis of forces based on the strength of materials, became more and more important, so that it would not be an exaggeration to claim that the main difference between architecture and engineering has, since 1750, lain essentially in disparities of scale.

Probably the first writer to apply the principles of mathematics to problems of construction in a popular treatise was Bernard Forest de Bélidor, a military engineer, whose *Science de l'Ingénieur* was published in 1729. There had indeed been a number of learned memoranda published by mathematicians at the turn of the century, such as that by Philippe de la Hire (who, incidentally, succeeded François Blondel as professor of architecture at the French Academy of Architecture's school), which attempted to solve problems of statics relative to the stability of vaulting. But before Bélidor's book appeared, no author had written a systematic treatise on building construction which was based on algebraic methods instead of on traditional rules, or which laid more emphasis on technology than on what was then called 'the decorative parts of civil architecture'. Admittedly Bélidor's book, being intended for military engineers, was more concerned with the design of retaining walls and bomb-proof shelters than with the more ordinary buildings of garrison towns. But he nevertheless devoted a large section of his text to the design of barracks, guard-houses, city gates and other purely architectural constructions. It is possible that few architects read it or were even capable of understanding the more recondite parts of his treatise; but by making a direct plea to architects to abandon their unscientific methods; by inviting them to take advantage of the help which mathematics could give, there can be little doubt that he greatly influenced the creation of a modern architecture, for such pleas, repeated at intervals by engineers for over two centuries, eventually had their desired effect.

More important, perhaps, than the new tendency to solve problems of statics mathematically was the practice introduced at this time of making experiments to ascertain the strength of materials. In 1707 and 1708, Antoine Parent had made tests on the resistance of timber beams, and had published the results in a learned paper submitted to the French Academy of Science. By 1729 there was available to those who sought them a complete and accurate set of tables showing the ultimate compressive, tensile and bending strengths of different kinds of wood, metal and glass. Once again, only the engineers were to take advantage of this scientific information at the time, and nearly two centuries were to elapse before architects as a body even gave serious attention to the possibilities inherent in this type of information; but the seeds of these new architectural ideas were undoubtedly sown in the mid-eighteenth century, even though they took so long to ripen and produce their full effect.

It would be unwise to be too critical of the architects of the nineteenth century for neglecting the help which the engineers could give them. Even Léonce Reynaud, one of the most assiduous promoters of scientific methods of architectural analysis, and a graduate of the École Polytechnique, pointed out in his *Traité d'Architecture*, published in 1850, that 'one should not conclude that it is appropriate to submit all the parts of our constructions to the laws of mechanics, for it is evident that the prescriptions of science might lead to great difficulties in execution, and would not always be reconcilable with the exigencies of the building's purpose'. A knowledge of the strength of materials was undoubtedly essential to the development of the new structural systems which appeared soon after 1880, especially when these involved buildings of immense height or tremendous span; but it is probably fair to say that most of the rule of thumb methods evolved for masonry structures of moderate dimensions were still quite adequate for the majority of buildings constructed between 1750 and 1900, and that even if precise scientific methods had been applied to such buildings, the results would have been much the same. It cannot be too strongly emphasized that the engineers in the nineteenth century were not interested in such problems of vital importance to architecture as the insulation of heat and sound; nor were they greatly concerned with the economy of small-span structures, or with the materials most clearly indicated for such structures, namely masonry and wood. The architects of the time may justifiably be condemned for their backwardness in failing to adopt the methods of engineering research to their own problems; but it would be wrong to assume that all the information they required had already been ascertained by the engineering profession, and needed only to be applied. Moreover, even when the information was ascertained, it did not always lead to conclusions favourable to the use of new materials. For example, when John Robison, one of the most distinguished scientists of the late eighteenth century, lectured on 'Mechanical Philosophy' at Edinburgh University, he tempered his recommendation of the use of iron for roof trusses by observing that 'iron is only about twelve times stronger than red fir, and is more than twelve times heavier; nor is it cheaper, weight for weight or strength for strength'.

Perhaps the most influential aspect of the engineers' approach, as regards architectural design, was at this time their abstract way of considering structural elements. Before 1750, columns and piers were thought of as simply standard elements of the Classical Orders, and since both were traditionally associated with rules laid down since remote Antiquity, it seldom occurred to any architect that the proportions or shapes might be changed. After 1750, however, the term 'point support' came more and more frequently to be used by French engineers, and was also used by J. F. Blondel in his *Cours d'Architecture* (1771) and by Rondelet in his *Art de Bâtir* (1802) the standard architectural textbooks of the period. This clearly helped rid architects of the notion that a pier or column must necessarily have some predetermined shape and proportion, regardless of the material of which it was made. Thus Perronet's pupil E. L. Gauthey, when discussing Soufflot's design for the church of Ste. Geneviève, compared the columns which supported the dome to the piles used as foundations for heavy buildings, adding that, 'piles are nothing else than a multiplicity of very small point supports, and it is enough if one distributes these point supports so that none will be useless in providing a solid foundation'. He therefore approved Soufflot's method of placing twelve columns close to each triangular pier, and justified this arrangement by claiming that they were arranged and spaced in the way that piles were ordinarily arranged in engineering constructions.

The church of Ste. Geneviève was not the first building to be subjected to scientific methods, for in 1742 three mathematicians had analysed the structure of St. Peter's, Rome, to try to determine the cause of cracks which had been noticed in the dome. But it was probably the first building to be actually designed scientifically, and to be analysed by a professional civil engineer as a result of doubts as to its eventual stability when it was still in its early stages of conception. The methods used by Soufflot and Perronet to determine the crushing resistance of the stone must unquestionably have had a considerable influence on subsequent architectural thought; certainly the lessons to be learnt from civil engineers were not lost on the more perspicacious architectural theorists of the following century, and many practising architects will have made use of Léonce Reynaud's elaborate statical analyses of masonry vaults. The only trouble was that instead of exploring ways in which the new information provided by engineers could be applied to their problems, architects only too often wasted their time trying to minimize the distinction between the two professions, pretending that no division had taken place.

This attitude was largely encouraged by amateur theorists and historians. Thus James Fergusson claimed that there was 'no real demarcation between the two branches of the building profession', and that 'if architecture were only as truthful and as living an art as engineering, the distinction would entirely disappear'. He then went on to claim that an engineer was merely an architect who 'occupied himself more especially with construction', and the more utilitarian class of works, whilst the architect, properly so called, was 'the artist who attended to the ornamental distribution of buildings and their decoration when enriched'.

Professor Donaldson also denied any distinction between the two professions, for in 1842 he insisted that since engineering and architecture were intimately connected, their practice should be the same, their studies the same and the buildings and constructions in which they were engaged common to both. Yet these observations were prompted by the fact that he was talking to a mixed class of engineering and architectural students, and it could hardly be claimed that he put theory into practice. It was to be many years before the teaching of this particular structural engineering was systematically integrated into the teaching of architecture in England, even though at King's College, London, evening lecture courses on civil engineering and architecture were given in a joint syllabus.

Instead of reflecting on the nature of the very real differences of scale which had inevitably separated architecture from civil engineering, the architectural profession tended to waste its time platitudinously deploring the 'schism' which had taken place. This was partly because architects were jealous of the popular esteem in which engineering was held by a materialistic populace (especially in England, where the distinction between civil engineering and mechanical engineering was nebulous, and where the engineers' reputation for progress was based more on machinery than on static structures), and partly because lay critics like Fergusson added bitterness to their frustration by pointing out triumphantly how bridge-building had advanced whilst other forms of construction remained relatively stagnant. Even Edward Cresy, a distinguished architect, antiquary and sanitary inspector, wrote in the preface to his *Encyclopedia of Civil Engineering* (1847) that 'the future historian of Britain will not refer to her architectural remains, but to the vast works of the engineer, by which to judge the habits and civilization of the age'.

Thus the architectural profession was overwhelmed by a sense of inferiority—if not by a sense of inadequacy—into seeking a closer alliance with their separated brethren, hoping that by closer co-operation they might share with them some of the glory they had shared in the past.

The demand for a closer alliance between the two professions was most articulate and insistent in the new architectural magazines. The preface to the first issue of the *Revue Générale de l'Architecture* (1840) began by lamenting that architects and civil engineers were completely isolated from one another, and announced an editorial policy of promoting the exchange of technical knowledge between the two professions. In the following year Alfred Bartholemew, the author of *Specifications for Practical Architecture* (1841), deplored the proposed foundation of a College of Civil Engineers, claiming that it would increase still more the severance between architecture and engineering, the reunion of which he was labouring to effect. The ninth volume of *The Builder* (1851) published the lengthy remarks of Sir William Tite (spoken after a lecture given by an engineer to the Royal Institute of British Architects on the subject of tubular bridges) in which he 'regretted exceedingly the severance which had taken place between architects and engineers', and reflected wistfully on the public's willingness to allow engineers to spend large sums of money on experimentation—a luxury the architectural profession was invariably denied. Considerable controversy on the whole relationship between engineers and architects was aroused by the appointment of a military engineer, Captain Francis Fowke, to design the 1862 International Exhibition, especially when Henry Cole, who had been responsible for the appointment, made a violent attack on the architectural profession to the Royal Society of Arts. The climax was reached in the 1870s, when, interestingly enough, the initiative for a *rapprochement* seems to have come from the engineers rather than from the architects. Thus Captain Seddon of the Royal Engineers expressed himself eloquently on the theme of professional co-operation when lecturing to the Royal Institute of British Architects in 1871 on 'Our present Knowledge of Building Materials', and his sentiments were echoed by J. Scott Russell, the famous naval architect, when lecturing on the great iron dome he had designed for the Vienna Exhibition of 1874.

There were two reasons why the engineers were beginning to regret the rupture between the two professions. One resulted from the numerous popular criticisms levelled against the engineers' own work on aesthetic grounds. The other resulted from a growing awareness among the more perspicacious engineers that the differences between the two professions had arisen, not through any conflict of interest but purely from disparities of scale. In this respect, it is worth noting that J. Scott Russell, in his lecture just referred to, announced that he would confine his remarks to 'the peculiar principles which it seems should govern the proportions, and indicate the structure, of very large buildings, as distinguished from ordinary small ones'. Thus, with more acumen than was usual at the time, he made clear that the distinction between architecture and engineering was not, as Fergusson had claimed, the distinction between a Fine Art and a utilitarian art, but between two types of creative design, whereby the quality of genius required to create beauty was equally meritorious in both instances, and where the distinction of techniques was influenced only by the requirements imposed by the need to design for very different spans.

Few engineers rose to the challenge offered by the aesthetic problems of bridge design, and even today we find that any engineer who designs beautiful structures, such as Pier Luigi Nervi, tends to be designated as an architect *honoris causa*. Thus Fergusson probably voiced the dissatisfaction of all his more sensitive readers when he asserted in his *Historical Inquiry* (1849) that scarcely one of the many viaducts, bridges and railway stations then being erected had attempted more than 'merely to effect the useful purpose for which it was designed, with sufficient durability and the least possible expense'. It was true, he confessed, that these structures were unrivalled for their magnitude and magnificence. It was also true that this somewhat mundane attitude on the part of the engineers was the reason their work had escaped from the affectation, and the servility to archaeology, which characterized the work of architects. But he persisted in claiming that engineers were neglecting the 'vast opportunity afforded for artistic treatment', and this same criticism was continually levelled against civil engineers during the whole of the nineteenth century. It occurs even as late as 1901.

In that year, Montgomery Schuyler wrote an article on 'Monumental Engineering' for the *Architectural Record*, in which he deplored the fact that the most conspicuous man-made structures in the landscape were the least affected by any conscious attempt to produce a pleasing design. This deficiency was due, he thought, to the fact that American engineering education completely ignored problems of aesthetics, and the only way to correct this was by adding lecture courses on artistic expression to the training in practical construction. In his view, the only well designed urban bridges were to be found in France, and he attributed this success to the fact that there was a professorship of architecture attached to the Department of Bridges and Roads.

It is no part of the purpose of this chapter to discuss the advantages to be gained by teaching aesthetics to civil engineers, or to examine the plausibility of Schuyler's claim that French engineers showed superiority in design through the persistence of their tradition of having lectures on architecture given at their schools. But it is important to consider the influence of this branch of engineering education on architectural education, since clearly the continuous interaction between the architectural education given to engineers and that given to architects has necessarily had an enormous influence on architecture itself. It is of more than accidental significance that Henri Labrouste's greatest friend at the French Academy in Rome (E. J. Gilbert) had been trained first at the École Polytechnique. Similarly, it may be argued that much of J. F. Blondel's Rationalism might well be due to the fact that from the time his school of architecture was established in the rue de la Harpe, Paris (long before he became the Academy professor), he was officially responsible for training young men destined for the corps of civil engineers.

When the School of Bridges and Roads was established by Louis XV's ministry in 1747, only candidates already trained in the rudiments of architecture were admitted, and government bursaries were therefore established to enable promising candidates to obtain preliminary instruction at Blondel's school. In course of time, attendance at this school was the recognized official preparatory course. After Blondel's death in 1774, the system was continued by his assistants, Dumont and Daubenton, so that it was not until the time of the French Revolution (when the whole system changed due to the establishment of the École Polytechnique) that French engineering students were not actually trained as architects before beginning their instruction as engineers.

The École Polytechnique, founded in 1795, was modelled on the School of Military Engineering (which had always paid considerable attention to building construction, and had employed an architect to teach this course), since it was designed to be a preparatory school for the various professional schools which trained military and civil engineers. Thus from its inception, it included courses on architecture given by J. N. L. Durand (a former pupil of Pierre Panseron, the professor of architecture at the School of Military Engineering, as well as a pupil of Boullée and Rodolphe Perronet) whose revolutionary importance has been discussed in the first chapter of this book. Initially, Durand's course only accounted for eight per cent of the total tuition, and many of the peculiarities of his course, such as his rather facile technique of axial planning by means of graph paper, can be attributed to the need to condense the curriculum into a short period of time. But these architectural courses eventually increased in importance, and though they were never preponderant, it would be fair to say that building construction came (if we include the lectures given on applied mechanics) to occupy a major part in the curriculum. It is not surprising, therefore, that the lectures eventually given there by Léonce Reynaud, and elaborated in several published editions after 1850 under the title *Traité d'Architecture*, became eventually the most complete and up-to-date course on architectural theory to be found anywhere in the world.

Reynaud's career was in certain respects curiously similar to that of Perronet. He started out to be an engineer by enrolling at the École Polytechnique (where he was for some time a pupil of Durand), but being obliged to leave hastily because of his political activities, he decided to work as an architect, and was employed by J. N. Huyot, who in addition to being a practising architect was professor of the history of architecture at the École des Beaux-Arts. After the liberal revolution of 1830, he was reinstated at the École Polytechnique, and subsequently entered the School of Bridges and Roads. Thus, when he was made professor of architecture at the École Polytechnique in 1837, he had not only a profound knowledge of current architectural problems and a sound background of architectural history, but also a complete familiarity with current engineering practice, and it is this which makes his lecture course such a valuable synthesis of contemporary constructional ideas.

Reynaud's treatise is divided into three main parts. The first part deals with structural materials and with the scientific analysis of their properties; the second part deals with the elements of architecture (that is to say with columns, beams, apertures, vaults and so on, considered as much from the point of view of statics as from that of aesthetics); the final part deals with composition, that is to say with various building types, and the way in which different programmes of requirements had been fulfilled at the time at which he wrote. Reynaud, though by temperament a scientist, was at pains not to underrate the emotional content of architectural creativity; but his method was the quintessence of what is meant by Rationalism, as he himself makes clear in his introductory remarks. No form, he claims, is advocated without reference to the rational data which caused it to originate, and he defines architecture as 'an eminently rational art'. Nevertheless, he also claims that architecture 'demands a lot of our imagination'. Similarly, he insists that there must be 'a complete harmony between form and function', and that just as there exists an intimate relationship between form and function in God's creatures (whereby 'the exterior is the result of the interior composition'), so architecture demands that the form shall be the result of satisfying a given purpose with order and simplicity, admitting nothing except what appears founded on real needs.

Such was the architectural training given to students at the École Polytechnique in the 1840s; yet even this was merely a preparation for further training in building construction given at such specialized schools as the School of Military Engineering and the School of Bridges and Roads, to which most of the students then proceeded. It may at first seem surprising that so much emphasis should be given to building construction, especially in view of the fact that little formal education in this subject was given at either the French École des Beaux-Arts or even the British School of Military Engineering at Chatham. Yet it had been a tradition in France ever since the eighteenth century for officers of the corps of military engineers to design the buildings in garrison towns, just as it was common for the Department of Bridges and Roads to design occasional buildings for the small communities within their territorial domain.

Probably the most important architectural course to be given in the mid-nineteenth century, apart from Reynaud's, was the course in construction given by Captain (later General) Paul-Joseph Ardant at the School of Artillery and Engineering at Metz. This was never published in book form, and its contents are only known to us through duplicated manuscripts. Hence its influence can only have been slight. Yet it is worth analysing as an example of the tuition then given to engineers, in view of the fact that engineering was eventually to dominate the architectural speculations of the modern age.

The first thing one notices is that, like Reynaud's course, it follows unquestioningly the doctrines of Classicism, though Ardant was at pains to insist that he held no brief for any particular 'style', and wished, as he put it, 'to make abstraction of every system of architecture'. The significance of the engineers' bias towards Classicism will be discussed more fully in the chapter on Classical Rationalism; but it is worth emphasizing here that for all the more practical constructors of the period, apart from those involved in archaeological repairs, the virtues of Classical forms were never in any doubt. Secondly, one notices the great emphasis given by Ardant to Durand's ideal of economy. Construction is defined as the art of making solid buildings with all the economy desired, and the first rule for obtaining this economy is 'never to admit in the planning and decoration of a building any combination which is not in perfect harmony with the usages, climate and constructional materials of the locality'. Thus according to Ardant, many of the notions popularized by Boullée and Ledoux were reprehensible, since they were contrary to the demands of economy. Similarly it was wrong to borrow from foreign countries or from Antiquity such architectonic systems as modern needs no longer justified. He therefore condemned flat roofs, top-lighting and peristyles (all favourite Boulléesque features), which, he claimed, were only justifiable in hot climates.

Many of Ardant's strictures suggest that he was greatly influenced by J. F. Blondel's published lecture course. Thus he claimed that a properly adorned building should 'announce its destination', that its architectural style should be analogous to this destination, that its construction should be demonstrably solid and expressed on the exterior, and that its parts should be symmetrical, regular, well proportioned, tasteful and simple—rules which, he claimed, were independent of any system of architecture. Simplicity, for him, consisted in the absence of every constructional element and every ornamental accessory which was not of some obvious utility. A building could be both rich and simply designed, just as it could be poverty-stricken yet pretentious. One should thus not confuse simplicity with nudity (as was only too common in the first quarter of the nineteenth century), or believe that to preserve a building's simplicity, one must deprive it of the parts most essential for its real and apparent solidity, such as cornices, bases and *chaînages*—that is to say, the vertical and horizontal masonry elements which in French Classical buildings constituted a sort of skeleton frame of ashlar.

Ardant strenuously opposed the notion that it was possible to create a new style of military architecture. No one, he claimed, could have the pretension of creating any new architecture all of a piece, since centuries had been required for each ancient or modern system to develop. He therefore advised his audience to limit themselves to following the meanderings of contemporary architecture, which consisted, he said, in employing in each building the constructional processes most in harmony with local needs and materials, and combining these with the decorative system transmitted by the Romans. He considered that climatic conditions in France made it necessary for solids to dominate over voids (a conclusion which was then fashionable, but which was in fact at variance with historical precedent, and with the conclusions later to be enunciated rather more logically by Julien Guadet), just as the climate made it advisable to provide sloping roofs. Here, he claimed, was the clear difference between the physiognomy of French dwellings and those of Greece or southern Italy, where external apertures were rare, porticos open and roofs flat. Since architecture was an art whose main purpose was utility, its forms and techniques should always conform to the customs of each nation and to the climatic and geological milieu for which it was created. 'No nation', he asserted, 'can create voluntarily its own style of architecture, nor borrow from other nations those architectural forms developed according to particular circumstances and needs'. There could be no such thing as a national architecture in Europe, especially as the current tendency of civilization was to create a greater uniformity of customs, religion and political institutions.

Even more interesting than his reflections on the possibilities of a new architecture is his explicit exposition of the Classical doctrine that the Orders are essentially a skeleton frame, since this idea, as we shall see, was to dominate the Classical Rationalists when confronted with the problem of employing steel and reinforced concrete frames at the end of the century. If, said Ardant, we compare northern buildings with those of the south, we shall see that their construction is founded on the same principles; everywhere the skeleton (*ossature*) of a house is composed of vertical supports, placed at the angles of the building, and at the points most heavily loaded by vaults or timber trusses. In the south these intervals between the vertical supports can remain open, to produce colonnades or arcades, whereas in the north the intervals are filled in with walling pierced by apertures. Thus although in the latter case we have a system of pilasters between which occur doors and windows, the vertical supports in both instances fulfil the same destination. Hence the arrangement of pilasters and columns and continuous architraves must be carefully related to the essential parts of the structure so that they are seen to be its actual constituent elements, set in relief and adorned with greater or lesser elegance. Hence also both free-standing columns and pilasters must be given the same form, the same ornamentation and the same mouldings. This was why, he said, the Greek and Roman system of architecture was still valid for the era in which he lived, apart from certain modifications imposed by reason and good taste.

Not that his preference for Classical forms was rigid or exclusive. He admitted that there reigned at that time in architecture considerable latitude regarding the choice of historical 'styles', and he referred specifically to the design of Gothic prisons in the United States. He was moreover prepared to admit the suitability of Gothic for churches. But he considered that Classical architecture had overriding advantages in every other type of building, and it was thus with Classical architecture that his lecture course was essentially concerned.

It is worth noting that Ardant nowhere dealt with new structural materials, and this might be regarded as a major defect of his course. Yet even Reynaud, who had had considerable experience with advanced metal construction in the design of lighthouses, devoted very little space to iron construction in his published treatise, and then only dealt with metal roofs. The fact is that metal construction had a very small role to play in the evolution of architectural design before the commercial exploitation of rolled steel in the 1880s, and most of the speculation regarding a new architecture of iron and glass originated solely in the writings of enthusiastic amateurs, not in the works of architectural practitioners and practising engineers.

The history of iron, steel and reinforced concrete construction has been succinctly told by Sigfried Giedion in *Space, Time and Architecture*, and there is no need to re-tell it here. At the same time, in view of the importance rightly attached to the influence of new engineering materials on architectural design, some brief comment is necessary, if only to explain why these materials were so slow in producing the new architecture for which so many theorists clamoured.

As is well known, the greatly increased use of iron from the middle of the eighteenth century onwards was due to the substitution of coke for charcoal as a means of smelting iron ore, whereby cast iron was henceforth produced in large quantities. Before 1750, cast iron was seldom deliberately manufactured, only malleable iron, and the system then normally adopted was to place alternate layers of charcoal and ore in a furnace, and heat them by means of bellows driven by water power. The main disadvantage of this primitive process was the immense cost and wastage of charcoal used to smelt the iron ore; but an additional disadvantage was the small amount of ore which could be smelted at each operation. If too many layers were superimposed, the lower layers of charcoal were crushed and absorbed into the newly smelted iron, whereby instead of malleable iron, iron with such a high carbon content was produced that it was only capable of being cast.

The difference between the two types of iron is crucial to an understanding of the architectural problems involved. Cast iron, which was the easiest and cheapest to produce, was brittle, had a negligible tensile strength, and melted at relatively low temperatures. Only wrought iron, which was strong in tension, malleable and relatively fire-resistant, was of real use to architects, but this could only be made either at considerable cost and effort by the method just described, or from cast iron, by means of the process known as 'puddling' which reduced its carbon content. It is significant that no iron 'I' sections were rolled before 1847, and that not until 1854 were wrought iron beams made sufficiently deep to fulfil any but the simplest architectural requirements.

The next development in metal construction only occurred when Henry Bessemer invented an economical method of turning cast iron directly into steel; but although this event took place in 1856, it was not until 1879 that anyone invented a cheap method of removing phosphorus from the iron, and it was not until the end of the nineteenth century that manganese steel and other modern alloys became available for constructional purposes. The first railway bridge to be constructed entirely of steel was that at Glasgow, South Dakota, built in 1878, and it was another six years before steel sections suitable for buildings were rolled. The first steel frame building to be constructed in England was built in 1904. Even the Eiffel Tower, which is often described as the first monumental structure in steel, was in fact built of wrought iron, and Gustave Eiffel went to great pains to explain why he considered this material more reliable. Indeed, nothing could justify more clearly the relatively late date at which the new engineering material entered the architectural domain than the fact that Eiffel himself distrusted the current methods of manufacturing steel.

A similarly late development occurred with reinforced concrete, but having already discussed the history of this material at length in *Concrete: the Vision of a New Architecture*, there will be no need to repeat any of this information here, especially as the main facts have already been admirably summarized in the latest edition of Nikolaus Pevsner's *Pioneers of Modern Design*. It will be sufficient, in order to conclude this chapter, to say that until 1880 the influence of engineers on architecture was more due to the example of their rational approach than to their use of new materials, and that it is with this Rationalism that we should be mainly concerned.

19

Rationalism

The best definition of Rationalism is to be found in an article written by César Daly in 1864, and published in translation in *The Builder* in the same year. In this article, devoted to the subject in general, he defined it as the belief, held in common by all French Gothicists, Classicists and Eclectics, to the effect that architecture was ornamental or ornamented construction (a definition, it will be remembered, already given of architecture by Fergusson in his *History of Architecture*), but more specifically as the belief that architectural forms not only required rational justification, but could only be so justified if they derived their laws from science. He added that the Rationalist School had the strange characteristic of existing 'without being well known to the greater part of its own members', even though it could be identified by the common beliefs which a great number of architects shared.

In other words, the Rationalists were simply that vast body of architects who believed that architectural form was essentially structural form, however ultimately refined and adorned those basic structural forms might be, and they found their most eloquent apologists in France, where architects had held this doctrine consistently throughout the Classical period as a result of its having been bequeathed to them by the master masons of the Middle Ages, from whom many of them could trace a lineal descent. French Classical doctrine, whether literary or architectural, had always equated truth with beauty, for as Boileau wrote in his *Art Poétique*: 'nothing is beautiful but what is true'. This idea had expressed itself architecturally by a particular regard for the tectonic integrity of buildings; and the same attitude continued even when the decline in the authority of Antique prototypes caused seventeenth century doctrines also to decline.

According to César Daly, the self-imposed task of the Rationalist School was to reconcile modern architecture with modern science and industry; a conciliation which, he said, was impossible for those who blindly imitated temples, cathedrals and castles. He thought Rationalism was purely an interim measure, for when this essential work of creating concordance between architecture and science was accomplished, the Rationalist School would then, according to him, disappear, and be re-absorbed into a more elevated School, of which it would have prepared the advent. What, he asked rhetorically, was this School which was to come? It was easy to foretell; for once the alliance between architecture and reason had been accomplished, only one further advance was possible, namely 'the alliance of architecture and sentiment', and this, he claimed, alone merited for architecture the name of art in its spiritual connotation.

In retrospect, it must be admitted that César Daly was extraordinarily perspicacious in his prophecy, for undoubtedly the pursuit of structural Rationalism has, within the last forty years, been widely tempered by the pursuit of arbitrary abstract form, to such an extent that pure Rationalism may be regarded historically as an essentially nineteenth century phenomenon. Nevertheless it may be argued that Rationalism is still, and must always be, the backbone of any valid architectural theory, for however deeply the alliance between architecture and sentiment may be explored, the alliance between architecture and science must always be its ultimate basis of existence. It is still, therefore, an important subject of study even in the present day.

Historically, it is worth noting that although Classical Rationalism preceded Gothic Rationalism in time, the former was always, from its formulation in the mid-eighteenth century, greatly influenced by Gothic architecture. Eventually the Gothic Rationalists and the Classical Rationalists formed two distinct and at times hostile schools; but in the 1750s, when the general principles of Classical architecture were still (especially in France) unquestioned, it was by reference to the economy and virtuosity of mediaeval vaulting that the Classical theorists first enunciated their specifically Rationalist ideas. Thus J. G. Soufflot, the first and perhaps the greatest architect of the Classical Rationalist School, made elaborate researches into such buildings as Notre-Dame, Dijon (later to be singled out for special study by Eugène Viollet-le-Duc) before designing his great church of Ste. Geneviève, Paris (1756). In 1762 he announced to the Paris Academy that 'by using the Orders in the early Greek manner one can approach the lightness which members have admired in several Gothic monuments, and arrive at a great saving in materials'. As early as 1741 he had given a lecture on Gothic architecture to the Lyons Academy, when he had asked his audience both to admire the bold logic of Gothic constructions, and to make '*quelques raisonnements*' as to their relevance to current designs. 'As regards their construction,' he remarked, 'however superficially we examine Gothic churches, we can see that they are more ingenious, more daring, and even more difficult to construct than our own.' The columns of Gothic buildings were, he said, so pierced by passageways as to be reduced to almost nothing, despite having to support great stone vaults and, above these, timber roofs; and he noted that the mediaeval architects knew how to direct thrusts to the points of greatest resistance (especially in vaulting) by the use of slender shafts and ribs. In his view Roman architecture, on the contrary, was heavy; a defect, he said, not only due to the proportions of the spaces enclosed, but to the character of the supports and the vaulting, which were neither as delicate nor as difficult to execute as those in mediaeval buildings. He therefore tried to overcome these defects in his church of Ste. Geneviève, and we have already seen how he enlisted the services of engineers of the Department of Bridges and Roads in order to make his building as structurally daring as possible.

It is important to notice that Soufflot did not do this by over-simplifying the composition, or by abandoning the established Classical rules governing the proportions of standardized structural masonry elements. Rationalism did not mean for him (nor has it ever meant for any reputable theorist of this School) the type of structural economy expressed by adopting naïvely elemental shapes and constructing them out of cheap materials; it simply meant limiting aesthetic effects to those which logically followed from the nature of the structural components, and designing those components in accordance with rational criteria. Thus even J. F. Blondel (who was not particularly absorbed by the subject of building construction, but who was probably the first theorist specifically to teach that 'good architecture is inseparable from reasoning') defined architecture in 1752 as an art of which 'the first excellence is to express solidity, having for its object construction; then commodity, relative to each type of building; and finally decoration, which consists in the appropriate disposition of the building in general, and, in particular, in the distribution of the ornaments'. It is not without relevance to the later history of Rationalism that French theorists had most consistently, since the time of the elder Blondel (1672) defined architecture as 'the art of building'; a definition which was never part of orthodox Vitruvian doctrine, and was noticeably lacking from Italian writings which elaborated on the Vitruvian text.

Before discussing some of the French Classical Rationalist text-books devoted to building construction (books which constitute one of the novelties of this period as far as theoretical writings are concerned), mention must again be made of the most important speculative writer of the time, Marc-Antoine Laugier, whose *Essay on Architecture* was first published in 1753. A detailed discussion of this perspicacious Jesuit's ideas would be superfluous, since an excellent monograph has been published recently on the subject by Wolfgang Herrmann. But some outline of Laugier's basic contentions is necessary if the thread of the Rationalist argument is to be maintained; otherwise the theoretical basis of many nineteenth century contentions may be unnecessarily obscured.

Laugier began his book by insisting that in those arts which were not purely mechanical, it was necessary above all to learn how to reason, for 'an artist must be able to justify by reasons everything that he does'. This statement in itself is enough to justify us in regarding Laugier as a pioneer of the Rationalist School, but he then proceeds to a thoroughly Rationalist exposition of Classical and Gothic construction (though he shows himself to be a confirmed Classicist, in his assumption of the use of the Five Orders) since he asserts that 'the parts of an architectural

J. G. Soufflot: Church of St. Geneviève (Panthéon) Paris (1757)

RATIONALISM

Illustrating the structural temerity of the Classical Rationalists,
inspired by Gothic prototypes

XXI

H. Labrouste: Library of St. Geneviève, Paris (1843)

RATIONALISM

Illustrating how Classical proportions were modified by the Rationalists
in accordance with new structural materials

E. E. Viollet-le-Duc: Illustration from *Entretiens* (1863)

RATIONALISM

Showing one of the attempts made in the nineteenth century to create a new architecture of iron

XXIII

E. E. Viollet-le-Duc: Illustration from *Entretiens* (1863)

RATIONALISM

Showing another attempt made in the nineteenth century to create a new architecture of iron

XXIV

Order are the very components of the building; they must therefore be employed in such a way as not only to decorate a building but to constitute it, whereby if a single element is removed, the whole building will collapse'. It was, he thought, easy to distinguish those elements which entered essentially into the composition of a Classical Order from those which had no practical necessity and were attributable to some kind of artistic whim. The essential elements comprised free-standing columns, the entablatures which these supported, and the superimposed pediment terminating the sloping roof.

At first sight this assertion might appear as nothing more than a plea for the Greek Revival in its most ingenuous form, that is to say, as an encouragement for using temples to encase every type of accommodation from small houses to public edifices. But Laugier's argument was considerably more subtle, since he was concerned with Greek *elements*, not Greek compositions. For example, the design he proposed for a church was based on Gothic prototypes, in that he envisaged a system of slender free-standing supports between which the infilling walls would consist solely of large sheets of glass. His ideas, doubtless inspired by Jules-Hardouin Mansart's chapel at Versailles (which he knew well, and which was in turn based on the Sainte-Chapelle), were thus exactly comparable to those held by Soufflot. 'Gothic buildings', wrote Laugier, 'have sometimes carried delicacy to absolute extremes, going beyond even the limits generally accepted. But these buildings are no less stable than those built in more recent years, as is proved by their durability. It is certainly time we took note of the spirit of this architecture, ridiculous though it may appear, and studied the surprising artifices used in this manner of building, where everything is consistent, even though extremely slender'.

The main difference between the architectural system he proposed and the Gothic churches which inspired his compositions lay in his insistence on the use of Classical entablatures instead of arches. Now this complete exclusion of the arch in a country such as France, where megalithic construction was impracticable, inevitably necessitated the use of what may be called pseudo-entablatures, that is to say, of flat arches held in position by metal reinforcement; a contradictory and somewhat illogical process which was to be triumphantly assailed by the Gothic Rationalists when they argued in favour of the pointed arch.

For some reason—probably the early eighteenth century's unshakeable faith in Classical values—the architects of the time saw nothing paradoxical in using voussoirs shaped to simulate beams. As early as 1687 the Academy had asserted that architraves made up of several voussoirs were preferable to those made from a single stone, since such monoliths would have to be face-bedded. As late as the mid-nineteenth century, engineers such as P. J. Ardant, with no aesthetic axe to grind, had expressed their complete faith in the universal validity of trabeated expression. Admittedly, by the nineteenth century, trabeation was not in itself an important issue, since the Renaissance Revival had brought light semi-circular arches back into favour as part of the repertoire of Classical motifs when supported on free-standing columns rather than piers; but the notion of not merely carving the appearance of a frame on the surface of a building (as practised by the Romans), but constructing such buildings as genuine frames, continued to dominate Classical Rationalist thinking, and we find it expounded by such authorities on building construction as J. A. Borgnis and Léonce Reynaud. According to Borgnis's *Elementary Treatise on Construction* (1823), engaged columns and engaged pilasters which merely formed an 'architecture in relief' had neither the beauty nor magnificence of isolated columns, and it was only permissible to use them provided one did not lose sight of the fact that this architecture in relief constituted, like an open peristyle, an integral part of the building. Thus, according to his doctrine, the parts in relief must actually be the horizontal and vertical *chaînages* which 'constitute the carcass of the building', and which consequently must be composed of solid materials carefully worked. The rest of the building, 'being only an infilling', could thus be of flimsy materials without the solidity of the building noticeably suffering. Hence a good architect should regard architecture in relief not as simply decoration, but as something utilitarian, and composed of fundamental elements which would guide him in the positioning of apertures and partitions when the building was being planned.

Borgnis's Rationalism is evident from the very beginning of his treatise, for he announced in his preface that 'architecture is an art which demands more reasoning than inspiration, and more factual knowledge than verve'. The avowed aim of his book was to enable architects to fulfil 'economically and suitably' all the conditions demanded by nature and by the client. According to him, the close analogy which some people had tried to establish between architecture and the imitative arts, such as painting and sculpture, was completely unjustified, for whereas the main pursuit of architecture was utility, painting and sculpture limited themselves to giving pleasure to the eye, or to charming the understanding. Thus, he claimed, a false analogy had been made, which had slowed down the progress of architecture by directing the studies of young architects into false paths. They had been persuaded that first of all the principal purpose of architecture was to produce agreeable sensations by the elegant and picturesque combination of masses, and had thus tended to become decorators rather than architects. He assured his readers that it was an error to believe that an architect only produced dull and inelegant designs if he subordinated the choice of forms, relationships and dimensions to the essential purpose of the building. Architecture, he insisted, was like nature; for 'the sovereign Master of the universe has established that in organized beings, the parts which best fulfil their special destination are also most pleasing to the sight'.

It will thus be seen that Borgnis's argument was not only an attack on the romantic architecture of Boullée and Ledoux, and a defence of the views of Durand (who was almost certainly his master); it was also an attack on the current system of education then given at the École des Beaux-Arts, where building construction was notoriously neglected, and where the main effort was directed towards designing lavish projects for the *Prix de Rome*. In this respect it is worth noting that before the French Revolution, architecture had been taught in complete independence of the Academies of Painting and Sculpture, and had consisted simply of lectures on theory and mathematics given at the Academy of Architecture, combined with a system of articled pupillage directed by the members of the Academy themselves. But after the Revolution, the three disciplines had been combined to form a single Academy of Fine Arts, and it was against the subjection of architecture to the 'arts of drawing', characteristic of the early Italian Renaissance (and doubtless inspired in part by the Renaissance Revival) that Borgnis clearly rebelled.

Nevertheless, in fairness to the École des Beaux-Arts, it must be admitted that the bad habit of treating architecture as simply a matter of dramatic pictorial representation and lavish ornamentation had been growing increasingly evident long before Napoleon's administrative reforms were put into effect in 1806, for an attack on such abuses was contained in a memorandum distributed to the National Assembly in 1789 by J. B. Rondelet, the supervising architect for Soufflot's Ste. Geneviève. From the time of the Renaissance, he wrote, architects had been far too preoccupied with decoration, and had made this accessory part of architecture their principal aim. The origin of the abuse, he said, could be traced to the fact that when Gothic architecture was abandoned in Italy, the first architects to follow the new fashion had been painters and draftsmen, who thus had had nothing but decoration in mind. Hence this part of architecture was more congenial to them than planning and construction, because the latter demanded specialized knowledge. Hence also, the products of these first architects consisted mainly of decorative elements, which did not form an essential part of the building, and resulted in a heavy and expensive veneer of architecture in which everything was subjected to the decorator's caprice. Unfortunately the special favour accorded to specialist decorators since this time had caused many architects to abandon the study of planning and especially that of construction. Distinctions and prizes were lavished on those who excelled in architectural decoration, and one could not escape the impression that they regarded the two other parts of architecture as degrading and beneath their contempt, even though, in Rondelet's view, these were in fact the most essential parts of the art of building.

Rondelet therefore proposed that instead of just having one professor at the proposed new school of architecture (who, he felt certain, would deal only with decoration), there should also be professors of planning and construction. Projects and competitions could then emphasize each of these three aspects in turn, whilst the *Prix de Rome* could demand the union of all three.

To some extent his recommendations were accepted, for he himself was eventually appointed professor of stereotomy at the new École des Beaux-Arts as soon as it was established, and he profited from the appointment to interpret the term 'stereotomy' (which means in fact the applied science of solid geometry relevant to masonry and carpentry) in its widest technological sense. But the tendency to emphasize superficial skills in draftsmanship, and to ignore the more practical aspects of building, continued unabated, despite attempts at reform by Rationalist studio-masters such as Henri Labrouste. As a result, the École des Beaux-Arts was subjected to violent criticisms throughout the nineteenth century (especially from the ranks of the Gothic Rationalists) in the pages of the architectural magazines. In 1840, even such a confirmed Classicist as Henri Labrouste wrote to the *Revue Générale de l'Architecture* complaining that the constructional studies made by his students at the École des Beaux-Arts had no relationship to their design projects (a system which, it will be recalled, had unwisely been recommended by Rondelet), and he lamented the impression this created that design and construction were entirely separate disciplines. Similarly, in the following year, the editor of this same magazine (who also favoured Classicism) commented acidly on the fact that those who entered for the *Prix de Rome* had to isolate themselves from the world in which they lived in order to remain in constant contemplation before an ideal of academic art; and he supported his complaint by pointing out that the programme for that year, entitled 'A French Embassy for an Oriental Capital', included the instructions that 'it must be assumed that this embassy will be organized with all the pomp which was customary in the age of Louis XIV'!

Yet during the first quarter of the nineteenth century, French architectural students had at least the opportunity of studying Rondelet's *Theoretical and Practical Treatise on the Art of Building* (first published in 1802), and this, being the first comprehensive textbook on building construction, was undoubtedly one of the greatest rationalizing influences of the age. Like the engineers of the period (with whom he had been in close contact during the construction of Ste. Geneviève), he claimed that the essential purpose of architecture was to construct solid edifices by employing exact quantities of selected materials, and setting them in position with skill and economy. Architecture was not, like painting and sculpture, an art whose sole aim was to please, and in which the artist, executing his own projects, could abandon himself to the fire of his own imagination. Architecture was a science, and its essential aim was to construct solidly and commodiously; to build edifices which combined in the most beautiful form all the parts necessary for its destination.

Rondelet's book was eventually reprinted in several editions, and was widely imitated, notably by the German engineer C. F. Wiebeking (whose *Civil Architecture* was published in 1827) and Peter Nicholson (whose *New Practical Builder*, which first appeared in 1823, was almost a plagiarism in translation of Rondelet's *Art de Bâtir*). Moreover, Léonce Reynaud's *Treatise on Architecture*, which has already been discussed in the previous chapter, was clearly a reflection of the tendency which Rondelet had so auspiciously inaugurated. Reynaud himself claimed that his purpose was to show that 'the principal forms of our architecture are eminently rational in their fundamentals', and that the historical truth of this would have been long before demonstrated by science if the scientists of the epochs in which earlier forms had been developed had been sufficiently knowledgeable. By this he presumably meant the same thing as was later to be claimed by Auguste Choisy (another distinguished engineer, who eventually became professor of architecture at the École des Ponts et Chaussées) when he asserted in his *History of Architecture* (1899) that the Hellenic age had brought the structure of its marble temples into harmony with the archaic timber forms already established by pious tradition. Thus Reynaud also asserted that the spirit of the Doric Order consisted 'in seeking ornamentation by setting in evidence the system of rational construction'.

There is no doubt that the Classical Rationalists merited both parts of their title, since they were undoubtedly temperamentally inclined to rationalize every element of design, whilst they were equally clearly reluctant to reject any traditional Antique forms. But what, it may be asked, was the practical advantage of this combination of ideals? Did it help produce a new architecture? Did it even produce an architecture suitable for the age in which their theories were evolved? Or did it just serve to intoxicate its advocates by the lucidity of its intellectual demonstrations, whilst at the same time confirming them in the perpetuation of superannuated traditions, hallowed by age?

It must be confessed that Classical Rationalism did not produce any startlingly novel works of architecture, and critics who, like William Vose Pickett, considered that the criterion of progress was novelty, naturally considered that the theory had no value at all. But it would be wrong to assume that the ideals of the Classical Rationalists were not widely beneficial, or to assume that they failed to produce buildings appropriate to the age. In essence, the Classical Rationalists demanded three things of architecture: firstly, a reappraisal of the proportions of all structural elements with respect to the newly established science of the strength of materials; secondly, a logical approach to planning with respect to the actual needs of the intended occupants; and thirdly, a more flexible approach to the Classical notions of symmetry and regularity, whereby, for example, windows lighting stairways could be placed more often in relationship to internal landings, rather than with respect to a regular alignment on the exterior façades.

Apart from their attitude towards planning (which will be discussed in the next chapter), the Classical Rationalists' doctrine thus resolved itself into a philosophy inspired by what a correspondent to the *Revue Générale de l'Architecture* (anticipating Viollet-le-Duc by many years, and Frank Lloyd Wright by over half a century) was to call 'the nature of materials'. But it will be apparent that this new philosophy only became ostensibly applicable when necessity or economy dictated the use of new materials, such as metals, or (when it was invented) reinforced concrete. Thus Reynaud, like the other Classical Rationalists, was well aware that new forms and new proportions would be necessary for the materials which industry had just given them, and that, for example, iron columns needed to be more widely spaced than stone columns. This was why Labrouste's libraries, with their cast iron Corinthian shafts thirty diameters high, were so rightly regarded as of revolutionary importance at the time. Yet it must never be forgotten that Labrouste also built several other buildings which, superficially at least, might seem simply examples of neo-Louis XIII; for where the use of new materials was not logically indicated, a novel form of expression seemed to the Rationalists to be automatically excluded, and it was only those who deliberately sought a 'new architecture' at any price, and who used new systems of construction without any rational justification from the point of view of convenience or cost, who could hope to produce a new architecture visible in every kind of building they erected. As Labrouste expressed it: 'architectural elements, which are truly the organs of the whole building, are modified according to the particular functions they have to fulfil, and from this fact they demand a choice of materials which are most suited, in accordance with their aptitudes, to make these functions possible. The special aptitudes of building materials thus have the most direct influence on the form it is appropriate to give them, and decoration thus finds itself intimately linked to construction. The beauty of a monument resides in the harmonious expression between needs and the means of satisfying them'.

Rationalism, whether Classical, Gothic or Eclectic, was the most widespread and certainly the healthiest architectural movement of the nineteenth century, and many buildings which appear to be simply examples of Revivalism are in fact honest attempts to put Rationalist ideals into practice. This can even be deduced from the idealistic appeal launched by the Royal Institute of British Architects in 1849, when the problem was squarely placed before the whole profession. According to this official statement, the aesthetics of every distinct period of history had to be considered as growing out of the principles of construction observed at the time. But since society, in the middle of the nineteenth century, was undergoing a marked transition as regards new standards of construction, new materials and new needs, the architecture of the day was faced with boundless requirements which had not existed a century before. The Royal Institute therefore considered it time that all architects who wished to keep pace with contemporary progress should study the problem in co-operation with one another. The Council was determined, it said, to render the ensuing session remarkable by a more distinct aim and activity of purpose. They ventured to anticipate that members of the Institute would consider it their duty, as well as a delight, to contribute to the intellectual advancement which they hoped to see in action; and that this contribution could only be made by each one turning his attention to the consideration of some particular aspect of contemporary architectural design, and communicating his discoveries to fellow-members.

It needed in fact no more than this to create an architecture in harmony with the age; but Rationalism did not produce the startlingly visible and tangible results the pundits were expecting until the commercial exploitation of steel and reinforced concrete frames began in the early 1890s. Here, clearly, were the ideal materials for Classical Rationalism, for by the very nature of these structural systems, and of the spaces normally to be enclosed by them, they were trabeated, and hence possessed potentially all those aesthetic qualities possessed by the Classical buildings of the past. In addition, the fireproof nature and weather-resisting qualities of concrete enabled it to be used without any exterior casing, such as was necessary for steel. It was inevitable therefore that sooner or later someone would use reinforced concrete in accordance with Classical Rationalist principles. In the event, that man proved to be Auguste Perret, an architect trained by Julien Guadet, the last great theorist of Classical Rationalism, and the author of the standard textbook on the subject published at the end of the nineteenth century. But Perret was also trained by reading Viollet-le-Duc's works on Gothic Rationalism, and by practical experience in his father's construction firm.

There is no need to discuss either Perret's principles or his career, since this has been amply accomplished in several languages. But it is perhaps worth while reflecting on the reasons why Perret's example was so little followed, and why he may appropriately be regarded as the last great Classical Rationalist of the nineteenth century (just as Ludwig Mies van der Rohe, the apostle of glass and steel, may be regarded as the first great Classical Rationalist of the twentieth century). One might argue that Perret's principles became obsolete once Maillart discovered that reinforced concrete was technologically more effective when used as thin slabs rather than as a frame (though this argument would seem to be demonstrably refuted by the large number of reinforced concrete frame buildings still being constructed in our modern cities). One might argue that Perret's forms became unfashionable once the public became finally tired of cornices, string courses, pilasters and all the other elements of his system which, however logical, were too reminiscent of the past. Yet in fact the abandonment of traditional Rationalist principles in reinforced concrete construction goes far deeper than any of these considerations, and is intimately related to the whole revolutionary change which has taken place in the nature of the graphic arts.

According to J. A. Borgnis in his *Elementary Treatise on Construction*, architecture differed from painting and sculpture in that the former used methods deducible from the physico-mathematical sciences, whereas painting and sculpture relied on 'the faithful and ingenious imitation of nature's most beautiful productions'. Similarly, Léonce Reynaud had asserted in his *Treatise on Architecture* that architecture presented one peculiarity, as compared with painting and sculpture, in that the forms from which it was called upon to extract its expressions were products of human intelligence, instead of being borrowed from creation. But with the invention of abstract painting and abstract sculpture, all this changed. Henceforth, as Reyner Banham has explained in his *Guide to Modern Architecture*, architecture was considered aesthetically as 'the creation of sculpture big enough to walk about inside', whilst architects such as Le Corbusier made no mystery of the fact that abstract painting was the basis of their architectural creativity. Thus all abstract theorizing about the rational proportions of structural members and the most logical refinements of such tectonic elements was henceforth considered a waste of time. Not everyone may agree with John Summerson's remark, in *Heavenly Mansions*, that 'technological progress has really very little to do with advances in architectural design', or that 'it is by no means true that the "new materials" of our time have changed architecture'. Indeed, no Rationalist, from the very nature of his beliefs, could possibly agree with such a point of view. But there is no doubt that the reliance on structural justifications for architectural forms is no longer as fashionable as it was, and that despite the work of Mies van der Rohe and his numerous disciples, Classical Rationalism, as an ideal, is temporarily overshadowed by the search for more emotionally-inspired abstract shapes.

*   *   *

Gothic Rationalism, as has already been pointed out, was, in the mid-eighteenth century, theoretically indistinguishable from Classical Rationalism, since both were manifestations of the same belief that architecture derives its finest expression from the most economical use of structural forms. But it was inevitable that the two should eventually separate, because of the general disagreement which arose between Classical Revivalists and Gothic Revivalists in the following century. Ostensibly, the Gothicists' reason for precipitating the schism was their objection to the Classicists' use of flat arches, since they argued, with some justification, that this was structurally irrational, and was a blatant example of an alien structural system being fitted into a preconceived tectonic form. But the real reason for the schism was the fact that they believed so fervently in Gothic for religious, sociological or nationalistic reasons, as well as for structural reasons, and were thus unwilling to compromise by making a rational synthesis between Classical and Gothic ideals. The synthesis was not again to be accomplished until the end of the nineteenth century, with the historical works of Auguste Choisy and the theoretical works of Julien Guadet. But by this time new structural systems were already making any architectural speculations based on masonry construction virtually obsolete, so that although the synthesis was by no means wasted, it did not have the immediate beneficial value it might have had fifty years before.

The weakness of the Gothic Rationalist position, when urged independently of Classical Rationalism, was that in the nineteenth century it implied resuscitation rather than reform; for however extravagant Classical stereotomy might seem in its complicated techniques for constructing trabeated forms out of voussoirs, it did at least constitute a system of masonry construction which had been developed continuously from the end of the Middle Ages until the modern age. It may be argued that when the Gothic Rationalists insisted that building craftsmen should be completely re-trained, they were demanding nothing unreasonable, and were in fact showing remarkable prescience, in that within recent years the training of building craftsmen has become radically different from what it was a hundred years ago. Nevertheless it should be noted that even the Classical Rationalists never denied that building technology would have to change and evolve; they simply denied the necessity of going back to the Middle Ages in order to set this evolutionary process into motion properly. As Léonce Reynaud put it: 'the art of the Middle Ages is dead, and although one can galvanize a corpse, one cannot bring it back to life. It is precisely because thirteenth century architecture was true in its day that it would be completely false now'.

The dilemma became very apparent in France during the controversy which raged over the construction of the church of Ste. Clothilde in Paris in 1845. The Academy, when asked specifically to pronounce on this problem, contended that despite the undeniable appropriateness of the religious atmosphere created by Gothic churches, it was not permissible to retrogress four centuries in order to give monumental expression to a society which by this time had acquired new needs, customs and habits. There was only one natural and legitimate means for society to be artistically productive, it claimed, and that was to be of its own time, to live with the ideas of its own century, and to appropriate all the elements of civilization to be found within its grasp, as, for example, 'by collecting from the past and the present all elements which can serve a useful purpose'. Naturally this latter Eclectic doctrine did not satisfy the more convinced Gothic Revivalists, and their leader, Eugène Viollet-le-Duc, who was then at the beginning of his career, retorted with a pamphlet entitled *On the Gothic Style in the Nineteenth Century* (1846), which, after criticizing Eclecticism for its lack of unity, asserted that unity could only result, as in Gothic architecture, from a consistent system of construction.

To justify the imitation of Gothic, Viollet-le-Duc claimed that since art progressed by gradual transitions, it was permissible for architects, in order to liberate themselves from the shackles of the immediate past, to copy buildings based on the most rational structural system they could find. They would thus produce original masterpieces in due course. But the hollowness of his argument became only too apparent in the ensuing fifty years, for it was not until the end of the century, with the construction of Anatole de Baudot's concrete church of St. Jean-de-Montmartre, that any disciple of Viollet-le-Duc succeeded in abandoning the mere imitation of Gothic forms. In fact the only solid defence of the Gothic Rationalist position (as will be remembered from the controversy already reported between G. G. Scott and James Fergusson) was that Gothic was the most scientific system of masonry construction, and should therefore be adopted without further delay in masonry buildings. But it was very difficult in practice, and perhaps even illogical in theory, to make a real distinction between the adoption of mediaeval masonry principles and mere conformity with mediaeval tectonic prototypes, and many must have shared the disillusionment of theorists like J. L. Petit, who, with exquisite tact, remarked to Scott in 1856 that 'when few modern Gothic works of merit were in existence, I thought the revival possible, and that a careful study of ancient examples might enable us to work in the ancient spirit; but after having seen many new Gothic works of great merit, I consider that the attempt to revive the style will not be successful'.

Another reason for Gothic Rationalism's relatively modest influence in the mid-nineteenth century was the defection of John Ruskin. In *The Seven Lamps of Architecture*, particularly in the chapter entitled 'The Lamp of Truth', it had seemed as if Ruskin would champion the view that architectural form was essentially structural form; but we have already seen how, as a result of the attractions of Venetian polychromy, he soon decided that 'the science of inner construction' was to be abandoned, and that just as Protestantism had despised the arts, so 'Rationalism has corrupted them'. His arch-enemy E. L. Garbett expressed the view, in his *Rudimentary Treatise on the Principles of Design* (1850), that this attitude resulted in two widely different arts bearing the name 'architecture', and that the more common of them could be defined as the art of clothing or masking buildings, of whatever class, with scenic representations of the features of a superior class, erected in some past age. Many Gothic Revivalists made a gallant attempt not to fall into this error; but despite the efforts of A. W. N. Pugin and G. E. Street, neo-Gothic architecture in England was mainly a costume, applied for religious, sociological or nationalistic reasons. The most powerful advocate of the principles of Gothic Rationalism was the Frenchman whose name has already been mentioned: E. E. Viollet-le-Duc.

Not that England lacked occasional writers who were anxious to put the Gothic Rationalist point of view before the British public. As early as 1805 Dr. John Robison, in a series of university lectures on *Mechanical Philosophy*, had asserted that 'the Gothic architecture is perhaps entitled to the name of rational architecture', and had told his audience that they might profitably assess the appropriateness of this title by studying the construction of Gothic vaults, and by examining its component parts: 'not as ornaments, but as useful members; for all this cannot be understood without mechanical knowledge, a thing which few of our professional architects have any share of'. Yet Robison's attitude was more characteristic of the eighteenth century point of view, in that it did not accept everything Gothic uncritically. Thus he was astute enough to observe that mediaeval architects, for all their Rationalism, frequently imitated masonry forms in timber, just as the architects of Antiquity had imitated timber forms in stone. It was this which led him to point out to his students the relationship between rational forms and good architecture, and he even anticipated the theory of vernacular architecture, by pointing out that 'since stone is the chief material of our buildings, the members of ornamental architecture ought to be refinements on the essential and unaffected parts of simple stone-building'. For this reason, he thought that masonry and not carpentry should constitute the basic design principles of contemporary architecture, and since masonry was the characteristic feature of Gothic, he thought

Gothic principles should prevail. Similarly, he noted that the mediaeval architecture of northern Europe was characterized by high-pitched roofs, and he challenged his audience to prove that the principles on which these were based were false or tasteless.

Another equally unbiased British supporter of Gothic Rationalism at this early period was Humphrey Repton, who, in his book on *Landscape Gardening and Landscape Architecture* (1795) announced that the leading principle of construction in Gothic architecture was the fact that every arch exerted lateral thrust, so that Gothic architecture depended on a system of abutments. He also perceived that Gothic pinnacles, 'which have often been mistaken for ornaments', exerted a structural function in loading the summits of these buttresses. But Repton was probably the last British theorist to write intelligently about Gothic construction without becoming emotionally involved in the sociological or religious implications of Gothic forms, and henceforth, books on Gothic architecture constituted a sort of *littérature engagée*, in which constructional principles represented only a minor aspect of the lessons to be taught.

Probably the first book to expound in a coherent form the notion that Gothic architecture was the only true architecture, and that it was true partly because its forms were alone derived from structural laws, was A. W. N. Pugin's *True Principles of Pointed or Christian Architecture*, a series of lectures published in 1841 and translated into French in 1850. It started off by explaining that the two great rules for design were, firstly, that there should be no features about a building which were not necessary for convenience, construction or propriety, and secondly, that all ornament should consist simply of the enrichment of the essential construction of a building. This construction itself would vary with the material employed, and designs should therefore be adapted to the material in which they were executed. Only in 'pointed architecture', he insisted, were these great principles carried out, and he announced his intention of demonstrating this by reference to every type of building constructed in the Middle Ages, from cathedrals to simple cottages.

According to Pugin, Gothic architecture did not conceal its construction but beautified it. Thus a Gothic column was an architectural member which was only employed when a superincumbent load was required to be sustained without the obstruction of solid walling. Hence engaged Classical pilasters were always wrong. Similarly, Gothic buttresses at once showed their purpose, diminishing naturally as they rose with less compression to resist, whereas Classical pilasters, being on the contrary of more or less constant width, were illogical as a form of exterior modulation. Flying buttresses showed the way in which the essential supports of a building could be converted into light and elegant decoration, for 'who can stand among the airy arches of Amiens, Cologne, Chartres, Beauvais or Westminster', he rhetorically asked, 'and not be filled with admiration at the mechanical skill and beautiful combination of forms which are united in their construction?' A number of rival theorists could do this quite well, and they said so; but their views were airily disregarded by Pugin, who was more of a draftsman than a constructor, and was too enamoured of Gothic forms to accept Léonce Reynaud's sober contention that flying buttresses were an unnecessary luxury, just as he was indifferent to the fact that they were difficult to calculate accurately, and impossible to maintain in good repair without constant supervision.

Pugin returned to the attack in 1843 with his *Apology for the Revival of Christian Architecture*, when in addition to the many religious and nationalistic arguments marshalled in favour of Gothic, he again put forward the Rationalist point of view. Architectural skill, he wrote, consisted in embodying and expressing the structure required, and not in disguising it with borrowed features. Thus the peasant's hut, the yeoman's cottage, the farmer's house and the baronial hall could each be perfect in its own way, in that 'every building that is treated naturally, without disguise or concealment, cannot fail to look well'. As an example of how appropriate Gothic was for a modern city, he even appended an illustration of a neo-Gothic merchant's house inscribed above the lower windows with the legend 'G. Edwards, Grocer and Tea Dealer' (or, in the French edition, 'Edouard Marlet, Epicier') in Gothic capitals. But in practice the Gothic Rationalist theory was mainly of service as a justification for a certain type of ecclesiastical architecture, and it was for this reason that so many of its arguments misfired when attempts were made to adapt Gothic principles to the more mundane requirements of the modern world.

Another important British writer at this time was Alfred Bartholemew who, according to Eastlake, the first historian of Gothic Revivalism, was 'the first to enunciate the principle that the conditions of true taste in architecture have always been intimately associated with those of structural excellence'. Thus in his *Specifications for Practical Architecture* (1841), a book very much influenced by Rondelet's *Art de Bâtir*, he announced that it was his intention to prove that pure taste in architecture had in all past ages been purely structural, and that 'in Pointed Architecture all is structural'. But he was not particularly gifted as a speculative writer, nor did he make any real attempt to analyse the structural virtues of the great buildings of the past. There can in fact be no doubt that the first really important apostle of Gothic Rationalism was Eugène Emmanuel Viollet-le-Duc, a man who spent the early part of his career repairing and studying existing mediaeval monuments, and who was thus enabled to ascertain more correctly than any of his contemporaries the structural principles on which a theory of Gothic architecture should be based.

Viollet-le-Duc had precursors in his own country, and we have already seen how the ground had been prepared by the Classical theorists of the eighteenth century. He himself acknowledged his debt to an obscure author named Frémin, whose structural description of Notre-Dame and the Sainte Chapelle had been published in 1702. Moreover, although the architectural aspects of Gothic Romanticism had never gained much popularity in France (where it was known derisively as 'the

Troubadour Style'), there had been a considerable amount of scholarly research into mediaeval archaeology by the 1840s, and a number of popular works on the subject had been published, such as J. B. Seroux d'Agincourt's *History of Art from the Fourth Century to the Renaissance* (1823) which, though highly inaccurate, and biased in favour of Italian Romanesque, nevertheless put forward Gothic architecture as a coherent system. In 1842, the *Revue Générale de l'Architecture* had published a translation of Willis's study of mediaeval vault construction, whilst at the same time considerable interest in the Rationalism of Gothic architecture was stimulated by the publication of Lamennais' essay *On Art and Beauty* (1841), in which it was asserted that what characterized Gothic architecture was the organic way in which so many diverse elements were united in a single form. It is not surprising, therefore, to find enthusiasm for mediaeval architecture among a few of the younger architects of the early 1840s, as was manifested, for example, by the drawings of mediaeval buildings exhibited in the Salons of those years.

There is no need to elaborate here on the general theories expounded by Viollet-le-Duc, since a comprehensive study of his doctrine has already been admirably written by John Summerson, and published in the series of essays entitled *Heavenly Mansions*. It will be enough simply to indicate the specific nature of Viollet-le-Duc's Rationalism as expounded in his *Lectures on Architecture*, first published in 1863, and subsequently reprinted in English translation in the United States in 1889.

First it should be made clear that although Viollet-le-Duc was essentially concerned with Gothic architecture, he was not, like Pugin and Ruskin, either a romantic or a religious enthusiast, and was perfectly willing to admit that even Greek temples were rational in so far as they went. He had no hesitation in asserting that in Greek architecture 'the visible exterior form was simply the result of construction', or, elsewhere, that 'the exterior form of Greek architecture was simply the result of reasoned construction'; and whilst he despised Roman architecture (because it was veneered concrete) and Renaissance architecture (which, though not of concrete, was in his view derived from it), he was unstinting in his praise of such unlikely buildings as Gabriel's palaces in the Place de la Concorde, where there were free-standing Classical columns supporting reinforced flat-arch entablatures and a flat masonry vault. 'The Orders of architecture invented by the Greeks are the very structure itself', he proclaimed, in words which almost paraphrase Laugier; 'thus the structure and appearance of Greek buildings are essentially united, since it is impossible to remove any part of the Order without destroying the monument itself'.

Naturally this principle was best expressed for him in Gothic architecture. It could properly be asserted, he wrote, that it was impossible to separate the form of thirteenth century architecture from its structure, since every member of that architecture was the consequence of a structural need. Hence it was impossible to remove or attach any decorative forms without doing harm to the building's solidity, or, as he put it, to its 'organism'. Thirteenth century architecture had, in his opinion, the virtue of being true and universally applicable, because its forms evolved from reasoned principles, and not from arbitrary shapes. Thus the forms could never be capricious, since they were simply the expression of the structure. 'I cannot give you rules to impose on form', he remarked (implying thereby an unspoken criticism of Vitruvian rules), 'because the essential quality of architectural form is to adapt itself to every necessity of the structure. Impose on me a structural system, and I will naturally find you the forms which should result from it. But if you change the structure, I shall be obliged to change the forms; not in their spirit, since that spirit is precisely to express the structure, but in their appearance, since the structure has changed'.

On the basis of such principles Viollet-le-Duc speculated on the nature of an architecture appropriate to the new age in which he lived, but unlike most Gothic Revivalists, he not merely welcomed cast iron, but assumed that it was only by using some such new structural material that a new architecture could evolve. 'Architecture', he wrote, 'can only equip itself with new forms if it seeks them in the rigorous application of a new structure'. Unfortunately, however, his anxiety to discover new forms betrayed him into devising combinations of iron and masonry which no experienced building contractor would have countenanced for one moment, and into devising systems of triangulation which any engineer would have laughed to scorn. In this respect it is worth comparing his achievement with that of Auguste Perret, who found so much inspiration in Viollet-le-Duc's ideals. Perret's superiority rests on the fact that he simply adopted and refined a structural system *which had already been evolved by engineers and building contractors*; hence his system conserved its validity until more economical and more rational ways of using concrete had been devised. But Viollet-le-Duc's system was a figment of his own untrained speculation, and received no support from the building industry of his day; hence his imaginative projects had little evolutionary significance. Nevertheless, though Viollet-le-Duc found himself incapable of devising a new architecture (mainly through the misfortune of being born half a century too soon), his writings were the main source of the Structural Rationalism of his successors, and it may justly be claimed that no one has ever put forward so coherently and so plausibly the Rationalist point of view.

Viollet-le-Duc's main influence on the young architects of the following generation, such as Anatole de Baudot and Auguste Perret, derived principally from the careful studies of mediaeval masonry construction published in his *Dictionary of French Architecture from the Eleventh to the Sixteenth Century*, especially in the chapter entitled 'Construction', two hundred and seventy-eight pages long. Here he asserted that his entire method was based on the assumption that 'the architecture and construction of the Middle Ages cannot be separated, in that the architecture is nothing else than a form commanded by the construction itself'. Similarly, in the same chapter, he explained how the flexible principles applied by mediaeval architects could, if carefully studied, place his readers in the paths of progress, since such a study permitted every innovation, and the use of every type of material. 'Mediaeval principles consist precisely in submitting everything—materials, forms, plans and details—to *reasoning*', he wrote. But his influence on Perret resulted not only from his Rationalism, but from his insistence on the need to study architecture as a process which took place on building sites, rather than solely as an aspect of delineation and academic research. It so happened that Perret was one of the few students of the École des Beaux-Arts whose father was a building contractor. He was therefore forced to gain practical knowledge at first hand, and to become a 'skilled constructor' of the type Viollet-le-Duc admired. It was this experience, combined with the extraordinary coincidence of reaching maturity just at the time engineers and building contractors were bringing the techniques of reinforced concrete frame construction to perfection, which enabled him to accomplish that role of a pioneer which has been universally and so justly attributed to him. But one should not overlook the fact that this emphasis on building crafts-manship was also influential elsewhere, notably at the Bauhaus, and it is worth noting that Mies van der Rohe also had a rigid practical training before he evolved an architecture of his own. One may perhaps regret that this basic notion of the early Bauhaus curriculum has been generally abandoned in architectural education, although it may of course be argued that practical skill in building technology is only of vital importance in periods of radical architectural change.

A less beneficial aspect of Gothic Rationalism, but one which was to have considerable influence in the subsequent development of architectural ideals, was the notion that structure was something dynamic. The term 'architectural dynamics' was probably first used by Alfred Bartholemew, when he illustrated it by super-imposing a sketch of a human skeleton on the diagram of a Gothic buttress; but the idea was also put forward by Viollet-le-Duc, who compared the stability of a Gothic cathedral to the stability of a human frame. Just as the human body, he said, is supported on the ground by means of two slender point supports, occupying the least possible space, so a Gothic building stands on a sort of system of pins (*quillage*), the stability of which is only maintained by the combination and development of the upper parts. Thus one cannot remove one of these upper 'organs' without seeing the whole building perish, for it only acquires stability through the laws of equilibrium.

Now there were at this time many reputable engineers who rejected this idea that dynamic equilibrium, in its Gothic Revival sense, was structurally desirable. Léonce Reynaud, for example, in condemning flying buttresses, preferred earlier mediaeval buildings in which the system of buttressing was sheltered by the roof, or, better still, where the structure was sufficiently massive to require no counter-thrusts at all. Similarly, he poured scorn on the so-called daringness of Gothic supports, which he claimed was purely artificial, in that Gothic piers were not really extravagantly slender at all, but were simply made to look slender by the decorative display of composite shafts. But it will be perceived that the opposing attitudes of Viollet-le-Duc and Reynaud stemmed not so much from mathematical analysis and structural logic as from the opposing aesthetic prejudices which were linked to the Classical and Gothic points of view. The Classicists had always favoured the deliberate pursuit of visible repose, and as early as 1676 the French Academy had laid down the rule that 'one must not only pay attention to the real and effective solidity of a building, but also to the appearance of solidity, in order to avoid those Gothic caprices which display an affected search for what is marvellous and surprising'. But it was precisely effects which made men marvel, and filled them with surprise, which had delighted the romantic precursors of Gothic Rationalism, and caused them to favour Gothic daringness even before Rationalists such as Viollet-le-Duc justified it from a structural point of view. That the latter attitude has prevailed in the ensuing years is only too obvious to anyone with the least familiarity with twentieth century architecture, for nowadays it is almost obligatory to support a building on what Viollet-le-Duc would have called *quillages* (and which Le Corbusier has called piles or *pilotis*), whilst cantilevers, which to the early Classicists were always suspect (and hence called *porte-à-faux* or false bearing) are now more popular than any other aesthetic device. Indeed, one of the most paradoxical differences between Perret and Le Corbusier, which explains the former's eclipse and the latter's persistent success, is the fact that whereas Le Corbusier always ostensibly rejected the historical lessons of Gothic architecture (because 'the cathedral is not a plastic work, it is a drama—a fight against the forces of gravity which is a sensation of a sentimental nature'), he nevertheless adopted the sentimental notion of placing every building on *pilotis*, whereas Perret, under the Classical influence of Guadet, always sought for visual effects of repose. Classical Rationalists like Reynaud claimed that it was irrational for the thirteenth century masons to have sought difficulties of execution; but it was precisely the difficulties of execution which most excited the Gothic Rationalists, even though few of their buildings were ever more daringly constructed than those of the Classicists they despised.

Perhaps the most influential aspect of Gothic Rationalism was its ethical message expressed in its emphasis on 'truth'. Nineteenth century Classicists like E. M. Barry, the son of Charles Barry, might well contend that it was 'not truth but affectation to display ostentatiously in a building all the rude features of construction'; but in an age which professed itself tired of shams, the call for truthful expression had an irresistible appeal. When Auguste Perret boasted that there was not a square inch of plaster in his Museum of Public Works (1938), he was not merely attacking the fondness for stucco of the 'International Style'; he was affirming his faith in an ideal that had been the pride of every Gothic Rationalist since the middle of the preceding century. John Robison, in the lectures on *Mechanical Philosophy* referred to earlier, had drawn attention to the truthfulness of Romanesque timber roofs, the essential parts of which were, he said, 'exhibited as things understood and therefore relished', and he praised these slender interlaced timbers as being 'naturally pretty', and as forming an object which no carpenter, nor any enlightened person for that matter, could view without pleasure. The fulminations of Ruskin against shams in his chapter of *The Seven Lamps of Architecture* entitled 'The Lamp of Truth' confirmed and articulated a general sentiment which was already widespread in that integritous and hypocrisy-fearing age. Thus the last of the great English Gothic Revivalists, G. E. Street, speaking in the discussion which followed the first lecture on mild steel construction ever given at the Royal Institute of British Architects (in 1880), voiced his dislike for concealed girders, and criticized Scott's Albert Memorial because, he said, 'we architects know how it stands and why, but it is only because we have been told of the box girders which carry the superstructure'.

Today, the ideals of Gothic Rationalism assert themselves most clearly in a fondness for structural acrobatics and in a delight in rough surfaces. Just as in 1862 Fergusson demanded that the doors in dwellings should be of plain deal and that the timbers of the drawing-room ceiling should be 'exposed, rudely squared, with the bolts and screws all shown', so the so-called New Brutalists today demand that concrete shall be poured into rough formwork, rather than into formwork with its surfaces in any way refined. Indeed, in the United States there are known cases of admirers of Le Corbusier nailing special coarse planking to the interior surfaces of their smooth plywood formwork in order to obtain this roughness artificially and at considerable expense. One can, of course, dismiss all such attitudes as temporary fashions, and there is no doubt that the taste for crude surfaces is to some extent a momentary reaction against the plastered surfaces associated with the International Style of the 1930s. But it would be unwise to underrate the very profound influence which the taste for Structural Rationalism, whether Classical or Gothic, has had on contemporary architectural speculation. However much the emphasis on structural expression may have been exaggerated in the past by a craving for ostentation, or reduced by the competing emphases on spatial effects, sculptural effects and new planning requirements, it is still potentially one of the most vigorous ideals of the modern age, and it would not be an exaggeration to say that it is the notion which offers the most fruitful prospects for the future development of modern architectural thought.

20

New Planning Problems

It has been necessary to employ the term 'Functionalism' in various differing contexts in this book, since it has several meanings. It can mean the general philosophical notion that an object which fulfils its function properly is automatically beautiful, as when Archibald Alison asserted that 'in useful forms, beauty is proportional to expression of character'. It can mean the general philosophical notion that an object which fulfils its function properly is automatically of its era, however superficially unattractive, as when Frederick Etchells, in his introduction to *Towards a New Architecture*, wrote that 'it is inevitable that the engineer, preoccupied with function and aiming at an immediate response to new demands, should produce new and strange forms, often startling at first, bizarre and disagreeable'. It can mean the general philosophical notion that an object made to fulfil its function economically possesses structural integrity (although in this sense 'Functionalism' becomes virtually synonymous with what has just been described in the previous chapter as 'Rationalism'). But its most important meaning relates to planning; to the notion, first expressed by the biological analogy, that the internal organization of a building (or of a city) is the source of its external appearance; or as Le Corbusier succinctly expressed it: 'the plan proceeds from within to without; the exterior is the result of an interior'.

Naturally even seventeenth and early eighteenth century critics realized that planning had an important formative influence on visible architectural character (indeed, the notion of the aesthetic importance of *utilitas* goes back to remote Antiquity), and J. F. Blondel's first book (1737) was entitled *On the Planning of Country Houses*. Tiercelet's *Modern Architecture* (1727) was specifically designed, so its publisher tells us in his preface, to deal with the new modes of planning which had given a specifically modern character to the domestic architecture of the time. Even laymen such as William Mitford claimed that the first principle of design in building must be utility; a term which Alexander Gerard had defined in 1756 as 'the fitness of things for answering to their ends, constituting another species of beauty distinct from that of figure'. Similarly, J. C. Loudon, in his *Encyclopedia of Cottage, Farm and Villa Architecture*, asserted that 'every building should appear to be what it is, and every part of a building ought to indicate externally its particular use'. But the planning requirements of the eighteenth and early nineteenth century were so elementary, when judged by present standards, and were so easily fitted into conventional geometric shapes, that function could only be expressed by using more superficial means than the total composition of the building, as for example by the choice of decorative ornaments. Admittedly J. F. Blondel tried to find some more fundamental means whereby the plan could indicate precisely a building's general appearance, and he included in his lecture course a series of analyses of current building types; but these were so elementary as to be virtually useless. For example, all he could find to say under the heading 'Stock Exchanges' was to the effect that 'the Bourse in the rue Vivienne has nothing more remarkable about it than a courtyard surrounded by porticoes, and a few rooms on the ground floor'. Similarly he excused himself from dealing with factories, on the grounds that each type comprised special conditions which determined the orientation, situation and arrangement of the blocks which composed them, so that there was thus nothing particular about them to be said. Blondel was probably right in implying that no general principles could be formulated with respect to such buildings, and that the programme of each would have to be established individually in the light of local requirements. But it is nevertheless important to realize that in the middle of the eighteenth century there seemed in fact only two kinds of building relevant to a general theory of architectural planning, namely domestic architecture (which ranged from palaces to garden pavilions) and religious architecture (which ranged from monasteries to wayside shrines).

In the middle of the eighteenth century, however, a revolution in architectural practice occurred through the need experienced by an evolving civilization to develop new building types. This was the era when developments in public administration demanded the creation of proper city halls, when developments in public hygiene demanded the establishment of proper hospitals for the poor, and when developments in public entertainment demanded the construction of proper theatres. A century later, a whole host of new building types made their appearance, such as hotels, banks, offices, railway stations and so on, whilst the rapid increase in population even brought the problems of public housing out of the control of local craftsmen and building contractors, and into the hands of the architectural profession.

Curiously enough this revolution was first reflected architecturally in the academic studies made in the middle of the eighteenth century for the French *Prix de Rome* competition. It was for these competitions that the idea of a 'programme', or detailed list of requirements, was first evolved, and the notion of standardized scales for drawings first introduced. Until 1744, the kind of subject usually proposed in these programmes consisted of either religious buildings or domestic buildings, or, more usually, of fragmentary parts of either of these, such as 'a church porch' (1732), 'a high altar' (1734), 'a stairway' (1737) or 'a stable for a royal palace' (1739). But by the middle of the eighteenth century the subjects were already becoming more complex and more grandiose, so that in 1748 the subject was 'a stock exchange', in 1757 and 1761 'a concert hall', in 1764 'a college', whilst between 1767 and 1789 large public buildings predominated, and consisted of such subjects as customs houses, theatres, arsenals (i.e. armament factories), hospitals, thermal baths, medical schools, prisons and museums.

To some extent the introduction of these new building types was due to the natural tendency of academic competitions to become more and more complex and grandiose. It was also due to the influence of the Roman Revival, in that the complexity of Roman public buildings, and the Roman fondness for extravagance in this domain, had a strong attraction for the artists of the time, especially Piranesi, Boullée and Ledoux. But this academic trend also reflected the first glimmerings of a real public need, and its only defect was its disregard for the more mundane practical requirements of the buildings involved, in that it encouraged the students to prefer grandiose images of a purely imaginative and picturesque kind.

It is important to draw attention here to the reasons for the impracticability of so many of the *Prix de Rome* projects, for a similar impracticability is only too often characteristic of academic projects today. In its favour, it can be argued that by limiting a student to very strict requirements, compatible with those encountered by practising architects, his imagination is cramped, and he is forced to produce a banal design. But it can also be argued that by giving a student complete freedom of invention, he will be unfairly tempted (especially in a competition) to produce unrealistic drawings which have no relevance except as pictorial works of art. This is precisely what happened at the French school of architecture in the eighteenth and nineteenth centuries. Since the programmes frequently contained only relatively vague indications of the sizes of the accommodational requirements, and stipulated virtually unlimited sites, the projects were usually nothing more than vast symmetrical blocks arranged only according to the massing and fenestration patterns dictated by current fashions. In general it was the freedom of siting which represented the greatest danger. For example, though the programme for a hospital issued in 1771 was two pages long, and contained an exceptionally detailed list of the accommodation needed, its only allusion to the site was the remark that 'an isolated area of about 36,000 square yards' was available, and no indication was given as to the topography of the terrain or its shape. Now it may be argued that the ideal site for any hospital is precisely a large open flat site of generous dimensions, so that there was nothing unreasonable in this approach. But if we examine the *Prix de Rome* projects in detail from 1787 onwards (and they have all been published by A. P. Prieur, P. L. van Cléemputte and their successors), we find that they were all essentially composed of the same sequence of regular volumes, lacking that very integrity which well-defined usages must necessarily impart to truly functional shapes.

The *Revue Générale de l'Architecture* expressed the dilemma well in an article published in 1842. 'At the École des Beaux-Arts', it announced, 'little concern is shown for the utilization of the different parts of a large building, and the students scarcely deign to bear in mind the purpose of the edifice. What is sought, above all, when developing a plan, is a certain pictorial disposition, the rigorous symmetry of which is agreeable at the first glance. They try to evolve graceful graphic patterns rather than reasonably planned monuments'. From 1750 to 1900, all the projects seem to have been composed more with a view to this monumental variety, rather than with a view to the function they were supposed to perform, and this is particularly apparent when we compare *Prix de Rome* projects with buildings of the same type actually constructed at the same time. During the period 1750 to 1880, that is to say before new structural systems permitted the development of high-rise office buildings, it was usual for any public building actually constructed to consist of a large number of rooms compressed into a restricted, irregular and enclosed site, whereby the main challenge to the architect's skill consisted in creating the most pleasing volumes, the most efficient circulations and the most spacious courts out of the limited space allotted. Thus, for example, if we compare the *Prix de Rome* project for a medical school submitted in 1775 with the medical school actually constructed by Gondoin at the same time, we see that despite the awkwardness of many of Gondoin's rooms (due to the fact that his building was constructed on a site where no two sides were parallel) the whole design has an authenticity and integrity, due to the limitations of the site, which the academic projects of the same subject invariably lack.

The arbitrary academic attitude towards planning begun in the eighteenth century was perpetuated and aggravated by the peculiar technique taught by J. N. L. Durand. Admittedly his method was deliberately designed for rapidity of production (since he had to fit his lectures into the short time allotted by the curriculum of the École Polytechnique), and it was for this reason that he introduced the practice of designing on graph paper, with the lines representing the axes of columns, and the whole plan built up on a series of squares. But although he was lecturing to engineers, and had thus every incentive to be as practical as possible, the 'functional' quality one might expect of his plans is noticeably absent. The students were first of all given a series of abstract ideal room shapes, and were then shown how these could be assembled to form picturesque and well-balanced assemblages or compositions, reminiscent of the type created nowadays by children with wooden blocks. But these compositions were purely abstract, and Durand did not bother to indicate, even summarily, the usage to which such compositions might appropriately be put.

In fairness to Durand, it should be pointed out that he seems to have exerted a salutary influence on such excellent planners as Leo von Klenze, and he also published a *Compendium and Parallel of Ancient and Modern Buildings* (1800) in which the examples were arranged according to building types, all drawn to the same scale. He was thus in fact a pioneer of functional planning studies as far as historical research was concerned. But few useful lessons seem to have been drawn from this publication in academic circles, and the tendency of schools of architecture during the nineteenth century was always to neglect the formative potentialities of function in favour of more facile means of external display. Even such important factors as climate were ignored, to such an extent that when the Academy proposed 'a governor's palace in Algeria' as the subject for the *Prix de Rome* of 1840, the results, according to Henri Labrouste, showed no influence of the climate whatsoever, and each design could have been erected on a Parisian boulevard without exciting any public comment. The fact that today the same attitude is common in reverse (as may be judged from Le Corbusier's Visual Arts Centre at Harvard University, which is barely distinguishable from his cotton manufacturers' headquarters in the Punjab), does not render Labrouste's criticism any less valid.

In retrospect, it seems so obvious to us that the essential quality of all modern buildings is constituted by the distinctive functions they serve that the small attention given to this factor by the theorists of the eighteenth and nineteenth centuries seems incomprehensible. It seems obvious to us now, for example, that the essential distinction between a neo-Gothic hospital of the 1860s and a mediaeval infirmary is to be found not in any radical differences of structure or detailing, but in the differences in the way the two are planned. Yet few nineteenth century theorists realized, despite their undisguised admiration for these magnificent new buildings, that new planning problems were producing a new architecture beneath their eyes, and although there were indeed a number of perspicacious writers who did vaguely suspect what was taking place, the majority were so obsessed by archaeology, and by the importance of creating datable fragments for the future, that the true nature of contemporary architectural developments was seldom perceived.

Moreover, there were at this time a number of men of reactionary temper who, despite their progressive tendencies in other respects, resolutely rejected the notion that new planning problems were capable of creating the new architecture of a modern age. For them, architecture was still essentially concerned with creating monuments, by which they ideally envisaged such structures as churches, triumphal arches and obelisks; hence they attached little importance to new planning needs. It is not perhaps surprising that Sir William Chambers should have considered industrial architecture, such as forges, kilns, glassworks and so on, to be 'objects of the horrid kind', since he was the last of the great Classicists of the Georgian era, and may be excused his reactionary opinions. Nor is it surprising that Sir John Soane, despite his revolutionary ideas with respect to the Classical Orders, should have denounced all multi-storey buildings devoid of giant Orders as calculated to give the idea of large factories, or that he should have condemned the new variety in the functions of buildings because it was a cause of the orgy of Revivalism which was the fashion of his day. But it seems strange that as late as 1832, A. T. L.

Vaudoyer, who had designed or remodelled so many important public buildings, should have declared before the French Academy that there were only two kinds of architecture: civil architecture (consisting of domestic architecture, factories and farms) and monumental architecture (comprising temples, basilicas, theatres, obelisks, columns, tombs, prisons, aqueducts and bridges), or that César Daly, writing in 1842, should have viewed the schism between industrial architecture and monumental architecture with equanimity, rejoicing that even dwellings of humble artisans were now so ornate that they could henceforth be regarded as monuments.

Occasionally, seemingly progressive and farsighted notions as to the importance of planning were expressed in the century between 1750 and 1850; but when studied in their actual context, they seldom show any appreciation of the true problem. Thus Laugier advised greater variety in plan forms (as compared with the ubiquitous rectangle, which was virtually obligatory in all but churches before 1750), and enunciated the aphorism that 'forms are determined by plans'; yet it is clear that his aim was simply to encourage the type of arbitrary sculptural variety later associated with Boullée and Ledoux. Borgnis, in his *Elementary Treatise on Construction* (1823) took the unprecedented step of devoting over a hundred pages to planning; yet most of his examples of public buildings were taken from Antiquity, and few were related specifically to contemporary usages. It was not in fact until Reynaud's *Treatise on Architecture* appeared in 1850 that any textbook was available in which building types applicable to the new age were illustrated and discussed, and the first really thorough study of the subject was Julien Guadet's *Elements and Theory of Architecture*, which was not published until 1902.

By the middle of the nineteenth century, some awareness of the true nature of the problem began to be shown in the new architectural magazines, and it is significant that it was the Classicists and Eclectics who first appreciated it, rather than the social-reforming Gothic Revivalists (who found mediaeval compositions so much more satisfying, and so much in harmony with their mediaeval details). Even the Gothic Rationalists showed themselves less interested in new compositional forms than in new structural forms, and as late as 1863, Viollet-le-Duc was still proclaiming that 'the essence of programmes changes little, for men's needs in a civilized state are approximately the same'. On the other hand, the first issue of the *Revue Générale de l'Architecture* contained a discussion by César Daly, the apostle of Eclecticism, concerning the problem of giving character to new domestic architecture, in which he stated that 'since the main architectural lines which imprint each structure with its essential character spring from the *plan*, one is tempted to conclude that our domestic architecture must necessarily be more beautiful than what it was in the past'. In the next issue of the magazine, Daly criticized certain conditions stipulated in a programme issued by the École des Beaux-Arts by observing that 'it seems obvious that the character and style of any kind of architectonic construction resides essentially in its overall shape which results, it seems to me, from the arrangements of the plan'. By 1845, he was reassuring his readers that the need to satisfy new requirements had frequently led to the adoption of forms and proportions which were not to be found in the traditional architectonic alphabet, and he stated that it was time architects paid more attention to new building-types, such as public markets, factories, warehouses and stations, rather than to 'triumphal arches and temples dedicated to Fame'. In 1856, he contended that since modern society was an industrial society, its monuments were none other than those very railway stations, department stores, restaurants, hotels, colleges, libraries, museums, law courts and theatres which were then being built in such profusion. The following year he asserted that the characteristics of the architecture of the future would be found in buildings devoted to public assembly, such as hotels and clubs; an opinion republished two years later by *The Builder*, when it issued a translation of César Daly's description of Barry's Reform Club. Even enlightened laymen of the time, such as the Vicomte de Laborde, perceived that as soon as architects had established the proper character required by buildings of the nineteenth century, 'contemporary architecture will have taken its place in the history of art'.

Indeed, by the 1860s, architects were beginning to become more aware of the distinctive contribution which new building-types were making to the architecture of their century, to such an extent that they started to neglect external expression altogether, and concentrated entirely on planning. Thus it was not uncommon, in the architectural competitions of the era, for each competitor to establish his plan, and then submit several façades to go with it—an attitude which may be regarded as an expression of cynicism or indifferentism, but which was often simply a manifestation of the new overriding importance attached to the organization of space. Even in domestic architecture, where many traditional values necessarily persisted, this same attitude can be seen. Thus Robert Kerr, in *The English Gentleman's House* (1864), dismissed the whole problem of external appearance in a short and witty chapter illustrated by ten different 'styles' all based on the same plan, and devoted the rest of the book to planning requirements. Only the archaeologists, still preoccupied by ornamental details to the exclusion of new planning problems, disregarded completely the distinctions arising from total compositional forms, and their oversight in this respect is still perpetuated today, as is witnessed by the frequency with which art historians discuss the evolution of modern architectural forms without any reference to the evolution of the building-types to which they belong.

The greatest revolution in planning occurred round about 1890, when new structural systems made it unnecessary to ensure that partition walls in the upper parts of a building were continued right down to the ground. There were of course reactionaries such as G. E. Street, who regretted these new developments, and deplored the fact that architects were no longer required to show the ingenuity in planning they had been forced to possess when there were no such convenient means of carrying walls over voids. But the younger, more enterprising, and less pedantic architects welcomed these aids to freer planning, and, by substituting point supports for load-bearing walls in every type of building, used them to produce plans which were even more functional than before. Some architects naturally abused these facilities, using their new-found freedom to produce arbitrary and eccentric shapes which had no functional *raison d'être*, and were only 'modern' in respect of their novelty. But in general the notion of 'Functionalism' can be said to date from the era when a truly functional plan really became possible, even though the ideals of Functionalism had, as has been shown, been adumbrated many years before.

Perhaps the main changes in ideals of planning brought about by steel and reinforced concrete concerned the traditional interpretation of the words 'composition' and 'programme', the first of which fell into disrepute at the beginning of this century, and the second of which has suffered a complete change of meaning within the last few years. It is not entirely clear why 'composition' should have become such an unpopular term, for the application of the biological analogy to the principles of planning is still as popular as ever, and since 'decomposition' is an approved way of describing the cessation of life in something organic, 'composition' would seem to be an equally appropriate way of describing the way something organic is created. Perhaps the word 'composition' ceased to be popular only because it was associated with the methods of design taught at the École des Beaux-Arts. At any rate the triple division of the École des Beaux-Arts' system ('elements', 'composition' and 'detailing') is now no longer universally accepted as a reflection of the contemporary philosophy of architectural design. To understand why not, it is necessary to study the techniques of academic planning in force from the eighteenth century to the end of the First World War.

With the establishment of the *Prix de Rome* at the beginning of the eighteenth century, and the need to ensure that each competition was conducted fairly, the practice arose whereby the establishment of the main dispositions of the masses of the building (or *parti* as it came to be called) took place in locked cubicles or *loges*, and after the completion of the time allotted for this drawing, a duplicate sketch was then submitted to those in charge. This compositional *parti*, once determined, could not be departed from; hence the elaboration and detailing of the *parti*, and the preparation of the final drawings, was strictly circumscribed. Those who accepted the system could argue, with some justice, that by designing compositions under such conditions, students were forced to set out their ideas rapidly and clearly, and to learn a discipline which would enable them to produce a scheme possessing consistency and unity in a short space of time. But opponents of the system argued that the time allotted for composition, and the restrictions on research which physical isolation entailed, were unrealistic as far as architectural education was concerned, and hence that the system should be replaced by one in which composition and detailing took place concurrently, or were in some way combined.

The eighteenth century system still persists in France at the École des Beaux-Arts, but it has been abandoned at most other schools of architecture, partly because the Anglo-Saxon system of full-time academic supervision, developed at the end of the nineteenth century, rendered redundant the disciplinary problems the method was originally designed to combat. But quite apart from the question as to whether or not the older system was or was not a good method of architectural education, it is worth noting that the basic idea of 'composition' always had an undesirably close affinity to the techniques traditionally used in schools of painting. If, for example, we compare the original organization established at the British Royal Academy (where architecture was taught in company with painting and sculpture forty years before the 'Beaux-Arts' system was adopted in France), we find that the techniques laid down for teaching architecture were virtually identical with those prescribed for teaching painting. In article XI of the Academy's charter (1768), provision was made for a professor of architecture who would 'form the tastes of the students and instruct them in the laws and principles of composition'. But this was precisely the same wording as that used in article XII with reference to the professor of painting. In practice, therefore, 'composition' always tended to imply pictorial grouping, and it was thus scarcely a coincidence that the debasement of the architectural ideal of composition became particularly noticeable in France under the influence of Piranesi and in England during the professorship of Soane. Nor is it surprising that the term was eventually abandoned as a means of describing the method of establishing a functional plan.

Nevertheless, the abandonment of the idea of 'composition' has had one serious drawback in that in place of the ideal of *combination* it has substituted the ideal of *subdivision*: what Reyner Banham calls 'subdividing a bulk volume to create functional spaces out of it'. Now it will be obvious that although the traditional idea of composition was by no means incompatible with the creation of a bulk volume (indeed, it frequently happened that, after a nineteenth century architect had assembled the various elemental volumes which composed his building, the final result was a simple prismatic block), the fashion for subdivision inevitably led to formalism, or the adoption of arbitrarily shaped envelopes for their own sake. The great virtue of 'composition' lay in the sequence of operations by which internal spaces were functionally related to one another by the designer, and it must be admitted that whatever its defects, the Classical notion of composition implied, as its basic ideal, the very sensible technique of establishing a number of functional volumes and then relating them to constitute an organic and pleasing whole. With the abandonment of the term 'composition', the notion rapidly gained credence that planning is essentially a technique for situating partitions within an all-embracing pre-conceived container. At its best, this technique can be justified analogically by reference to the way an animal's vital organs are fitted into an enclosing shell or skeleton, or the way an internal combustion engine is fitted into an automobile. But it is clear that this type of planning favours an arbitrary external wrapping even more insistently than the techniques used by the nineteenth century Revivalists, and the implications of this method, which industrial designers exploit under the name of 'styling', will be made even more evident in the chapter dealing with the twentieth century subjection to abstract art.

Curiously enough, the term 'composition' was also disliked by romantic theorists such as Goethe and Ruskin, and by romantic architects such as Frank Lloyd Wright, despite the fact that they might have been expected to favour any method guaranteed to produce picturesque effects. Ruskin specifically objected to the word 'composition' in *The Stones of Venice*, saying that the word was used merely in order to express a scientific discipline and inventive arrangement instead of a natural or accidental one. Wright, in his essay entitled 'The Cause of Architecture' (1925), also objected to the word, asserting that 'we may no longer speak of "composition" ', and claiming that a work of architecture should be regarded as a plastic thing modelled like a fluid, and not as something superimposed, aggregated or composed. It is probable, however, that such attacks on the notion of composition were not based on very profound motives, but were simply devious ways of combating the whole traditional Classical doctrine epitomized in their minds by the teaching vocabulary of the École des Beaux-Arts.

Compared with the notion of 'composition', the notion of a 'programme' presents a very different problem historically, and it will be advisable to consider it under four headings: firstly, with respect to the way it should be drawn up; secondly, with respect to the way it should relate to the distribution of interior spaces; thirdly, with respect to the way it should relate to the arrangement of exterior spaces and façades; and finally, with respect to the way it should take account of surroundings. Only by studying the concept of the programme from these four points of view can we understand the aims and dilemmas of nineteenth century architects, and be in a position to sympathize with the problems they had to face.

First, then, let us consider the various techniques whereby a programme has been established during the last two hundred years. At the beginning of this period, it was assumed that a programme was simply the expression, in concise terms, of a client's wishes, enumerating the spaces required for specific usages. The architect's task was thus conceived as being simply a matter of determining the proper shape and allocation of these spaces with respect to their intercommunication and appearance. It was not for him to enquire too closely as to what had been done in similar circumstances in earlier periods, what had been done in similar circumstances elsewhere, or what ought to be done in similar circumstances at some future date. His task was simply to fulfil the conditions given him, and this was well expressed by the traditional formula used for academic programmes at the École des Beaux-Arts, where the students were informed that 'the Professor of Theory proposes such and such a subject', and were then told of the purpose of the spaces to be included, with occasional indications as to the levels at which they were to be placed.

RATIONALISM

It was theoretically feasible in the eighteenth century to elaborate magnificent edifices without any programme whatsoever (as occasionally happened at the French Academy in Rome—the classic example being Renard's 'Palace for a Conclave' of 1779), but it had become necessary by the mid-nineteenth century for teachers of architecture to face reality. As early as 1823, Louis Bruyère had remarked in his *Studies Relative to the Art of Constructions* that it was extremely difficult to determine all the needs of a building, or in other words, to establish a good programme; hence this programme must be the result of the most positive information provided by the interested persons, and discussed in their presence. When this was not possible, it must result from a careful study of buildings of the same type known to have been executed elsewhere with a reasonable measure of success. 'The architect may doubtless co-operate in drawing up the programme', he wrote, 'but in so doing he must try to forget the fact that he is a creative architect, so as not to get any preconceived ideas before having fully mastered the problem. It is very useful', he continued, 'to have books which contain detailed programmes and the plans of well designed buildings, and it is for this reason I have tried to provide the latter in the present publication, where will be found the programmes and plans of markets, storage sheds, abattoirs, private houses, hospitals and so on'.

The advantages of such a straightforward attitude towards the relationship between programme and client or programme and student will be obvious. It imposed a strict discipline on the designer, especially in academic projects, where designs could be rejected out of hand if the conditions were blatantly disregarded. Even as early as 1779, fifteen of the twenty-eight submissions for the *Prix de Rome* were set aside because they did not fulfil the conditions which the programme sought to impose. Yet it eventually became apparent, even at the École des Beaux-Arts, that no one could adequately design a large building without having previously studied the requirements of the particular type of building involved, and this led to the idea that lecture courses on the theory of architecture should consist of some kind of programmatic research with respect to building-types. In an age dominated by historiography, this research was naturally thought of historically, and thus Julien Guadet, for example, in the three volumes devoted to building-types comprising the second part of his *Elements and Theory of Architecture* (1902) considered it his duty to describe and illustrate his theme with respect to all eras, including Antiquity and the Middle Ages. Admittedly, there were certain buildings, such as schools, for which he had no choice but to confine himself to recent examples; but he rarely included the work of contemporary architects, for he thought it indelicate and improper to discuss the works of living colleagues. Still less did he speculate as to what should be done in the future, for he was not concerned with indicating what programmes *ought to* comprise, but simply to describe what they *had* comprised and *did* comprise at that date. This attitude was very much influenced by the fact that, like most nineteenth century theorists, he still regarded a programme as essentially something prescribed by a client, and based more on common sense than on expert research. He was well aware, from his own considerable practical experience, that clients were frequently uncertain as to what they wanted, and that when buildings had to fulfil the needs of a large number of people, there was frequent disagreement as to the conditions to be fulfilled. But he still considered it a client's duty to state his needs fully, and asserted that in public buildings it was the responsibility of the relevant authorities to give full and detailed expression of their requirements to the architect they commissioned. For example, with respect to the design of prisons, he wrote: 'the architect is the servant of a programme which does not emanate from him; for it is the legislature, preceded by the moralist, who says what a prison must be'. Thus Guadet did not regard the architect as a social reformer, but only as an instrument of social reform.

Within recent years, the attitude towards such situations has completely changed. Original programmatic research, particularly when it can lead to social or organizational improvements, is now considered in academic circles to be an architect's primary duty, and clients are regarded as ignorant, inarticulate, insensitive laymen who, through force of habit and conservatism of temperament, neither know what they want nor are able to express those needs even if they are farsighted enough to perceive them dimly. 'Modern society,' asserted the Professor of Architecture of London University recently, 'is too complex for the architect to have an automatic understanding of what is wanted in a building; the client does not know this either, although he sometimes thinks he does . . . The client's brief is nearly always wrong, and a bad brief inevitably results in disastrous architecture'. The most radical current opinions thus seem to have moved a long way from the nineteenth century attitude which, on the contrary, attributed 'disastrous architecture' only to the way a programme was implemented, and never to the programme itself.

Moreover, there is a growing tendency among certain architectural theorists to regard the 'programming' of buildings as comparable to the 'programming' of electronic computors. In its most naïve form, this comparison is simply an up-to-date extension of the romantic notions already analysed with respect to the Mechanical Analogy. In its more sophisticated form, it is an attempt to reduce the number of 'design decisions' which can occur in the more complex types of buildings such as hospitals, thus making the designs themselves less arbitrary and more efficient. In both forms, it implies that architectural design is more a matter of analysis and research than of drawing; or in other words, that practical considerations exert a determining influence on architectural form well beyond that understood by earlier designers.

There were of course occasional theorists, even in the nineteenth century, who perceived that architects were strategically well placed to initiate social reform, and there were even some who suggested the idea which was to become so common among *avant-garde* theorists after 1919, namely that the easiest way to create a new architecture was to change the public's way of life. Thus César Daly remarked in

1840 that since domestic architecture resulted from social habits, 'the way to modify the effect is to begin by modifying the cause'—a revolutionary concept which was eventually to result in the so-called 'functional' domestic architecture of the 1920s, when every workman's dwelling designed by Le Corbusier was like an artist's studio. It may be doubted to what extent architects are justified in initiating changes in ways of living in domestic architecture; to what extent, that is to say, they are entitled to force people to adopt new social habits independently of the recommendations of social workers and scientifically conducted sociological research. But there is no doubt that various types of human environment have profited from architects' initiative in this matter, even though few examples are in fact to be found in which the architect was alone responsible for conceiving the basic principles behind the particular kind of social reform.

Three types of building constitute particularly good historical illustrations of the way functionalist idealism has influenced modern architecture, namely prisons, hospitals and theatres. All were essentially creations of the era beginning in the mid-eighteenth century (for before this date the accommodation was provided in *ad hoc* premises), and all possessed the common quality of demanding that certain clearly defined functions be fulfilled. The new prisons imposed an overriding demand for maximum supervision, the new hospitals imposed an overriding demand for maximum ventilation, the new theatres imposed an overriding demand for good visibility and audibility, and all except the first demanded easy egress in case of fire. It was in buildings such as these that modern Functionalism best expressed itself, and as a result, the nineteenth century subjected them to a considerable amount of architectural research.

To discuss adequately the evolution of prisons, hospitals and theatres during the last two hundred years—or of any other modern building-type for that matter—would require a whole book of the kind best exemplified by Carroll Meeks's *The Railroad Station*. Moreover, it is worth noting that prisons and theatres were the first buildings to be dealt with in such monographs, whilst hospitals constitute the first type of building to be the subject of serious scientific research. An *Architectonography of Prisons, or Parallel of the Different Systems of Planning of which Prisons are Susceptible* was published by Louis-Pierre Baltard in 1829 (inspired by John Howard's famous *State of Prisons* published in 1777). Pierre Patte published his *Essay on Theatre Architecture* in 1782. The French Academy of Science published its lengthy report on Poyet's project for a new city hospital (Hôtel Dieu) in Paris in 1785. All three works are interesting in that they show the part played by architects in initiating improvements, or, more frequently, in putting into tangible form the improvements envisaged by laymen. They also demonstrate the importance played by the Classical notion of standardization; a notion (so often and so paradoxically rejected by those architects who have always sought primarily to create dramatically original works of art) which implies that once a perfect planning solution has been found, there is good reason to repeat its dispositions with minor variations and improvements in every situation where it is required. For as Pierre Patte himself remarked in his *Essay on Theatre Architecture*: 'it may be objected that theatres will henceforth have only one form, and that it will then be necessary, as in Antiquity, for all theatres to look alike; but why not? Will it in fact be so great an evil to reduce all such structures to the character proper to their destination, which consists in seeing well and hearing well?'

Unfortunately the introduction of photography has artificially militated against this functional standardization; for whereas, in the days before illustrated architectural magazines, it did not seem unreasonable for two localities, many miles apart, to have similar public buildings, the ease of photographic juxtaposition has inevitably created a false sense of emulation among architects, whereby each community finds itself obliged to have public buildings which are 'original', whether or not the rational solution of the accommodational problem is best provided by standardized forms.

Pierre Patte was a Classical architect of the old school, so that for him, standardization was not distasteful. Moreover he may be regarded as a Rationalist in that he also published some interesting studies on fireproof construction and urban design, and wrote the two volumes on building construction which posthumously completed J. F. Blondel's published lecture course. Baltard was a former pupil of Ledoux, who had served in the corps of engineers during the revolutionary wars, and was appointed professor of theory at the École des Beaux-Arts in 1818. Few of the reforms Baltard proposed were of his own inspiration; yet he had the perspicacity to see that since the new prison system only existed in the minds of its originators, it was necessary, to avoid 'remaining in the rut of tradition', to carry out research from then onwards into the architectural elements of prison design, envisaging their consequences, and, considering the problem to be in principle solved, to base a new method of planning prisons on 'a programme analogous to the new ideas which could consequently be formed of them'. The English had already tried to give a lead in this matter by developing the 'panopticon', that is to say, a system (originally invented by Samuel Bentham in 1780 for supervising factory workers in St. Petersburg) whereby blocks of cells radiated from a central inspection post. But Baltard disagreed with this method, and in criticizing it, he had the insight to perceive the basic analogical fallacy upon which it, like so many other misleading aspects of the new theory of Functionalism, was based. 'The English,' he wrote, 'bring into all their works the genius for mechanics which they have perfected, and they thus want their buildings to function like a machine worked by a single motor.' Thus we see the beginning of the functional theory of the machine age, for this phrase could hardly have expressed more clearly the idea of a prison as a 'machine for living in'.

With respect to hospital planning, Poyet's project for rebuilding the Paris Hôtel Dieu also used the panopticon principle (though in this instance it was adopted to facilitate communications rather than to allow centralized supervision). But the principle was rejected by the Academy of Science, since its members had a practical example of the panopticon type on which to base their objections, the idea of radiating wings having been used two centuries earlier for the Hôtel Dieu at Lyons (where the arrangement was employed to enable all the patients to see the central altar). The Academy objected to the panopticon principle on the grounds that it prevented good ventilation, and preferred a system of isolated pavilions as being better calculated to check the spread of disease. Ventilation was always difficult to attain in this era; moreover, the public had little understanding of its therapeutic value, and considered it quite in order for six persons to occupy one hospital bed, or for a hundred and ten such beds to occupy a room 85 ft. square in the old Hôtel Dieu in Paris. Interestingly enough, the development of artificial ventilation at this time was largely due to research on hospital and prison design. In 1753 Dr. Stephen Hales had introduced mechanical ventilation into Sir John Oldcastle's smallpox hospital, as well as into the Winchester, Durham, Shrewsbury, Northampton, Newgate and Maidstone county jails, whilst in about 1830, an engineer named Charles Sylvester was to introduce a most ingenious system of ventilation into Derby Infirmary, whereby fresh air was brought in by means of an underground tunnel, 200 yds. long, where it was heated in winter by means of a large stove.

The problems of theatre design were clearly of a rather different order from those confronting the designers of hospitals and prisons, since the reforms to be introduced were not concerned with the eradication of incontestable evils but with the improvement of existing, though admittedly clumsy, amenities. Nevertheless all three building-types had this in common: they were a challenge to architects to substitute ideal arrangements for what had previously been *ad hoc* adaptations of existing buildings. Just as the earliest hospitals had usually been modified dwellings or monasteries, and the earliest prisons modified fortresses, so the earliest French theatres had usually been modified tennis courts, and no adequate provision was made for proper acoustics, proper ventilation, or proper protection against the hazards of fire. Moreover, little attention was given to such details as stage lighting. It is to Pierre Patte's credit that he not only made a serious effort to come to grips with the scientific problems of acoustics, but also made an ingenious attempt to solve problems of illumination, as for example by suggesting that reflectors should be used instead of the smoky lamps which usually dangled in front of the scenery. Moreover, perceiving that well-dressed women were, as they always will be, the principal ornaments of auditoria, he proposed rings of boxes instead of galleries, and preferred them to be cantilevered over the main arena rather than supported by columns which would block the view.

It should be noted that Patte's book on theatres contained no illustrations, whilst Baltard's *Architectonography of Prisons* was illustrated solely with plans. But this should not obscure the fact that one of the concerns of the epoch, of particular relevance to the whole aesthetic theory of Functionalism, was the way such planning

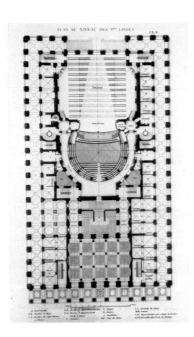
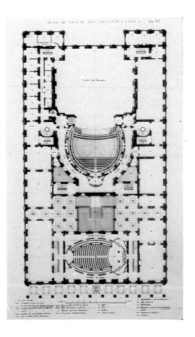

V. Louis: Theatre at Bordeaux (1777)

NEW PLANNING PROBLEMS

Illustrating how the rational approach to new planning problems created new and characteristic compositions (compare Plate III)

XXV

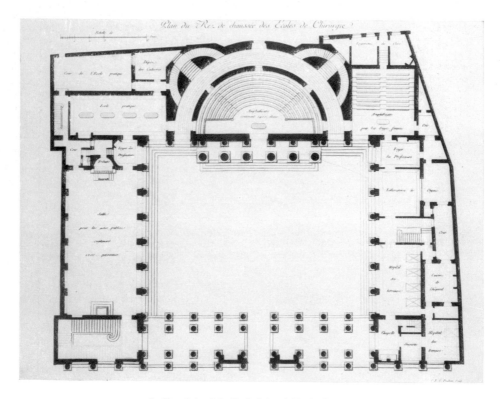

J. Gondoin: Medical School, Paris (1771)

NEW PLANNING PROBLEMS

*Illustrating the ingenuity of Classical Rationalists in creating
regular spaces out of irregular urban sites*

XXVI

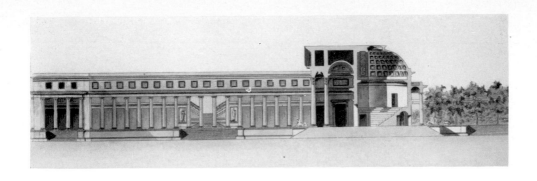

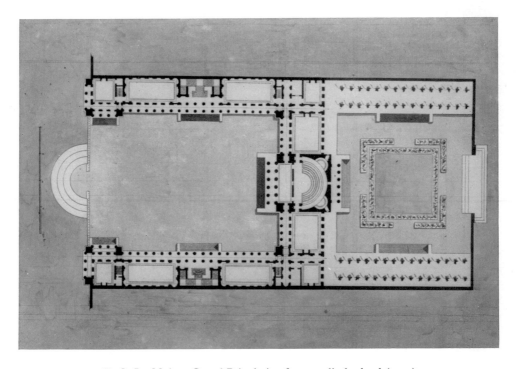

P. G. Le Moine: Grand Prix design for a medical school (1775)

NEW PLANNING PROBLEMS

*Illustrating the characteristic approach to planning and composition when academic projects
initiated the practice of assuming regular geometric sites*

XXVII

W. K. Harrison and others: United Nations auditorium, New York (1950)

NEW PLANNING PROBLEMS

Illustrating the new compositional shapes created by new planning requirements and new structural systems

XXVIII

arrangements could and should be expressed on the outside. We have already seen that early nineteenth century theorists such as Durand considered that a good plan automatically produced a good elevation. Later architects, under the influence of Revivalism, showed an apparent indifference to the expression of function in their lax attitude towards the choice of 'style', but many architects did indeed realize that one of the problems of the age was to discover how an efficient plan could produce not merely a good elevation but an expressive elevation. Sometimes they simply adopted the somewhat arbitrary techniques of expression proposed by those Romantics who attached importance to the association of ideas, as for example, when they designed prisons in the Gothic 'style' because this was calculated to inspire the observer with awe and horror. Even quite enlightened theorists such as E. L. Garbett thought it impossible for a building to express its function more accurately than this because 'the destinations of modern buildings are more numerous than the distinguishable varieties of expression'. But many others perceived that a fundamental relationship must exist between a functional plan and its architectural expression, and some even perceived that the determination of this relationship was one of the crucial problems of the modern age.

The problem of unequivocally creating an architectural expression which is both functional and varied might seem insoluble because of the possibility of three mutually exclusive attitudes. For example, one can claim that every programme is susceptible of several solutions (and hence that a single authentic functional expression is unthinkable), one can claim that a modern building needs to be as adaptable as possible (and hence that the exterior must express this so-called 'flexibility'), or one can take the view (already expounded with respect to theatres, hospitals and prisons) that Functionalism implies standardized compositional shapes. But in fact these distinctions have little effect on the basic problem of the architectural expression of a building, for it is clear that each attitude can have an aesthetic integrity of its own. If a building is designed to allow for easy internal modifications it can perfectly well express this 'flexibility' externally; if it is designed to fulfil an unexacting set of requirements, the general purpose of the building can still be made perfectly clear outside; if, finally, each building-type is considered to be as standardized as a Greek temple or a Roman theatre, the variations between one such building and another can result from changes of dimension or differences due to the site.

The idea of the uniqueness of every design problem was justified quite early in the nineteenth century by Captain Ardant in his *Course on Construction* (1840). 'Luckily the programme for a building project is susceptible of several complete solutions', he wrote, 'so that with perseverance a designer is always assured of finding one which is completely satisfying'. Paradoxically, however, the military engineers were the pioneers of standardization, for standardized barrack plans had been common since the middle of the eighteenth century, even though these standards were not officially formulated until the Napoleonic wars. Then it was simply a matter of codifying existing military regulations which determined the number of square feet per soldier, the number of soldiers per barrack-room, and the number of barrack-rooms per block.

Nevertheless, the fear of standardization became almost an obsession in the mid-nineteenth century, and we can only understand the self-conscious variety of Victorian architecture if we realize that it was essentially a reaction against the simple Classical buildings of the preceding age. In London in 1840, Baker Street (one of the most striking examples of the dignified standardization achieved by contractors and speculators still working in an uninhibited Classical tradition) became a by-word for domestic drabness, whilst in France, violent criticisms of standardized urban façades were made in the *Revue Générale de l'Architecture*, where houses based on a standard pattern were ridiculed as comparable to 'the ramblings of an old dotard, which consist in the incessant repetition of the same idea conceived more or less in the same terms'.

'Flexible' planning is of fairly recent origin, since it only assumed importance after 1890 when steel and reinforced concrete frame construction made it unnecessary for dividing walls to be also load-bearing partitions. However, James Fergusson had envisaged something comparable to 'flexible' planning when he proposed Marshall's Flax Mill as a model for the British Museum in 1849. 'If we apply this plan to the purposes of a museum of natural history', he remarked, 'you have two acres of floor, on which you may arrange your kingdoms and classes in any form or according to any system you may think it best to adopt'. Flexibility is, of course, in its own way a type of Functionalism. Museums and offices need to be adaptable in order to fulfil their functions properly in a way that other types of building do not. Even buildings which might seem to imply a precise compositional form, such as theatres, are occasionally designed to be 'flexible', as for example Walter Gropius's 'Total Theatre' of 1927, which was designed so as to be adaptable to various dramatic relationships between the actors and the audience. It may therefore be said that the ideal of expressing the function of a building implies more ambiguities than it did a century ago, even though it is still presumably an unambiguous stimulus during the formative stages of any architectural design.

It may well be, however, that future generations will consider the relationship of a building to its environment as more important than the way it expresses its function when considered in isolation. If this is so, we shall see a return to the nineteenth century ideals of urban design which were gradually abandoned after the First World War. Before 1919, an urban building was almost always considered as part of a street; in other words, it was not simply an object standing isolated in space but one section of two contiguous façades at front and rear, separated from the adjoining buildings by invisible party walls. Thus urban architectural form was thought of in terms of *enclosures* of space, which might vary in size from a light well to a plaza, which might vary in shape from a square to a passageway, which might be ugly or pleasing, unified or disparate, but which were always immediately affected for better or for worse by the remodelling of any of its sections, or by the completion of gaps which still remained to be filled.

The reaction which occurred in the third decade of the twentieth century was a reaction against the traditional concept of the city, and the importance of the ideas of such theorists as Le Corbusier, who claimed that streets were unnecessary evils, cannot be minimized. Henceforth, cities were envisaged by the most influential theorists of the decade as a sequence of isolated buildings surrounded only by grass and trees. 'Imagine', wrote Le Corbusier in *The City of Tomorrow* (1929), with reference to an air photograph of one of the most luxurious districts in Paris, 'imagine all this junk, which till now has lain spread out over the soil like a dry crust, cleaned off and carted away and replaced by immense clear crystals of glass, rising to a height of over 600 ft. . . . instead of a flattened out and jumbled city such as the aeroplane reveals to us for the first time, terrifying in its confusion, our city will rise vertical to the sky, open to light and air, clear, radiant and sparkling'. Thus was unwittingly reborn the ideal, so dear to the old Academy school and the early École des Beaux-Arts, of a formal symmetrical layout, comprising a series of buildings each regarded as an isolated piece of sculpture, to be seen, admired, and especially drawn or photographed, in isolation from all sides.

Large public buildings, such as theatres or city halls, are clearly most appropriate when they stand in isolation; but it has been argued, by several distinguished writers such as Jane Jacobs, that dwellings and shops are most congenial as human environments when they form part of a continuous enclosed space. However, these are problems which fall more within the domain of sociology and city planning than of architectural history. All that needs to be said here is that the problems of planning buildings, and hence the expression of their functions, are inextricably bound up with problems of contiguity and isolation in urban design, though it may fairly be asserted that the ideal of expressing the purpose of a building becomes very much easier to fulfil when a building can be seen from all sides, and is not merely visible as a component element of a city street.

*   *   *

In conclusion, something must be said about the development of mechanical services which, though they seldom affected the planning of buildings until the twentieth century, originated in the late eighteenth century and early nineteenth centuries, and must therefore be taken into account when the history of functionalist ideals between 1750 and 1950 is under consideration.

First in order of invention seems to have been the cast iron stove, invented in Russia and first introduced into western Europe in 1767. In itself it does not seem to represent a very radical departure from the systems of heating used before 1750, for today such stoves would be regarded as representing little advance on open fires. Yet in fact they were revolutionary, for they initiated the principle of heating by means of radiation or convection from hot metal surfaces, and this principle, immeasurably improved upon in subsequent decades, may be regarded as the characteristic method of space-heating used in the modern age.

Not that this revolutionary method met immediately with universal approval; on the contrary, it seems to have been stoutly resisted by a large proportion of the populace. The stoves installed in the Bank of England (where the smoke was ingeniously sucked downwards under the floor), had to be removed in 1787 because the employees protested that the warmth emitted from the surface of the cast iron was unwholesome, that the air in the room was not changed and purified as it would be by a common fire, that the stoves produced disorders of the lungs, and that they were afflicted with a new disease described as 'the iron cough'. Later, a gloomy correspondent to *The Architectural Magazine* complained that when he installed an iron stove in his bedroom, 'my sleep became disturbed, my appetite declined, I was stricken with a furious cough with pains in the chest, and my bowels were obstinately constipated'. Customs officials complained that when stoves were installed in the Customs House in London, these caused them to suffer from 'a sense of tension or fulness in the head, throbbing of the temples and vertigo, followed not infrequently by a confusion of ideas' which, as the editor of *The Architectural Magazine* sympathetically pointed out, 'must be very disagreeable to officers occupied with important and sometimes intricate calculations'. Nevertheless, despite these objections, the trade in the new heating equipment seems to have flourished, if we can judge from the number of patent stoves and radiators advertised in the architectural periodicals of the mid-nineteenth century, and by the variety of inventions exhibited in the various International Exhibitions after 1851.

The next most important invention in this respect concerned the use of a gravitational hot water system as a means of circulating heat. The first such apparatus to be installed in an English building probably dated from 1816, but its invention can be traced at least to 1777, when an inventor named Bonnemain used it as part of a patent incubator he had devised for hatching eggs. By the fourth decade of the nineteenth century both low pressure and high pressure hot water systems were widely popular, especially after cast iron radiators were substituted for coils of pipe. Nevertheless architects showed little interest in such technicalities; no courses in heating or ventilation were given at the École des Beaux-Arts, and even Léonce Reynaud, at the École Polytechnique, suggested that the subject was of more concern to specialist craftsmen (or *fumistes*, as they were called) than to architects.

Experiments were made by engineers in steam heating as early as 1784. James Watt heated his study by means of a hollow iron box fed with steam from a boiler in the basement, and he used a modification of the system in 1800 for the cotton factory he designed for a Mr. Lee of Manchester, where the steam was circulated through the hollow iron columns used to support the floors. A primitive method of steam heating was also used by the Marquis de Chabannes at the beginning of the nineteenth century to heat Covent Garden theatre, but here the air was simply allowed to circulate through small pipes enclosed by cylinders which constituted the jackets through which the steam was forced.

It will be appreciated that to begin with, such inventions had little influence on the planning of the more modest types of building except in so far as they obviated the need for fireplaces and chimneys. Admittedly, in 1838, Charles Barry had excited considerable admiration for the amount of mechanical equipment incorporated into the Reform Club (which included steam heating, gas lighting, an intricate system of bell-wires, widely distributed hot and cold water, and a number of service elevators), but such refinements were rare even in the most palatial domestic architecture, and were generally lacking in the smaller types of public building. On the other hand, the need to ventilate large public buildings, such as hospitals, had a very profound effect on planning indeed. Reference has already been made to the experiments carried out with respect to hospitals and prisons in the early nineteenth century. The first serious attention given to this matter in a monumental building occurred during the planning of the new Palace of Westminster, when parliamentary commissions studied the problem, and invited anyone with any ideas on the subject to suggest the most effective way it could be solved.

The ventilation of the British House of Commons was already a problem of venerable antiquity; indeed, when one reads of the inefficiency of the ventilation of the original building as it existed before the fire of 1834, one cannot help but wonder that British government policy in the eighteenth century was not more disastrous than some historians now suggest. In 1723, Dr. Desaguliers had tried to improve the primitive system originally introduced by Sir Christopher Wren in the seventeenth century by installing a centrifugal fan operated by hand. Unfortunately, however, this apparatus occupied a space which the janitor considered to be his own by prescriptive right, and he therefore sabotaged the system by ingeniously ensuring that it would produce the opposite effect to that intended. It is not surprising, therefore, that after the destruction of the original building, the Members of Parliament should show particular concern with the ventilation of the new structure, and should have appointed a committee to make a full enquiry into the matter, published by W. S. Inman under the title: *Report of the Committee of the House of Commons on Ventilation, Warming and the Transmission of Sound* (1836).

From this report it is clear that although evidence was given by a number of architects and scientists, including Michael Faraday, only one man had any positive and constructive proposals to make on the subject, and that person was David Boswell Reid, a Scottish physician, who lectured on chemistry at Edinburgh University, and whose researches into the ventilation of his own lecture theatre had long before drawn his attention to the combined problems of heating, ventilation and acoustics. It was he who was finally engaged as a consultant to Sir Charles Barry when the new Palace of Westminster came to be built, and who made all sorts of ingenious suggestions, such as that the air should be drawn over bags of ice in summer so as to keep the building cool. He also considered that a large air chamber or reservoir should be provided and furnished with purifying washers and heaters.

The basic system he finally envisaged, and which was also used in the temporary House of Commons erected in the meantime, was of the type then called 'thermo-ventilation'; that is to say, instead of the air being propelled by fans (which before the invention of the electric dynamo were extremely inefficient, although occasionally used, as at the Whitechapel Public Baths (1846) and the Criterion Theatre (1872)), it was set in motion by the convection of heat generated by a furnace. This necessitated large ducts and tall chimneys, and it was not long before a bitter quarrel developed between Reid and Barry as to the amount of such space to be allotted. The latter claimed that if Reid had his way, the greater part of the building would consist of nothing but ventilation ducts, whereas Reid, like so many later enthusiasts in this field, considered the perfection of his own speciality to be the only thing that mattered. Eventually a compromise was reached, but the quarrel is interesting, not only as demonstrating an unusual aspect of Rationalism as a creative force in the Gothic Revival, but as marking the first occasion when mechanical services had a real influence on architectural design. For this reason, the architectural treatment of the ventilation shafts of the Palace of Westminster, which can be seen above the central portion of the river façade, is well worth studying.

There were many public buildings of the era, notably the law courts erected in London and Manchester, where thermo-ventilation was also used, and where tall towers were incorporated in the design, thus serving an eminently practical purpose, even though today they may appear simply as picturesque elaborations of a pseudo-mediaeval feature. Ten years ago, this fact might well have seemed to have little historical importance; but in the last decade, a whole aesthetic based on the emphasis on ventilation ducts has been exploited by Louis Kahn and his followers, so that the subtlety of the distinction between ventilation shafts serving a practical purpose and towers providing a picturesque silhouette will be only too apparent.

It is probably fair to say that the real revolution in mechanical services occurred only when electricity was harnessed to the needs of heating and ventilation, and in this respect it is worth noting that by an extraordinary coincidence this revolution occurred in the same decade that saw the development of the steel and reinforced concrete frame. The Gramme dynamo was invented in 1875, the incandescent bulb in 1879; and although to begin with electric light flickered and fluctuated too much to inspire universal confidence, the Savoy Theatre was entirely lit by electricity in 1881, and it is from this year that we can date the revolutionary era when artificial light was no longer provided by a flame.

The importance of electricity in improving ventilation and in accelerating the functioning of elevators (invented, for all practical purposes, by E. G. Otis in 1853, though used before this in cruder forms) need not be emphasized; nor is there any need to insist on the contribution of such inventions as air conditioning (first introduced in 1902 and developed initially as a means of regulating the humidity of factories) in the evolution of tall buildings. But one final word must be said about the integration of mechanical services into buildings, particularly with respect to ventilation ducts, for there are clearly two ways of achieving this in a modern building. One is to fix the ducts to the structure and then cover them with false ceilings and false columns; the other is to integrate them within the structure itself. Auguste Perret was probably the first architect to achieve complete integration (which he accomplished in his Museum of Public Works, Paris (1938)). Similarly it was he who, in the Théâtre des Champs-Élysées (1913) was probably the first architect to design a building entirely illuminated by concealed lighting. But it was not until the 1950s that the solution of this problem was seen as of crucial importance to architecture, and given realization in such splendid interiors as Louis Kahn's art gallery at Yale University. Here, however, we leave the realm of history and enter the realm of theory, and since it will not be possible for an objective historical assessment of these developments to be made for many years, a discussion on their historical significance may appropriately be left to a future date

Part Five

===

THE INFLUENCE OF THE ALLIED ARTS

21

The Influence of Literature and Criticism

<hr>

The influence of the allied arts on architectural design raises ethical problems of considerable gravity, for whilst this influence can bring about, and undoubtedly has brought about, certain benefits, it can also vitiate the nature of architectural creativity by leading to the production of forms which are not strictly architectural at all. This is not to say that the influence of the allied arts has always been totally absent in the best architecture of the past. On the contrary, since an architect has the right to seek artistic inspiration from any source which may be forthcoming, he can just as well obtain it from, say, Japanese prints, as from contemplating buildings of the present or the past. But it seems nevertheless fair to say that when the allied arts have exerted an excessive or even predominant influence on architectural design, the result has often been pseudo-architecture, in the sense that it is difficult in such instances to tell where the genuine tectonic virtues of the work are to be found.

It is perfectly admissible for John Burchard and Albert Bush-Brown, in *The Architecture of America*, to assert that 'a building of high artistic merit measured solely in visual terms is architecture, even if it is badly built or if it performs its practical functions indifferently', for there undoubtedly exist one or two buildings of widely acknowledged artistic merit which are both shoddily constructed and uncomfortable to live in. But if the artistic merit of a building depends mainly on literary romantic allusions, or is due to the arbitrary 'sculptural' quality of the forms, it may reasonably be argued that such buildings are not architecture at all, but simply whimsically conceived constructions disguised in the borrowed aesthetic trappings of another art.

It will have been perceived from the preceding chapters that there have been, during the past century at least, three main straightforward sources of inspiration for architectural form: firstly, the authority of the traditional architecture of the past (which resulted in Revivalism); secondly, the desire to escape from this authority by means of functional analogies (which were mainly of influence to planning); and thirdly, a reliance on the selection of structural components justified by reason (which resulted in Eclecticism and Rationalism). But none of these three philosophies provided any real source of inspiration for envisaging *novel* forms, so that those who considered novelty to be the essence of a new architecture were often tempted to turn their thoughts towards the other arts: painting, sculpture, industrial design and literature. Literature naturally exerted the least influence, since it is not, like the first three, a visual art. But certain fundamental ideas connected with modern literature, such as a feeling for the artistic virtues of ugliness, and a hypersensitivity to the importance of sincerity, were to have a drastic influence on architecture, and indeed affected all the visual arts. Similarly, the growth of literary criticism helped to create architectural criticism, and this naturally affected architecture itself.

The idea that art and ugliness are not necessarily incompatible was bound sooner or later to be developed as a positive aesthetic doctrine, once it was believed that aesthetic emotions are not solely concerned with beauty (as the terms 'beaux-arts' and 'belles-lettres' had formerly implied), but could also be aroused by the sublime or the picturesque. Moreover, the Platonists' definition of beauty as 'the splendour of truth', when coupled with certain novelists' increasing concern with the more sordid facets of urban life brought into being by the Industrial Revolution, allowed the notion of artistic beauty to be interpreted in extremely unconventional terms. It had of course long been appreciated that what was ugly in real life could be beautiful in art. Uvedale Price had devoted a whole chapter to this problem in his book *On the Picturesque* (1794), whilst Denis Diderot had long since argued that ugliness and horror could be tolerated in poetry. But the great change was brought about by the leading Romantic writers in the 1830s, due to the fact that they defended the merits of ugliness itself. Victor Hugo, in the preface to his play *Cromwell* (1830), asserted that beauty was simply that small and almost negligible part of nature which was pleasing to man, whereas everything organic was pleasing to God. Christianity, he wrote, had demonstrated, in the pursuit of truth, that everything in God's creation was not humanly beautiful, since ugliness existed there side by side with grace, the grotesque behind the sublime, evil with good, and shadow with light. Why then should not these aspects of life, rejected by the Classical dramatists, be the essence of works of dramatic art? Thus was born the school of literary Realism, when whole novels were written about the more heart-rending aspects of human degradation, and the scenes of dramas were laid in slums: a *genre* which is now so familiar that we take it for granted, but which was revolutionary a century ago.

It was useless for Victor Cousin, the apostle of Eclecticism, to condemn 'that enervating literature, by turns gross and refined, which delights in painting the miseries of human nature, which caresses all our weaknesses, which pays court to the senses and the imagination, instead of speaking to the soul and awakening thought'. The spirit of the age was enthralled by what it took to be the contact with reality which the analysis of the cruder human instincts permitted, and henceforth coarseness and ugliness were no longer comic elements (as they were in Shakespeare's plays) but came to be almost synonymous in *avant-garde* circles with the noble vigour of spiritual life.

There were of course historical precedents for the artistic exploitation of ugliness, and there have been several historical treatises published on 'Ugliness in Art', in which such ugliness is justified by reference to mediaeval religious sculpture or the grotesque paintings of Hieronymus Bosch. But it is probably fair to say that there was no real historical precedent for the type of ugliness introduced by certain nineteenth century Revivalist architects, such as William Butterfield. In their work, ugliness was achieved partly by the deliberate distortion of traditional forms, and partly by simply ignoring the problem of 'design' altogether. The latter technique was partly influenced, no doubt, by the current vogue for 'vernacular' buildings already mentioned; but it was facilitated by the fact that Butterfield himself possessed neither a drawing board nor a T-square, and created most of his designs from small sketches, or by personal intervention on the site. He was thus a pioneer of what in recent years has been called 'Action Architecture'; that is to say, architecture which is left to find its own organic order without too much human forethought or graphic research.

The immediate connection between Butterfield's architecture and the writings of literary Realists is not blatantly obvious, but it was noted several years ago by no less an authority than John Summerson. 'To suggest comparison between architects and writers is risky at any time', he wrote in an essay on Butterfield in *Heavenly Mansions*, 'and if I go on to say that the inartistic verbosity with which Charles Dickens hammers out his characters always strikes, in me, the same chord as do the copious devices which Butterfield requires for his effects, I may very well be accused of careless talk. But in Dickens the "aesthetic" appeal of hardness and cruelty is evident both in the choice of his material and in its handling, and I think there is no escaping the general conclusion that during the middle decades of the nineteenth century, there was a singular attraction on the part of some painters, architects and writers towards ugliness'.

This ugliness was quite apparent to Butterfield's contemporaries, and was frequently remarked upon, sometimes with admiration, but more often with distaste. *The Ecclesiologist*, as we have seen, liked it, and in a long and laudatory article on Butterfield's church of All Saints', Margaret Street, London, remarked: 'Curiously enough there is here to be observed the germ of the same dread of beauty, not to say the same deliberate preference of ugliness, which so characterizes in fuller development the later paintings of Mr. Millais and his followers'. But Scott, in his *Remarks on Secular and Domestic Architecture* (1858), objected to 'that intentional queerness and artistic ugliness which some of our young architects labour to produce'. Similarly Robert Kerr, in *The English Gentleman's House* (1864) remarked that 'there has been growing up an incredible worship of what can only be fitly called The Ugly'; and although he acknowledged the merits of the reaction against sham colonnades and stuccoed walls which had introduced this love for undisguised honesty, however crude, and for masculine simplicity, however unrefined; and although he agreed that the 'Ugly Style' had at least the merit of not being effeminate, he was discerning enough to perceive that one of the less healthy results of this pursuit of ugliness was that its exponents 'set common criticism at defiance'. Indeed, it is this group's disdain not merely for traditional canons of criticism, but for all canons of criticism, which relates the nineteenth century esoteric vogue for architectural ugliness so closely to nineteenth century literary anti-Academic trends, and also to certain nineteenth century philosophical theories, as for example those of the Positivists, who showed the same indifference towards what was traditionally good and bad.

This *laissez-faire* attitude towards architectural criticism was singled out for attack by *The Builder* in 1869. There were, according to the editor, designs then being produced which were referable to no principles that ever existed, and which, though rapidly achieving a temporary popularity, could only be described by him as 'barbarisms'. The mere revival of mediaeval styles had evidently, he said, become too tame and commonplace a source of effect in the craving for novelty which had beset so large a portion of the architectural profession, and he shrewdly apportioned a large part of the blame for this trend on architectural competitions, where 'each man feels that his best chance of distinction is to put forth something more wild and startling than his neighbours have done'. All attempts at giving refinement of character to a building by carefully proportioning the various parts, and by design-ing each detail with reference to its effect on the whole, were now, he complained, scouted as so much child's play calculated to interfere with the vigour and picturesqueness of the design, and he instanced the contemporary fashion of obtain-ing originality by perpetually shortening the shafts in pseudo-Gothic designs. This barbaric mania (which, he perceived, was clearly divorced from all considerations of structural logic) had spread to furniture design, and his contemporaries were being beset with designs for furniture of the most clumsy and unwieldy type, with studiously ugly outlines, such as 'bookcases inlaid with different woods, with an absence of all definite design, just as we might expect to find them in the Sandwich Islands, or among any other barbarous people'. It was of the essence of barbarism, he concluded (little dreaming of the future twentieth century European interest in Polynesian sculpture), to rejoice in all such gewgaw displays of colour and jumble of intricate forms.

This pursuit of ugliness was not confined to England. It was even more popular in America, and is probably best exemplified in the work of Frank Furness, whose historical significance has hitherto rested on the fact that Louis Sullivan worked for him for a short time after leaving the Massachusetts Institute of Technology. Furness's work is in fact interesting only because it exemplifies how the pursuit of ugliness was so often merely a perverted aspect of Eclecticism, in that whereas the true Eclectics chose historically ill-assorted elements because they were functionally appropriate, Furness and those who shared his attitude chose them simply because they produced visually exciting and novel compositions. Professor Hitchcock has described Furness's Philadelphia Provident Trust Building (1879) as 'an intensely personal work, original and impressive'. Original it certainly is, but whether one is impressed by it or not will depend on whether one welcomes the tendency of the extremists of the age to throw all traditional aesthetic criteria into the melting pot.

The new attitude towards criticism was important, because although the nine-teenth century's grotesque miscombination of decorative and structural motifs, both mediaeval and antique in origin, might seem at first to have little relevance to twentieth century designs, the rejection of aesthetic criteria was an essential pre-requisite for the acceptance of the new abstract forms produced in the 1920s by the Bauhaus and by Le Corbusier. Thus the nineteenth century intellectual atmosphere which ignored aesthetic criticism allowed the leaders of the new movement in the twentieth century to experiment with new architectural forms, new materials, new structural systems and new building techniques in comparative freedom. This is not to say that they themselves ever publicly professed a belief that the traditional distinctions between ugliness and beauty were of no importance; but there is no doubt that the more radical exponents of the New Architecture ignored this distinction in their early experimental work.

Sometimes, of course, nineteenth century ugliness was not due to a deliberate search for this quality but resulted simply from the insensitivity of the designer. On the other hand, in fairness to many of these designers, one may suspect that the bitterest complaints about architectural ugliness were inspired more by historically motivated prejudices than by a real appreciation of the inadequacies in the archi-tectural solutions evolved. Thus the editor of *The Builder*, in 1847, was not merely content to castigate the design of the new public baths in Goulstone Square, Whitechapel, by calling them 'downright ugly', but went on to lament that the designer had not endowed this working-class district with something comparable to the thermae of ancient Rome, 'the rendezvous of men of letters, which, with their galleries of sculpture and painting, were nurseries of taste'.

Moreover, many capable architects whom we would now consider exponents of the philosophy of deliberate ugliness were themselves convinced that they were producing works of exquisite beauty. No architect of the nineteenth century ever produced more brutal designs than William Burges, yet in a lecture he gave in 1867, he criticized those of his contemporaries who tried 'to get an appearance of strength by using forms which were known to our ancestors, but rejected by them as being ugly'. The problem of deciding which architects subscribed to the doctrine of ugliness and which did not is thus fraught with difficulty; but it can be asserted without any hesitation that those who today are described as 'Brutalists', and who today advocate 'Action Architecture', are not exploiting ideals which either emanate from machine-age technology or even reflect a reaction against earlier manifestations of this technology; they are simply reviving a romantic aesthetic craving which can be traced back over a hundred years.

A more subtle, but more widely pervading literary influence of the modern era was the craving to express sincerity, which Henri Peyre has described as 'the most potent *idée-force* in the literature and psychology of the age'. It is not surprising therefore that it should have been expressed during the last century by a number of architects and architectural theorists, from Eugène Viollet-le-Duc to Marcel Breuer. Viollet-le-Duc, in his *Entretiens* (1863), used the word 'sincerity' several times, and remarked in particular that 'à coup sûr, aujourd'hui, un parti pris de sincérité absolue serait très nouveau et probablement très piquant'. Frank Lloyd Wright, in *The Natural House*, asserted that 'the first feeling was hunger for reality, for sincerity'. Marcel Breuer, in a lecture reprinted in the monograph devoted to his work declared: 'to sum up, to us clarity means the definite expression of the purpose of a building and a sincere expression of its structure. One can regard this sincerity as a sort of moral duty'. J. M. Richards, in his *Introduction to Modern Architecture*, praised H. H. Richardson for compositions 'whose sincerity did much to free American building from the trivialities of current antiquarian fashions', and asserted that 'the important thing in the future is that modern architecture should blossom into full maturity without losing the sincerity which is at present its special virtue'. Reyner Banham considers in his *Guide to Modern Architecture* that the most important feature of C. R. Mackintosh's Glasgow School of Art is its 'brutal frankness', and that it is this frankness which makes the building specifically modern. Undoubtedly many other such quotations could be found if one troubled to look for them; but there is no need. Every architect and every architectural student knows the important part played by the notion of sincerity (or by the fear of accusations of lack of sincerity) in his creative work, even though he may not be aware of the far-reaching implications which such an attitude of mind entails.

Before discussing these implications, it is important to emphasize the distinction between sincerity and truth. The urge towards sincerity in the mid-nineteenth century was, like the taste for ugliness, greatly influenced by the distaste for Regency shams, and this in turn led to a belief in some quarters that all Renaissance architecture was, to quote Geoffrey Scott, 'bad in itself, inherently, because it is insincere'. But sincerity and truth are not the same thing, even though the *Concise Oxford Dictionary* treats them as synonymous. Ruskin's 'Lamp of Truth' does not contain one word about sincerity, and for good reason; for the notion of truth, in architecture, has usually implied an *objective* correspondence between what a structure is and what it appears to be, whereas sincerity is *subjective*: it suggests an integritous relationship between the artist and his work of art, and has thus only assumed artistic importance since Benedetto Croce's subjective theory of aesthetics became the most fashionable theory of art. Truth is what we owe to others, whereas sincerity is what we owe to ourselves. The sincere architect is the architect who designs a building the way he believes it should be designed, and not just the way

F. Furness: Provident Trust Building, Philadelphia (1879)

INFLUENCE OF THE ALLIED ARTS

Illustrating the influence of literary explorations into the aesthetic merits of ugliness

XXIX

E. André: Huet House, Nancy (1903)

J. Hoffmann: Stoclet House, Brussels (1905)

INFLUENCE OF THE ALLIED ARTS

Illustrating the influence of furniture design on architectural composition and detail

XXX

M. Breuer: Belfrey, St. John's monastery, Collegeville (1953)

INFLUENCE OF THE ALLIED ARTS

Illustrating the influence of furniture design on architectural composition

XXXI

F. L. Wright: Detail of ornament, Coonley House, Riverside (1907)

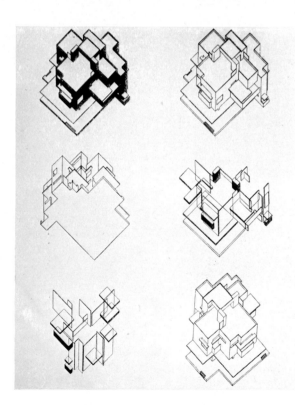

T. van Doesburg: Design for a house (1922)

INFLUENCE OF THE ALLIED ARTS

*Illustrating the influence of research into abstract patterns on new notions regarding
the spatial relationship of planes*

XXXII

his client or the public will most readily accept it. No modern architect questions the sincerity of the original architects of York Minster, even though he may have reservations about the propriety of imitating a stone vault in wood; but he suspects the sincerity of those who have built Gothic cathedrals in the twentieth century because he rejects the idea that it would be sincere for him to build something comparable if he were invited to undertake such a task. He does not deny that Scott's Liverpool Cathedral is a true expression of its structure, that it is well proportioned or endowed with qualities which stimulate emotions of piety; he simply doubts that anyone can still build according to these same structural and ornamental methods without sacrificing that sincerity which modern man owes to himself as a creature of his age.

For artistic sincerity is characteristic of the modern age (which, as explained in the chapter on Historiography, is appropriately dated from 1750), and first appears in the writings of Jean-Jacques Rousseau, whose *Confessions* constitute the first example of a work of art in which sincerity is treated as a dominant artistic quality. 'To this day,' writes Henri Peyre, 'no other revelation by the legion of self-confessed, self-incriminating egotists in love with sincerity who followed Rousseau has surpassed the *Confessions*, the *Rêveries*, and the *Dialogues* in originality. To Rousseau must be traced back the worship by many moderns of sincerity as a test of greatness or as a substitute for almost any other quality, moral or aesthetic.'

Now if one examines the nature of Rousseau's sincerity, one cannot help but be struck by the correspondence between Rousseau's temperament and that of the more famous revolutionary architects of the present century. For example, it seems of more than casual significance that Rousseau was not merely an extremely ardent personality, overflowing with the urge to enshrine, in monumental form, an experience he deemed unique, and consumed with the urge to communicate a message of human redemption to mankind, but that, paradoxically, he was a person who also considered himself a typical sample of humanity. According to Henri Peyre, the stress laid by Rousseau on sincerity may be accounted for by several reasons, one of these being the fact that 'sickness contributed to make him an introvert and directed him to the acceptance of himself as both a sample and as a model for mankind'. But this inner conflict, however pathological, must nevertheless suggest to any architect who reads these words a curious similarity with the careers of some of the men now referred to as 'The Masters of World Architecture'. Le Corbusier, for example, has always thought of himself in this dual role: firstly, as a super-intellectual, seized with a unique awareness of the needs of humanity, and secondly, as the creator of environments which are always ideal essentially for himself; that is to say, artists' studios with one large window and a mezzanine of the traditional type which he and his friends occupied in the 1920s in Paris, and which he has transmuted into workers' dwellings and luxury flats.

Another interesting aspect of sincerity as an artistic stimulus is the emphasis it lays on an artist's own artistic development, since clearly there is no weightier evidence of sincerity than the proof that an artist has pursued a consistent path throughout his career. It may be argued that the biographical method of art-historical study goes back to Vasari, and that it is a natural and sensible way of studying the development of the literary and graphic arts. Yet it can hardly be denied that the urge to demonstrate sincerity is producing more and more architectural biographies of the type best exemplified by the recent biography of Eero Saarinen, and is leading more and more architects to publish their *Oeuvre Complète*. There is clearly no harm in this biographical method, provided it is not exploited to excess. But it will be readily perceived that it militates against the more traditional interpretation of the notion of evolution, such as was common among nineteenth century architectural theorists like Fergusson (largely because mediaeval architecture was thought of as anonymous). It also militates against more recent ideas concerning the evolution of architecture by anonymous collaboration, such as has been urged for many years by Walter Gropius.

The third interesting parallel which can be drawn between Rousseau and the leading exponents of modern architecture stems from the fact that Rousseau, like Viollet-le-Duc, Frank Lloyd Wright, Le Corbusier and Bruce Goff, was virtually self-taught. He had no formal education, and had to acquire the elements of a normal education without a teacher, discovering the elements of music, of grammar and of philosophy through slow and devious paths, and learning about human nature the hard way. Now obviously the need to acquire a professional education in this manner did not make it inevitable that Rousseau would be the first apostle of sincerity; but it is significant that he signals the beginning of a deeply-rooted feeling, which has lasted for the past two centuries, that academicism is in some way a breeding ground for insincerity, and that one can only be sincere by resisting the influence of academic training, or drawing from such training only those purely technological or methodological notions which it imparts.

Fourthly, we find, in the cult of sincerity, a tremendous emphasis given to the virtues of spontaneity. Whereas in the traditional teaching of the École des Beaux-Arts, most of the time spent on a project was devoted to 'study'—that is to say, to developing a composition by refining it and adjusting its details—the last century has seen the growth of a tendency to consider that a composition loses its spontaneity if studied too carefully, and as a result, many contemporary buildings look like small-scale sketches blown up to full size. Even when intricate detailing appears to exist, it only too often turns out to consist of bric-à-brac, which is another characteristic of sincerity as a literary *genre*; for, as Henri Peyre remarks, 'the reader who buys the diaries of Gide, Green or Léautaud is reassured that his own trivia—how he eats and talks and fails to sleep and hates his relatives and is "crucified by sex"—are in no way different from those that are deemed worthy of note in a "great" man's diary'. This paucity of detailing, in its traditional sense, and the emphasis on the decorative interest of trivia, are not of course readily apparent in photographs, and can only be appreciated when one actually visits a recent building. But it is very evident that a world of difference exists between small-scale photographs of, say, the Chase-Manhattan Bank in New York and the building itself, for the former look so rich and the latter so barren and empty; and there can be few visitors, even devoted admirers of Skidmore, Owings and Merrill, who have not nostalgically compared the opulence of the various nineteenth century banks surrounding it with the bleakness of its own details, and regretted that the sincere expression of structure and materials has not provided something more substantial to caress the eye.

Finally, as regards the last of those aspects of sincerity which affect the architect's attitude towards his own work, mention must be made of the emphasis on frankness, by which is usually meant a rather brutal kind of sincerity. In its mildest form it implies a belief in the importance of being earnest; in its most common form it implies an indifference to other people's more sensitive feelings; and in its extreme form it implies a deliberate desire to hurt. The high seriousness of modern architecture, and the fear of frivolity (except in exhibition pavilions), is only too apparent, so that it is interesting to see how, in the history of literature, seriousness has so often been linked with the urge towards sincerity. According to Wordsworth, writing about epitaphs: 'when a man is treating an interesting subject, and one which he ought not to treat at all unless he be interested, no faults have such a killing power as those which prove that he is not in earnest. Indeed, when the internal evidence shows that the writer was moved, in other words when this charm of sincerity lurks in the language of a tombstone and secretly pervades it, there are no errors in style or manner for which it will not be, in some degree, a recompense'. Similarly Matthew Arnold spoke of 'the high seriousness which comes from absolute sincerity', and regarded this as the source of power behind much noble verse.

Indifference to others as created by the search for sincerity is eloquently explained by Henri Peyre with reference to literature. 'The march onwards and downwards in ourselves is fraught with perils,' he writes, 'the readiest of them being narcissism and its consequent failure: the inability to locate the self in its relation to its surroundings'. In architectural terms, this notion may perhaps be interpreted as meaning that the more an architect strives to make his buildings sincere, the less are they likely to harmonize with their environments; for sincerity, being a matter of personal conviction, is impatient of external servitudes, and perhaps one of the most striking characteristics of these 'Masters of World Architecture' who have prided themselves on their sincerity is their indifference to what is already in existence near the site. 'A modern building,' wrote Walter Gropius, 'should derive its architectural significance solely from the vigour and consequence of its own organic proportions; it must be true to itself.' But this sort of truth, alas, is only too often achieved at the expense of truths of a wider and more harmonious kind.

The relationship between sincerity and brutality is even more obvious in modern architecture, since sincerity, as Simone de Beauvoir has observed, often conceals a desire to provoke. It may be that the recent fashion for rough concrete surfaces, or for the type of detailing described by some authors as 'The New Brutalism', can and should be justified by other motives than the desire to give pain to those critics who persist in prizing carefully-worked surfaces and carefully modulated transitions; but undoubtedly, in its origin at least, such brutalism was influenced by, on the one hand, the extremist and exhibitionist elements present in the cult of sincerity, and, on the other hand, the puritanical hatred of all that is coquetry and charm. Interestingly enough, these elements, at one stage in the history of art, combined to produce 'anti-art' (or in other words, to produce the shock-therapy against those artistic values which were then thought of as insincere). But it makes no difference whether we regard rough concrete, crude details and a studied lack of elegance as art or anti-art; the element of shock, as part of the element of sincerity, is still there.

In brutal detailing we see most clearly the confusion which can exist between the notion of sincerity and the notion of truth; for whereas those who believe that good architecture implies structural truth may well consider brutalism as simply the emphatic expression of structure, those who deny nineteenth century Rationalist ideals, and consider the expression of structure immaterial, will hold, like Montherlant, that truth, in this sense, is non-existent; that 'the object of our affirmations hardly matters, for what counts is only the arrogant sincerity with which we assert them'. The Classical theorist was less concerned with what was true than with what was likely (that is to say, he preferred *le vraisemblable* to *le vrai*); but the writers of modern memoirs, diaries and confessions often make every effort to convince their readers that their aim is not so much to display what is true as to display what is unseemly, and one can hardly fail to observe that this literary fashion of undressing in public is matched by the architectural fashion of not merely exposing what needs not be covered, but of deliberately seeking out complicated techniques for exposing the 'guts' of a building, whether these be ventilation ducts or merely the knot-holes of the woodwork in which the concrete elements were cast.

Inevitably, the search for sincerity has also contributed to the modern distrust of 'style'; for in the Classical age, when art was taken to imply the conscious stimulation of an emotion of beauty, it also indicated the deliberate use of devices calculated to obtain it, whereas after the Romantic revolution, style was soon regarded as an artificial device inimical to sincere expression. Rousseau admitted that he dreaded the weakening influence of style, which tended to make everything monotonous and artificial. He wanted to respect and preserve spontaneity in writing; an attitude not very different from that of Walter Gropius, who never discusses 'style' except in the sense of 'historical style', as when he asserted that a 'Bauhaus Style' would have been a confession of failure and a return to the stagnation which his educational system had been created to combat.

Gropius's reasons for rejecting the notion of style were undoubtedly justified in their day; but the dangers of the continued disdain for style in the interests of sincerity are becoming increasingly apparent, and have been elaborated upon by Henri Peyre. 'The will to annihilate style', he writes, 'implies an unflagging awareness of style itself designed to eschew its flourishes and to sift the most genuine in our experiences or in our emotions from what might be borrowed, assumed, feigned. It tends to stress the author's analytical scrutiny of himself at the expense of his free inventiveness, and thus may impair his sincerity, which might be at its greatest if he followed his own inner necessity instead of distrusting it. It also leads to a writer's straining of his own originality, in his anxiety not to imitate technical devices of previous authors. In the past, borrowing such devices had seldom detracted from creativeness, provided the results (reached through such resort to a form already polished and well refined) remained original. The fanatics of literary sincerity in the present age have oscillated around two opposite poles. On the one hand there are the Puritans and the Jacobins, who aim at banishing effects, superfluity and emotional intemperance; at the other extreme stand the Whitmanesque lovers of words and tenants of spontaneousness.'

In practice the disdain for style has meant that, in literature, the man and the author have been merged into one. Similarly, in architecture, the architect now creates by direct experience rather than by the application of a system of rules based on a common fund of knowledge. Just as the sincere author ceased to be, or to wish to appear as, a fastidious craftsman, but lived first as intensely as he could, and enriched his writings by the experience thus gained, so in architecture, the architect designs according to his own personal experience, whereby the notion of a theory of architecture, or even of the discipline of a client's programme, has ceased, under the impulsion of the search for sincerity, to have any real meaning at all in the sense that it had in the past. Professor Llewelyn-Davies has made clear that in his view, what was at one time thought to constitute the theory of architecture is seen, on closer inspection, to be simply an accumulation of disparate ideas best treated as part of other disciplines or ignored altogether. Thus sincerity in architecture has meant, in effect, starting from scratch, or, as Reyner Banham puts it, 'the freedom to live in a house designed as if houses had just been invented'. It has meant rejecting the acquired experience of our ancestors, and thus paradoxically relates, in the realm of the history of ideas, to those notions of Greek Revivalism which can also claim Rousseau as their ancestor, and which were responsible, two centuries ago, for a type of Primitivism which sought for new architectural roots in the most remote past.

When considering this primitivistic aspect of Revivalism, it is interesting to note the affinity between the cult of sincerity and the cult of vernacular poetry, since a yearning for vernacular architecture has also been characteristic of the modern age. In an earlier chapter, I attempted to show the influence of vernacular architecture on the theories used to support the 'Queen Anne Revival'. In this present context, it is important to make clear that the emphasis on vernacular writing, and the abandonment of literary ornaments, was largely dictated by the quest for sincerity.

Moreover, this emphasis led to another attitude which is also characteristic of certain modern buildings, namely the notion of a work of art as a kind of soliloquy, in which the artist cares little for the public, and does not deign to address his works to them, but creates only to justify his own innermost urge, as a result of which the artist is the work of art's only judge.

For it is in its devastating effect upon criticism that the influence of sincerity has been most clearly marked. How can a critic assess the merits of a building if its value is mainly to be assessed by the sincerity which went into its creation? Such an assessment merely substitutes the artist for his work, and makes the study of the history of art, which at its best is a study by means of criticism, virtually impossible. What is henceforth the value of deciding whether the work of François Mansart is superior to the work of Jules-Hardouin Mansart if the pertinent facts about these architects' careers is that the former was universally admired for his integrity whereas the latter was lampooned by Saint-Simon as an obsequious lackey of the court? Reyner Banham claims that one of the merits of Denys Lasdun's flats in St. James's Place, London, is that the architect 'worked with complete conviction'; but sincerity itself will not suffice for posterity, for as Henri Peyre pertinently remarks, 'El Greco behaved like any commercial artist, painting just the saints and martyrs he was asked to portray, whilst Mozart composed precisely the religious music requested from him, utilizing lighter and purely pagan passages from his other works in a Mass or a Kyrie. He would not have posed as a dishevelled, haggard artist waiting for inspiration to strike his forehead. Like most musicians of his day, and others since, he filled orders. Emperor Joseph II commissioned *Così Fan Tutte* and Mozart delivered it.' In other words, the Classical artist's ambition was not to be sincere but to please, though he could do this perfectly well by lampooning insincerity, as is evident from Molière's *Tartuffe*. If, then, the literary cult of sincerity has a lesson for us, it is this: that sincerity is only a virtue when it is unselfconscious. When the artist becomes so priggishly aware of his own sincerity that it dominates his work, other values, of equal importance, become pushed into the background; and whilst no one would deny that an architect must have integrity to achieve greatness, this integrity must be incidental to his desire to please, or (if this word seems too obsequious to modern ears) to his desire to create environments which will give genuine pleasure to those for whom they are built.

We have seen that one of the most important effects of the pursuit of ugliness and the pursuit of sincerity was that both tended to set criticism at defiance. There were of course a number of philosophers who, long before these fashions established themselves, asserted that criticism was dangerous in that it inhibited the artist from creating spontaneous works of art. Archibald Alison, in his *Essay on the Nature and Principles of Taste* (1790), contended that the exercise of the critical faculty diminished or destroyed the perception of beauty, and he asserted that 'the mind, in such an employment, instead of being at liberty to follow whatever trains of imagery the composition before it can excite, is either fettered to the consideration of some of its minute and solitary parts, or pauses amid the rapidity of its conceptions, to make them the objects of its attention and review'. Similarly Payne Knight, in his *Analytical Enquiry into the Principles of Taste* (1805), declared that 'the whole history of literature obliges us to acknowledge that, in proportion as criticism has been systematic, and critics numerous, the powers of composition and purity of taste have gradually decayed'. Even Wordsworth, one of the first great poets to be also a critic, was notoriously distrustful of contemporary critical opinions of his own verse, and in this his attitude was characteristic of the whole Romantic movement. Indeed, the big difference between the Romantics and the Classicists lay in the fact that the latter had traditionally put reliance on the critical faculties of the common reader, whereas the former did not.

Yet it must be emphasized that the distrust for, or disregard of criticism was not shared by the general public in the nineteenth century, and this explains why the growth of criticism was one of the most influential features of the age. This was the great era of popular critical literature, especially in periodicals, which started in the mid-eighteenth century with the duplicated manuscript criticisms circulated by Grimm and Diderot to their aristocratic correspondents, and reached its full flowering with such magazines as the *Quarterly Review*, the *Edinburgh Review* and the *Revue des Deux Mondes*.

Before discussing the influence on architectural ideals of architectural criticism, it will be appropriate to consider first some of the reasons for the upsurge of artistic criticism in general. Clearly criticism is as old as art itself, since the idea of establishing critical standards can be traced back (particularly in the realm of literature) to ancient Greece, even though popular literary criticism does not seem to go back further than Joseph Warton's *Adventurer* essays (1753). On the other hand, the whole notion of publishing detailed criticisms of individual paintings, sculpture and works of architecture is relatively recent, and can be traced back only to the beginnings of the modern age: to the 'Salons' of Diderot (that is to say, to his criticisms of the bi-annual Parisian art exhibitions which he circulated to a select body of correspondents from 1759 onwards), and to J. F. Blondel's *Architecture Française*; a four-volumed illustrated folio published in 1752. Blondel's treatise is particularly important in the history of architecture because it reflects more clearly than any other writing of the period the Rationalist didactic method. This book was primarily intended for students, as is stated in the first volume, for here he announced that 'the diverse reflections I intend to make, concerning the many buildings of which this work is composed, will doubtless be of some use to those who intend to be architects, and it is for them that I make these observations'. Moreover, there is good reason to suspect that his published remarks were simply a transcription of those he voiced as he conducted his groups of students round

Paris, declaiming on the merits and defects of each building as he passed. But the theory on which they are based belongs more to the type of Classicism that was then dying, than to the new architecture with which this book is concerned. For to Blondel there was no generic distinction to be made between sixteenth century buildings and eighteenth century buildings, since all were united by a common obedience to the architectural principles of Antiquity. No sense of history troubled his criticism, nor were doubts expressed as to the intrinsic validity of the stan- dardized tectonic elements which he so often considered to be treated with undue licence or abused; from this point of view his *Architecture Françoise* is thus not only the first book of architectural criticism but the last great compendium of the Classical age.

The reason for the popularity of art criticism in the second half of the eighteenth century is doubtless to be found in the new study of aesthetics, and the influence on it of historiography; for whereas before 1750 criticism was simply a matter of reference to universally accepted objective rules, after 1750 it became a subjective literary exercise in which history, psychology and literary allusions provided intellectual ingredients with which artistic judgements came to be inextricably mixed. The influence of historiography resulted inevitably from the fact that so many early literary critics, such as J. G. Herder, Friedrich Schlegel and A. W. Schlegel were also historians of literature; indeed, the latter contended that there cannot be history without theory, since history, if it is not to be a mere chronicle, requires a principle of selectivity. As a result, criticism not merely became in- extricably bound up with theory but also (in an age when all theoretical speculation was dominated by history) inextricably bound up with history. In this respect, it is worth noting the number of eighteenth century historians who also wrote about philosophy or aesthetics. The most influential modern writers to put forward a purely subjective theory of art—Croce and Collingwood—have both been primarily historians. Similarly, the mid-eighteenth century group of English critics who first started studying the history of mediaeval poetry were also responsible for creating the new 'free theory' of literature. The leader of this latter group was the poet Thomas Gray, one of the most important influences on the Gothic Revival; and as George Saintsbury remarks of him in his *History of Criticism*: 'small as is the extent of deliberate critical work he has left us, we may perceive in it nearly all the notes of reformed, revived, we might say reborn criticism. The two dominants of these have been the constant appeal to history, and the readiness to take new matter, whether actually new in time, or new in the sense of having been hitherto neglected, on its own merits'.

The influence of Rationalism was more marked in criticisms of architecture than in the critical writings on any of the other arts, and this was to be expected in the age of the *Encyclopédistes*, since architecture is a science as well as an art. Neverthe- less it is worth noting that Rationalist criticism declined as soon as the techniques and fashions of art criticism and literary criticism became influential in architectural circles. In the eighteenth century, the few architectural criticisms published had been mainly written by practising architects (and in this respect it should be noted that J. F. Blondel was not only a practising architect but contributed to the *Encyclopédie*). In the middle of the following century, however, historians, art-critics and professional journalists took over this task, from which time onwards the theory of architecture became bound up more with the history of architecture, just as criticism became essentially a form of literature. James Fergusson, who was an amateur in every sense of the word, wrote his *Historical Inquiry* (1849) because of 'the immense strides that have been made during the last half century in the true principles of artchitectural criticism.' Yet it was not from authors such as he that modern architecture had most to lose, for Fergusson was at least a convinced Rationalist, and was simply using history as a convenient instrument for justifying Rationalist ideals. The writers who proved the greatest menace to the uninhibited evolution of Rationalist ideals were those who regarded architectural criticism as an art form in itself; that is to say, those who considered that the critic's task was to absorb a work of art into his system in order to create another work of art (this time literary) which was entirely of his own making.

The merits of this approach have been most eloquently put forward by Oscar Wilde in his essay entitled *The Critic as an Artist*, but the idea itself is quite old, and was expressed in the early nineteenth century by the literary critic William Hazlitt, according to whom 'the critic, in place of analysis and an inquiry into causes, undertakes to formulate a verbal equivalent for the aesthetic effects of the work under consideration'. This, in its least dramatic form, means that a criticism is the transmutation of a painting, or some other work of visual art, into a prose poem; in its most dramatic form it implies the vivid outpouring of the writer's own sensations, which are activated by the work of art he had just seen or heard.

The first art critic, as has already been mentioned, was Denis Diderot, the leading *Encyclopédiste*. He deliberately interpreted the critic's task in the terms of Horace's well-known aphorism: *ut pictura poesis*. Now the danger of this technique of transmuting pictures into poetry is that it encourages the critic to prize the anecdotal elements of a work of art to the prejudice of its more formal qualities. Undoubtedly, the nauseatingly anecdotal quality of so many nineteenth century Romantic paintings and works of sculpture was the main cause which para-doxically led to a reaction in favour of completely non-representational art in the following century; but it was due to the fact that the critics who followed Diderot could only expatiate on subject matter, and found little stimulus in the subtleties of composition and proportion, or in the dispositions of colours and tones. It is indeed characteristic of Diderot's method that he found virtually nothing to say about the more practical architectural drawings exhibited in the Salons he appraised. Regarding the design of a stair by de Wailly, he could only observe that 'the drawing is quite cleanly done and I have no doubt that it can be built solidly;

but as regards its agreeableness, I make no decision whatsoever'. For him, the Orders had simply been invented 'to lead to monotony and stifle genius', and he warned his readers to beware of architects who were not great draftsmen, since 'although architecture gave birth to painting and sculpture, it is to these latter arts that architecture owes its great perfection'. Clearly the only kinds of architectural drawing which interested a critic of his temper were perspectives of Piranesian splendour, and there is thus no doubt that the vogue for this kind of scenic architectural drawing, as exploited by Hubert Robert and Boullée, must be largely attributed to the new type of art criticism which appeared at this time.

Diderot's most distinguished successor was Charles Baudelaire, whose first criticism of a Salon appeared in 1846, and was deliberately modelled on Diderot's method. The importance of Baudelaire in the history of art criticism lies not so much in the fact that he was a poet of considerable distinction (though this is clearly of immense significance), but in the fact that, unlike Diderot, he propounded a specific aesthetic doctrine, though he himself did not know how to paint. Being a poet, the test of good art, for him, was whether or not it demanded 'the application of imagination and the introduction of poetry', and whilst there was evidently a good deal of sense in his point of view, one can see why it inevitably made him favour Romanticism to the exclusion of Classicism, and why it made him prefer Delacroix to Ingres. Indeed, the influential importance of all this kind of criticism was that it encouraged the Romantics of the period to delight in the more sensual qualities of materials and compositions: in lush foliage, awe-inspiring ravines, rich brocades, gorgeous jewellery, and, in architecture, the kind of building epitomized by the Paris Opera House.

Baudelaire, like Diderot, seldom mentioned architecture, because, as César Daly remarked, whereas it was only too easy for a critic with even a slight familiarity with literary forms to take his readers on a tour of pictures and statues, 'expatiating on the colour of one and the form of another, and intermingling more or less amusing anecdotes with each remark', the analysis of an architectural project did not offer the same facilities as those offered by paintings, since an architect's lines were usually traced with straight-edges and compasses, and the forms developed in accordance with scientific laws. In other words, he perceived the purely practical literary reasons, sequential upon the essential nature and technique of journalistic criticism, why art critics had no sympathy with Rationalism, and were only interested in picturesque architecture (thus following the lead Sir Joshua Reynolds had earlier given, in his well-known remarks on Vanbrugh's painterly approach to the problems of architectural composition).

The only famous art critic of the nineteenth century to occupy himself predominantly with architecture was John Ruskin, and his writings are extraordinarily illuminating, in that they show just how tendentious the architectural criticisms of an impassioned amateur can be. Ruskin, it will be remembered, originally made his reputation by winning a poetry prize at Oxford and then promoting the paintings of Turner, and the kind of argument which he used to make his art-critical views prevail is clearly echoed in the description he gives in *The Stones of Venice* of the façade of St. Mark's. This description is quite extensive, even though it is only two sentences long, but it deserves to be quoted in full, since it shows better than any other of his writings how his deeply felt emotion could transmute architecture into literature without contributing anything at all to the public's understanding of the problems of architectural design, or of the nature of building as such:

'A multitude of pillars and white domes, clustered into a long low pyramid of coloured light; a treasure-heap, it seems, partly of gold, and partly of opal and mother-of-pearl, hollowed beneath into five great vaulted porches, ceiled with fair mosaic, and beset with sculpture of alabaster, clear as amber and delicate as ivory —sculpture fantastic and involved, of palm leaves and lilies, and grapes and pomegranates, and birds clinging and fluttering among the branches, all twined together into an endless network of buds and plumes; and, in the midst of it, the solemn form of angels, sceptred, and robed to the feet, and leaning to each other across the gates, their figures indistinct among the gleaming of the golden ground through the leaves beside them, interrupted and dim, like the morning light as it faded back among the branches of Eden, when first its gates were angel-guarded long ago. And round the walls of the porches there are set pillars of variegated stones, jasper and porphyry, and deep-green serpentine spotted with flakes of snow, and marbles, that half refuse and half yield to the sunshine, Cleopatra-like, "their bluest veins to kiss"—the shadow, as it steals back from them, revealing line after line of azure undulation, as a receding tide leaves the waved sand; their capitals rich with interwoven tracery, rooted knots of herbage, and drifting leaves of acanthus and vine, and mystical signs, all beginning and ending in the Cross; and above them, in the broad archivolts, a continuous chain of language and of life— angels, and the signs of heaven, and the labours of men, each in its appointed season upon earth; and above these, another range of glittering pinnacles, mixed with white arches edged with scarlet flowers,—a confusion of delight, amidst which the breasts of the Greek horses are seen blazing in their breadth of golden strength, and the St. Mark's Lion, lifted on a blue field covered with stars, until at last, as if in ecstacy, the crests of the arches break into a marble foam, and toss themselves far into the blue sky in flashes and wreaths of sculptured spray, as if the breakers on the Lido shore had been frost-bound before they fell, and the sea-nymphs had inlaid them with coral and amethyst'.

Now no one could deny that these lines are amongst the most beautiful in the English language; but as an architectural appraisal they clearly suffer from the defect of being concerned only with the external surfaces, not to say superficial decorative veneer, and even his contemporaries were nonplussed by the essentially anti-Rational philosophy which his description, by its omissions, implied. Professor Robert Kerr, for example, after remarking that it was most dangerous to believe that there was anything in common between the poet and the architect, observed that although he had originally held the same views as those put forward by Ruskin, he had grown out of them as a result of twenty years' practical work. He considered that practising architects ought to discourage the younger members of the profession from associating architecture with such romantic and visionary notions as Ruskin's writings conjured up, and he argued in favour of the architect as 'a servant of the public for the efficient design of buildings, precisely like the engineer'. Similarly, when discussing 'Architectural Criticism' three years later at the Royal Institute of British Architects, he remarked acidly that 'Mr. Ruskin's thoughts soar high enough in the poetry of visionary art, because poetry is his business, but they cannot stoop down to the plain prosaic details of the structuresque, because building is not his business'. Even the review published by *The Builder* of Ruskin's *Seven Lamps of Architecture* in 1849 (when the book first appeared) remarked that the author 'seems to attach little value to the beauty resulting from proportion, fitness and propriety, but finds charm only in the massive, the rude and the ruined'; a remark which might equally well have been applied to all the other amateur critics who delighted more in the sublime and the picturesque than in structural integrity and functional plans.

Within recent years, there have not lacked other exponents of this literary *genre*, and as an example, one cannot do better than quote from the recent book entitled *Modern Architecture* by Vincent Scully. Discussing Antonio Gaudi's Casa Milà, an apartment building in Barcelona, he writes:

'The Casa Milà, both in plan and elevation, is like a sea-hollowed cliff, its rock-cut façade water-smoothed and eroded, hung with metal seaweed and dug with windows like eyes. The whole "rolls round" like Wordsworth's early nineteenth century image or a late painting by Van Gogh. It seems to embody a total human participation in the rhythms that infuse the natural world. This is why the strange gods that crowd the roof of Gaudi's sea-formed acropolis enjoy such an eerie life. They come, as icons and guardsmen, from somewhere underneath—hollow, plated and helmeted—and take their places above and beside the broken stairs. Gaudi's forms, like those of the best of *Art Nouveau* as a whole, are infused with the action of nature and are therefore somehow real.'

Now it may well be argued that such literary effusions are harmless, whilst at their best they constitute a help to insensitive or inexperienced laymen, by giving them an understanding of the beauties architects are trying to create. But it may also be argued that they are extremely dangerous to the healthy development of architectural ideals in that, from the Rationalist point of view, they not only mislead the public by giving it false criteria, but encourage architects to favour forms which will incite future critics to similar verbosity. There can be no doubt that they tend to encourage the more loquacious architects to substitute purely verbal concepts for solid structures, as is evident from Le Corbusier's proposal for rebuilding the cathedral of St.-Dié:

'I propose to make the charred and ruined cathedral a living torch of architecture; to take deferent charge of the misfortunes which have struck it, and make it a perpetual witness of the tragic event for the rest of time. The roof has fallen in, and the choir and transepts, cut to pieces against the sky, allow through their jagged shreds of red stone a glimpse of mountains and of the waving foliage of great trees. The nave is henceforth full of light, so that now we shall see clearly the beautiful Romanesque capitals which obscurity hid from our sight. Reinforced concrete, combined with clear and coloured glass, offer us the chance of saving all this, and of handing on to the future a quivering symphony of stone and of souvenirs'.

As a piece of descriptive writing, this is sheer poetry; but one may question the architectural merit of creating a new church by simply enclosing a few archaeological remains in a large glass case. No one would deny the drama and romance of preserving ruins as a war memorial; indeed, the idea was put forward as early as 479 B.C. by the Athenians after the battle of Plataea. But we may wonder what would have been the course of architectural history if Pericles had not broken this vow, or what would have been the development of mediaeval architecture if the prelates of the Middle Ages had tried thus to preserve every Romanesque church damaged by fire. There is no doubt that all good architecture must contain within itself an element of poetry; but this poetry is of a kind peculiar to architecture, and there is a threat to architecture when architects convert it too facilely into words.

Nevertheless it is clear that architectural criticism cannot exist unless architectural values are verbalized in some form or another. In this respect, it may therefore be contended that the greatest services have been rendered by the architectural periodicals, which have always aimed their remarks more at architects than at the general public, and have thus generally eschewed the more extravagant phraseology of the popular commentators. Interestingly enough, the first architectural magazine to endure for any length of time (namely the *Revue Générale de l'Architecture*) began in 1840 with the avowed policy of avoiding architectural criticism, and of confining itself solely to factual information; but this policy was due more to the editor's modesty than to any doubts as to the ultimate efficacy of criticism as a technique of architectural reform. The influence of critical writings, he explained, was proportional to the author's reputation and to that of the periodical in which such views were printed; hence he preferred to 'acquire a reputation for competence and loyalty' before publishing any criticisms of his own. But it was not very long before he considered that his reputation had been acquired, and before he indulged in architectural criticisms of considerable length. Even so, his critical writings were usually of a fairly broad character, and seldom dealt with specific buildings. He felt that it was his duty not merely to criticize current artistic and technical developments (which he regarded as the magazine's purely passive role), but to 'fulfil an active mission of "scouting the path of the future" '. Now this notion of a magazine as a 'scout' (*éclaireur* is the word he uses) is curiously suggestive of the more recent notion of an architectural periodical as constituting an active element of the *avant-garde*, for both these military expressions mean much the same thing. We thus see why, of all the influences brought by literature to bear on architectural developments, that of the architectural magazine has been the most important of all.

The architectural magazines of the past hundred years constitute a particularly interesting source of study if they are compared with the architecture they reflect. It seems clear, for example, that architectural developments have been very much influenced by the techniques of reproducing illustrations. There can be little doubt that the coarseness of English detailing in the mid-nineteenth century was very much influenced by the fact that all the illustrations in *The Builder* were reproduced from wood engravings, just as the relatively greater delicacy of French detailing of the same period was undoubtedly influenced by the fact that the *Revue Générale de l'Architecture* was illustrated by steel engravings. Similarly, one can hardly over-emphasize the importance of the introduction in 1856 of photographic reproductions into architectural periodicals, since not only did this obviate the need for periodicals to rely on architects providing them with their own perspectives (usually drawn before the building was even started), but it encouraged their editors to show a preference for photogenic buildings, and a corresponding lack of enthusiasm for buildings which, however excellent, did not provide flattering points of view for the camera. Mention has already been made of the way poly-chromatic adornment was influenced by the crude techniques used in the mid-nineteenth century for printing in colour. Colour reproductions, though rare in the earlier issues of periodicals, were provided often enough from 1851 onwards to suggest that, here again, architectural magazines played a considerable part in influencing the architectural fashions of the age.

Moreover, the part eventually played by architectural magazines in promoting certain esoteric fashions was, during certain periods, so preponderant as to suggest that the documentary evidence they provide for historical assessments is at times extremely unreliable, particularly if the aim is to determine the tastes of the age. It was many years before architectural periodicals began systematically reporting any contemporary buildings, or reproducing illustrations of them; indeed, this habit only took hold in the 1860s. But by the end of the nineteenth century, they had virtually abandoned their original role as diffusers of technical knowledge to become fashion magazines, and this change is well exemplified in the exaggerated publicity given to Art Nouveau, which was certainly never as popular as its publicists contended, or as the numerous magazines devoted to this ephemeral and rootless vogue might lead the uninstructed observer to believe.

After the collapse of Art Nouveau, the influence of architectural periodicals suffered a temporary eclipse, though they were more numerous than ever. This was partly because of the hesitancy shown by many editors in espousing the more revolutionary trends, but mainly because of the virtual abandonment of architectural criticism altogether. Even the more progressive editors rightly felt that, at this juncture, the new forms then being evolved were so devoid of roots that any adverse criticism might be fatal to their further development. However, the period of uncertainty came to an end in the 1940s, when an awareness of the renewed need for systematic appraisals (coupled, it is probably fair to say, with the difficulty of finding any new buildings to publicize during and immediately after the war) prompted architectural magazines to adopt a new policy. For example, in an article entitled 'Criticism', in the *Architectural Review*, published in 1940, the editor explained that the stage had been reached when it was possible to take most of what modern architecture stood for for granted, in that it was no longer necessary to explain the functional basis on which the modern architect worked. Thus, as maturity developed, it became essential to restore the practice of what he called 'pictorial criticism', that is to say, of appraisals concerned with the appearance of buildings. In undertaking this function, he would not, he said, be retreating from the principles which gave modern architecture its validity; on the contrary, these principles were now so well founded that it was no longer the business of an onlooker to enquire in each case whether they had been adhered to or not. He admitted that when criticizing in 'literary' terms, the practical study which gave the appearance of architecture its meaning would still have to be borne in mind, otherwise the public would find itself back in the period when the planning and construction of buildings was one thing, and the architecture of their façades another. But he considered himself justified in judging buildings largely according to their 'appeal to the eye' since, for the man in the street, he said, this was the only approach open to him.

The decade which saw the end of the Second World War thus marks a definitive stage in the evolution of modern architecture, since it is probably fair to say that the ability to criticize individual buildings according to accepted principles, in the manner initiated by J. F. Blondel two centuries before, implies the existence of a genuine style—one might almost say of a genuine Classicism. This sense of assurance did not exist between the mid-eighteenth century and the mid-twentieth century, despite the valiant attempts of certain critics to assert principles which they felt *ought* to be universally accepted by their contemporaries; yet we have apparently reached the stage now when we are as sure of our principles as the Classical architects were before 1750. If this is so, then the history of architectural criticism provides us with additional evidence for regarding the last two centuries as a historical entity, and for considering them as essentially the period of gestation of the present architectural age. Architectural criticism, like all forms of criticism, has always existed, and must always exist, if only in spoken form, where there are men cultivated enough to reflect upon the aesthetic experiences architects provide for them; but the type and quality of criticism inevitably varies according to the age, and it is by studying the critical writings of the past two centuries that we are best able to assess the hesitancies and backslidings which characterized the transitional period from 1750 to 1950, and brought about the growing sense of confidence which gives the architecture of the present day so much in common with the great Classical eras of the past.

22

The Influence of Industrial Design

It is perhaps characteristic of recent trends in architectural theory, and of the growing influence, since 1890, of industrial design, that about sixty years ago, the ultimate test of architectural genius became whether or not one could design a new kind of chair. There were of course architects in earlier eras who made names for themselves as chair designers, such as Robert Adam. Moreover, as early as 1883, Montgomery Schuyler had criticized a building by McKim, Mead & White as looking 'less like a work of architectural art than a magnificent piece of furniture'. But it was only when the German Arts and Crafts Movement was established at the beginning of this century that the ability to design chairs was regarded as important evidence of architectural aptitude, and the idea of regarding a man like William Morris as the first of the 'Pioneers of the Modern Movement' would have been inconceivable before the era of what industrialists call 'styling'.

By a curious paradox, it was largely because of the unquestioned belief, in the mid-eighteenth century, that architecture was the Mother of the Arts that this new idea asserted itself. Immanuel Kant, in his *Critique of Pure Reason* (1781), used 'Architectonics of Pure Reason' as the title of the penultimate chapter of his book, because 'architectonics' was the best word he could think of to express the notion of a complex system of rationally assembled components in the domain of abstract ideas. But a century and a quarter later, the word 'architectonics' came to be used by German industrialists as a synonym for what they also called 'pure functional art' (*reine Zweckkunst*)—presumably because, in some vague way, they thought that 'pure reason' could be equated with 'pure form'.

It was in this sense that Hermann Muthesius, the Prussian civil servant who was sent to London in 1896 to study British architecture and industrial design, used the word 'architectonics' when justifying the establishment of the *Deutscher Werkbund*. Form, he proclaimed, was above all 'architectonic', and he cited the Greek temple, the Roman thermae, and the Gothic cathedral. Most significantly of all, he also cited 'the princely salon of the 18th Century'—i.e. the decoration and furnishing of luxurious interiors, with which, at that time, industrial design (or, as it was then

265

called, 'decorative art') was mainly concerned. Thus the re-establishment of an 'architectonic culture' was for him a basic condition for the improvement of all the products of industry. 'Germany's vocation is to resolve the great problem of architectonic form . . . the whole class of educated Germans, and above all wealthier private individuals, must be convinced of the need for pure Form'.

Ideals such as these were responsible for the general philosophy of the Arts and Crafts schools founded in Germany at this period, the most influential being the school at Weimar directed by Henry van de Velde, the famous exponent of Art Nouveau.

The role played by Art Nouveau in reinforcing the idea that architectural forms are analogous to, if not interchangeable with, those of furniture is only too obvious, as anyone can see by comparing Art Nouveau furniture and Art Nouveau buildings as illustrated in S. T. Madsen's well-documented monograph. Sigfried Giedion has remarked that 'in Austria around 1900, the movement was from handicrafts to architecture and from architecture to handicrafts', and that 'as late as 1914, in Hoffmann's Stoclet House in Brussels, the influence of the cabinet-maker is still evident'—a fact also remarked upon by Eric Mendelsohn. Now Art Nouveau's principal ancestor was unquestionably the Rococo style of the mid-eighteenth century, and Madsen very properly draws attention to the fact that the city of Nancy, which contains some of the finest architecture of the Rococo period, is also the city where French Art Nouveau first emerged. What he fails to emphasize, however, is that the characteristics generally described as Rococo were, in France at any rate, specifically confined to the *interiors* of buildings, and that the only Rococo features on the *exteriors* of the buildings surrounding the plazas at Nancy are confined to the ornamentation of the keystones and the vases which surmount the balustrades.

This fact is of considerable importance in the present context. The façades constituting the two main plazas at Nancy were by Emmanuel Héré de Corny, who based them on those of two buildings in Nancy by his master, Germain Boffrand. Boffrand was not only one of the greatest architects of his day, but, together with Jean-François Blondel and Robert de Cotte, was one of the first to establish himself as an interior designer. His interiors, to which his designs for furniture (such as console tables) were carefully fitted, have been described by one recent author as being among 'the great masterpieces of Rococo art'. Yet his exterior façades, and those of his pupil Héré de Corny, are as severe and as Classical in their use of standardized tectonic elements as those of his own master, J. H. Mansart, and indeed depart little from the French tradition of the previous hundred years.

Boffrand's own views on this matter are quite explicit, and, in view of the popular misunderstanding of the nature of French Rococo, are well worth quoting. 'Fashion, at various times (and especially in Italy) has taken pleasure in torturing all the parts of a building, and has often tried to destroy all the principles of architecture, *whose noble simplicity should always be preserved*', he wrote in his

Livre d'Architecture, published in 1745. 'Ornamentation has (in the work of Guarini and Borromini) passed from the interior decoration of houses, and from the carved woodwork for which delicate work is suitable, to exteriors, and to works in masonry, which require to be worked in a more vigorous and more masculine way.'

Since the notions which Boffrand condemned were also popular in Germany, Spain, and the Spanish Netherlands, it is not surprising that a Belgian Art Nouveau decorator should so easily introduce into Germany the idea that architecture and furniture are designed in much the same manner, especially after Muthesius had paved the way. Van de Velde, whose training and experience prior to opening his Decorative Art Workshop near Brussels in 1894 had been that of a painter, naturally showed himself less sensitive than Boffrand to the distinctions between architecture and furniture, or to those between the private, ephemeral interiors of buildings and the public, permanent character of exterior structures. Moreover, not having even been trained as a craftsman in wood or metal, he had no sense of the nature of materials, as Auguste Perret soon demonstrated with respect to his project for the Théâtre des Champs-Élysées (a commission which van de Velde then resigned in Perret's favour). Thus, when van de Velde's attention was called to the fact that his furniture was constructed in open conflict with the nature of wood, he declared, according to Kurt Behrendt, that for a long time he had been convinced of wood's inadequacy as a material for his designs, and that he anticipated the discovery of a more suitable material which could be cast.

Since cast furniture can be mass-produced with ease, few people will regret that the influence of Art Nouveau was so short-lived. Indeed, it would not have lasted as long as ten years had not its reputation been artificially inflated by the energetic enthusiasm of Sigfried Bing, who made a living out of selling its more exuberant manifestations, and by the sudden appearance of a number of new Decorative Art magazines. What is surprising is that it was succeeded not by something more rational, but simply by something more angular. Thus whereas van de Velde's chairs, though structurally irrational, were at least sufficiently sinuous to accommodate themselves to human posteriors, those designed by Constructivists, and Neo-Plasticists, such as Gerrit Rietveld (who should have known better, since he was a master cabinet-maker), were pure geometric abstractions, and seem to have had no merit except in terms of the Dutch art movement that was known as *De Stijl*.

The *De Stijl* movement, which will be discussed more fully in the next chapter, was, in general, undoubtedly instrumental in promoting the cause of non-representational art (if by this one means painting and sculpture). But the *De Stijl* chair was not; for all chairs are non-representational, from the most archaic three-legged stool to the more sophisticated masterpieces of fibre-glass and foam rubber produced today. Where the *De Stijl* movement was original, as regards furniture design, was in creating the first chair deliberately designed, not for comfort, not for dignity, not for elegance, not for rational assembly according to commonly accepted principles of woodwork, but simply 'designed'. Even Theodore Brown, Rietveld's biographer, has had to confess, in the five lengthy pages he devotes to this chair, that 'the jagged, angular quality of the piece, as well as its hard surfaces, are not conducive to bodily comfort, and those who have used it, including Rietveld himself, have complained about bruising their ankles on it. Obviously factors other than comfort determined its design'.

These factors were, according to Brown, economic, social, and aesthetic, but it seems fairly clear that the aesthetic motive predominated, and it was this which caused the chair to be the 'determinant' (as Brown calls it) of the much publicized house that Rietveld designed for his friend and collaborator, Mrs. Truus Schröder, in 1924. The historical importance of this house (and this is at least the sixty-ninth time, to my knowledge, that it has been discussed in print) resides essentially in the influence it exerted on the teaching methods of the Bauhaus. But it is also important in being the first architectural monument to be designed by a cabinet-maker; that is to say, by a man whose only architectural training, after working as a cabinet-maker for twenty years, was gained during three of those years by studying architectural drafting at evening classes. By 1928, he was sufficiently influential to be a founder-member of Le Corbusier's Congrès Internationaux de l'Architecture Moderne.

The influence of Rietveld's chair on the work produced by the Bauhaus under the influence of Walter Gropius—the last of the 'Pioneers of the Modern Movement'—is only too apparent. Gropius, unlike his precursor at Weimar, van de Velde, was an architect by training, and has always been an architect to his very fingertips. But after graduating, he went to work immediately for Peter Behrens, a painter, who at the age of thirty-nine had just been appointed industrial design consultant to the German General Electric Company, and who designed not only their trademarks, type-faces and electric kettles, but their factories and probably their furniture as well.

Doubtless because of Behren's influence, Gropius not only accepted Muthesius's interpretation of the word 'architectonics' in its totality, but saw the Arts and Crafts schools as the ideal places in which a New Architecture could be created. He therefore accepted with alacrity the offer to succeed van de Velde in 1919, and, by combining the Weimar School of Arts and Crafts with the Weimar Academy of Fine Arts (i.e. the school of architecture, painting and sculpture), he was not only able to take responsibility for training designers of furniture, stained glass, pottery, metalwork, weaving, stage-scenery, wall-painting, and typography, but also for training architects, who had never been linked academically to the so-called 'decorative arts' before. No machine technology was introduced into the Bauhaus until 1923, and after abstract 'basic design' courses, the architectural students were trained essentially as building craftsmen (whereby 'the pupil, if proficient enough, obtained his Master-Builder's Diploma from the local Trades Council'). It is therefore evident that, for Gropius, the principal virtue of the

Bauhaus (or 'School of Design', to give it its official title) was that all these specializations could be treated as variations of the same kind of activity. The world of furniture could be treated not only as a microcosm of the world of architecture, but also as a laboratory for experiments in the organization of urban space.

When Gropius was established at Harvard University (where virtually every element of the Bauhaus curriculum, except for the Basic Design courses, or *Vorlehre*, was abandoned), he still contended that 'the approach toward any kind of design—of a chair, a building, a whole town or a regional plan—should be essentially identical, not only in respect to their relationship in space but to social aspects as well'. In 1947, he was even more explicit, insisting in his essay 'Is There a Science of Design?' that 'the process of designing a great building or a simple chair differs only in degree, not in principle'.

Whether or not Gropius's assertion is true, it is a fact that the only graduate of the Bauhaus to have signally furthered his ideal of 'realizing a modern architectonic art' in the purely architectural sense has been Marcel Breuer, who studied only furniture design there (or rather taught himself, since the carpentry workshop seems to have been virtually unsupervised until he took charge of it himself, on graduation, in 1925). Breuer's architecture is probably no more like furniture than that of the other European 'Form-Givers'. But it is certainly no less. His UNESCO Secretariat stands on legs; its façades may not unfairly be likened to a filing cabinet with the drawers removed; and its compositional form, though obligatorily curved on one side to relate to the Place de Fontenoy, is curved likewise on the other two sides to look good from the air: i.e. from the point of view from which one normally sees furniture when entering a room.

'Aside from the obvious differences in scale,' writes Theodore Brown, in *The Work of G. Rietveld, Architect*, 'chairs are as much spatial creations as buildings.' But the difference in scale is crucial to the whole problem. Whereas architecture is related fairly directly to structural engineering by techniques of assembly, as well as by other factors and objectives (although here again it is differences in scale which make the two disciplines essentially distinct), it is related only *analogically* to the discipline of furniture design. Undoubtedly, between 1900 and 1930, furniture design, being both functional and non-representational, and requiring a pleasing appearance, proved to be an analogy of the utmost value in allowing architecture to escape from the more inept aspects of Revivalism, and was heuristically far more successful than the other well-known analogies—biological and mechanical—by which architectural theorists had tried to escape from Revivalism during the preceding fifty years. But the linking of architecture so closely to furniture, pottery, weaving, typography, etc., would seem now not only to be less defensible but in some cases demonstrably harmful.

In other words, as soon as Revivalism no longer constituted a living issue, there seemed no good reason why architectural students should not simply study architecture from the very beginning of their course, as they did in the days when the art of building evolved steadily and rationally in harmony with the technological and sociological evolution of the people it was intended to serve. Indeed, such is in fact what generally happens in our leading schools, despite the lip-service paid to the Bauhaus ideal. This is not to say that architectural students should not also study the design of interiors. On the contrary, the architect's role as a co-ordinator of interiors and exteriors is more vital than ever before, because of the increased use of glass. But co-ordination, as Gropius has been the first to insist, must be by means of collaboration, and collaboration implies respect for the peculiar skills which each member of the team brings to the task.

The criticism levelled here is thus aimed not at the idea that certain gifted architects are capable of designing good furniture (which would be nonsensical), but at the notion that there is some mystical skill called 'design' which, once it has been mastered, entitles one, without further ado, to design anything from a toothpaste tube to an ocean liner, and which obviates the need for a prolonged, specialized study of the respective techniques and materials by which various structures and artifacts are made. It is aimed at the sort of attitude best exemplified by John 'Buonarotti' Papworth—painter, furniture designer, architect, landscape gardener and town planner—who in 1836 was appointed director of the British government's new School of Industrial Design. 'In common with the great architects of that age which he so greatly admired', we are told by one of his biographers, 'he could turn his hand to pretty nearly anything; from the designing of handkerchiefs for the great merchant, Mr. James Morrison of Fore Street, to the decoration of the first paddle steamer that plied on the River Thames, or to directing the manufacture of a Chair of State all of glass for the Shah of Persia.' For brilliant, versatile, and enterprising in the use of new architectural materials (such as iron and plate glass) as he was, he was still essentially an ornamentalist, and ornament in this sense is always superficial, whether its surfaces be riotously intricate as they were in the Victorian era, or absolutely smooth as they are today.

23

The Influence of Painting and Sculpture

The dominant influence on architectural design during the second quarter of the twentieth century has undoubtedly been that of painting and sculpture; a fact incontrovertibly demonstrated by Reyner Banham in his *Theory and Design in the First Machine Age*. At the beginning of this period (that is to say between 1920 and 1935), the technique of using abstract pictorial and sculptural devices as a means of creating novel architectural forms was exploited only by a few men who built little, and who achieved few rewards except the honour of being apotheosized as pioneers of the modern movement. By the middle of the century, however, the publicity given to their endeavours, and the popularity which their ideas excited among the new generation of students (often involving the official adoption in schools of architecture of the methods of preliminary architectural instruction invented at the Bauhaus), resulted in the technique becoming a new orthodoxy, to such an extent that only a book which aims at reviewing all the changing ideals which have occurred in architecture during the last two hundred years could dare question the fundamental value of this influence, or embark on a critical appraisal of so ingrained a contemporary phenomenon in terms of absolute worth.

The precise nature of the influence is so complex that it demands more than a cursory examination; but before analysing the large element of novelty it contained, it is worth recalling that the doctrine that painting and sculpture possess a natural affinity with architecture (regarded here as a sister art), and that this affinity implies some kind of reciprocity, formed not only the basis of that Italian Renaissance tradition re-injected into European and American culture during the Renaissance Revival, but also the basis of much of the speculation by amateur reformers who were fundamentally opposed to Renaissance ideals. For example, Ruskin, in an appendix to his *Edinburgh Lectures* (1854), announced that 'no person who is not a great sculptor and painter can be an architect, for if he is not a sculptor and painter he can only be a builder', whilst in the preface to the second edition of the *Seven Lamps of Architecture*, he similarly asserted that the architect who was not a sculptor or a painter was nothing better than a frame-maker on a large scale, since 'there are only two fine arts possible to the human race, sculpture and painting'. 'What we call architecture,' he added, 'is only the association of these in noble masses, or the placing them in fit places; all architecture other than this is, in fact, mere building.' The same theme was urged by his disciple T. G. Jackson in the last two chapters of his book *Modern Gothic Architecture* (1873), and became a commonplace among the anti-Rationalists of the age. It became particularly prevalent in Germany, where Oswald Spengler proclaimed that 'architecture is simply the highest form of pure ornament'.

There was thus nothing essentially revolutionary in the idea that the regeneration of architecture was to be achieved through a closer contact with the 'allied arts'. What was new in 1920 was the character which had been given to painting and sculpture by a few revolutionary artists during the previous decade. Before 1910 there had only been two kinds of sculpture, namely naturalistic sculpture (consisting usually of representations of the human body, and regarded as a branch of the 'Fine Arts'), and non-representational sculpture (consisting of objects of daily use such as spoons, forks and jugs, and regarded as a branch of the 'Useful Arts'). Similarly, there were only two kinds of two-dimensional design, namely naturalistic paintings (consisting usually of perspectives of people, natural objects or landscapes) and non-representational patterns (consisting of adornments to textiles, pottery and other household objects). The revolution occurred when Vasily Kandinsky, catching sight of one of his own naturalistic paintings lying upside-down in an obscure light, was inspired to paint a series of amorphous shapes on canvas which represented nothing whatsoever. It was not the birth of non-representational art; it was simply the birth of a non-representational art which had no practical purpose.

The problem was thus raised as to whether it was possible to justify an art which was both non-representational and useless, and one of the philosophical devices used to answer this question in the affirmative was to define the word 'usefulness' in purely aesthetic terms, and then to justify abstract shapes by saying that they alone constituted 'significant form'. According to Clive Bell, the leading exponent of this point of view, 'significant form' meant 'a combination of lines and colours which moves one aesthetically', and any such deliberate combination which would lead the observer to a state of euphoristic detachment from the concerns of life was therefore art. Hence art was said to have nothing intrinsically to do with the natural world or with functional criteria, so that the emotion transmitted by an artist could be expressed in any sort of form—'in pictures, sculpture, buildings, pots, textiles and so on'. It will be seen then that not only did the new theory of abstract art lead to a wider interpretation of Muthesius's ideal of 'pure form' (as discussed in the last chapter), and to the complete interchangeability of artistic disciplines; it also inevitably suggested that the Vitruvian qualities of usefulness and stability were artistically of little importance as compared with the abstract aesthetic value which every building potentially possessed.

The revolutionary character of this approach, and its subversive effect on Rationalist doctrines, can easily be appreciated by the sort of statement which is now considered axiomatic by thoughtful and serious architects, such as that 'architecture is above all an Art, and only as such will it produce significant forms', or that 'Le Corbusier's Carpenter Centre at Harvard transcends mere architecture into the realm of pure art'. Now for the Rationalists, it would have been nonsense to suggest that a building could 'transcend architecture', just as it would have been nonsense to suggest that a building's significance (as opposed to its beauty) depended on anything more than the fact that a client had commissioned it, and that it was built. This is not to assert that 'significance' cannot have special implications for painters and sculptors which are foreign to architecture. For example, even with respect to the more traditional notions of Fine Art, it can reasonably be argued that the painting of a human portrait, or the carving of a human bust, inevitably requires some additional 'significance' if it is to be distinguishable in aesthetic value from the actual face and bosom portrayed. But a building derives its significance merely by existing, since architecture, not being an imitative art, contains within itself the justification of its own primary forms.

Inevitably, however, it was this very non-representational quality possessed by architecture which induced many of the artists who followed in Kandinsky's footsteps to draw their inspiration for paintings and sculpture from buildings, whereby their works often have a curiously parasitic 'tectonic' quality, as the titles they gave their works often indicate. Mondriaan painted a number of pictures entitled 'Façade'; Malewitch depicted abstract rectangular masses entitled 'Architectonics'; Vantongerloo carved and modelled abstract statues to which he gave a similar name; Boccioni asserted that the basis of Futurist sculpture was 'tectonic'; and there was a whole group of statues entitled 'constructions', produced by a coterie of artists who called themselves Constructivists or Elementarists. Thus was laid in the minds of certain architects the seeds of the idea (already foretold by Robert Kerr in his lecture on 'The Architecturesque') that architecture was not, as in the nineteenth century, structural form *modified* aesthetically by sculpture i.e. ornamented construction) but that it was structural form *constituted* aesthetically by sculpture (i.e. constructed ornament): an idea well exemplified in Le Corbusier's church at Ronchamp, and which assumed a peculiarly twentieth century aspect by virtue of the fact that the materials used for many of these sculptural experiments were not stone or marble, but sheet metals, glass, wire, and other materials which, though by no means invented in the present century, were becoming increasingly associated by the more enterprising architects with the new machine age.

The ideal of a complete fusion of abstract sculpture, abstract painting and building technology was expressed by J. J. P. Oud in his manifesto *On the Architecture of the Future*, published in 1921, in which he announced that 'a self-created architecture is possible at last, to which the other arts are no longer subordinated, but work organically with it'. The greatest and most influential exponent of this theory was Walter Gropius, whose curriculum of instruction at the Bauhaus was deliberately designed to achieve this ideal. 'Our ultimate goal', he wrote in *The New Architecture and the Bauhaus* (1935), 'was the composite but inseparable work of art, the great building, in which the old dividing line between monumental and decorative elements would have disappeared for ever'. Thus his students were initiated into the study of architecture by manipulating abstract shapes without any reference to building functions or the ultimate strength of materials, but solely with a view to achieving ornamental appeal in terms of 'significant form'. By this means, the art of architecture became, at its least effectual, a kind of large-scale abstract sculpture, and at its best, the art of utilizing the vocabulary of the newly fashionable sculptural shapes to serve the functional and structural requirements of a specific architectural programme. In both cases a three-dimensional design was created which had the advantage of not requiring additional ornament, since it constituted a total ornament in itself.

The most distinguished exponent of these new techniques was Le Corbusier, and Fello Atkinson is doubtless right to link his name with that of Michelangelo, for not only did Le Corbusier originally justify much of his theory by reference to Michelangelo's work at St. Peter's, Rome, but he has consistently pursued those same Mannerist devices which have given Michelangelo such a peculiar place in the history of Renaissance architecture. Yet before discussing Le Corbusier's ideas, it will be appropriate to discuss some of the new qualities which abstract art seems to possess, and these may conveniently be studied under seven headings: art as 'research', art as an end in itself, art as an expression of 'modernity', art as 'avant-gardisme', art as a means of creating 'surprise', art as 'non-art', and art as 'pure art'. In addition, it will be appropriate to say briefly something about the three main manifestations of abstract art which were considered relevant to architecture at this time, namely in its angular forms (Cubism and Neo-plasticism), its structural forms (Constructivism and Elementarism) and its sinuous forms (Expressionism).

The idea that art is a form of research seems to have originated with Cézanne. Admittedly, long before his day, painting had often involved a type of experimentation which might be described as research, as for example when Renaissance painters produced drawings which seem to have had little purpose except the study of fore-shortening and perspective. But never, before Cézanne, had any painter talked about his work as if he were some kind of scientist heroically pushing back the frontiers of knowledge. It can be imagined, therefore, how congenial it was for those painters and sculptors who followed Cézanne's methods to perpetuate his idea that there was something comparable to the more dramatic aspects of scientific research in their pictorial or sculptural dissections of nature, and how congenial it was for the small groups of revolutionary architects which established themselves after the First World War to collaborate with these successors of Cézanne, particularly once they had accepted Cézanne's notion (so reminiscent of

Boullée) that natural forms are ideally interpretable in terms of cubes, cylinders, spheres and cones.

Secondly, we find a particular emphasis on the idea that art is an end in itself. This again was not peculiar to the era, since the term *l'Art pour l'Art* had been coined by Victor Cousin, and was quite common even in architectural circles in the mid-nineteenth century, as is evident from César Daly's use of the term in the *Revue Générale de l'Architecture* of 1857. Moreover, it was the most prominent doctrine of the aesthetes who flourished at the end of the nineteenth century. But in the 1920s the idea assumed an additional significance by the invention of *collages*: pictures which were not simply delineations of still life, but fragments of real objects, such as pieces of newspaper and fragments of cloth, actually glued to the canvas. Thus the traditional distinction between the depiction of a group of objects and the objects themselves disappeared; a development which again cemented the bonds between architecture and the Fine Arts; for architecture also contains no inherent distinction between its quality as a work of art and the formal elements of which it is composed: a fact which was equally obvious even to the reactionary theorists at this time, when abstract carvings and mouldings were still fashionable on traditional façades.

Thirdly, we find the emergence of the idea that abstract art was peculiarly 'modern' in that it was not merely something invented by the age but was alone truly expressive of the spirit of that age. Admittedly, the whole validity of the latter notion has been disputed on philosophical grounds, and George Boas, in particular, has written a spirited essay on *Historical Periods* in which he points out the folly of characterizing any esoteric art movement as 'modern', asserting that the question should not be 'what is modern art?' (which he says is a meaningless conundrum) but 'how much unity is there in modern art?'. From this statistical point of view, abstract art can hardly be considered as expressive of the age, since during the last half century it has represented only a fragment of the total pictorial and sculptural output of civilization, and this is true even if we limit our terms of reference to works generally accepted as 'progressive' by European and American connoisseurs. Nevertheless, there has been fostered in many minds the impression that because total abstraction is an exclusive characteristic of twentieth century art, architects must pursue the same ideals and use the same shapes as abstract artists if they are to construct buildings in keeping with the times.

Fourthly, we have the notion that the best abstract artists are essentially ahead of their times, or, to employ the popular expression, that they constitute an *avant-garde* (a term meaning, literally, the scouts who precede an invading army so as to survey the land and gain contact with the enemy). At first it might seem as if this heroic notion was opposed to the idea that abstract art is something contemporary, since presumably one cannot be both abreast of one's era and ahead of it simultaneously. In fact, however, this dilemma (which has already been referred to in a previous chapter) is illusory and largely verbal, for it was long ago resolved by the automobile industry, which found it good business to sell the latest model car a year ahead of its stated date. In other words, the general notion is not so much that by being *avant-garde* one is ahead of one's time, but that, in an age of rapid mechanical obsolescence, the general populace is slightly behindhand. In industrial terms, it corresponds at best to the lag in production whereby an aeroplane designed in 1965 will not be ready to fly until 1970, and this attitude has seemed particularly appropriate to architects impatient to construct a new world, yet conscious of the growing dependence of architecture on changes in industrialization. Hence, also, the scientifically-minded *avant-garde* painter and sculptor similarly regards himself somewhat romantically as a designer for the future, and as long ago as 1917, in an essay entitled *l'Esprit Nouveau* (which powerfully influenced Le Corbusier), Guillaume Apollinaire, the apologist of Cubism, wrote: 'The new spirit struggles to open new views on the exterior and interior universe which shall not be inferior to those which scholars of every category are discovering each day, and from which they extract so many marvels. These marvels impose on us the duty of not leaving imagination and poetic subtlety behind that of the artisans who improve a machine'. In other words, just as the most unusual machines constituted *ipso facto* the most advanced machines, so the most unusual art became the most advanced art—expressing ideas which would be exploited only by future generations, and using forms whose 'significance' would only be widely appreciated in later years. The artist thus to some extent assumed the role of a prophet; not interpreting what was, but imagining what would be, and we can therefore see again how attractive such ideas were to the revolutionary architects of the 1920s, who, whilst envisaging a new world for their contemporaries, appreciated that their Utopias could not be built in a day, and who in fact were forced to design for generations yet unborn, despite the impatient appeals of their propaganda for immediate change.

Inevitably, even the most rational architectural shapes produced by the *avant-garde* seemed surprising when contrasted with the more traditional buildings of the period, but it is worth noting that among the more articulate apologists of abstract painting and sculpture in this era, there were several who claimed that the element of surprise should be deliberately sought after for its own sake. 'It is by the important place given to surprise that the new spirit distinguishes itself from all the artistic and literary movements which have preceded it', wrote Guillaume Apollinaire, showing a curious ignorance of what had happened in the late eighteenth century. Nevertheless, although the element of surprise had been a commonplace in the *jardin anglais*, it was novel in its application to painting, sculpture and architecture, and particularly novel in the brutal way it was sometimes achieved in the 1920s; a brutality fostered by a group calling themselves 'Dada'. According to Louis Hautecoeur, 'only artists who invented hitherto unpublicized relationships or forms now seemed to be valid and to have a future. The term "living art" was given to everything which freed itself from normal standards.

This myth was encouraged by art dealers, who multiplied in this period of monetary inflation, when purchasers were no longer the old connoisseurs, but speculators out for quick profits; and the art magazines, which had to advertise in order to exist, often became accomplices of the dealers. Art critics exerted themselves to discover the young hopefuls, and vaunted them in a style whose brilliance was often more "enlightened" than enlightening. Never were painters so drunk with gratuitous words, or told so many theories about their own work'.

The exponents of Dada should perhaps be excluded from Hautecoeur's general condemnation, since, far from professing high artistic ideals, they claimed on the contrary that their aim was to destroy art, that their activity would best be called 'anti-art', and that their sole purpose in producing their various artefacts was to ridicule the bourgeois prestige which the Fine Arts had attained in the nineteenth century. It may of course be argued that the problem as to whether their works are to be considered as a form of art or as non-art has long since been settled in favour of the former interpretation, for paradoxically enough, art dealers and museum curators now compete strenuously to possess them, and pay dearly for these objects of derision whenever they appear on the market. Nevertheless it seems fair to say that at the time they were created, their main purpose was to shock the public into rejecting all traditional artistic values, and this shock was administered not so much by creating novelties as by desecrating what was familiar, as for example when a replica of the Mona Lisa was exhibited adorned with a moustache, or when an ordinary lavatory pedestal was submitted for an exhibition of sculpture in New York.

Naturally Dadaism was short-lived, for as William Gaunt has wittily observed in *The March of the Moderns*: 'mental suicide committed periodically by the same people, with a pistol loaded with blank cartridge, lost its power to horrify'. But it undoubtedly exerted an important influence on architecture in that it was at the root of much of the topsy-turvydom which, as John Summerson has observed in *Heavenly Mansions*, constitutes so telling a feature of Le Corbusier's technique. Apart from those designs of his which are pure Dada (for example the walled roof-garden on the Champs-Élysées equipped with a Rococo fireplace that does not work), most of Le Corbusier's basic revolutionary ideas also imply what Summerson describes as Alice-in-Wonderland inversions, and which, despite their elaborate rationalization, are essentially examples of a logic turned upside-down. In other words, when compared with traditional building methods, they constituted a kind of 'anti-architecture'. For example, whereas in traditional architecture, a villa is situated in a garden, in Le Corbusier's architecture, the garden is situated in the villa. Whereas in Classical architecture colonnades are placed on a base of solid walling, Le Corbusier places solid walling on top of his columns. The whole technique is comparable to that of some of Marcel Duchamp's Dadaist paintings, such as his canvas depicting a jagged rent which is then 'secured' with a genuine safety pin. These devices are extremely witty and refreshing; the only reservation one may have about them is the extent to which permanently pleasing architectural environments can be continually created out of the proliferation of such Rococo jokes.

However, in contrast to the Dadaist attitude of treating art as an excuse for fun, the most influential group of abstractionists regarded art, on the contrary, with high seriousness. Their principal aim seems to have been the achievement of the greatest austerity, since for them, the virtue of abstract painting and sculpture seems to have been that it was 'pure' art (a term which should not be confused with 'Purism'—the label which Le Corbusier attached to his paintings, and which means something else). This purity was evidently mainly conceived in terms of apparent economy of effort, so that it was an ideal related to the current popular notion that chamber music is 'purer' than orchestral music because fewer instruments are involved in making the noise. Hence it was considered a great achievement when Kasimir Malewitch painted a white square on a white canvas—a feat only surpassed by that of Alexander Rodzhenko, who triumphantly painted a black square on a black canvas.

This search for purity was also very characteristic of the more revolutionary architecture of the period, when it often involved the complete suppression of the structural realities of a building. Surfaces were left completely unmodulated in the interest of 'pure' surfaces, and when structural features existed they were plastered to a uniform smoothness; tiled roofs and cornices disappeared; glazing bars were attenuated; interiors were reduced to blank walls hung with one or two abstract paintings; and the whole of architecture was given the aseptic quality of an operating theatre. Indeed, a picture of an operating theatre was included by Frederick Etchells in his preface to Le Corbusier's *Towards a New Architecture*, with a triumphant quotation from a current periodical to the effect that 'because of its absolute fitness to purpose the modern hospital's operating theatre—like the engine room of an ocean liner—is one of the most perfect rooms in the world'.

The idea of purity also had other architectural connotations at this time. Reference has already been made to Le Corbusier's definition of 'pure art' as 'a concentrated thing free from all utilitarian motives'. The word also occurs in the correspondence which the Berlin *avant-garde* circulated among themselves in 1919 and 1920. For example, Hans Luckhardt, in a circular letter dated July 15th, 1920, wrote: 'Pure form is that form which, detached from all that is decorative, is freely fashioned out of the basic elements of straight line, curve and free form, and will serve the purpose of any expression—be it a religious building or a factory'. We thus see that pure form had nothing to do with function and little to do with structure, and that it was only 'architectonic' in the sense that it bore a superficial resemblance to some of the more austere funeral monuments of the past.

*   *   *

There is little need to describe the nature of Cubism, or to discuss what its exponents were trying to achieve, since everyone is now familiar with the main facts which constitute this aspect of the history of modern art. There are, however, two things about it which need emphasizing in the present context. Firstly, Cubism was not, strictly speaking, abstract art, since the Cubist painters continued to portray natural objects; for as Henry-Russell Hitchcock has observed in *Painting Towards Architecture*, their work relied more on distortion than abstraction. Secondly, Cubist sculptors did not, as is sometimes suggested, create a new art of 'space-time'. High-relief sculpture, unlike painting, can never, from its very nature, be limited to a single view-point; hence it is absurd to state that the Belgian Cubist sculptor Vantongerloo 'demonstrated with the prisms, slabs and hollows of his plastic of 1918 that contemporary sculpture, like painting, was not limited to a single point of view'.

The architectural importance of Cubism lies mainly in the fact that it was the source of the *de Stijl* (or Neo-plastic) and Constructivist movements, since it was the first attempt in painting to imply the existence in nature of angular space-defining planes. It would be an exaggeration to assume that the original Cubism of Picasso had any direct and immediate influence on architecture, for as Reyner Banham remarks in his *Theory and Design in the First Machine Age*: 'Attempts to compare buildings of the "International Style" with Cubist paintings are never very convincing'. Cubism, in fact, was only of direct importance to architecture because it was developed by Le Corbusier into 'Purism': a type of painting which, by its interpenetration of contours, suggested what Giedion has called 'the interpenetrations of inner and outer space', and which, by its use of traditional standardized objects, such as bottles, glasses and guitars, suggested the aesthetic possibilities of manipulating simple standardized geometric forms.

As opposed to Cubist and Purist paintings, Mondriaan's 'Neo-plastic' paintings were complete abstractions, consisting of flat patterns and coloured rectangles, in which the affinity to natural three-dimensional objects was no longer directly perceptible. It might be assumed from this two-dimensional quality that their main influence on architecture was to provide new façade patterns and new planning patterns, and in fact a number of elevational designs and plans of Mondriaanesque inspiration did result, notably in the work of Mies van der Rohe. But Mondriaan's influence extended far beyond this, for it was his belief, shared by the *de Stijl* group which clustered round him, that his paintings expressed a three-dimensional reality whereby the whole of nature was to be conceived as essentially a series of planes, and that even architectural composition must be thought of as a similar series of planes, rather than as volumes and masses bounded by traditional façades. 'Moving around or within a rectangular building or object', wrote Mondriaan, 'it can be seen as two-dimensional, for our era abandons the static vision of the past. By moving around, the impression of a two-dimensional aspect is directly followed by that of another two-dimensional aspect'.

The aim of the *de Stijl* group was thus to destroy the isolation of objects in space and to treat form and space as something universally integrated; for in Mondriaan's words, 'in plastic art, the reciprocal action of determining forms and determined space establishes the objective expression of reality'. 'Space determination,' he added, 'and not space expression, is the pure plastic way to express universal reality.' Thus the *de Stijl* group experimented with isometric drawings of spaces which were defined by planes cutting and interpenetrating one another, in such a way that the box-like volumes of traditional architecture were superseded by more open plans.

Nevertheless, despite the real contribution to the problems of space analysis made, in pictorial terms, by the *de Stijl* theorists, it can hardly be denied that the germ of their spatial ideas, and in fact everything about their compositions which was truly architectural, was derived from Frank Lloyd Wright, whose designs were made known in Holland through a monograph published in 1910. It was Wright who, perhaps as a result of the Froebel training he received as a child, had first conceived the idea of 'destroying the box' and of making architectural compositions out of space-defining planes. It was in his suburban houses (built, it should be noted, with little recourse to new technological processes,* and with a great display of traditional masonry and timber surfaces) that he had first exploited and exposed the aesthetic possibilities of widely cantilevered roofs, broad cantilevered balconies and space-defining partitions. It was in his early churches and factories that he had first explored the aesthetic possibilities (anticipated, it must be admitted, by the Greek Revivalists) of destroying traditional fenestration patterns in favour of apertures which seemed simply the voids separating pilasters. It could thus cogently be argued that *de Stijl* painting got as much from architecture as architecture got from *de Stijl* painting, and that the principal contribution of the *de Stijl* movement was in the graphic exploration of the aesthetic possibilities of very thin planes which the new techniques of steel and reinforced concrete frame construction—virtually ignored by Wright—now made possible.

Moreover, it should be noted that if Mondriaan disregarded his debt to Wright, it may well have been simply because he himself had little patience with the architectural profession, and considered that architects were incapable of creating the new beauty which the age demanded, since they were not true artists. Whereas Wright boasted that he had never been a painter, and thus had seldom ever drawn without the aid of a T-square and set-square, Mondriaan, who had reached rectangularity only by way of a long discipline of brushwork, had eventually concluded that true architectural beauty could only be brought about by direct collaboration between artists such as himself and engineers. The essential thing, in his view, was to take aesthetics as the point of departure; not traditional aesthetics (for this, in his opinion, had caused the decadence of architecture) but the new aesthetic resulting from the evolution of art. If one took technology and utilitarian require-

* Nevertheless, his dependence on the new technology should not be overlooked. The Robie House (1908) only achieved its daring cantilevers by concealing four fifteen-inch welded steel channels, each 110 ft. long, within the roof.

Salon, Hôtel d'Evreux, Place Vendôme, Paris (1750)

L. I. Kahn: Art gallery, Yale University (1954)

NEW CONCEPTS OF SPACE

Illustrating the illusion of parallax created by mirrors, and the effects of parallax created by screens

XXXIII

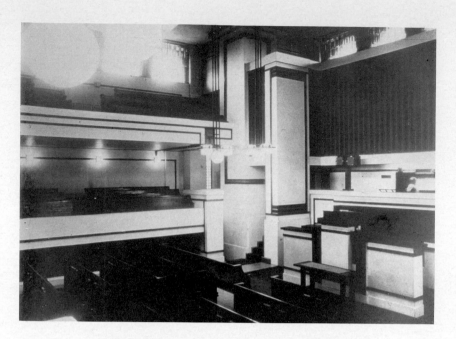

F. L. Wright: Unity Temple, Oak Park (1904)

F. L. Wright: Falling Water, Bear Run, Pennsylvania (1936)

NEW CONCEPTS OF SPACE

Illustrating the effects of parallax produced by introducing widely cantilevered balconies

XXXIV

R. M. Hunt: Studio Apartments, New York (1856)

Le Corbusier: Unité d'Habitation, Marseilles (1946)

NEW CONCEPTS OF SPACE

Illustrating the influence of the 'studio window' on modern domestic architecture

XXXV

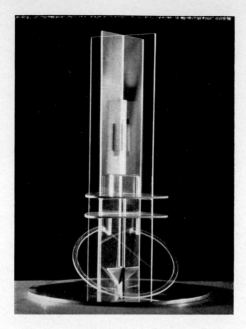

N. Gabo: Model for glass fountain

W. K. Harrison and others: United Nations secretariat,
New York (1950)

NEW CONCEPTS OF SPACE

*Illustrating the influence of transparent sculpture on the design
of wall surfaces*

XXXVI

ments as the point of departure there was a risk, he contended, of losing every chance of success, 'for intuition is then troubled by intelligence'.

The number of people who actually designed buildings at this time by using their intuitions untroubled by intelligence were mercifully few, but the doctrine that architecture is essentially the combination of abstract sculpture and engineering has by no means been discarded, and has received considerable impulsion from the Bauhaus method of treating abstract art as what is called 'Basic Design', that is to say, as a substitute for what traditional theorists like Guadet called 'Elements' (columns, walls, windows, roofs and so on—the study of which originally constituted the tuition given to architectural students in their early years). Yet in favour of the abstract art taught at the Bauhaus, it should be pointed out that it was not of the type developed by Mondriaan, but was of a kind labelled variously as 'Constructivism', 'Elementarism' or 'Suprematism'; a type clearly more applicable to architectural problems than *de Stijl*.

Constructivism seems to have been mainly a Russian phenomenon, and its austere forms may well have owed something to the Nihilism which preceded the Russian revolution, whilst its more positive qualities probably derived something from the contemporary research into illusionistic perspectives for stage sets. Malewitch, the originator of Suprematism, said it was founded on 'the supremacy of pure sentiment translated without representation of the exterior world by means of plane geometry'. Basically, then, it had much in common with *de Stijl*, but from an architectural point of view it had the virtue of conceiving sculpture as *constructed*, rather than as modelled, and it produced many ingenious assemblages of metal and glass which seem to have been very successful as a stimulus to architectural invention. There can be no doubt, for example, that many Russian buildings in steel and glass of the 1920s were directly inspired by this type of sculpture, and that these buildings were much admired by *avant-garde* architects in Europe at the time. Indeed, it is worth noting, in parenthesis, that most of the designs for Constructivist buildings prepared by European architects at this period were submitted for competitions organized by the Soviet Union, and that there were grave misgivings among the pro-Bolshevik intelligentsia when, in 1935, this kind of design was officially condemned as bourgeois and reactionary by the Soviet authorities.

As a method of architectural research, Constructivism was undoubtedly very useful as a means of throwing off the legacy of Revivalism; nevertheless, it suffered from the faults inherent in any system based on the arbitrary manipulation of small-scale elements. Firstly, it naturally paid no attention to the spatial requirements of specific accommodational programmes, whereas this, as John Summerson has observed, can now be seen as the essence of modern architecture. Secondly, it paid no attention to the eventual dimensions of the various components which constituted the models, so that however stable these miniature structures might be, they carried no guarantee that their stability would persist when the model was translated to a larger scale, or, conversely, that the components would still be economically dimensioned when proportionately enlarged. Thus even Constructivism had a very limited use when applied to architectural research, whilst as a type of pure sculpture its popularity was never very great.

We thus come to the only other art movement to influence architecture at this time, namely Expressionism. As an architectural idiom, it may well have derived from Art Nouveau (which was itself a derivation from the Rococo) whilst art-historically it was related to a sculptural fashion called 'dynamic plasticity', in which sensual forms emerged imperceptibly from neutral backgrounds in the way that many of Rodin's carvings seem to emerge from the living rock. Technically it depended on the fact that the designers studied their projects with the aid of soft wax. But whatever its diverse origins and peculiar techniques, it was essentially a *plastic* form of expression: an adjective used here to mean a shape that looks as if it had been modelled by hand, and which should not be confused with the term 'neo-plastic' (which Mondriaan attached to his angular theory of painting) nor with the German word *plastik* (which is simply a synonym for sculpture, often erroneously transliterated into English in this sense).

Thus several buildings of the first half of the present century seem 'plastic', as for example Antonio Gaudi's Casa Milà and Eric Mendelsohn's Einstein Tower. Neither were in fact moulded, since the former is of carved stone, whilst the latter is of plastered brick. But many people have seen this 'plasticity' as expressive of plastic materials, such as adobe or reinforced concrete, and undoubtedly the development in recent years of reinforced concrete shells has given greater force to the contention that reinforced concrete is most logically expressed in sinuous, rather than angular forms.

Nevertheless in the 1920s, the influence of concrete technology on Expressionism was negligible, and it would perhaps be truest to see Expressionism as a kind of 'symbolic functionalism'. It seems more than coincidental, for example, that the more dramatic Expressionist projects produced by Eric Mendelsohn were for buildings connected with movement, such as automobile factories, film studios, railway stations, and so on. Mendelsohn himself described them all as examples of 'Dynamism', a word which was one of the main catch-phrases of the age; for as Reyner Banham has pointed out, speed was the quality of the new Machine Age which most excited the Italian Futurists, and F. T. Marinetti, their leader, used the expression 'plastic dynamism', just as Sant'Elia used the term 'architectonic dynamism' with reference to his urban designs.

The number of Expressionist designs actually constructed in this era were few, and in general, the main influence of painting and sculpture on architecture in the 1920s was due to the presence of one or two architects among the coteries of painters just described (as for example J. J. P. Oud's membership of the *de Stijl* group) or to the presence of painters and sculptors on the teaching staffs of schools of architecture (as for example the appointment of Kandinsky and Moholy-Nagy to the Bauhaus). The only architect of this period who ever seriously practised as a painter was Le Corbusier, and he, after working as an architectural draftsman for ten years, only took up painting under the influence of the Cubist painter Amedée Ozenfant in 1918. But henceforth he devoted his mornings to painting and his afternoons to architecture; thus his achievements deserve special consideration in the present context, for it is worth considering how extensively his painterly vision has influenced his designs for buildings, and how much his theory of architecture has depended on his constant exploration of pictorial techniques.

That Le Corbusier's buildings have been influenced by his paintings can hardly be denied for he himself, in his book on *The Modulor*, has specifically explained how the façade of his proposed business centre for Algiers (1939) was based on an abstract painting he made in 1931. But it may well be argued that all that is best in his architecture derives from the Rationalism he learnt from the writings of Anatole de Baudot, from the example of Auguste Perret (for whom he worked in 1909), and from the theories of the German *Werkbund* (about which he wrote a book in 1912), and that it is this Rationalism, rather than the eccentric pictorial qualities of his more individualistic creations, which inspire the works of his most influential disciples.

We can clearly distinguish, for example, between his rational buildings, such as the Swiss Pavilion for Paris University or the Unité d'Habitation at Marseilles, and his more arbitrary sculptural compositions, such as the church at Ronchamp or the public buildings at Chandigarh. Admittedly there are sculptural elements at Marseilles (such as the detailing of the roof structure and the way the building is mounted on stilts like a museum specimen on a pedestal—an analogy he himself has observed), just as there are elements of an obviously functional derivation at Chandigarh. But it seems fair to say that the fusion between Rationalism and abstract sculpture is never complete in any of his buildings (which usually tend towards either one extreme or the other) for the good reason that these two ideals are antithetical: a dichotomy which is already apparent in *Towards a New Architecture*, the first treatise on architecture he ever wrote.

The opening chapters of *Towards a New Architecture* are almost entirely Rationalistic in tone, and contain little which could not also be found in the teachings of de Baudot and in the current German theories on industrial design with which he was so familiar. Their originality, apart from the forceful manner in which the ideas are expressed, lies in the significant omission of anything to do with Gothic architecture (and hence Gothic construction, the basis of de Baudot's Rationalism) and the uncharacteristic inclusion of a chapter in praise of the more sculptural aspects of St. Peter's, Rome. But this sculpturesque attitude is heavily reinforced at the end of the book in an analysis of the Parthenon, where the contribution of Phidias, the sculptor, is alone regarded as having given this building its architectural qualities. Nevertheless, Le Corbusier's plea for the primacy of sculpture is here tempered by an insistence on the virtues of standardization, of a kind which had already been achieved in the Greek temple before Phidias's era. Indeed, it is this standardization which is the real theme of his chapter, even though such standardization is something Le Corbusier has seldom himself been able either to accept from others or to provide for the rest of mankind.

It may be said in conclusion, therefore, that despite the example given us by Le Corbusier, there seems little reason to believe that the contribution of painting and sculpture in the 1920s was anything more than a useful means of rejecting all vestiges of Revivalism. Hence today (when, thanks to the efforts of the Bauhaus, the new tectonic forms appropriate for reinforced concrete and steel have been fully accepted) painting and sculpture may well prove more of a hindrance to architectural creativity than an aid. Perhaps Bruno Taut was right when he wrote that 'with all due appreciation of Le Corbusier, his great weakness lies in the fact that he is not an architect alone, but an abstract painter as well, and that in consequence he confounds the problems of building with those of studio-painting'. There is no doubt that architects can learn a lot from painters and sculptors, just as they can learn a lot from biologists and mechanical engineers; but they will do well to bear in mind that such specialists can only provide them with *analogies*, and that these, however fruitful in ideas, can seldom provide valid prototypes for architectural forms themselves.

For the danger to architectural design of laying too much emphasis on abstract painting and sculpture as formative disciplines is that they lead to the idea of a building as simply an object in space, instead of as part of a space. They thus accentuate the evil, already described when discussing the mechanical analogy, of considering architecture as something isolated from its environment, and from the other buildings among which it must find its place. This danger did not exist before 1750, because painting and sculpture were still thought of largely as architectural decoration. Thus when Boucher painted a picture, it was more often than not a *dessus de porte* for a drawing-room, just as when Anguier or Tuby carved a *bas-relief*, it was frequently the spandrel of an arch. Hence they thought of these objects as parts of environments, and considered their work as simply elements with which other works of painting, sculpture and architecture were to harmonize. Today it is rare for an abstract painter or sculptor to actually create a work of art with a specific environment in mind (other than the blank wall of an art gallery), and it is this divorce of painting and sculpture from other paintings and sculptures which makes abstract art such a dangerous analogy for those who see architecture not as a series of disparate *objets d'art*, but as the component elements of a harmonious urban or rural scene, much of which will be already found existing, and much of which will be modified in centuries to come.

24

New Concepts of Space

The notion of space as an essential element of architecture must have existed in some rudimentary form from the time man first built enclosures or made structural improvements to his caves; but it is a curious fact that until the eighteenth century no architectural treatise ever used the word, whilst the idea of space as a primary quality of architectural composition was not fully developed until the last few years. What mattered to Classical theorists, in an age which defined architecture as the art of building, was structure, and this did not neecssarily imply the enclosure of space, but might equally well be a solid object such as an obelisk or a triumphal arch (where space-enclosure was non-existent or negligible). Complex sequences of inter-related courtyards and rooms, incorporating extremely subtle spatial relationships, were often built by Classical architects; but these were only discussed by theorists in terms of structure and proportion, and if the word 'space' was used at all, it was only with respect to their decoration, to indicate amorphous unproportionable surfaces, such as the blank areas of a painted ceiling, and had no three-dimensional significance whatsoever.

The change in outlook probably first occurred in the middle of the eighteenth century as a result of the introduction of romantic gardens, since here the spaces, though equally amorphous and unproportionable, clearly had a more positive quality than those flat surfaces just described. Thus R. L. Gérardin, in his treatise *On the Composition of Landscapes, and the Means of embellishing Nature in the Neighbourhood of Dwellings* (1777) criticized those who tried to produce great variety by 'piling up the productions of every climate, and the monuments of every century, in a small space'. But the word 'space' or '*espace*' itself was seldom used even in this context; and although it does occur once or twice in J. F. Blondel's lecture course, it does not begin to come into fashion with any precise three-dimensional sense until the mid-nineteenth century. Even then it was not very generally employed by English-speaking or French-speaking authors. Horatio Greenough referred to 'a scientific arrangement of spaces and forms' in one of his essays. Constant-Dufeux used the term 'distribution des espaces' in an essay on

285

planning written in 1847. Two years later Professor Donaldson claimed that Roman architecture had originated as a result of the need 'to cover in larger spaces'. Auguste Choisy, in his *History of Architecture*, described Roman concrete construction as a technique for 'moulding in space'. But despite these random examples, it is fair to say that the concept of architectural space was completely foreign to the English and French way of thinking, and its introduction into the history of architectural ideas derives almost entirely from its use by German theorists at this time.

The German comprehension of the significance of architectural space, or *Raumgestaltung* (i.e. the spatial design of rooms as opposed to the solid surfaces circumscribing them) doubtless resulted to a large extent from native perspicacity, but it can also be attributed to the interesting linguistic coincidence whereby the German word for 'space' is similar to the word 'room'. Thus it required no great power of the imagination for a German to think of room as simply a small portion of limitless space, for it was virtually impossible for him to do otherwise. We thus find, from the beginning of the nineteenth century, a number of German writers on aesthetics using the term 'space' in its modern architectural sense. The best example is Hegel, whose *Philosophy of Art* (based on lectures given in the 1820s) contains numerous uses of the term, as when he refers to buildings as 'limiting and enclosing a defined space' or describes a Gothic church as 'the concentration of essential soul-life which thus encloses itself in spatial relations'. This somewhat mystical notion of space was developed to its greatest extent as a technique of art criticism by the German art-historian Heinrich Wölfflin, and it is probably through his English-speaking disciples that the idea spread through the Western world.

Nevertheless, it is probably fair to say that Wölfflin's concept of space would never have achieved its present architectural significance had it not been for the intuitive creative endeavours of Frank Lloyd Wright. It was he who, at the beginning of the century, by the judicious application of new structural materials, first exploited the spatial possibilities which had lain dormant since the end of the Baroque, and applied them to buildings appropriate to the new age. Not that his concept was entirely unprecedented, for his Larkin office building (which he himself claimed to be the first expression of this new ideal) was simply the adaptation of the traditional interior of a non-conformist church to a more modern and materialistic function. However, if we compare the interior of the Larkin building with his contemporary Unity Temple in Oak Park (1906), with its cantilevered reinforced concrete balconies, we can see not only a similarity of composition but a good reason for giving the latter building primacy of place when considering Wright's contribution to modern architectural spatial developments. For it is clear that whereas the Rationalists, such as Viollet-le-Duc, could conceive only the *structure* of churches as providing the archetype for a new way of building, Wright took the *space*; and it is this which distinguishes Wright from the other great architects of his generation (such as Perret) as the first great architect of the twentieth century.

Another pioneer in the modern evolution of space has been Ludwig Mies van der Rohe. From many points of view he can be regarded as essentially a Rationalist, in that his methodical researches into the architecture of steel closely parallel those researches made by Perret into the architecture of reinforced concrete; but partly through the influence of contemporary developments in abstract sculpture, and partly through an accident of fate, whereby his professional life was at first mainly concerned with designing exhibitions, he developed, in addition, a great sensitivity to those new spatial relationships which could be achieved with thin solid planes and transparent sheets of glass. Indeed, no better example of the influence of exhibitions on architectural design could be found than the way the essential features of Mies van der Rohe's Barcelona Pavilion have been adapted to buildings of every variety of use.

From the era of the Larkin building and the Unity Temple onwards, then, the whole conception of architecture began to assume a radical change, and we even find men like H. P. Berlage (who was essentially a nineteenth century Rationalist, but was profoundly influenced by Wright) asserting in an essay in 1908 (written, significantly enough, in German) that 'the art of the master builder lies in this: the creation of space, not the sketching of façades'. Henceforth, space was regarded as a twin partner with structure in the creation of architectural compositions, and the sensation of spatial relationships resulting from successive viewpoints (which had been such an important feature of the *jardin anglais*) became the principal aesthetic experience sought. We have already seen that Mondriaan claimed that when moving around or within a rectangular building, the impression gained is that of a sequence of two-dimensional aspects. It is probably truer to say, however, that the impression we gain results from a rapid sequence of *three*-dimensional aspects, and this is borne out by physiological research.

Those architects who base their theory of architecture on Giedion's analysis of its modern developments will doubtless describe this as 'Space-Time', and be so used to the idea that 'Space-Time' is an essential element of contemporary architecture that they may consider it an impertinence to enquire whether, outside the realm of astronomy and nuclear physics, the term means anything at all. Yet Giedion himself is curiously vague about the precise way this new space concept operates. Part VI of *Space, Time and Architecture* is called 'Space-Time in Art, Architecture and Construction', and its first chapter is called 'The New Space Conception, Space-Time'. Yet in this first chapter, the hyphenated word does not occur at all, whilst in the remaining eighty pages of Part VI, it occurs only four times, namely with reference to the three famous buildings and one famous project in which its characteristics are apparently to be discerned.

Paul Rudolph believes that the concept of Space-Time has been the motivating force behind much of the International Style, and that in the hands of a great man, this concept can be immensely successful. On the other hand, John Burchard and Albert Bush-Brown contend that even the serious efforts of Giedion have been unable to build believable connections between Gropius's *Werkbund* building at Cologne and the recondite Space-Time of Einstein. It seems worth enquiring, therefore, what Space-Time really does signify in terms of architecture, and whether, if it means anything, the meaning could be more accurately expressed in simpler terms. This enquiry aims neither at philological hair-splitting nor at substituting one catchword for another. Its purpose is to give a clearer idea of what the fundamental aesthetic nature of contemporary architecture is, whereby it can be more accurately studied and its future possibilities more effectively explored.

One difficulty of analysing the implications of Space-Time in architecture is that it seems to mean different things to those who use it. In some passages of *Space, Time and Architecture* it evidently means 'related to Einstein's theory of relativity', whilst in others it seems to mean only 'related to *avant-garde* paintings of the 1910s and 1920s'. Sometimes it is used as a synonym for 'four-dimensional', sometimes as the equivalent of 'non-Euclidian geometry', and on at least one occasion it is used to explain the architectural significance of Zen Buddhism. I propose to look briefly into each of these various meanings in an attempt to isolate those ideas which seem to have some application to architectural design.

Firstly, we can, as Burchard and Bush-Brown rightly observe, dismiss as an illusion any idea that using the words 'Space-Time' establishes a firm analogy with Relativity. Indeed, Giedion in one instance seems to dismiss this relationship himself as a 'temporal coincidence'. However inspiring the announcement of Einstein's initial theory must have been to painters and writers when it was published in 1905, and however exhilarating his startling experimental proof of the final theory (published a decade later) must have been in 1919, the fact is that neither had anything to do with the kind of space that painters, sculptors and architects are involved with, but were a development of the algebraic techniques of analytical geometry, extended to solve problems in dynamics. Moreover, although Einstein's general theory of relativity (which is concerned with accelerated motion) involves non-Euclidian geometry, his 'special' theory of relativity (which is concerned with uniform velocity) does not.

It is clear therefore that when Giedion talks about non-Euclidian geometry as if Euclidian geometry were limited to three dimensions, and claims that 'like the scientist, the artist has come to recognize that classic conceptions of space and volume are limited and one-sided', or that 'the essence of space as it is conceived today is its many-sidedness', he is not talking about anything which would have been intelligible to Einstein; for Einstein never claimed that space was many-sided, or that 'in order to grasp the true nature of space the observer must project himself through it'. On the contrary, it was precisely because of the impossibility of measuring our absolute velocity through space that he engaged upon his famous research. His great feat was to demonstrate why it was that the true nature of space was not apparent to observers moving through it, and the truths he enunciated were more to the effect that problems of measurement involving mass and light are not so much a matter of geometry as a matter of history. 'The past,' wrote R. G. Collingwood in his *Philosophy of History*, 'consisting of particular events in space and time which are no longer happening, cannot be apprehended by mathematical thinking because mathematical thinking apprehends objects that have no special location in space and time, and it is just that lack of peculiar spatio-temporal location that makes them knowable.' Einstein's theory may, without unduly broadening the meaning of 'history', be said to constitute the ultimate extension of Historicism to our interpretation of nature by relating it to astronomy and nuclear physics.

In such circumstances one would not expect to find any detailed explanation of the Space-Time qualities of modern architecture in Einstein's own writings, but he makes one remark in his introduction to Max Jammer's *Concepts of Space* which provides a useful clue as to his own ideas concerning the relationship between architecture and space. 'Now as to the concept of space,' he wrote, 'it seems that this was preceded by the psychologically simpler concept of place. Place is first of all a small portion of the earth's surface identifiable by a name . . . a sort of order of material objects and nothing else.' Now this is precisely the kind of space involved in architectural design, and one might contend that a 'place' (plaza, piazza) is the largest space that an architect is able to deal with as a unified work of art.

Closely related to the analogy with Einstein's theory of relativity is the notion that modern architecture is characterized by its use of a fourth dimension. 'The fourth dimension,' wrote Le Corbusier in *New World of Space*, 'is the moment of limitless escape evoked by an exceptionally just consonance of the plastic means employed', and whatever this may mean exactly, it is obviously related to Giedion's notion that the 'fourth dimension' enables us not merely, like the Cubists, to depict the world in a new way, but to *see* it in a new way. The four-century-old habit of seeing the outer world in terms of three dimensions, Giedion tells us, rooted itself so deeply in the human mind that until quite recently no other form of perception could be imagined. No wonder, he concludes, that the modern way of seeing the world in terms of four dimensions should be so difficult to comprehend.

Now 'fourth-dimensional' in architecture presumably means time considered as a measure of displacement, and since buildings do not move (although Moholy-Nagy defined Space-Time architecture in terms of automobiles, trains and trailers), the 'fourth-dimensional' component must necessarily be contributed by the observer. Yet Giedion states not only that to appreciate a Space-Time structure in its entirety one must move through it and around it; he also states that one can appreciate both the inside and outside simultaneously by staying in the same place —a seemingly contradictory distinction which depends in fact on the extent to which the structure is sheathed in plates of glass.

According to Giedion, it is impossible to comprehend Le Corbusier's Villa Savoie by a view from a single point, since 'quite literally', he says, it is a construction in Space-Time; the body of the house has been hollowed out in every direction—from above and below, within and without—so that a cross-section at any point shows inner and outer space penetrating each other inextricably, in a way which Borromini had been on the verge of achieving in some of his late Baroque churches. Le Corbusier gives much the same interpretation of it, although he does not use the expression Space-Time, and considers that his building exemplifies the exact opposite of Baroque principles (which, according to him, produced an architecture conceived on paper around a fixed theoretical point). Moreover, far from considering his own principles exclusively modern, he derives them from Arab architecture. 'Arab architecture gives us an invaluable lesson. It is appreciated *whilst walking*, and it is only thus, in moving around, that the observer sees the architectural dispositions develop'.

Giedion's other great Space-Time paradigm, the Bauhaus, is also, according to him, too complex to be summed up at one view, so that it is necessary here again to go around it on all sides, to see it from above as well as below. This means, he says, new dimensions for the artistic imagination; 'an unprecedented many-sidedness'. But for him, the specific Space-Time quality of the building is attributable to the fact that the extensive transparency permits interior and exterior to be seen simultaneously *en face* and *en profile* 'like Picasso's *L'Arlésienne* of 1911–12'.

Perhaps, then, Giedion's views might be summarized by saying: modern architecture is characterized by the fact that the inside of a modern building can often be appreciated from single external viewpoints, and the external totality of a modern building can only be appreciated as a sequence of visual impressions. If this is so, it is the converse of what occurs when one looks at traditional buildings of similar purpose; for in a typical Renaissance villa comparable to the Villa Savoie, the totality of the outside of the building is intelligible from a single viewpoint (because of the axial symmetry), whereas the interior can only be appreciated as a sequence of visual impressions obtained by moving from room to room. But 'fourth-dimensional' does not, for Giedion, simply refer to the movement of an observer. In an introductory passage, he makes clear that he regards it as evidence of the evolution of art. The Renaissance manner of seeing the world three-dimensionally, he tells us, was an important step forward, because the art of previous centuries had been two-dimensional. Thus our contemporary four-dimensional vision is in one sense revolutionary, but in another sense it is simply an inevitable advance in the evolutionary progress of civilization.

Disregarding the question whether all the art of pre-Renaissance cultures really was in fact two-dimensional, whether even painting was then two-dimensional, and whether, for example, a mediaeval Italian painting depicting the same person participating in several sequential events on the same panel is to be called two-dimensional, three-dimensional or four-dimensional; disregarding also the logical extension of Giedion's theory which would seem to imply that the next development of art is to become five-dimensional, then six-dimensional (as in the dynamic theory of gases) until eventually it becomes *n*-dimensional; it is surely enough to say that this evolutionary theory is only possible if one considers the *creation* of space to be indistinguishable from the *depiction* of space. That painters have found new ways of 'conquering' space, first by mastering perspective and then by discovering techniques for producing the illusion of infinity, is a matter of common knowledge. But to suggest that architects before 1400 actually *created* only two-dimensional architecture, in the way that between 1500 and 1750 they were creating three-dimensional architecture, and that the Baroque heralded the creation of four-dimensional architecture, is to divest the words of any real tectonic meaning, and nobody except Moholy-Nagy has ever been rash enough to try to demonstrate the theory by reference to historical examples. He illustrates the theory by asking us to believe that Egyptian architecture was 'one-dimensional' because their temples could be comprehended by walking through the sphinx alley leading towards its façade; that Greek architecture was 'two-dimensional' because the architects of the Acropolis designed a two-dimensional approach to 'the temple'; and that the spectator inside a Gothic cathedral became the centre of co-ordinated space cells of all directions, whilst the Renaissance and the Baroque brought man into closer contact with the inside and the outside of its buildings. 'In our age of airplanes,' he concludes, 'architecture is viewed not only frontally and from the sides, but also from above—vision in motion'; i.e. Space-Time.

It is significant that when Wölfflin (from whom Giedion derived his basic ideas about the primacy of space in art-historical analysis) discusses architectural space most eloquently, it is with reference to the *painting* of an architectural interior, rather than to an architectural interior itself. Altdorfer's early sixteenth century painting of the birth of the Virgin, he tells us, characterizes well the fundamental difference between the German and Italian conceptions of space, since here 'space is undefined and in motion', whereas with Brunelleschi all forms are defined and distinct. In Altdorfer's interior, he continues, the nave and aisles flow into one another, 'and what is more, a rotating, whirling movement throws the entire space into a turmoil'. The church's ground plan remains intentionally unclear, and the painting, he therefore concludes, compensates for the completeness of the diverse views offered to the spectator wandering on the spot 'by transforming finite into infinite form'.

When Wölfflin discusses Baroque interiors, his descriptions are almost indistinguishable from Giedion's description of the Space-Time experience of the Villa Savoie. 'We move round them,' he writes, 'because in the intersections new pictures constantly arise. The goal cannot lie in a final revelation of the intersected form—that is not even desired—but in the perception, from as many sides as possible, of the potentially existing views.'

Nevertheless, Giedion's interpretation of Baroque clearly differs from Wölfflin's in that Giedion sees Baroque only as the anticipation of Space-Time, and I suspect that the immediate source of Giedion's theory is to be found not in Wölfflin's lectures or Einstein's theory, but in an extremely influential and popular German book which appeared in 1918, when Giedion was a student in Munich, namely Spengler's *Decline of the West*. If specific evidence were required to demonstrate Spengler's influence on Giedion, it could be adduced by the term 'Faustian', that most Spenglerian of expressions, which occurs in *Space, Time and Architecture* with reference to the League of Nations competition. But for readers of Giedion nothing could be more conclusive than the following quotation from *Decline of the West*:

'The Temple of Poseidon at Paestum and the Minster at Ulm . . . differ precisely as the Euclidian geometry of bodily bounding-surfaces differs from the analytical geometry of the position of points in space referred to spatial axes. All Classical building begins from the outside, all Western from the inside . . . There is one and only one soul, the Faustian, that craves for a style which drives through walls into the limitless universe of space, and makes both the exterior and the interior of the building complementary images of one and the same world-feeling . . . The Faustian building has a *visage*, and not merely a façade.'

'Faustian' might well be an appropriate substitute for the increasingly unpopular word 'International' as a stylistic identification of twentieth century architecture, but regardless of 'style', I would suggest that in fact the visual effects usually referred to as Space-Time, Fourth-Dimensional, and so on, *are nothing more or less than modern developments of the exploitation of effects of parallax*, which was discussed in the first chapter. The phenomenon of parallax (whereby an apparent displacement of objects occurs when the point of observation changes) is also, like Space-Time, a device for astronomical measurement, but unlike Space-Time it has been an important element of architectural composition, and has been manifest in architecture ever since the first hypostyle hall was constructed. It occurs in every large space containing rows of free-standing columns, and must have produced particularly striking effects in the great mediaeval churches and halls when these were also subdivided by low screens, or spanned by deep hammer-beam roofs.

The aesthetic revolution which has occurred in architecture within the last century has consisted firstly in the reversal of the traditional method of exploiting parallax, and secondly in its extension by means of a greater use of cantilevers and glass. Reversal of the traditional method is best exemplified in Le Corbusier's work, and it is probably this which relates it so closely to Cubism; for, as John Summerson has observed, 'just as Picasso's work is, as he has said, a sum of destructions, so, in a sense, is Le Corbusier's; for to him the obvious solution of a problem cannot possibly be the right solution . . . he sees the reverse logic of every situation'. Extension of the traditional method is best exemplified in the works of Gropius, and particularly of Mies van der Rohe, that greatest of all pioneers of modern parallax, whom Giedion, with regard to Space-Time, completely neglects. But all the leading architects of the century have exploited it to some extent, whether it be Frank Lloyd Wright's use of large balconies or free-standing mushroom columns, or even Perret's emphasis on isolating point supports. Its most striking development today is in the use of high towers which change their apparent relationship as one moves round the building, as introduced by Louis Kahn.

Giedion's terminology will probably persist, whatever interpretation we give it, because of the modern credulous appetite for pseudo-scientific mumbo-jumbo, and the fact that it was used recently to explain traditional Japanese architecture and its relation to Zen Buddhism will occasion no surprise. It is even to be found outside architectural writings, as for example in a recent sociological periodical where, in an article entitled 'A Study of Free-Time Activities of 200 Aged Persons', their Space-Time activities are carefully described. Yet here, on close examination, it is apparent that 'space-time activities' was simply a misprint for 'spare-time activities', and one may perhaps be excused for wondering whether a similar typographical transposition has not occurred in one or two recent books on modern art.

Epilogue

In the preceding pages, an attempt has been made to trace the history of architects' and critics' ideas about architecture from the 1750s to the 1950s: dates which may appear just a little too neat, but which really do correspond to the beginning and end of a historic period. The reasons for beginning in the middle of the eighteenth century have been amply discussed and, it is hoped, justified. The decision to end in the middle of the twentieth century is perhaps less conclusive, but it seems fair to insist that it is just as sound. It was only in the decade following the Second World War that the architectural ideas of the men described by Nikolaus Pevsner as 'The Pioneers of the Modern Movement' were established; hence we may fittingly describe this decade as the beginning of a new era. From this time onwards, architecture was to have about it all the features of stability and orthodoxy we associate with Classicism; for despite the immense differences between early Georgian vernacular architecture and the vernacular architecture of the modern building contractor, a universal architecture of sorts does exist, whereas for the previous two centuries it did not. 1750 to 1950 may thus be considered as a formative period, to which the period after 1950 is a natural but quite distinct sequel, and it is not for the historian to pry too closely into its nature until he has some idea how it will develop and how long it will last.

Nevertheless, there may be readers who would argue that even if this interpretation is correct, it is no more sensible to halt the study of modern architecture at the beginning of its Classic period than it would be to halt the study of Gothic architecture at the year 1250. To these I would reply that there is one crucial difference between the two instances, namely that we are actually living in the Classic age of modern architecture, whereas the Gothic era is dead and gone. Not merely is there something unseemly about the current frantic eagerness to take history up to the very last minute (for there are some historians who even include and illustrate in their textbooks projects yet to be built), but there is a grave danger that modern architecture may be maimed and devitalized if we allow historians to breathe too heavily down practising architects' necks. Such eagerness overlooks the crucial difference between the theory and the history of architecture; between the way buildings *are* built and the way they *were* built. There is much that the theorist of architecture can learn from the historian, and *vice versa*; but this is no justification for confounding the distinctive task of each.

The dangers of this confusion can clearly be seen in recent attempts at art-historical witch-hunting in pursuit of new manifestations of Revivalism, and one of the most striking and perhaps most disquieting paradoxes of modern architecture is that whereas the 'Pioneers of the Modern Movement' considered that their principal victory lay precisely in the overthrow of the nineteenth century concept of 'styles', no generation of architectural historians has ever classified its contemporary architecture into so many stylistic subdivisions as our own. 'The "styles"', wrote Le Corbusier, 'are a lie. Style is a unity of principle animating all the work of an epoch'. Yet despite this widely accepted definition, and despite Walter Gropius's vehement assertion that a 'Bauhaus Style' would have been a confession of failure, the works of these men, like those of their contemporaries, are now being classified stylistically by architectural historians with such chrono-logical exactitude that Pevsner has detected at least eighteen recent examples of what he calls 'a return to Historicism' involving 'the imitation of styles which had never previously been revived'; that is to say, of recent buildings constructed in 'styles' presumably to be considered authentic only in the first quarter of this century. There is already, he explained in a lecture to the Royal Institute of British Architects, 'neo-Art Nouveau (which includes neo-Liberty and neo-Gaudi) neo-*de-Stijl*, neo-School-of-Amsterdam, neo-German-Expressionism, and finally to a certain extent, neo-Perret'; and he hinted darkly at the prospect of a Ronchamp Revival and the imminence of neo-Maison-Jaoul.

It must be said at once that the essence of Pevsner's total argument is an entirely convincing plea for the return to the principles of 'form related to function', and as such no practising architect could possibly quarrel with it. On the contrary, most of those who have read his lecture as published in the April 1961 issue of the *R.I.B.A. Journal* will have fully endorsed his general thesis, especially his tacit admission that Art Nouveau and German Expressionism are not only bad in their revived form, but were bad in their original form, and always will be bad, since neither 'share with the early Modern Movement the regard for function'. But one may wonder whether some of his examples of 'Historicism' really are revivalistic (for that is what 'Historicism' means for him), or whether these returns to earlier forms are not occasionally justifiable within the principles of modern architecture.

Let us take, for example, one of the most striking buildings included in Pevsner's lecture, namely, the Torre Velasca in Milan by Belgiojoso, Peressutti and Rogers. Since this building is constructed of reinforced concrete, with an exposed, cast-in-place frame, with intermediate precast mullions spaced at regular intervals, and with precast infilling panels, it might fittingly be included in the category he entitles 'neo-Perret', especially in view of its structural similarity to Perret's apartment

G. Howe and W. Lescaze: P.S.F.S. Building,
Philadelphia (1932)

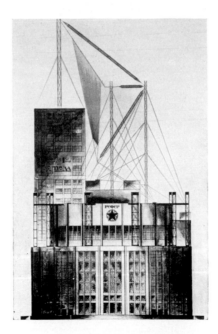

A. L. and V. Vesnine: Design for a
Palace of Labour (1923)

CONSTRUCTIVISM

*Illustrating the influence of constructivist sculpture on
architectural composition*

E. Rogers and others: Torre Velasca, Milan (1957)

G. P. Chédanne: Offices, rue Réaumur, Paris (1903)

PSEUDO-REVIVALISM

Illustrating similarities of forms which have been misconstrued as stylistic imitation

XXXVIII

A. Perret: 51-55, rue Raynouard, Paris (1928)

PSEUDO-REVIVALISM

Illustrating the harmony which can be achieved between a modern building and its environment without relinquishing the ideals of functional planning and new methods of construction

XXXIX

Skidmore, Owings & Merrill: Hancock Building,
San Francisco (1958)

PSEUDO-REVIVALISM

*Illustrating the harmony which can be achieved between a modern
building and its environment without relinquishing the ideals of
functional planning and new methods of construction*

block in the rue Raynouard, Paris, built thirty years before. Moreover, the fact that one of the three architects responsible for the Torre Velasca published a biography of Perret in 1955 would seem to give weight to such an interpretation. Yet not only does Pevsner not classify it as neo-Perret (a term he reserves for Edward D. Stone's Raincid precast tracery); he labels it 'neo-Art Nouveau' because it bears a superficial formal resemblance to a metal framed office building constructed by G. P. Chédanne in Paris in 1903.

The formal similarity between the upper part of the Torre Velasca and the upper part of the 'Le Parisien' office building in the rue Réaumur is indisputable; but it can be fully justified on purely functional grounds. The top six storeys of the Torre Velasca are apartment floors, whereas the lower part of the building consists of office space; hence the enlargement of the upper part corresponds quite rationally to the increased size of floor area demanded. Consider, for example, how the shape of the Torre Valasca was justified by G. M. Kallman at the time of its completion. 'It is not a self-sufficient structure that could be located anywhere,' he wrote in the *Architectural Forum* in February 1958; *'instead, it is a valiant essay in the neglected art of fitting modern architecture into a historic continuity of building, within which it seeks its own status.* Unlike most modern architecture, which is displaced, rebellious, and alien to its immediate environment, the Milan tower shows a definite response to the forms and figuration of its surroundings. . . . The giant mushroom shape of the tower recalls mediaeval machicolated defense towers. The cagelike appearance of the exterior frame is more reminiscent of Gothic structure than it is of skeleton frame and curtain wall. . . . *But the tower does not have a deliberately historicized silhouette.* . . . The more closely the tower is studied, the more apparent its complex dialectic becomes—between function and form, construction and ornament, new technology and ancient forms'.

It seems therefore opportune to consider the whole question of 'stylistic' imitation in the twentieth century, because it may well be that the depressing conclusions of modern art-historical analysis result simply from a refusal by art historians to distinguish between changes *of* style and changes *within* a style; to distinguish, in other words, between what biologists would call mutations and variants. In architecture, this distinction corresponds to buildings which are stylistically of a different species, and to buildings which, though stylistically of the same species, are unfashionable or archaic. I shall try to show that whereas stylistic imitation is as reprehensible as ever, variations within a style (that is, within 'the unity of principle animating all the work of an epoch') constitute simply what William H. Jordy aptly calls 'the overlapping gamut of expressive possibilities'.

First, let us consider the meaning of the word 'archaic'. The notion that all living styles develop like living organisms, 'and have their birth, growth, maturity and death', is at least as old as Vasari (from whom this quotation is taken), and seems a commonplace of every phase of architectural history except our own. Now archaism (birth and early growth) has two meanings in architecture, since architecture is both a science and an art. Either it means that a form has been scientifically or technologically superseded, in which case we say it is obsolete: or it means that a form has been artistically superseded, in which case we say that it is unfashionable. The first kind of archaism is purely objective, in that what is technologically obsolete can never cease to be so for a given state of society (though it can nevertheless legitimately be employed—indeed, in my opinion, it should invariably be employed—whenever architects are obliged by circumstance to build with traditional building materials and methods). The second kind of archaism is purely subjective, since what was fashionable twenty years ago may well become fashionable again tomorrow. Thus architects should feel no shame at adopting archaic forms and techniques in order to harmonize new buildings with an existing architectural environment, *provided that they do not betray the contemporary principles of stylistic unity*; a unity which, in the twentieth century, is best defined by what John Summerson calls 'obedience to the programme' (or, as we usually say—Functionalism) but which is also to be defined, to my mind, as the notion of the honest expression of the structural means employed.

This problem of creating environmental harmony with new buildings was the subject of a most interesting lecture given at the AIA Seminar at Cranbrook in 1961 by Dean Holmes Perkins. Why, he asked in effect, can we not learn the lesson of Assisi, of Venice, and of Paris, where all the buildings, of whatever age, seem infused by some *genius loci* so as to exist in harmony with one another? Why, he asked, as he projected a sequence of splendid coloured photographs of these cities on to a screen in rapid succession, do we not still consider it our duty to fit new buildings into existing urban patterns and textures, as was done so successfully in the past? He gave no examples of how anyone had achieved such harmony in the twentieth century, and when questioned specifically on this point, with respect to Paris, said he did not know of any work by a reputable twentieth century architect which fulfilled this condition.

Now it is not surprising that he was unable to give examples of harmonious modern buildings in either Assisi or Venice, since these cities are in no sense modern, and indeed for this reason were poor examples to take. But in Paris there is surely a very striking example of this kind of harmony to be found in all the later works of Auguste Perret, and perhaps in years to come, when architects are more concerned with creating humane environments than with becoming Form-Givers, his achievement in this respect may attract the attention it deserves.

There is no need for me to waste time justifying the twentieth century character of 51–55 rue Raynouard from a structural or a functional point of view, since I have already done this in *Concrete: The Vision of a New Architecture*. I would simply observe that by designing the building in accordance with the absolute limitations imposed by the Municipal Building Code, and by proportioning the fenestration in accordance with local traditions, Perret produced a building which is so unostentatious that those who travel through this old suburb of Paris would hardly appreciate that it was designed by a 'Pioneer of the Modern Movement' unless their attention were specifically drawn to the plaque recently affixed to the wall. In this respect, it is vastly different from Perret's earlier and universally extolled apartment building in the rue Franklin. Everyone knows the practical reasons why he was led to encase the reinforced concrete frame of the latter building in coloured tiles, and why he recessed the façade in the centre. But though this building is 'stylistically' acceptable to the art historians (presumably because it is covered with the Art Nouveau decoration of the era, and possesses spatial qualities shared with some of Victor Horta's houses in Brussels), it is, from the point of view of urban environmental harmony, deplorable, since it is completely alien to the other apartment buildings in the same street.

Perret, who in his later years was accused by Le Corbusier of betraying the Modern Movement, undoubtedly lacked that abstract vision of a New Architecture which enabled Le Corbusier to envisage destroying the whole of Paris north of the Seine, and substituting a symmetrically arranged group of widely spaced cruciform glass prisms, six hundred feet high. He was conservative, perhaps even prosaic, and he may well have inherited too many inhibiting traits from the parsimonious peasant stock from which he sprang. But he was a Parisian who loved Paris; who delighted in its character, its traditions, its atmosphere, and the way of life of its people; and it was in Paris that he mainly built.

Now if we are to draw any lessons from these examples, and from the architectural history of the last two hundred years in general, it must surely be this: that among all the conflicting ideals of modern architecture, none has proved today of such importance that it can take precedence over the task of creating a humane environment. Doctrinaire arguments concerning the authenticity or otherwise of individual buildings, individual techniques or individual mannerisms can never be unimportant; but they seem of secondary importance when compared with the problem as to whether or not a new building fits harmoniously into the environment into which it is set. Not that I am recommending that same indifference towards the ethical problems of architectural design which was the worst failing of the early nineteenth century; on the contrary, I consider obedience to principles to be never more urgent in an age when there are so many temptations to seek architectural novelty for its own sake. But it is surely worth noting that, in the buildings just described, the architects were able to discipline their architectural forms to harmonize with earlier forms without sacrificing any of the principles of the modern age. Admittedly, they did not produce anything which art historians could recognize and classify as a 'paradigm'. On the contrary, they produced works deliberately intended to be banal, if one uses the word in its strict etymological sense as meaning 'common to all' the buildings around them. But it might not be a bad thing if more façades in our cities were as banal as these, for as Perret once remarked: 'He who, without betraying the modern conditions of a programme, or the use of modern materials, produces a work which seems to have always existed, which, in a word, is banal, can rest satisfied. Astonishment and excitement are shocks which do not endure; they are but contingent and anecdotic sentiments. The true aim of art is to lead us dialectically from satisfaction to satisfaction, until it surpasses mere admiration to reach delight in its purest form'.

Bibliographical Note

In addition to the sources of information alluded to in the text, special acknowledgement must be made for information provided by the following recent publications:

ABRAMS, M. H.	*The Mirror and the Lamp*
BERTRAND, L.	*La Fin du Classicisme et le Retour à l'Antique*
CANAT, R.	*L'Hellenisme des Romantiques*
CROW, W. B.	*The Principles of Morphology*
CUST, L.	*History of the Society of Dilettanti*
HIPPLE, W. J.	*The Beautiful, the Sublime and the Picturesque in 18th Century British Aesthetic Theory*
LANSON, R.	*Le Goût du Moyen Age en France*
LEVIN, H.	*The Broken Column*
LOVEJOY, A. O.	*Essays in the History of Ideas*
MALAKIS, E.	*French Travellers in Greece, 1770–1820*
MORRISON, H.	*Louis Sullivan*
NEEDHAM, H. A.	*Le Développement de l'Esthétique Sociologique en France et en Angleterre au 19e Siècle*
NORDENSKIÖLD, E.	*The History of Biology*
PANOFSKY, E.	*Renaissance and Renascences in Western Art*
RUSSELL, E. S.	*Form and Function*
SANDYS, J. E.	*A History of Classical Scholarship*
SEZNEC, J.	*Essais sur Diderot et l'Antiquité*
SMITH, W. H.	*Architecture in English Fiction*
WELLEK, R.	*A History of Modern Criticism, 1750–1950*
WOODGER, J. H.	*Biological Principles*

Index of Illustrations

303

INDEX OF ILLUSTRATIONS

Index of Text

v

INDEX

INDEX

INDEX